REDEEMING MEN

REDEEMING MEN
RELIGION AND MASCULINITIES

Stephen B. Boyd
W. Merle Longwood
Mark W. Muesse
editors

Westminster John Knox Press
Louisville, Kentucky

Scripture quotations from the New Revised Standard Version of the Bible are copyright © 1989 by the Division of Christian Education of the National Council of the Churches of Christ in the U.S.A. and are used by permission.

Book design by Jennifer K. Cox
Cover design by Kevin Darst
First edition

Published by Westminster John Knox Press
Louisville, Kentucky

This book is printed on acid-free paper that meets the American National Standards Institute Z39.48 standard. ♾

PRINTED IN THE UNITED STATES OF AMERICA

96 97 98 99 00 01 02 03 04 05 — 10 9 8 7 6 5 4 3 2 1

Library of Congress Cataloging-in-Publication Data

Redeeming men : religion and masculinities / Stephen B. Boyd, W. Merle
  Longwood, Mark W. Muesse, editors — 1st ed.
      p.   cm.
  Includes bibliographical references and index.
  ISBN 0-664-25544-2 (alk. paper)
  1. Men (Christian theology).   2. Masculinity (Psychology)—Religious
aspects—Christianity.   3. Identity (Psychology)—Religious aspects—
Christianity.   4. Men's movement.   I. Boyd, Stephen Blake.   II. Longwood,
W. Merle, date.   III. Muesse, Mark W. (Mark William), date.
BT703.5.R43   1996
261.8′3431—dc20
                                                                    96-21403

Contents

Contents

Contents

PREFACE

Many people have provided us with insights, inspiration, and support as we solicited and edited these essays to make them a coherent collection. We have been sustained by other scholars, colleagues, friends, and family, who have given us what we needed to see this project to completion. The men, women, and children whose lives have touched ours, stimulating us to think more deeply about the issues raised in this book, are too numerous to list, but we do know that whatever wisdom we have achieved owes much to the great cloud of witnesses that surrounds us.

We received encouragement to create this volume from Jon L. Berquist, our editor at Westminster John Knox Press, and we thank him. At an early stage in our collaborative work he helped us to develop a clear focus for this project, and along the way he continued gently and persistently to nudge us toward the completion of this book.

We express our appreciation to the institutions within which we work for the support they have provided us. Steve is grateful to Wake Forest University for financial assistance and for a leave to work on this manuscript. Merle expresses his gratitude to Siena College, particularly the Faculty Committee on Teaching and the Office of Academic Affairs, for two summer research grants to work on this book. Mark acknowledges his indebtedness to Rhodes College and its Department of Religious Studies for invaluable technical and clerical support during the four years this book was being developed.

Among the many friends and colleagues who have given us assistance, we want to give a special thanks to David Schoeni at Wake Forest University, who read many parts of the manuscript, made valuable editorial suggestions, and researched some of the notes; to Sarah Frierson at Rhodes College, who masterfully assisted in the manuscript preparation; and to William J. Kanalley at the Father Jerome Dawson Memorial Library of Siena College for his expert bibliographical assistance. At a crucial stage in the development of our project, Anna Nobeck offered us her condominium at Wrightsville Beach, North Carolina, where we spent a memorable week in August in a scholars' paradise. We thank her for providing such an idyllic setting, where we managed to achieve an appropriate balance between disciplined work and spirited play, and from which we emerged with a clearer vision of how all the parts of our book did indeed fit together.

We are grateful to our contributors, from whom we learned much in dialogue, and who responded graciously to our suggestions for revisions of their essays to make them fit into the larger whole that we became better at imagining as time went by. Finally, we have been inspired and informed by our colleagues in the American Academy of Religion, particularly the Men's Studies in Religion Group and its steering committee; the Consultation that preceded it for two years; and the Gay Men's Issues Group. We have had important connections with all these men and women, and we have been enriched by their friendship and their wisdom.

Finally, each of us acknowledges the important support of the circles of family and friends who have made the research, writing, and editing of this book a far less lonely activity than it otherwise could have been.

Steve expresses his gratitude to the Monday Night Men's Group, John Collins, Richard Fireman, Jay Foster, Chris Ingalls, Russ McGhee, and Mark Retherford; the Leadership Group, John Rowe and Frederick Whitmeyer; his sister, Beth, and nephew, Jason Campbell; and his friends Lynn Rhoades, Linda McFarland, Lisa Allred, and Joe Foster, for their support, challenge, and loving presence along the way.

Merle gives special thanks to his mother and late father, Judie and Walter; his brother, Lester, and his sisters, Shirley, Marlene, Mary Ellen, and Carol; his daughters, Wendy and Leda; his friends, both near and far, Jim Nelson, Larry Vallet, Larry Rasmussen, Fareed Munir, Jean Hynes, Susan Johnson, and Elaine Ognibene; and his students over the years in the evening course "Modern Men, Meaning, and Morality." Their presence provided support, nurture, and gentle criticism, and helped him maintain a sense of humor during difficult times.

Mark is grateful to the members of the Tuesday Night Men's Group, Kerrel Ard, Ralph Chumbley, Patrick Crow, Tom Curry, Ken Mareck, Richard Popp, Greg Russell, Bobby Taylor, Rick Webb, and Mark Willis; his friends Clark Buchner, Diane Clark, Steve Haynes, Tracy René Helms, Beth Kamhi, Steve McKenzie, Laura Miller, Baine Palmer, David Peacock, Steve Sparman, and Herb and Betty Smith; his parents, Lemma and Billy; his brother Mike and his family, Andrea, Scott, Candice, and Collin; and his sister Lori. Most especially, he thanks Libby Robertson for her wisdom, humor, and delightful companionship.

Contributors

STEPHEN B. BOYD is associate professor of history of Christianity at Wake Forest University, Winston-Salem, North Carolina.

WILLIAM F. BRANTLEY is a retired newspaper editor and investor relations consultant who is active in HIV/AIDS-related work.

HARRY BROD is assistant professor of philosophy at the University of Delaware, Newark, Delaware, where he also teaches in the women's studies, Jewish studies, and honors program.

J. MICHAEL CLARK is adjunct assistant professor in the human and natural ecology program at Emory University and in the freshman English program at Georgia State University, Atlanta, Georgia.

HOWARD EILBERG-SCHWARTZ is associate professor and director of Jewish studies at San Francisco State University, San Francisco, California.

JOHN C. FOUT is professor of history at Bard College, Annandale-on-Hudson, New York.

DOUGLAS GILLETTE is an author, lecturer, counselor, mythologist, and artist in Chicago, Illinois.

CARTER HEYWARD is professor of theology at Episcopal Divinity School, Cambridge, Massachusetts.

CHRISTOPHER RONWANIENTE JOCKS is assistant professor of Native American studies and religion at Dartmouth College, Hanover, New Hampshire.

EVELYN A. KIRKLEY is assistant professor of theological and religious studies at the University of San Diego, San Diego, California.

W. MERLE LONGWOOD is professor of religious ethics at Siena College, Loudonville, New York.

SETH MIRSKY is an editor for *The Sun: A Magazine of Ideas* and lives in Pittsboro, North Carolina.

ROBERT MOORE is professor of psychology and religion at Chicago Theological Seminary, Chicago, Illinois.

MERLYN E. MOWREY is associate professor of social ethics at Central Michigan University, Mount Pleasant, Michigan.

MARK W. MUESSE is associate professor of religious studies at Rhodes College, Memphis, Tennessee.

FAREED MUNIR is assistant professor of religious studies at Siena College, Loudonville, New York.

JAMES B. NELSON is emeritus professor of Christian ethics at United Theological Seminary of the Twin Cities, New Brighton, Minnesota.

TIMOTHY NONN is founder and director of the Urban Justice Institute, San Francisco, California.

MIKEAL PARSONS is associate professor of New Testament studies at Baylor University, Waco, Texas.

ALTON B. POLLARD, III, is associate professor of religion at Wake Forest University, Winston-Salem, North Carolina.

STEVE SMITH is professor of philosophy at Claremont McKenna College, Claremont, California.

ULRIKE WIETHAUS is associate professor of humanities at Wake Forest University, Winston-Salem, North Carolina.

MEN, MASCULINITY, AND THE STUDY OF RELIGION

Twenty years ago, a book like this would have been unthinkable. The notion of assembling a volume of critical studies on men and religion had certainly not yet occurred to the three of us. Even if it had, the resources available then would have been insufficient to create a book-length collection of essays. At that time, studies on the relationships between gender and religion were focused on women—and rightly so. Feminist theologians were appropriately calling attention to the failure of religious traditions and scholarly reflections on religion to take into account the experiences of women. The suggestion that one should investigate the matter of men and religion might have been met with the response, "Why? Hasn't all religious reflection been about men?"

The New Men's Studies

In the intervening years, critical gender studies in religion and other disciplines have begun to acknowledge the value of the study of men as a specific group, and as a result, the new interdisciplinary field of men's studies has emerged.[1] This field owes a tremendous debt to the influence of feminist theory. From feminist perspectives, we have learned that males have been prone to regard themselves as generic humans rather than gendered persons conditioned by historical and cultural processes. The tendency to view themselves as generic has often led men to assume that their experiences are universal and that men—especially socially dominant groups of men—can and should speak for others.

Men's studies implicitly and explicitly challenges these assumptions by examining men's experiences as specifically male rather than generically human. Harry Brod, one of the pioneering theorists in this field, defines men's studies as the investigation of "masculinities and male experiences as specific and varying social-historical-cultural formations. Such studies situate masculinities as objects of study on a par with femininities, instead of elevating them to universal norms."[2] Brod further argues that the new men's studies

> does not recapitulate traditionally male-biased scholarship. Like women's studies, men's studies aims at the emasculation of patriarchal ideology's masquerade as knowledge. Men's studies argues that while women's studies corrects the exclusion of women from the traditional canon caused by androcentric scholarship's elevation of *man* as male to *man* as generic human, the implications of this fallacy for our understanding of men have gone largely unrecognized. While *seemingly* about men, traditional scholarship's treatment of generic man as the human norm in fact systematically excludes from consideration what is unique to *men* qua men. The overgeneralization from male to generic human experience not only distorts our understanding of what, if anything, is truly generic to humanity but also precludes the study of masculinity as a *specific male* experience, rather than a universal paradigm for *human* experience.[3]

Key Concepts in Men's Studies

Maleness and Masculinity

Central to the methodologies of men's studies is the distinction between maleness and masculinity. This distinction follows the analytical separation of sex and gender in the study of human sexuality. As these terms are generally used in academic discussion, "sex" refers to a biological category, one's genetic makeup as either male or female. "Gender," on the other hand, denotes a cultural construct, the expectations and ideals of behavior and modes of being believed to be appropriate to each sex.[4] Masculinity and femininity are terms of gender.

Men's studies views masculinity—whatever else it might be—as a social construction that varies by culture and by historical periods. As cultural constructs rather than a biological inevitability, masculinities are inextricably connected with the economic, political, social, psychological, and religious dimensions of human life.

Social Constructionism versus Essentialism

Many theorists maintain that gender has no intrinsic or ontologically necessary relationship to sex. They argue that males are not aggressive, competitive, emotionally restricted, and rational by nature. Rather men are molded by cultural dynamics to think and behave in these ways. This perspective on gender and sex is commonly known as the "social constructionist" position. This perspective prevails among North American feminists and most academic studies of gender.

Yet not all theorists of sexuality hold the social constructionist position. In polar tension with this view is "essentialism." Essentialists argue that sexual differences and dynamics are grounded in innate psychic and physical qualities. Thus, they contend, there *are* connections between the categories of sex and gender, though essentialists vary as to the extent and significance of these connections. Essentialism seems to be favored by the public at large. Although it is a minority perspective, some scholars in men's studies favor the essentialist stance.

Hegemonic and Nonhegemonic Masculinities

Scholars of men's studies frequently refer to "hegemonic masculinity." This phrase has come to be a technical term designating the dominant construction of masculinity in our culture. Specifically, hegemonic masculinity denotes the ideals considered appropriate for Euro-American, educated, middle- and upper-class, heterosexual, culturally Christian males—that group of men who have held the lion's share of public power in this country. Hegemonic masculinity is implicitly contrasted with nonhegemonic masculinities—the construction of appropriate male behavior for those outside this group, including poor and lower-class men; Native American, African American, Asian American, Hispanic, and Jewish men; and gay men. As some of the essays in this volume demonstrate, the hegemonic masculine ideals have a significant effect on males both inside and outside the hegemonic group.[5]

Masculinity and Masculinities

As the above discussion implies, men's studies generally concerns itself with "masculinities" rather than simply "masculinity." This distinction is merely an extension of the effort to study men as a specific, gendered group. Just as it is important to recognize that men's experience is not identical with human experience, so it is also important to appreciate that the experiences of all men are not the same. At different times, in different places and cultures, in different social and economic classes within the same culture, men have experienced their lives differently and have lived under different norms of appropriate behavior. To speak of masculinities in the plural reminds us of the diversity of men's experiences.

The Men's Movements

While men's studies has been developing as an academic enterprise, other currents in the wider culture have given rise to a number of significant men's movements. In *Contemporary Perspectives on Masculinity,* Kenneth Clatterbaugh identifies six such movements.[6] According to Clatterbaugh, the contemporary stirrings among North American men can be categorized as conservative, profeminist, men's rights, spiritual, socialist, and group-specific. Each of these movements differs significantly from the others, but there are also considerable areas of agreement among them.

Conservatism

The conservative perspective denotes less a "movement" and more the philosophical articulation of traditional beliefs about masculine and feminine characteristics and roles. Gender conservatism often relies on evolutionary biology to support the traditional view that the proper role of men is provider and protector of the nuclear family. Gender conservatives frequently justify their views by appealing to traits believed to be intrinsic to male and female natures. Because men are physically strong, aggressive, and competitive, argue gender conservatives, they are innately suited to protect and provide for women and children. Another variety of gender conservativism takes a perhaps more interesting, but far less flattering, view of male nature. According to those who hold this position, males are by nature excessively violent and destructive and require strict social controls to keep these tendencies in check. Gender conservatives of this stripe believe that the traditional male roles of provider and protector enable men to channel their antisocial aggression in more wholesome, society-enhancing ways. In the 1990s, gender conservatism has been given a religious spin with the Promise Keepers movement. Promise Keepers has become increasingly influential among evangelical Christian men who believe that most of society's ills stem from the failure of men to accept their God-given responsibilities as provider, protector, and spiritual head of the nuclear family.

Profeminism

In almost diametrical tension with gender conservatism is profeminism. Many profeminist men agree with the conservative description of men but disagree with conservative solutions. Profeminist men assent to the observation that men have been on the whole aggressive and competitive, and they point to the destructive effects these qualities have had primarily on the lives of women, children, the earth. As the name implies, contemporary profeminism developed as the appreciative response of men to the second wave of feminism begun in the 1960s. Like many feminists, profeminist men eschew the notion that male aggressiveness is somehow grounded in biological nature. The source of this and other traditionally masculine qualities is not male "nature" but centuries of patriarchal socialization. Profeminists are thus "social constructionists." Consonant with this assessment, profeminist men argue that masculine conditioning can and should be transformed in more creative and life-affirming ways. Because of its focus on the social factors that lead to traditional masculine gendering, profeminism advocates sociopolitical activism consistent with liberal or radical feminism.

Men's Rights

Like profeminism, the men's rights perspective arose as a response to the women's movement. And like profeminism, the men's rights movement tends to focus on social and political realities. In contradistinction to profeminism, however, the men's rights perspective addresses specific legal and cultural factors that put men at a disadvantage. Men's rights advocates, for example, target sex-specific military conscription and judicial practices that discriminate against men in child custody cases. To the degree that the men's rights movement has a philosophical grounding, it tends to share the profeminist view that traditional masculine qualities derive from socialization practices rather than innate biological elements. But whereas profeminism focuses attention on the deleterious effects of male conditioning on women, children, and disenfranchised groups, men's rights activists draw attention to its harmful effects on males themselves. This difference accounts for the different emphases of the men's rights and profeminist social agendas. Although at its extreme edge the men's rights perspective is sometimes antifeminist and even misogynistic, it is possible, at least in principle, to support both men's rights and a liberal feminist agenda.

Men's Spiritual Movement

The men's movement that has received the greatest attention from the mainstream media is what Clatterbaugh calls the spiritual movement. Indeed, the men's spiritual movement is commonly taken to be *the* men's movement. One of the reasons the spiritual—or as it is sometimes called, the "mythopoetic"—movement has received attention is what some consider the eccentric behavior of its participants. Weekend retreats, drumming, storytelling, and sweat lodges are some of the activities readily associated with this movement. The mythopoetic movement stems from the belief that modern men have lost a sense of the sacred in their lives. In an effort to recover the sacred, mythopoetic men often turn to premodern and non-Western traditions, which are believed to provide myths, symbols, and rituals for rediscovering authentic manhood. The poet Robert Bly, the mythopoetic movement's best-known though not sole representative, is most often credited with initiating the movement. In his book *Iron John,* an imaginative interpretation of an old fairy tale from the brothers Grimm collection, Bly argues that this and other myths and legends offer essential, but now mostly forgotten, clues about the psychic and spiritual development of men. Although the mythopoetic movement focuses attention on personal transformation, it tends not to place a similar stress on social and political change. For this, it has often been criticized by other groups, including profeminist men (see Michael S. Kimmel, *The Politics of Manhood: Profeminist Men Respond to the Mythopoetic Movement*). Like gender conservativism, the mythopoetic movement tends toward essentialism; nonetheless, the spiritual movement is not necessarily committed to essentialism.

Socialism

The socialist men's movement shares much with profeminism. Both see gender as a social construction and both are centrally concerned with political and social transformation. But whereas profeminists are likely to locate the problems of masculinity in male sexual violence, socialists see these problems deriving from the class structures of capitalism. According to socialists, masculinity and femininity are products of economic relations, principally the antagonistic relationship between the working and owning classes. Drawing primarily on the works of Marx and Engels, socialist men focus attention on the reproduction of various masculinities among different classes of men. Gender analysis, they remind us, cannot be complete without taking into account the matter of socioeconomic class. In theory, classical socialists believe that the problematic features of male conditioning, including the oppression of women, will not be sufficiently addressed until Western capitalist economic structures are dismantled and replaced by structures reflecting more egalitarian economic relations.

Group-Specific Movements

Finally, Clatterbaugh identifies what he calls group-specific men's movements. These are perspectives that deal with the special interests of particular communities of men, such as African American men, gay men, or Jewish men. Each group-specific movement is concerned with the ways certain social factors, such as racism, heterosexism, or anti-Semitism, affect the experience of males. African American men, for instance, focus on racist stereotypes about black male sexuality, "black-on-black" violence, and the impact of poverty and joblessness on African American masculinity. Since the protector-provider role is central to the dominant construction of masculinity, many African American men must grapple

with the meaning of their manhood when racial dynamics make it difficult to fulfill this role. The Million Man March, a rally of African American men who gathered in Washington, D.C., in 1995, called by Nation of
Islam minister Louis Farrakhan and supported by Benjamin Chavis and
Cornel West, has been the most dramatic demonstration of this group-
specific movement.

Similarly, because heterosexism is a key element of the dominant construction of masculinity in our culture, gay men have had to respond politically to institutionalized homophobia and personally to the way heterosexist attitudes have shaped their sense of maleness. In the cases of
both African American men and gay men, the unique forms of their exclusion from dominant ideals of society ally them with the women who
suffer similar forms of oppression. African American men make common
cause with African American women in opposing racism; gay men join
with lesbians to fight heterosexism. But their status as men sets them
apart in some key ways from the women who also face racism and heterosexism. Partly for this reason, group-specific men's movements frequently overlap the other men's movements. For example, African American men may participate in the mythopoetic and socialist movements or
gay men may find common ground with men's rights and profeminist
men.

Men's studies as an academic enterprise is not coterminous with any
one of these movements and, indeed, finds itself sometimes at odds and
sometimes in agreement with them. Both academic men's studies and the
wider cultural movements, however, share a concern to analyze the concept of masculinity critically and to suggest more constructive ways to be
male in our society. If the authors of this volume have anything in common, it is the conviction that contemporary masculinities are in dire need
of transformation.

Men's Studies and Religion

While men's studies scholars have produced impressive social scientific research exploring the construction of masculinities, little has yet
appeared that explicitly explores the relationships between religious
traditions and the experiences of masculinities. The few scholarly
monographs that have overtly made these connections include works by
James B. Nelson,[7] Philip Culbertson,[8] Patrick Arnold,[9] James Dittes,[10]
Eugene Monick,[11] and Stephen B. Boyd.[12] From the perspective of the
men's movements, a number of works have appeared, emerging
chiefly—and not surprisingly—from the men's spiritual movement.
These include works by Robert Bly,[13] Sam Keen,[14] and Robert Moore
and Douglas Gillette.[15]

The relative absence of major works in the area of men and religious studies has been a key motivation in our desire to produce this collection of essays. The majority of these essays have been commissioned especially for this volume, and in many cases the authors have read some of the works of the other contributors. Those essays that have been published elsewhere have been largely revised for the present work.

A collection of essays, we believe, is particularly important at this juncture in men's studies in religion. A collection is able to demonstrate a wide variety of perspectives and approaches that are possible when men and masculinities are taken seriously as categories for reflection in religious studies. By bringing together such a diverse array of works, we hope to stimulate further research by showing the fruitfulness of men's studies approaches and to contribute to an important conversation that is just beginning to emerge.

The essays we have selected include works by historians, biblical specialists, theologians, ethicists, and scholars of comparative religions. They include representatives from all of the perspectives identified by Clatterbaugh, except the conservative. Further, they are written by authors who represent a diversity of class, sexual orientation, gender, race, and religious tradition.

Outline of the Book

Redeeming Men comprises two major divisions: "The Problematics of Masculinity" and "Resources for Reconstructing Manhood." In the first, we explore the social, psychological, and theological dynamics contributing to the difficulties of contemporary masculinities for men and women. We begin with part 1, "The Dynamics of Power in Shaping Masculine Identity." The two chapters offered here examine the nature of male gendering in relation to the concept of power from explicitly theological perspectives. In part 2, "The Role of Religion in Shaping Masculine Identity," we begin to consider the impact of religion on male experience with three historical case studies taken from the three major Western traditions. In part 3, "The Role of Masculinity in Shaping Religions," the perspective is reversed, and we explore the ways male experiences have influenced the development of religious practices and thought. Here, three examples from nineteenth- and twentieth-century Euro-American culture illustrate the bearing of masculine constructions on specific Western religious traditions. In part 4, "The Effects of Masculinity," the contributors explore the influence of dominant masculinity on the experience of those not included by the definition of hegemonic masculinity. Specifically, we have included essays that concern women, Native American men, poor men, and Jewish men.

Having established some of the detrimental consequences of masculine conditioning on men, women, children, and the rest of the created order, in the second major division we consider resources from religious traditions for reimagining a more wholesome sense of maleness. In part 5, "Myth, Ritual, Spiritual Discipline, and Community," we begin this exploration with four chapters about male spirituality. In part 6, "Theology and Ethics," the investigation continues with several chapters that reflect on contemporary religious practice. Finally, we conclude with a brief chapter that contemplates the common themes and tensions among the essays and suggests trajectories for future exploration.

NOTES

1. Over the past decade, the interdisciplinary field of men's studies has gained increasing acceptance in American academic institutions and scholarly societies. Recent estimates from the American Men's Studies Association, a network of scholars and practitioners engaged in the critical discussion of men and masculinities, indicate that 400 to 500 men's studies courses are currently offered in U.S. colleges and universities.

2. Harry Brod, "The Case for Men's Studies," in *The Making of Masculinities: The New Men's Studies* (Winchester, Mass.: George Allen & Unwin, 1987), 40.

3. Brod, "Case for Men's Studies," 40.

4. For a more complete discussion of basic concepts in the study of gender, see Clyde W. Franklin II, *The Changing Definition of Masculinity* (New York: Plenum Press, 1984). For a challenge to the belief that sex is strictly a biological category, see Thomas W. Laqueur, *Making Sex: Body and Gender from the Greeks to Freud* (Cambridge, Mass.: Harvard University Press, 1990).

5. For a fuller elaboration of "hegemonic masculinity," see R. W. Connell, *Gender and Power: Society, the Person, and Sexual Politics* (Stanford, Calif.: Stanford University Press, 1987), 183–87; and R. W. Connell, *Masculinities* (Berkeley and Los Angeles: University of California Press, 1995), 77–78.

6. Kenneth Clatterbaugh, *Contemporary Perspectives on Masculinity: Men, Women, and Politics in Modern Society* (Boulder, Colo.: Westview Press, 1990).

7. James B. Nelson, *The Intimate Connection: Male Sexuality, Masculine Spirituality* (Philadelphia: Westminster Press, 1988).

8. Philip Culbertson, *The New Adam: The Future of Male Spirituality* (Minneapolis: Fortress Press, 1992).

9. Patrick Arnold, *Wildmen, Warriors, and Kings* (New York: Crossroad, 1991).

10. James Dittes, *The Male Predicament: On Being a Male Today* (San Francisco: Harper & Row, 1985).

11. Eugene Monick, *Phallos: Sacred Image of the Masculine* (Toronto: Inner City Books, 1987).

12. Stephen B. Boyd, *The Men We Long to Be: From Domination to a New Christian Understanding of Manhood* (San Francisco: Harper San Francisco, 1995).

13. Robert Bly, *Iron John: A Book about Men* (Reading, Mass.: Addison-Wesley Publishing Co., 1990).

14. Sam Keen, *Fire in the Belly: On Being a Man* (New York: Bantam Books, 1991).

15. Robert Moore and Douglas Gillette, *King Warrior Magician Lover: Rediscovering the Archetypes of the Mature Masculine* (San Francisco: Harper San Francisco, 1990).

THE PROBLEMATICS
OF MASCULINITY

PART I

THE DYNAMICS OF POWER IN SHAPING MASCULINE IDENTITY

We begin with two chapters that deal with the relationship of power to male roles and masculine identity. The authors of both chapters agree that men, at least in dominant cultural groups, are conditioned and expected to exercise a power over others—a power that, as many feminists and profeminist men point out, is often destructive. Both explore reasons why this is so and focus on the costs the use of this kind of power exacts from men, as well as noting the effects it has on women.

Steve Smith, a philosopher in conversation with feminist perspectives, attempts to provide some clarity about the definitions of power often implicit in discussions about men and their relation to masculinity. He distinguishes "threat power" from "integrative power" and argues that scarcity of resources and human egocentrism lead to the necessity of the use of coercive power as a human survival strategy. Observing that since men have historically carried the responsibility for exercising "threat power," men, more often than women, engage in its abuse, producing a "toxic masculinity" that is more life diminishing than life enhancing. He provides practical suggestions by which the destructive effects of "toxic masculinity" might be limited, including the critique of interpretations of primary religious texts of Western thought that legitimate the exclusive use of threat power by men. Smith stresses the value of recognizing threat and integrative power and the necessity of women and men sharing both the opportunities and responsibilities in exercising them.

Stephen Boyd's chapter is an example of one of Smith's suggestions taken up; he explores Martin Luther's interpretation of the biblical accounts of the creation and sin of Adam and Eve in the book of Genesis. He argues that Luther, consistent with one strand of historical Christian interpretation, believed that both woman (Eve) and man (Adam) were created in the image of God and had equal roles in ruling the institutions God had ordained to order human society. Because of the different nature of their sins, God punished the woman by denying her power in public institutions (the church, family, and state) and the man by requiring him to rule them in a coercive, dominating way. In Luther's tragic view, original equality between men and women is restored, not by the first advent of Christ, but only by the second. While Luther's interpretation of the creation accounts undermines a theological legitimation of male dominance, his pessimistic view of human nature has functioned to support it. Boyd ends the chapter by suggesting the need for building on Luther's insights.

From these essays, we lift up the following issues and questions. Smith believes that many men exercise "threat power" as the expression of their self-sacrificial love for others—women, children, and the earth. In that sense, it can be seen as a dutiful repudiation (Luther) of men's egocentrism. However, is it not more accurate to see men's insistent hold on these dominating institutional roles as precisely an expression of men's egocentric, self-aggrandizing, and therefore sinful nature? Or, is it possible that both of these perspectives express some aspect of the truth?

According to Smith, human egocentrism leads to the necessity of the restraining use of "threat power." He assumes a theological anthropology that agrees with Luther about the enduring effects of original sin. With Boyd, however, he is more optimistic than Luther about the redemptive healing of that human self-absorption in this world. For example, Boyd suggests that work against sexism and its concomitant sexual objectification contributes to the healing of Luther's "raging lust," or men's compulsive sexuality. Is he right? If so, how realistic is the elimination of sexism in the world as we know it? And what do we do in the meantime?

Given his belief in the continuing effects of sin and, therefore, the necessity of the use of "threat power," Smith argues that women, as well as men, should have the opportunity and share the responsibility for its use. We assume that he believes that women are as susceptible as men to the temptation to use that power in self-aggrandizing, abusive ways. He evidently believes that the sharing of responsibility for that power will provide checks and balances against its abuse.

Smith's discussion of power, though helpful, nevertheless invites further development and elaboration. Another framework, developed by Pamela Cooper-White, is compatible with Smith's analysis but expands it in fruitful ways. Drawing on philosophical and theological sources, Cooper-White delineates four kinds of power and describes their usefulness and limitations in the pursuit of justice.[1] Power-over is the power "to manage and control others [Smith's threat power]." Since power-over has often been death dealing, many feminists have simply affirmed alternative formulations of power—power-within and power-with—that contribute to the development of a notion of justice which stresses mutuality, responsibility, and care. Power-within is an "inner wisdom, intuition, self-esteem, even spark of the divine" that empowers acts of resistance to mistreatment and systemic forms of oppression. Power-with reaches out to affirm the sovereignty of the power-within of the self and the other and, therefore, strives for mutuality, rather than control, operating by negotiation and consensus.

Cooper-White, however, finds limits to this typology in providing adequate guidance for living. Power-within, without external reference, can become solipsistic; one can mistake one's own neurosis for the voice of the true self, or the image of God within. Power-with can devolve into "stifling merger" where one's envy, competition, and anger remain unacknowledged. An overemphasis, then, on power-with can lead to indecisiveness and leave groups "susceptible to manipulation, covert exercises of power-over, and psychological bullying." In addition, both power-within and power-within are often limited to the inner life of individuals or to relationships within smaller groups and, therefore, do not offer a viable alternative to power-over in the larger society.

In light of these limitations, Cooper-White believes, with Smith, that aspects of power-over can be used to make valuable contributions to right order. Referring to such aspects as power-for, she asserts that the legitimate exercise of "authority, responsibility, nurture, and stewardship" has positive roles to play in establishing justice in the world.[2] Power-for can be used to promote right order by promoting decisive action, limit-setting, and organization. Since power-for can easily devolve into unilateral and exploitative power-over, it must be "proportionally linked with service, and the purposes of that service must be defined by those served" by it. In other words, it must be directed and checked by structures of accountability that emerge from a fourth form of power, power-in-community.

Power-in-community, according to Cooper-White, holds individuality (power-within) and relationality (power-with) and transforms them toward a larger right ordering of things (i.e., the "kingdom of God" in her Christian perspective), thereby moving into the realm of the prophetic. In her vision of power-in-community, leadership, or the exercise of power-for, is "authorized by those served by that leadership and it is accountable to them." This notion of power-in-community may provide the checks and balances Smith calls for.

In the conclusion of this volume, we will have occasion to use Cooper-White's theoretical model to illuminate and relate the analyses by several other of our authors of the relationships among men, masculinity, religion, and power.

NOTES

1. The following summary and quotations are taken from Pamela Cooper-White's *The Cry of Tamar: Violence against Women and the Church's Response* (Minneapolis: Fortress Press, 1995), chap. 1.

2. Cooper-White is indebted to Martha Ellen Stortz, *Pastor Power* (Nashville: Abingdon Press, 1993) for the term *power-for.*

1

FEAR AND POWER
IN THE LIVES OF MEN

Steve Smith

My theme is power. I explore an apparent paradox: according to usual definitions, men are generally more powerful than women,[1] yet on average in the United States, men are less successful than women in meeting their fundamental needs of life, health, safety, shelter, and love. Men die, on average, more than seven years before women; their deaths are preceded by more severe health problems overall, especially those related to stress[2]; considering all categories of violent crime, men are more likely to be victims of violence[3]; men are more likely to be injured on the job or at play[4], and more likely to be homeless; men commit suicide at more than three times the rate of women[5]; and with its emphasis upon stoicism and denial of dependency and feelings, the male role in our culture inhibits men's capacities for giving and receiving love.

Powerful—yet lonely, vulnerable, sick, homeless, and dead: how are we to unravel the apparent paradox of men's power/powerlessness? I argue that the very pursuit and exercise of power as commonly defined tends to be destructive of those who exercise it, as well as often harmful to others. If power corrupts the powerful, it also tends to destroy them. Yet male and female alike, we are all complicit in social, political, and economic systems that hold up such power as both necessary and desirable. Indeed, if we are both clearheaded and honest, most of us will grant a need for the responsible exercise of power over others, despite its inevitable costs. So long as males disproportionately exercise such power, they will disproportionately suffer those costs.

I write as a white male, a citizen of the United States, a philosopher, and a member of the Religious Society of Friends (Quakers). From its beginnings in seventeenth-century England, Quakerism has preached a radical message on power and nonviolence; in refusing military service, George Fox (1624–1691), the founder of Quakerism, declared that he "lived in the virtue of that life and power that took away the occasion of all wars."[6] Not coincidentally, early Friends emphasized equality of the sexes. Though later generations of Quakers have not always lived up to this ideal, the founders of Quakerism—including George Fox and Margaret Fell themselves—explicitly maintained that men and women should be "helpmeets" for each other, and that every woman, as well as every man, may rightly serve as a minister of God's word.

Unlike other pacifist or "peace" churches, however, Quakers did not seek to withdraw from the world to create an isolated subculture; on the contrary, William Penn (1644–1718), a close associate of George Fox and the founder of the State of Pennsylvania, declared that "True godliness does not turn men out of the world, but enables them to live better in it, and excites their endeavors to mend it."[7] From the beginning, Friends have frequently been moved "to speak truth to power." Their efforts to sustain an authentic testimony of nonviolence while dealing realistically with existing power structures have generated among Friends an ongoing dialogue on power, peace, and justice, often accompanied by profound ambivalence and soul-searching. As a Friend I have inherited this legacy, and still struggle to find my place within it. In this chapter I offer no clear, unambiguous solutions; instead, I invite the reader to join in dialogue with me in an effort to live with integrity.

The dialogue begins with an enlargement of our concept of power. As feminist writers have frequently observed, power is more than simply "power over," that is, the ability to coerce others to act as one wishes. Bertrand Russell defined power in the broadest sense as "the production of intended effects,"[8] encompassing the ability to create or bring about *any* perceived good. Thus a relatively powerful person is one who usually can get what he or she chooses or needs, whereas a powerless person lacks such ability. Drawing upon economist Kenneth Boulding's *Three Faces of Power,*[9] we can distinguish between integrative power and threat power. *Integrative power* is the ability to bring about desirable results through affection, giving, loyalty, caring, and other forms of bonding. A person who is able to create and maintain strong friendships has a significant form of integrative power, for example. Perhaps the greatest of human goods, including self-esteem, appreciation of beauty, and love itself, are expressions of effective integrative power.

Threat power, the ability to coerce or control others through arousing fear of unpleasant consequences, is used to secure goods produced by other means. Threat power includes much more than blatant intimidation; for example, common forms of threat power are simple expressions of disapproval. Frowns, ridicule, coldness, ostracism, and other such displays are pervasive means by which societal norms are enforced; we conform because we fear rejection and exclusion. In particular, anger is often intended (and usually experienced by others) as a threat, suggesting possible withdrawal of love, limitations of freedom, or other forms of punishment or retaliation. When we get angry at others, we are exercising threat power.

To control their children, most parents use a variety of explicit and implied threats of unpleasant consequences, from simple disapproval to loss of privileges to corporeal punishment. At our workplace, our motivation to perform well typically includes fear of the consequences of failure, and in supervising others, we are likely to employ not only "carrots" but also "sticks." Indeed, reliance upon threat power is a central feature of any group or institution that exercises authority over potentially resisting others. The law itself is a massive and complex instrument of threat power, ideally rationalized by justice and fairness. We legislate penalties for murder, theft, rape, molestation, and so on to deter unwanted behavior and to establish guidelines for an acceptable social environment. Legalized threat power is deemed necessary in virtually every society to protect, maintain, and enhance valuable social bonds and economic goods. (As we know, not all uses of legalized threat power are benign; the mechanism of law may enforce exploitation and bolster unjust privilege.) Closely allied with legal sanctions are moral sanctions. Moral disapproval is generally experienced as unpleasant by those who are judged deficient, and it may indicate readiness to deter or punish the unwanted behavior. When we judge another to be morally lacking, we are usually exercising threat power.

Women and men in all societies exercise both integrative and threat power. In most societies, however, males are assigned a larger role in the use of threat power (particularly in its harsher forms) and females are usually assigned a larger role in the exercise of integrative power. In his wide-ranging review of manhood as an achieved status in cultures around the world, *Manhood in the Making: Cultural Concepts of Masculinity,* anthropologist David Gilmore identifies certain nearly universal features which may be regarded as training for the exercise of threat power.[10] In society after society, from aboriginal people of Oceania, South America, and East Africa to traditional cultures of India, China, Japan, and the Mediterranean, to modern North America, Gilmore repeatedly finds a culturally sanctioned emphasis for males on toughness, aggressiveness, bravery, and stoicism in the face of danger and pain, exacted at great physical and emotional cost to the boys who are made to undergo it. We may call this pattern "stressed masculinity," to reflect both the cultural pressures upon males to exhibit it, and its psychic and physical cost to males themselves.

If stressed masculinity is a cultural artifact (as Gilmore believes) rather than a biological necessity, why is it nearly universal? Gilmore notes that

"Those cultures that have a pronounced manhood ideology seem to be the ones that have chosen fight as a survival strategy. Without a genetic imprinting, men in those cultures have to be conditioned to be brave in order to fight."[11] This conclusion is reinforced by Gilmore's examination of two exceptions to the pattern: Tahiti and Semai. Both cultures have largely rejected fighting and belligerence, and not coincidentally display a high degree of sexual indeterminacy or androgyny.

Tahitian men "are no more aggressive than women; women do not seem 'softer' or more 'maternal' than men . . . men and women also have roles so similar as to seem almost indistinguishable . . . there is no stress on proving manhood, no pressure on men to appear in any significant way different from women or children."[12] "Men share a cultural value of 'timidity' which forbids retaliation, and even when provoked men rarely come to blows."[13] Perhaps Tahitian men are relatively peaceful partly because living is easy in their lush tropical climate; Gilmore notes that "The harsher the environment and the scarcer the resources, the more manhood is stressed as inspiration and goal."[14] Perhaps also the island isolation of Tahitian society provided natural insulation from marauding outsiders, so that fighting seemed unnecessary.

The second exception noted by Gilmore, the Semai of central Malaysia, are able to avoid most conflict with others simply by running away. Abhorring violence and conflict, the Semai have adopted a survival strategy of "fleeing rather than fighting."[15] Gilmore reports that Western observers invariably describe the Semais as "weak" and "timid": "Whenever trouble arises, they either immediately capitulate, or else they disappear into the forest."[16]

In summary, Gilmore observes that "when men are conditioned to fight, manhood is important; where men are conditioned to flight, the opposite is true. Just why most societies have chosen fight . . . probably is related to the general scarcity of resources and the inability of most societies to run away, like the Semai, into open wilderness."[17]

> Because of the universal urge to flee from danger, we may regard "real" manhood as an inducement for high performance in the social struggle for scarce resources, a code of conduct that advances collective interests by overcoming inner inhibitions. In fulfilling their obligations, men stand to lose—a hovering threat that separates them from women and boys. They stand to lose their reputations or their lives; yet their prescribed tasks must be done if the group is to survive and prosper. Because boys must steel themselves to enter into such struggles, they must be prepared by various sorts of tempering and toughening. To be men, most of all, they must accept the fact that they are expendable. This acceptance of expendability constitutes the basis of the manly pose everywhere it is encountered.[18]

The primary function of stressed masculinity is thus the exercise of threat power to serve and protect the in-group. In most societies, this task has fallen primarily upon males, perhaps because of their greater average size and physical strength, and because they are less needed for gestation, birthing, and nurturing children. (Women can, of course, be fully as fierce as men, especially for example in the direct defense of their loved ones.)

Requiring self-denial, risk, and pain, stressed masculinity does not come easily. Males must be initiated into their socially prescribed role, usually by older males in the society. For better or worse, the subjection of boys to stressed masculinity continues in our own culture—through athletic activities, ridicule of softness and of laziness and cowardice, and a conditional love that bestows approval only when demanding expectations are met.

Because it denies fear, stressed masculinity promotes exaggerated levels of anger. Much if not all of male anger is masked fear. Because it views men as expendable, stressed masculinity also invites denial of death itself; hence the exuberant and often foolhardy risk taking of many young men in our culture in a pattern of self-destructiveness that one author has dubbed "macho-psychotic."[19]

Stressed masculinity separates thought from feeling and destroys healthy self-care with a body-denying ideology—thus accounting for much of the disparity between men and women in longevity, health, and psychological well-being. The exercise of integrative power tends to enhance life and health, for self and others: we flourish more readily under conditions of love, trust, connectedness, and affiliation with nurturing others. In contrast, the exercise of threat power tends to be life- and health-diminishing, for self and others. In mounting a threat—whether of simple anger, or of a harsher sanction of some kind—one steels oneself against unpleasant reactions, closing off to empathy for others and to one's own fear and need. Threat power is the essence of objectification: for the person exercising threat power, the other becomes less a person, a center of self-governing will, and more an object or thing to be manipulated and controlled. In exercising threat power, one momentarily dies to a part of oneself, distancing from and objectifying one's own body and feelings. Threat power separates and alienates, promoting a fortress mentality of lonely autonomy and a demand for self-sufficiency. If the exercise of threat power becomes second nature over a lifetime of effort to meet stringent social expectations, the implications for longevity and health are not difficult to discern.

As we understand better the effects of exercising integrative and threat power, the paradox of men's power/powerlessness comes into better focus. Our culture tends to identify power exclusively with control based upon implied threat. In our own and most other cultures, such power is overwhelmingly in the hands of men. If power is exclusively threat power, men are indeed the more powerful sex. But power includes the ability to bring about *any* perceived good—including meeting one's own basic needs; and in this regard, men are often relatively powerless. Trained to exercise threat power, often themselves targets of threat power—at work and play, in public and private—men become sadly deficient in integrative power and consequently handicapped in taking care of themselves. Men thus become dependent upon women to meet basic human needs, while (in the service of threat power) denying their very dependency.[20]

Is threat power dispensable? May we improve the human condition by abandoning it entirely? Some perfectionist and utopian thinkers have answered yes to this question. The image of a benign anarchy in which all persons respond lovingly to one another without fear of punishment is a secular vision of the kingdom of heaven itself, or of the Garden of Eden. As told in Genesis, however, this myth suggests a negative answer to our question. Adam and Eve were expelled from paradise when they refused to abide freely by principles of rightness. By implication, we need threat power to maintain order, especially in a world of scarcities; otherwise, our greed and self-centeredness would turn anarchy into chaos.

Rejection of all threat power is one definition of absolute pacifism. Appeals for complete unilateral disarmament may be based upon a similar hope; likewise for certain forms of political anarchism and proposals to eliminate all punishment of children. Belief in the possibility of absolute pacifism tacitly rests upon a principle elucidated by the Indian sage Patanjali and espoused by Mahatma Gandhi: that violence ceases in the presence of nonviolence.[21] Patanjali's dictum implies that insofar as integrative power is successfully exercised, threat power becomes unnecessary. In the words of the First Letter of John (4:18), "perfect love casts out fear."

To abandon threat power entirely would mean not only to abolish all military forces, but also all police, prisons, and fines, and indeed, all punishment of any kind. In such an ideal world, no one would fear consequences from criminal behavior; workers would never worry about being fired; anger would never be used to influence others; and no parent would ever threaten to discipline a child. Gandhi knew that nonviolence in this exalted sense—in which all fear and intimidation are banished, leaving only acts of unconditional love—was a moral ideal to be approached as nearly as possible, but which seldom if ever is achieved by humans. (He frequently acknowledged that he himself had not achieved perfect nonviolence.) Gandhi emphasized that cultivating nonviolence requires extraordinary discipline, sacrifice, and suffering. A genuine pacifist is a kind of spiritual athlete who must be constantly in training.

In biological terms, absolute nonviolence would be a complete suspension of the fight-flight response: facing potential harm from others, one would respond neither by fighting nor by fleeing, but with loving readiness to experience all necessary suffering and still extend compassion. While urging constant self-discipline to become more nonviolent, Gandhi held that violence in the defense of important goods was to be preferred over cowardice. When a group of Indian men fled before an attacking mob, leaving family and possessions open to abuse and destruction, and afterward rationalized their flight by citing allegiance to nonviolence, Gandhi sternly replied:

> He who cannot protect himself or his nearest and dearest or their honor by nonviolently facing death, may and ought to do so by violently dealing with the oppressor. He who can do neither of the two is a burden. He has no business to be the head of a family. He must either hide himself, or must rest content to live for ever in helplessness and be prepared to crawl like a worm at the bidding of a bully.[22]

Gandhi also countenanced the use of a coercive police force to maintain law and order (though he termed it "a fall from the pure doctrine") until such time as society had mastered nonviolence sufficiently to render such coercion unnecessary.[23]

If the most successful proponent of nonviolence in modern times affirmed a qualified need for coercion under imperfect conditions, we should not rail self-righteously against all use of threat and force to protect goods that we hold dear. Historically, for example, Quakers have not generally objected to the existence of police, whose job is to enforce the law and maintain order.[24] Though they have worked to make punishment more humane, they have not advocated anarchy and the abolition of all social and political restrictions. For our personal safety, for the production and fair distribution of our food, for the preservation of our homes and the means of our livelihood, we depend upon expectations of civilized and orderly behavior, backed by the threat of sanctions of many kinds. To condemn all use of threat power while clinging to the benefits it secures is at best naive, and at worst, hypocritical.

So long as any good is scarce—food, water, comfortable and attractive living space, and so on—and so long as humans themselves fall short of complete altruism, it would appear that conflict can be averted only through an uneasy balance of competing threats—and some persons will need to be trained in the effective exercise of threat power. In this view, threat power is a necessary evil: unavoidable but costly, both to those over whom it is exercised and to those who exercise it. It is in this vein that we may understand Stephen Boyd's reading of Luther—that in the perspective of religious myth, male domination may be viewed as a punishment or consequence of sin.[25]

Thus the path of nonviolence is a high and stringent calling, no cheap shortcut to the peaceable kingdom. It is small wonder that most societies, groups, and individuals have felt justified in exercising force and the threat of force to secure certain goods. Parents discipline children; businesses fire irresponsible workers; states punish criminals; nations deter invaders; all in the service of cherished goods and values. The moral and spiritual task of those of us who are committed to nonviolence is to work wherever possible toward replacing hatred with love, violence with nonviolence, and threat power with integrative power, while recognizing that moralistic condemnations of all use of threat and coercion are dishonest. Our task is to journey in the direction of heaven, not to pretend membership in it.

To admit that we need threat power is not to justify its use in every situation, to any degree, of course. Much human suffering arises from gratuitous and excessive use of threat power, destructive rather than protective of the common good. Because men are assigned a larger role in the exercise of threat power, they are also its greatest abusers; for example, male prisoners outnumber female prisoners by a ratio of about eighteen to one.[26] The abuse of threat power by men has been called "toxic masculinity"[27]: swaggering macho belligerence, rape and sexual molestation, destruction of the natural environment, and a host of other evils. As Abraham Maslow once observed, if the only tool one owns is a hammer, then everything begins to look like a nail.

The wildly escalating culture of violence within the United States and elsewhere may seem to require ever-increasing levels of threat and punishment. Such "law and order" arguments overlook a more basic point: to glorify the exercise of threat in maintaining justice (for example, in *Rambo* and *Dirty Harry* films) is also indirectly to legitimize its unjust misuse. Reliance upon threat is a tacit admission of failure and weakness; we must learn to recognize it as such. Instead of being taught to admire toughness, dominance, repression of empathy, and extreme competitiveness, boys (and girls) need to learn the cost of such behaviors, and to engage in them only reluctantly, when all creative alternatives have been exhausted. Greater involvement of fathers in parenting; more training in nonviolent conflict resolution at every level; reduction of television, video, and other media violence; honest acknowledgment of the costs of highly competitive athletics—these and many other steps may help us to curb toxic masculinity and to reduce the exercise of threat power to that essential minimum required for discipline and order within the home and workplace, on the streets and abroad.[28]

To undercut the rationalization of toxic masculinity, we need also to question the interpretation of primary religious texts in Western thought. When both God and the first human are declared to be male, with woman originally created only for the sake of man; when the first woman was blamed for the first sin, and her punishment was for all time to be ruled over by man; when women were described as lacking the "image of God" (Augustine) and as "misbegotten males" (Thomas Aquinas),[29] it is not surprising that later generations of men have relied upon their understanding of religious authority to justify oppression and abuse of women. As Karen Bloomquist writes, "Exclusively male imagery and language for God continues to legitimize patriarchy and the paradigm of male 'control over' that undergirds the violence-laden situation we find ourselves in today."[30]

Stressed masculinity is not *ipso facto* toxic masculinity, however; nor is the essence of stressed masculinity a need to dominate and subjugate women, children, and nature itself.[31] Societies promote stressed masculinity to acquire and defend scarce goods, for the benefit of the group. The primary meaning of a masculine "denial of the feminine" is the effort by men to deny their own dependence, so that women and children may depend upon them. In fact, men's denial of the feminine originates paradoxically not in hatred, but love, for women and children. Nor is it surprising that a man who is trained to sacrifice his life for others will be tempted to "put them on a pedestal," to fortify his readiness.

Stressed masculinity must be purged of its toxic elements. Unless blinded by ideology or personal wounding, we know of the possibility of such a masculinity: men who are courageous, strong, and sensitive, able both to defend and to nurture loved ones. A persistent theme in the writings of Robert Bly on men is the effort to reclaim the fierceness and inner discipline of masculinity while rejecting its destructive, insensitive aspects. Bly writes of "a positive male energy that has accepted authority," encompassing "intelligence, robust health, compassionate decisiveness, good will, generous leadership"—"male authority accepted for the sake of the community."[32] Positive male energy in Bly's view involves the ability to establish clear boundaries and stand by them, a quality he finds missing in the "soft male" who has abandoned masculine energy altogether. In a dangerous world, we need good boundaries to manage our fear, both to ward off danger and to create a safe haven or home within which fear may be reduced, making space for the freer exercise of integrative power. In most cultures, establishing and maintaining boundaries has been the work of men.

If this sexual division of labor in the use of threat power is to be abolished, both sexes must be equally free on occasion to be needy and dependent, to lean on the other for nurturing and economic support, and both sexes must be equally prepared to risk themselves in the exercise of threat and coercive force, as needed for the good of family and society.

Men must be as free as women to be passive and emotional; women must be as ready as men to be threatening and coercive. If exercise of threat power is deemed essential, women must be permitted to exercise such power equally with men—for example, in military combat roles and as police, security guards, and firefighters—subject only to appropriate, genderless criteria of employment. If any such tasks become compulsory (for example, in the event of a military draft), women and men must be equally liable to serve.

With these concessions to an imperfect world, I return to my primary commitment. Complicit at a thousand levels with a society framed by the exercise of threat power, and unable honestly to affirm absolute pacifism, I nevertheless claim nonviolence as my path and goal. As we share the burden of threat, I invite my sisters and brothers to work with me on our essential moral task: to replace threat power with integrative power and fear with love, without endangering fundamental human goods of life, health, safety, compassion, and human flourishing. Viewed not as an absolute, unbending doctrine but as a working hypothesis inspired by faith, commitment to nonviolence may help us to realize more fully an ideal exalted in our various religious traditions: the primacy of love.

NOTES

A longer version of this chapter was published in *Men's Studies Review* 8, no. 4 (Fall, 1991). For copies please write to Steve Smith, Department of Philosophy, Claremont McKenna College, Claremont, CA 91711.

1. For a concise and comprehensive summary of the facts of male control of public positions of power and influence around the world, see R. W. Connell, *Gender and Power* (Stanford, Calif.: Stanford University Press, 1987), chap. 1.

2. See Herb Goldberg, *The Hazards of Being Male: Surviving the Myths of Masculine Privilege* (New York: Signet, 1976), esp. chap. 12; James Harrison, James Chin, and Thomas Ficarrotto, "Warning: Masculinity May Be Dangerous to Your Health", in *Men's Lives,* ed. Michael S. Kimmel and Michael A. Messner, 296–309 (New York: Macmillan, 1989); *American Health* (January/February 1989): 62f.

3. *Violent Crime in the United States,* U.S. Department of Justice Bureau of Justice Statistics, March 1991, NCJ-127855, 5–9.

4. See Warren Farrell, *The Myth of Male Power* (New York: Simon & Schuster, 1993), chap. 4, "The Death Professions." Farrell's book is a relentless detailing of the costs of the male role for men in this culture.

5. *American Health* (January/February 1989): 63.

6. *The Journal of George Fox,* ed. John L. Nickalls (London: Religious Society of Friends, 1975), 65.

7. William Penn, *No Cross, No Crown,* abridged by Anna Cox Brinton,

Pendle Hill Pamphlet 30, in *Quaker Classics in Brief* (Wallingford, Penn.: Pendle Hill Publications, 1978), 12.

8. Bertrand Russell, quoted in *Encyclopedia of Philosophy*, vol. 6, S.V. "Power," by Stanley I. Benn (New York: Macmillan, 1967), 424.

9. Kenneth E. Boulding, *Three Faces of Power* (Newbury Park, Calif.: Sage Publications, 1990). I have adapted and simplified Boulding's complex, nuanced analysis for my purposes here. Boulding's third major category, exchange or generative power, will not figure in my analysis.

10. David D. Gilmore, *Manhood in the Making: Cultural Concepts of Masculinity* (New Haven, Conn.: Yale University Press, 1990).

11. Ibid., 219.

12. Ibid., 203.

13. Ibid., 206.

14. Ibid., 224.

15. Ibid., 210.

16. Ibid., 211.

17. Ibid., 223.

18. Ibid., 223.

19. Herb Goldberg, *The New Male: From Destruction to Self-Care* (New York: Signet, 1979), 12.

20. These themes are richly explored in Catherine Keller's *From a Broken Web: Separation, Sexism and Self* (Boston: Beacon Press, 1986).

21. Mahatma Gandhi, "Discussion with Pacifists," February, 1940, in *The Collected Works of Mahatma Gandhi*, vol. 71 (Amedabad, India: Navajivan Press, 1978), 225.

22. Mahatma Gandhi, in *Young India*, 1928, reprinted in *For Pacifists*, ed. Bharatan Kumarappa (Ahmedabad, India: Navajivan Publishing House, 1949), 13.

23. Mahatma Gandhi, in *Young India*, 1925, reprinted in Kumarappa, *For Pacifists*, 27.

24. See Peter Brock, *The Quaker Peace Testimony: 1660 to 1914* (York, England: Sessions Book Trust, 1990), esp. 27–30. Fox wrote in 1679, "Caesar's weapons are for the punishment of the evil-doers and for the praise of them that do well; for which he is to have his tribute, his custom, his due." And William Penn declared, "For we believe magistracy to be both lawful and useful for the terrifying of all evil doers; and the praise and encouragement of those that do well" (Brock, *Quaker Peace Testimony*, 322 n. 5).

25. Stephen B. Boyd, "Domination as Punishment: Men's Studies and Religion," *Men's Studies Review* 7, no. 2: 1–10.

26. *BJS Data Report, 1989*, U.S. Department of Justice Bureau of Justice Statistics, NCJ-121514, 80.

27. Shepherd Bliss, "The Mythopoetic Approach to Men," *AXIS*, no. 4 (Winter, 1989–90): 1.

28. For an extensive, well-documented discussion of such strategies, see Myriam Miedzian, *Boys Will Be Boys: Breaking the Link between Masculinity and Violence* (New York: Anchor Books, 1991).

29. Rosemary Radford Ruether, "The Western Religious Tradition and Violence against Women in the Home," in *Christianity, Patriarchy and Abuse: A Feminist Critique,* ed. Joanne Carlson Brown and Carole R. Bohn (New York: Pilgrim Press, 1989), 32.

30. Karen L. Bloomquist, "Sexual Violence: Patriarchy's Offense and Defense," in Brown and Bohn, *Christianity, Patriarchy, and Abuse,* 67.

31. For an eloquent presentation of the view that masculinity is essentially premised upon sexual domination of women, see John Stoltenberg, *Refusing to Be a Man: Essays on Sex and Justice* (New York: Penguin/Meridian, 1990), esp. "Rapist Ethics," 9–24.

32. Robert Bly, *Iron John: A Book about Men* (Reading, Mass.: Addison-Wesley Publishing Co., 1990), 22.

2

MASCULINITY AND MALE DOMINANCE: MARTIN LUTHER ON THE PUNISHMENT OF ADAM

Stephen B. Boyd

> But [Adam's] position is burdened with a definite punishment, since it is the husband's duty to support his family, to rule, to direct, and to instruct; and these things cannot be done without extraordinary trouble and very great effort.
>
> —Martin Luther

According to Protestant reformer Martin Luther (1483–1546) men have inherited a condition from Adam that entails arduous and life-shortening responsibilities. Two of these roles—husband and pastor, or spiritual leader—Luther believed Adam exercised even in paradise, before the fall into sin. In other words, the family and church were ordained by God in creation and men had specific roles to play in them. The sins of Adam and Eve led, in Luther's view, to a pervasive egocentricity in humankind that destroyed the harmony that existed in the Garden of Eden. As a result, God ordained civil government as one means to constrain the destructive forces lodged in the hearts, minds, and bodies of every human being. In order to aid the state in managing these antisocial forces, the family and church were "institutionalized," or freighted with certain dominative dynamics, whereby husbands and pastors ruled and wives and laypersons obeyed. Because men, as the successors of Adam, were to fill the offices of magistrate, husband, and pastor, their lives were burdened with "the utmost difficulties"—difficulties Luther interpreted as men's punishment for sin.

In this chapter I will explore Luther's understanding of what it is to be a man and bear the various responsibilities required of manhood.[1] I will focus on the difficulties caused for men, and others, by explaining what the mature Luther said, in his Lectures on Genesis (1535–45), about men's responsibilities as pastors and husbands, both in paradise and after the fall into sin. I will briefly locate Luther's position in the context of the history of interpretation of key passages in Genesis, and then comment on some contemporary implications of his position.

My thesis is that, according to Luther, Adam's punishment requires a man, as pastor, to preach and uphold the Word of God to people who do not want to hear it and, as a husband, to have sexual relations with a wife who, for good reasons, resents him. The good news is that the quality of a man's participation in these spheres has nothing to do with his salvation; the bad news is that this grim situation will not get better in this life; it will get worse. To develop this thesis, I turn to Luther's exposition of the original state of humanity, the fall into sin, and to men's responsibilities as pastors and husbands after the Fall—focusing primarily on the husband role.

According to Luther, Adam, in his original state, had the "innocence of a child." He also had a choice; he could, in time, be translated to a deathless life or he could plunge into a curse, sin, and death.[2] Had he not sinned, his eating from the tree of life would have preserved his perpetual youth and there would have been none of those inconveniences which come with age: wrinkles, less active hands and feet, and, well, less "power for procreation."[3] In addition, he would have been translated, at a predetermined time, into a "virile innocence," wherein he would revert to the image of God and his physical activities would have come to an end as he entered an eternal and spiritual life.[4] Further, Adam had work to do. Luther says that Adam was created for work, not leisure, but that work would have been a supreme joy—more welcome than leisure.[5]

The two spheres of Adam's work were the institutions ordained by God before the fall into sin—the church and the family. As a physical being, Adam needed a physical form of worship by which to train his body in obedience to God. Therefore, God provided "the tree of the knowledge of good and evil" as Adam's altar and pulpit, where he was to admonish his descendants to live holy and sinless lives, to work faithfully in the garden, and to watch carefully the garden and the tree of the knowledge of good and evil.[6] In addition to his responsibilities in the "natural basilica," Adam had family responsibilities; he had a wife. Why is that? Since Adam was righteous, he had no need of woman.[7] Still, God said, "it is not good for man to be alone." Why? Well, because God decided that human beings, unlike angels who as spiritual beings did not procreate, would reproduce through sexual union, as did other animals. It is not clear why God made this decision, and Luther says that we should not be too inquisitive about it. But God did, and consequently God created "male and female."[8] So God was not speaking of Adam's personal good (he did not need a wife for that), but the "common good." A wife was needed to bring about the increase of the human race.[9]

According to Luther, the woman God created was paradoxically equal to Adam but dependent on him. The woman had mental gifts "in the same degree" as did Adam; she partook of both "the divine image and similitude" and of the "rule over everything."[10] Nevertheless, she was a "somewhat different being from the man, having different members and a much weaker nature." As the moon is less excellent than the sun, so the woman was not equal to the man in "glory and prestige." Luther gives two examples of the way in which the "male somewhat excelled the female." First, he asserts that had the serpent assailed Adam first, Adam would have said, "Shut up! The Lord's command was different."[11] So, there is implied a firmer will or more rational nature in the male, or at least a more independent, autonomous reason or will.[12] Luther also says that the woman "was so created that she should everywhere and always be around her husband . . . ; she so binds herself to a man that she will be about him and will live together with him as one flesh."[13] The implication is that the woman's dependency is a weakness that leaves her vulnerable to Satan. In fact, Luther says that Satan attacked her rather than Adam because "he sees that she is so dependent on her husband that she thinks that she cannot sin."

For Luther, there is a necessary complementarity between the sexes; therefore, he criticizes the institutionalization of celibacy in the Roman Church, because it implies that priests are not men in need of a female complement. God is the effective cause for the creation of woman and marriage; the final cause is "for the wife to be a mundane dwelling place to her husband." She is her husband's nest and home, where he stays; otherwise, men would not have reason for a dwelling and fixed habitation.[14] While the woman's duty was to provide a dwelling for her husband, Adam's duty was to fulfill the intention of God for human procreation by having intercourse with the woman. Since this procreative act would have been "a most sacred" act, devoid of the passion of lust and shame, it would have taken place publicly and produced offspring born in original righteousness and uprightness.[15]

So what happened? With the tree of the knowledge of good and evil, God also gave a command that human beings not eat from it. Worship at the tree, over which Adam was to preside, consisted of belief in that Word and obedience to it. Because she was not satisfied with the Word, Eve "drank with her ears" the poison of Satan and entered into a "dangerous discussion" about the command. Responding to the serpent's question about God's command, Eve said that they were not to eat of the tree "lest perchance we die (*ne forte moriamur*)." Right there, says Luther, with that little word "perchance," she has turned from faith to unbelief by distorting the Word of God.[16] This distortion of the Word led to a corrupted will and rebellion, which led to a corrupted intellect and doubt of the will of God, which led to a rebellious hand, reaching out for the fruit against the will of God.[17] There is a slippery slope leading from distortion to unbelief to blasphemy.

Luther identifies unbelief and sexual lust as the two most prominent manifestations of the pervasiveness and continuance of original sin. With respect to the soul, "death crept like leprosy into all of our perceptive powers"—the intellect, the will, and the conscience. The darkened intellect does not know God and cannot perceive God's works. The will does not trust God's mercy and does not fear God, disregarding the Word and will of God to follow the desire and impulse of the flesh. The conscience despairs in the face of God's judgment and "adopts illicit defenses and remedies."[18] The result is not only the abandonment of God's Word, but blasphemy, as the human beings follow gods of their own making.

To constrain original sin's destructive consequences of unbelief and sexual lust, God, in Luther's view, instituted the state and attached additional, and onerous, ruling functions to the pastor and husband roles.

Luther believed that, in his day, the pastor's role was the most difficult; like a soldier, he must hold the line against distortions of the Word that lead to sinful disobedience. Just as Augustine had to fight with the Pelagians, Donatists, and Manichaeans, so Luther and other Protestant pastors must do battle with Sacramentarians, Anabaptists, and "Papists," who, like the Arians of old, persecute the true church with the utmost cruelty.[19] The pastor must, then, teach and defend the Word, "lest they overthrow the teaching of Christ."[20] This work is the most difficult a man is expected to do. For those who wish to perform their duties faithfully, "there are daily dangers and countless burdens," so that "in one single day [pastors and magistrates] work and sweat more than a farmer does in an entire month."[21] The worries of a pastor are even greater than those of a magistrate because his duties are more important. Therefore, he must not be lazy or weak, but ever vigilant and ready to fight: "Such softness is not becoming to brave soldiers to throw down their weapons and run at the first attack of the enemy, as if we were intended for pleasures and idleness, not for work and activity."[22] And the work, Luther thought, would get more difficult. Since there was "almost no fear of God" in his day, Luther had the apocalyptic feeling that "either everything will be destroyed or Germany will pay the penalties for its sins in some other way."[23] So the pastor is faced with increasing indifference to the Word and even hostile aggression.

Adam's role as husband is similarly burdened with enervating dynamics as a result of sin. After the Fall, Adam experienced, among other things, intense shame—a shame that was apparently connected to his sexuality. Luther says that Adam realized that the glory of his nakedness was lost through sin; his shame is a witness "that our heart has lost the trust in God." Further, Luther says that the parts of the body remain the same, but "those which, when they were naked, were looked upon with glory are now covered up as shameful and dishonorable."[24]

Why does Luther associate sexual shame with the disobedience of Adam? He does not make this clear here, but we might infer the connection. Remembering that Luther says that Adam would have withstood the deceit of Satan and told him to "shut up," we might ask, "Why did he not withstand the woman; why didn't he tell her to shut up; why did he fall for her deceit?" Given that just after the Fall he is immediately ashamed of his genitals and sexuality, it may be that, in Luther's view, Adam's weakness was not his rationality, but his sexuality. Despite Luther's assertion of Adam's original sexual obedience, it is possible that, in Luther's mind, Adam caved in to Eve's offer of the apple because of a sexual weakness.

If this is true, one might say that that which, in Luther's view, led to the disobedience in the woman (rational weakness) and in the man (sexual weakness) is singled out for punishment by God. Put another way, those particular aspects of the woman and the man which led to disobedience suffer the most dire consequences of the Fall. Because of the woman's rational weakness and dependency, she is subjugated to the man; because of the man's sexual weakness, he suffers from an uncontrollable lust that, in some ways, makes him subject to the woman.[25]

Consequently, Luther says that, from within his own body, "the husband has a raging lust kindled by the poison of Satan in his body." Everything else in his body is "almost dead and without sensation." This raging lust is passionate not only "in its desire," but also "in its disgust after it has acquired what it wanted." Luther says that this "unavoidable leprosy of the flesh, which is nothing but disobedience and loathsomeness attached to bodies and minds, is the punishment of sin."[26]

Therefore, men, since the Fall, experience within themselves a "raging lust" and are "compelled to make use of intercourse with their wives to avoid sin." Those men who are married are to "restrain their passions and carefully guard their relations with their wives." So, although in paradise a man needed a woman as a help in performing his procreational duty only, now he needs her as an "antidote and a medicine." In addition, he needs her for companionship, which Luther explicates as the management of the household.[27] Therefore, those men who live outside of marriage "burn most shamefully" and, we might infer, have no reason for settling down (establishing a "fixed habitation").[28] They are figuratively and literally "loose cannons." In other words, men must get married or live a dissipated life in the most enervating shame.

Married men also encounter all sorts of temptations and difficulties. Because men are in the state of sin and death, they "cannot make use of woman without the horrible passion of lust." Even marital sexuality is "so hideous and frightful a pleasure that physicians compare it with epilepsy." Luther laments that "lust . . . can be cured by no remedy, not even by marriage which was ordained by God as a remedy for our weak nature."[29] Therefore, the performance of one's marital, procreational duty entails the guilt of sin.

One might say, then, that, in the post-Fall state, men's sexuality causes them to fluctuate between shame and guilt. And since even a Christian marriage does not provide a cure for the "leprosy of lust," there is no escape in this life. This is part of the punishment for sin men experience, but there is more.

External to himself—from the wife—the husband faces still further difficulties. Luther says that if Eve had not sinned, she would not have been subject to the rule of her husband and would have been a partner in the ruling functions that are now entirely the responsibility of males. However, because of her sin woman was "deprived of the ability of administering those affairs that are outside . . . she does not go beyond her most personal duties." She is like a "nail driven into the wall; she sits at home . . . as the snail carries its house with it, so the wife should stay at home and look after the affairs of the household." She unwillingly bears the punishment of having been placed "under the power of her husband." Luther says, "Women are generally disinclined to put up with this burden, and they naturally seek to gain what they have lost through sin."[30] So a power struggle ensues in the family. While the husband attempts to do his duty by ruling, directing, and instructing, the wife often tries to wrest whatever power she can from him. If she is unable to accomplish much of this, she "at least indicates [her] impatience by grumbling." As the man tries to carry out his responsibility to rule the family, he is met with, at worst, guerrilla warfare and, at best, grumbling resentment!

So, as successors of Adam, men are "burdened with a definite punishment."[31] In addition, Luther says that the earth endured a curse (Rom. 8:20) that made men's work increasingly more difficult. That, he believed, is why men of his day died much earlier than did men in the age of the Old Testament patriarchs.

One might anticipate that this dreary situation would change because of the redemption of Christ. After all, in Christ there is neither "Jew nor Greek, slave nor free, male nor female" (Gal. 3:28). However, Luther believes that original sin and its consequences—unbelief and raging lust—are "so deeply implanted in our flesh, and this poison has been so widely spread through the flesh, body, mind, muscles, and blood; through the bones and the very marrow; in the will, in the intellect, and in the reason, that they cannot be fully removed."[32] Therefore, although we are set free by Christ's death, acquire his merits through faith, and are reborn for righteousness, that righteousness "merely has its beginning in this life and it cannot attain perfection in this flesh." Christians, through baptism, are restored not so much to the life lost by Adam and Eve but to the hope of that life.[33]

So Luther believed that, until the final resurrection, men would continue to bear the onerous duty of ruling in the church, the family, and the state and endure its attendant debilitating effects. The work men do in fulfilling this duty does not save them—salvation is the work of Christ and comes through faith alone—but it is necessary work and somebody has to do it. This is an unhappy, even tragic, state of affairs, but, because of his estimation of the depth and extent of sin, Luther saw no way out this side of the eschaton.

Where does Luther stand in the history of Christian reflection on these issues? What have been the effects of his thought? And what can we make of his position today?

In his assertion that domination and subjugation are not a part of God's intention in creation, Luther said, to my knowledge, a new thing in the history of Christian theology. Other, earlier Christian writers had, with certain significant qualifications, asserted that women share in the image of God (e.g., Clement of Alexandria, Gregory of Nyssa, Augustine, Lombard, Bonaventure, and Thomas Aquinas).[34]

For example, Clement of Alexandria introduced an exegetical innovation when he interpreted Gen. 1:27b, "male and female he [God] created them," in light of Gen. 1:27a, "So God created humankind in his [God's] own image, in the image of God he created them." Earlier Jewish and Christian interpretation had related 1:27b not to 1:27a but to 1:28 "And God blessed them, and God said to them, 'Be fruitful and multiply, and fill the earth and subdue it.'" In other words, the sexual differentiation of 1:27b had been interpreted as being related not to the image of God but to God's plan for sexual reproduction among human beings. In fact, earlier Christian interpretation (e.g., Ambrosiaster) had explicitly denied that women were created in the image of God, citing 1 Cor. 11:7, "For a man ought not to cover his head, since he is the image and glory of God; but woman is the glory of man." In contrast, Clement, by relating Gen. 1:27b to 1:27a, argued that women were created in the image of God and interpreted 1 Cor. 11:7 not literally, but as an allegory with "man" representing higher reason and "woman" representing lower reason.[35] By spiritualizing the image of God, Clement can then claim that women share it insofar as they possess higher reason.

Augustine, building on Clement's innovation, also asserted that women, insofar as they possess higher reason, are in the image of God, but insofar as they play an inferior role in procreation (i.e., that of receptacles) and are subject to men, they are not in the image of God. Those who followed Clement and Augustine in this new interpretation advanced similar qualifications and also presumed that Adam, even in paradise, had an inherent ability, right, and responsibility to rule in the physical, temporal world.

Luther, by claiming that male domination and female subjugation were a result of the Fall and not God's intention in creation, introduced a further exegetical/theological innovation. This innovation has great potential for the transformation of Christian ideas and institutions insofar as they have been influenced by the debilitating effects of patriarchal assumptions. However, Luther's thinking continued to manifest a residual presumption of male dominance.

Luther's assertion that Eve would have shared equally in the ruling functions of the church and family is mitigated by other of his reflections on the pre-Fall state that betray an underlying assumption that she was not fully equal to Adam. For example, by conflating the Priestly (Genesis 1) with the Yahwistic (Genesis 2—3) accounts of creation, Luther focused on the *ha'adam,* the human being of Genesis 2, and presumed that the first specimen of the species was a male, who, in himself, was complete without need of a female. He thereby ignored the Priestly use of *'adam,* humankind without a definite article as a designation for a sexually undifferentiated species, which then is sexually differentiated for the purposes of reproduction.[36]

So, for Luther, Adam presided at the "natural basilica," not Eve; he did not mention any role she might have played. With respect to the family, Luther seemed to see in Adam a certain independence and autonomy that Eve did not possess. Adam was, apart from his relation to anyone else, except for God, wholly righteous. Apparently, this original righteousness did not involve human relationality, including a relationship with Eve. Eve was created only because of a completely free (autonomous) decision on God's part that human beings should procreate sexually.

In contrast, Eve was, from the beginning, dependent on Adam in a way that he was not dependent on her. Therefore, she was not equal to him in "glory and prestige." It seems, then, that in Luther's mind, maleness entailed a more autonomous reason or will—something he sees as God-like. This echoed Augustine's view that man, alone, was the full image of God, whereas woman shared that image insofar as she was related to man.[37] This independence of maleness was somewhat mitigated in Luther by his assertion that the man needed the woman as a "mundane dwelling place." There remained, though, an asymmetrical and hierarchical relationship between maleness and femaleness even before sin. Despite his innovative insight, Luther was not entirely successful in eliminating the presumption of male dominance from his thinking about the pre-Fall state. That may be one reason he did not think male domination and female subjugation could be eliminated from the world even after the advent of Christ.

The effects of Luther's presumption about the necessity of maintaining male dominance are many and far-reaching. I raise here a few questions on the effects that presumption has had on the church and family.

In the church, the male pastor is, in Luther's view, an embattled soldier contending mightily for what he assumes to be the truth of the unambiguous Word of God. To what degree did the masculine expectations and male experiences of early modern Germany shape Luther's sense of pastoral work as warfare? Is there a connection between this belligerent pastoral stance and Luther's insistence on the primacy of the historical/literal, rather than the allegorical, meaning of Scripture?[38] How has this emphasis on left-brain, technical reason in theology and worship limited the range and depth of religious experience in Christians influenced by this tradition? Finally, how does the residue of the presumption of male dominance obscure for Luther the effect of his own social location and life experience on his and others' interpretation of scripture? What effects has this naïveté had on women and men of other social locations (e.g., Jewish)?[39]

With respect to men's role as husband, Luther certainly was not blind to the difficulties that male dominance caused for both women and men. Both magisterial and radical Reformers decried the "unchristian" quarreling, disorder, and violence that sullied marriage in sixteenth-century Germany.[40] City councils, having passed ordinances supporting men's dominant positions in marriage, found that they had to undermine a husband's authority when he disciplined his wife too violently, unjustly, or both.[41] In addition, not all Protestant patriarchs managed to contain their "raging lust" in one, monogamous marital relationship. The most notable example of this was Philip, the Landgrave of Hesse, who on the basis of Luther's assertion that sexual desire is a natural aspect of men's constitutions argued that his nature demanded that he satisfy his desire with a woman besides his wife.[42] Luther privately counseled Philip to enter into a second, secret marriage rather than doing further damage to his conscience by continuing in adultery.[43]

Today, we might ask a question that Luther never seemed to have contemplated: "To what degree does male dominance in the estate of marriage contribute to compulsive male sexuality and its destructive potential?" Said another way, "Does what Luther considers to be a necessary, if imperfect, means to constrain men's 'raging lust' contribute to the very thing he abhorred?" If one assumes, as Luther did, that compulsive male sexuality is part of a biologically transmitted inheritance of original sin, then all one can do is make some similar uneasy truce with it. However, it is possible that Luther's solution—marriage characterized by male dominance—contributes to what he took to be an ineradicable lust or compulsive sexuality.

Mariana Valverde has argued that erotic tension is produced by the common desires in each human person to recognize another and to be recognized by another, to know and be known.[44] If this is true, and I believe that it is, the erotic inheres, then, in the tension produced by the dual desires to *both* know the other *and* be the object of another's knowing. Erotic tension requires then the maintenance of both roles for both persons in a relationship; that is, both persons must, simultaneously or alternatively, be both subject and object.

In a relationship, sexual fulfillment results from a communicative flow between two persons—a flow wherein there is a joining of the two, while the integrity of the subjectivity of each is preserved. The logical extension of Valverde's argument is that any attempt to dominate or objectify another (i.e., to affect the other without being willing to be similarly affected by the other) freezes the dominator in the role of subject and the dominated in the role of object. The other, as perpetual object, cannot know the dominator; the dominator's erotic desire to be known is, then, thwarted. This kind of objectification, or refusal to acknowledge the other as subject, creates a situation in which erotic desire can never be satisfactorily fulfilled. It leads to a dissolution of erotic tension and, therefore, to sexual frustration. This frustration may then be expressed in compulsive sexual behavior (Luther's "raging lust"), which attempts to create erotic tension in an objectified context, an attempt that is necessarily doomed to failure and can express itself in various forms of violence.[45]

Sexual relationships characterized by male dominance have the structural effect of frustrating men's authentic erotic desire, contributing to the production of sexually compulsive habits of thought, feeling, and behavior.[46] A way out of this tragic situation—more promising than the bigamy of Philip of Hesse—is the development of mutual sexual relationships in which there is not a structural power differential between the partners. For heterosexual men, that means rejecting the presumption of male dominance, sharing with women the "ruling" functions of our institutions, and working with them to overcome the significant structural impediments to the full expression of their public vocations. Luther built on Clement of Alexandria's innovative inclusion of women in the image of God and affirmed, to the extent he was able, the equality of women in creation. Our task is to build on Luther's innovative insight and extend that equality to the order of redemption here and now.

NOTES

All translations of Luther's text are from Martin Luther, *Works,* ed. Jaroslav Pelikan and Helmut Lehman (St. Louis: Concordia, 1958), which will be signified in the notes as AE (American Edition). For those interested in referring to the Latin text, I enclose in parentheses references to "Vorlesungen über 1. Mose von 1535–45," ed. G. Koffmane and D. Reichert, *D. Martin Luthers Werke; Kritische Gesamtausgabe* (Weimar, 1911). The standard abbreviation, *WA*, for this edition will be followed by numbers designating the volume and page numbers of the citation. Since this volume comprises edited student notes, the views here must be checked against less edited versions of what Luther says about these matters elsewhere. That will be done in a future, larger study. I am grateful to David Schoeni for his careful reading of this essay and for his editorial suggestions.

1. I am persuaded by Merry Wiesner-Hanks, who argues that, in using gender as a category of analysis, we need to go beyond women's and family history to gender history. Among the tasks she outlines are: a reexamination of women-identified categories (i.e., marital status, number of children, etc.) to see how "they determine men's experiences as well"; attention to male sexuality, familial roles, and gender restrictions on men; an examination of the "economic and ideological sources for the power of individual family members"; and analyses of gender, not "just as a physical or social fact, but as a way of organizing and discussing the social relations of power." See Merry E. Wiesner, "Beyond Women and the Family: Towards a Gender Analysis of the Reformation," *Sixteenth Century Journal* 18 (1987): 311–22.

2. AE 1:111 (WA 42:84–85). Luther seems, here, to assume that the original creation, *adam* in the Hebrew, was a male even before the sexual differentiation of Gen. 2:18ff. See Phyllis Trible, "Eve and Adam: Genesis 2—3 Reread," in *Womanspirit Rising: A Feminist Reader in Religion,* ed. Carol P. Christ and Judith Plaskow, 74–83 (New York: Harper & Row, 1979), for an interpretation that challenges that assumption.

3. AE 1:92 (WA 42:70).

4. AE 1:56–57 (WA 42:41–42); AE 1:111 (WA 42:84); AE 1:56–57 (WA 42:41–42); AE 1:65 (WA 42:48–49).

5. AE 1:103 (WA 42:78); AE 1:82 (WA 42:62).

6. AE 1:95–96 (WA 42:72–73); AE 1:105–6 (WA 42:80–81).

7. AE 1:115 (WA 42:87).

8. AE 1:112 (WA 42:85); AE 1:238 (WA 42:177). Here Luther conflates the two Genesis accounts of creation and rejects an androgynous understanding of the first exemplar of the human species. See also AE 1:170 (WA 42:52–53).

9. AE 1:116 (WA 42:87); AE 1:115 (WA 42:87).

10. AE 1:66 (WA 42:50) and AE 1:68–69 (WA 42:51).

11. AE 1:151 (WA 42:114).

12. Although Luther rejects the allegorical interpretation of the Genesis story that views Eve as the lower part of reason and Adam as the upper part in favor of a historical/literal meaning, he does seem to accept the notion that the woman possesses a lower form of reason than does the man.

13. AE 1:117 (WA 42:88).

14. AE 1:136 (WA 42:102) and AE 1:131–33 (WA 42:98–100).

15. AE 1:141 (WA 42:85–86). Luther says that sexual intercourse would have been as public as eating and drinking; AE 1:116–17 (WA 42:87–89).

16. AE 1:155 (WA 42:116–17).

17. AE 1:147 (WA 42:111).

18. AE 1:114 (WA 42:86); AE 1:84–85 (WA 42:64).

19. AE 1:156 (WA 42:118).

20. AE 1:213 (WA 42:159).

21. AE 1:212 (WA 42:158).

22. AE 1:214 (WA 42:160).

23. AE 1:207 (WA 42:154).

24. AE 1:167 (WA 42:125).

25. For a discussion of sixteenth-century views concerning the sexual power women held over men, see Lyndal Roper, *The Holy Household: Women and Morals in Reformation Augsburg* (Oxford: Clarendon Press, 1989), 109ff.

26. AE 1:203 (WA 42:152); AE 1:62 (WA 42:46–47); AE 1:71 (WA 42:54).

27. AE 1:116 (WA 42:88).

28. AE 1:118 (WA 42:89); AE 1:168 (WA 42:126).

29. AE 1:119 (WA 42:89); AE 1:168 (WA 42:126).

30. AE 1:203 (WA 42:151). In another place Luther makes a distinction between the public and private spheres and says the man is put in charge of the public, but the woman has dominion in the family (AE 1:67 [WA 42:51]). This reveals a more complex relationship between the husband and wife than Luther implies elsewhere. AE 1:200 (WA 42:149).

31. AE 1:204 (WA 42:152).

32. AE 1:166 (WA 42:124).

33. AE 1:64 (WA 42:48); AE 1:196 (WA 42:146).

34. See Kari E. Borresen, "God's Image, Man's Image? Patristic Interpretation of Gen. 1,27 and I Cor. 11,7," and "God's Image, Is Woman Excluded? Medieval Interpretation of Gen. 1,27 and I Cor. 11,7," in *Image of God and Gender Models in Judaeo-Christian Tradition,* ed. Kari E. Borresen, 188–207 and 208–27 (Oslo: Solum Forlag, 1991).

35. Borresen, "God's Image, Man's Image?" 194–96.

36. Phyllis A. Bird, "Sexual Differentiation and Divine Image in the Genesis Creation Texts," in Borresen, "God's Image, Man's Image?" 11–31, points out that the Priestly writers, though speaking of the species, probably have the male in mind as the "representative and determining image of the species." However, she contends that, for him, "maleness is not an essential or defining characteristic" (p. 18). For her, "Genesis 1 invites, and demands, renewed reflection on the meaning of sexual differentiation as a constitutive mark of our humanity and the meaning of God-likeness (image) as the defining attribute of humankind." Therefore, "it may serve as a foundation text for a feminist egalitarian anthropology, since it recognizes no hierarchy of gender in the created order" (pp. 24–25). Jane Dempsey Douglass, in "The Image of God in Women As Seen by Luther and Calvin," in Borresen, "God's Image, Man's Image?" 242, notes that the "theology of women's subordination in passages like I Cor. 11:7 and I Tim. 2:14 . . . influences [Luther's] reading of Genesis."

37. Augustine believed that Adam needed woman's help neither for his work, for it was not yet onerous, nor for companionship, for a man would have been better suited for that. See Borresen, "Patristic Exegesis," 202–3.

38. Medieval theologians recognized four levels of meaning in scripture—the historical/literal, allegorical, tropological (moral), and anagogical (eschatological). See Beryl Smalley, *The Study of the Bible in the Middle Ages,* 2d ed. (South Bend, Ind.: Notre Dame, 1964), and James Samuel Preus, *From Shadow to Promise: Old Testament Interpretation from Augustine to the Young Luther* (Cambridge, Mass.: Harvard University Press, 1969). Luther contends that the historical/literal is primary because it has the force of logic. In the fight against unbelief, it is, then, a better weapon than, for example, allegorical interpretations, for their use implies that the text is not univocal and unambiguous.

39. For a helpful assessment of Luther's relationship to Judaism, see Heiko Oberman, *The Roots of Anti-Semitism in the Age of Renaissance and Reformation* (Philadelphia: Fortress Press, 1984).

40. Lyndal Roper, "Sexual Utopianism in Reformation Germany," *Journal of Ecclesiastical History* 42 (1991): 394–418.

41. Roper, *Holy Household,* chap. 5.

42. Philip had earlier organized a military league of northern princes to protect the progress of the reform against the pro-Roman forces led by the emperor, Charles V.

43. Roper, in "Utopianism," 413–14, notes that Luther later denounced the Landgrave "not for having married bigamously, but for having publicly defended his act." He further observes that Luther's distinction between "public" adultery (an offense punishable by the magistracy) and "private" adultery (a matter for confessional discipline) reveals his uneasy acknowledgment that human sexual desire could not always be disciplined in a monogamous marriage.

44. Mariana Valverde, *Sex, Power, and Pleasure* (Philadelphia: New Society Publishers, 1987), 29ff. For a theological grounding and explication of Valverde's insight, with reference to the work of James Nelson, Beverly Harrison, and Carter Heyward, see my *The Men We Long to Be: From Domination to a New Christian Understanding of Manhood* (New York: Harper San Francisco, 1995), 119–22 and 219–20.

45. Parts of these two paragraphs first appeared in my "Domination as Punishment: Men's Studies and Religion," *Men's Studies Review* 7 (1990): 6.

46. I focus in this essay only on the effects of patriarchal sexual relationships on heterosexual men. For reflections on the effects of these dynamics on women and gay men, see the chapters by Merlyn Mowrey (9) and J. Michael Clark (19) in this volume.

PART II

THE ROLE OF RELIGION
IN SHAPING MASCULINE IDENTITY

Contemporary sociological and psychological research on men and masculinity often neglects to explore the influence of religious traditions and spirituality in shaping men's understanding of themselves as men. In part 2, we present three chapters that, among other things, analyze the effects of these traditions on masculine identities of their male adherents. These essays offer historical case studies from the three major traditions of the West, Judaism, Christianity, and Islam, and from three geographical locales, the Middle East, Europe, and North America. And they explore the conceptions of masculinity within three major time frames: the ancient world, the medieval period, and modernity.

Howard Eilberg-Schwartz, a Jewish rabbi and theologian, discusses the impact of a traditionally conceived male God on the lives of men in ancient Judaism. Eilberg-Schwartz advances the provocative thesis that the father God of Judaism and Christianity paradoxically legitimated male authority and tended to destabilize the masculinity on which it was based. The maleness of God, in other words, was problematic for men as well as for women. To allay the homoerotic anxieties provoked by the maleness of God, says Eilberg-Schwartz, the men of ancient Judaism employed several strategies. First was the taboo against depicting or imaging God's body, especially his sexual organ, despite the fact that an insistence

33

on the maleness of the supreme being logically entailed his corporeality. Second, to view themselves as proper partners and intimates of this God, ancient Jewish men had to understand themselves as in some sense feminized. Finally, because of the strong heterosexual imperatives of the Hebraic world, females would have been considered more "natural" consorts for a male deity. Eilberg-Schwartz speculates that to attenuate their anxieties about this more "natural" complementarity, the men of antique Judaism had to see women as relatively unsuitable for God by viewing them as ritually impure and spiritually unfit. In this way, the male experience of a male God served to reinforce patriarchal structures.

Like Eilberg-Schwartz, Ulrike Wiethaus, a historian of religious thought, discusses the dialectic between imagery of the divine and the construction of masculinity. Eilberg-Schwartz analyzes this relationship across a wide expanse of time and for an entire community, but Wiethaus focuses attention on a comparably smaller historical moment and on a representative individual of that period. The twelfth century, she claims, was a critical era for Western Christian conceptions of masculinity. In response to monumental cultural and economic developments, European monastics such as Bernard of Clairvaux developed a "bridal mysticism" that functioned to relieve male anxieties about their appropriate place as men in a society in ferment. Part of that response for Bernard was the creation of an idealized image of Woman, embodied in the Virgin Mary, and the concurrent devaluation of flesh-and-blood women.

Both chapters thus raise crucial questions about the nature of any construction of masculinity. Must all conceptions of masculinity, because they by definition involve the repression of human qualities defined as feminine, result in instability? Put in other words, must men who judge themselves by the standards of an ideal masculinity live their lives in a way that actually falls far short of that ideal? And what consequences result for those men whose "real" lives fail to measure up to the masculine criteria under whose judgment they stand? Further, is it reasonable to say that all conceptions of masculinity are, by their very nature, unstable?

When we turn to Fareed Munir's chapter, we encounter a different approach to understanding religion's effect on male self-identity. Munir, himself a former member of the Nation of Islam and now a Sunni Muslim, traces the spiritual evolution of Malcolm X from his origins in a sectarian Christian home, through his involvement with the black separatist movement inaugurated by Elijah Muhammad, and finally to his embrace of Islamic orthodoxy. Munir argues that at each step along the way Malcolm's understanding of himself as a man was profoundly influenced by the worldview of each religious tradition, as well as by the racist culture of twentieth-century America. Malcolm's ultimate acceptance of Sunni Islam galvanized a spiritual development that was destined to acknowledge the humanity of all persons—black and white, male and female—as equal before God.

In all three chapters, questions are raised, explicitly or implicitly, about the impact of conceptions of God on men's self-understanding. Eilberg-Schwartz and Wiethaus show some of the ways these conceptions often contribute to a deep ambiguity in the lives of men, which in turn fosters a devaluing of women. Munir's analysis also touches on some the difficulties men have submitting themselves to a God who is conceived as a higher male authority. But for Malcolm, according to Munir's interpretation, complete submission to the divine alone yields a more humane and inclusive perspective on life.

3

GOD'S PHALLUS AND THE
DILEMMAS OF MASCULINITY

Howard Eilberg-Schwartz

Most Jews and Christians think of God the father as lacking a body and hence as beyond sexuality. Without a body, God obviously can have no sexual organ. But from where does the idea of a disembodied God come? What if, historically speaking, it is discomfort with the idea of God's penis that has generated the idea of an incorporeal God? What if this uneasiness flows from the contradictions inherent in men's relationship with a God who is explicitly male? This in a nutshell is the argument of this chapter. This is why the title "God's Phallus" is a serious one that points to interesting questions about the nature of religious symbols and the way in which issues of gender, sexuality, and desire are inseparable from them. More specifically, this essay is about divine fatherhood and the ways in which the sexual body of a father God is troubling for the conception of masculinity.

It may, of course, seem counterintuitive to think of a male God as being problematic for the conception of masculinity. After all, dozens of feminist studies over the past twenty years have explored the way in which images of male deities authorize male domination in the social order.[1] As these studies have well demonstrated, a divine male both legitimates male authority and deifies masculinity. It thus may seem paradoxical to consider that the symbol of a male God generates dilemmas for the conception of masculinity. Nevertheless, I would argue that at the same time such a symbol works to legitimate masculinity—which may in fact be its primary and even original function—it also renders the meaning of masculinity unstable. In this chapter, I explore how tensions arising from the idea of the sexual body of the father God are expressed in the myth and ritual of one religious tradition, ancient Judaism.

Homoeroticism and Divine Imagery

What are those dilemmas? The first is homoeroticism: the love of a male human for a male God. The issue of homoeroticism arises in ancient

Israel because the divine-human relationship is often described in erotic and sexual terms. Marriage and sexuality are frequent biblical metaphors for describing God's relationship with Israel. God is imagined as the husband to Israel the wife; espousal and even sexual intercourse are metaphors for the covenant. Thus when Israel follows other gods, "she" is seen to be whoring. Israel's relationship with God is thus conceptualized as a monogamous sexual relation, and idolatry as adultery. But the heterosexual metaphors in the ancient texts belie the nature of the relationship in question: it is human males, not females, who are imagined to have the primary intimate relations with the deity. The Israel that is collectively imagined as a woman is actually constituted by men—men like Moses and the patriarchs. And these men love, in ways that are imagined erotically and sensually, a male deity.

This would not have posed a problem if human masculinity were not so strongly associated with procreation in ancient Judaism. Being a man in ancient Israelite culture involved marrying, having children, and carrying forward the lineage of one's father or tribe. Thus ancient Judaism's concept of masculinity was deeply entangled in images of what is now called heterosexuality.[2] In the culture of ancient Israel, woman was imagined as the natural counterpart of man, and sexual acts between men were condemned. Thus, at the heart of this religious system was a deep tension in the definition of masculinity. Men were complementary to women; marriage was a return to a primordial unity. At the same time, a man's relationship to God was conceptualized as loving and sensual.

It is for this reason, I propose, that various myths and rituals of ancient Judaism attempted to suppress the homoerotic impulse implicit in the male relationship with God. The denial of homoeroticism takes two significant forms: a prohibition against depicting God (veiling the body of God) and the feminization of men. By imagining men as wives of God, Israelite religion was partially able to preserve the heterosexual complementarity that helped to define the culture. But this also undermined accepted notions of masculinity. The feminization of men also disrupted what the tradition posits as a natural complementarity between a divine male and human women. When male-female complementarity is the structure of religious imagery, human women are the natural partners of a divine male, but this connection also renders human males superfluous in the divine-human relationship. The potential superfluousness of human masculinity may offer additional insights into the misogynist tendencies of ancient Judaism: women were deemed impure and men were feminized so as to disrupt what in this religious culture was a natural complementarity between the divine male and human females.

Monotheism and Masculinity

Still another set of dilemmas is generated by the monotheistic image of a sexless father God. As has been pointed out by many interpreters, the God of the Jews, unlike the gods of the ancient Near East and many other religious traditions, does not have sexual intercourse and father children, at least in the literature that made its way into the Hebrew Bible. The archaeological record suggests that many Israelites may have imagined the goddess Asherah to be a partner of Yahweh, but in the Hebrew Bible, and in the variety of Judaisms that flourished subsequently, Israel imagined God as having no sexual partners. Despite the fact that God metaphorically gets married (e.g., Hosea 1—2; Jer. 2:2), and even has sexual intercourse with the entity Israel (Ezek. 16:8), who is imagined as a woman, this metaphorical union differs from the couplings of male and female deities found in the mythology of many other religious traditions.

The sexlessness of the father God generated dilemmas in a culture defined by patrilineal descent. A man was expected to reproduce, to carry on his line, yet he was also understood to be made in the image of a God who was essentially celibate. Masculinity is an impossible achievement. The decreasing importance of patrilineage in late antique Judaism would have an enormous impact on the religious conception of masculinity. The story of the virgin birth of Jesus makes explicit what had always been a latent tension in monotheism: God fathers a son and the human father becomes irrelevant. This was intolerable to ancient Judaism, in which tracing the father's line remained important, but it was a perfect myth for certain forms of what would become Christianity, in which the father's line became less relevant.

God Sightings

To ask about the anatomical sex of the Jewish God is to formulate a question that strikes most interpreters of Judaism as absurd. For it is assumed that the Jewish God has no body. Raphael Patai illustrates how this ancient assumption has continued into the modern period. The God of the Jews, he writes, "being pure spirit . . . is without body, he possesses no physical attributes and hence no sexual traits. To say that God is either male or female is therefore completely impossible from the viewpoint of traditional Judaism."[3]

But in fact matters are much more complicated than this, for on a number of occasions various Israelites are said to have seen God. And in these "God sightings," or "theophanies," which is the more technical term for them, various Israelite leaders see the deity in what appears to be a human form. But it is a human form in which the sex of God is carefully obscured. The question of God's genitals was an extremely delicate one for ancient Jews, a question to which any answer would have been troubling and disconcerting. And it is in part an attempt to sidestep this question that explains why the divine body is so carefully veiled.

The literature of ancient Israel contains a number of reports in which someone sees God. In one early Israelite myth, for example,

> Moses, Aaron, Nadab, Abihu and seventy elders of Israel ascended and they saw the God of Israel: under His feet there was the likeness of a pavement of sapphire, like the very sky for purity. Yet he did not raise His hand against the leaders of the Israelites; they beheld God and they ate and drank (Ex. 24:9–11).

In another early myth, Moses alone requests permission to see God. But here, God permits Moses to gaze on him only from behind. This incident occurs after the Israelites have worshiped the golden calf. To Moses' request for assurance of divine favor, God answers, "I will make all My goodness pass before you ['before your face'] as I proclaim the name Lord before you. . . . But you cannot see My face, for man may not see Me and live."

> And the Lord said, "See, there is a place near Me. Station yourself on the rock and, as My presence (*Kavod*) passes by, I will put you in a cleft of the rock and shield you with My hand until I have passed by. Then I will take My hand away and you will see My back; but My face must not be seen" (Ex. 33:21–23).

Various prophets are also reported to have sighted the deity in dreams or visions. The prophet Amos sees God standing by the altar (Amos 9:1); Job sees God at the end of his long ordeal (Job 42:5); and the prophets Micaiah (1 Kings 22:19), Isaiah (Isa. 6:1–2), Ezekiel (Ezek. 1:26–28), and Daniel (Dan. 7:9–11) see God seated on a throne.

All the myths involving God sightings exhibit a discomfort about describing the deity's image. In most God sightings, such as those of Amos, Job, and Micaiah, the deity is not described at all or very little content of the vision is reported. When Moses and the elders ascend to the top of the mountain, the narrator describes only what is under God's feet. When Ezekiel describes God on the chariot, he couches his description in repeated qualifications that show a discomfort with describing God as a human figure: "such was the appearance of the semblance of the Presence of the Lord." And Daniel's sighting of God, although showing no explicit ambivalence, occurs in a dream, possibly a less direct medium of experience.

It is the nature of this ambivalence that has been subject to alternative interpretations. What does this veiling of the body mean? We find that much information is available about the gender of the monotheistic God, but the sex of this God is carefully obscured. In accounts of God sightings, the gaze is averted from the face and front, parts of the anatomy that are critical to an identification of a body's sex. Not only is there no indication that this God has a penis, but we don't even know whether this being has secondary sexual characteristics such as facial hair. We have no information about the divine anatomy. From bodily characteristics alone, it is impossible to say anything definitive about the sex of God.

At issue, then, is the significance of the sexual veiling of God. What is being veiled and why? The sex of God can be inferred from God's gender. God is primarily imagined in masculine gender images. Images abound of God as king, father, shepherd, and man of war. God is routinely described with masculine nouns, pronouns, and adjectives. To be sure, there are some feminine images of God, but they are few and far between. Moreover, the feminine gendering of God as mother or nursemaid can be construed as acts of male appropriation: God the father usurping the positive roles of women. Following the lead of Mary Daly, Rita Gross, Judith Plaskow, and others, I assume that the maleness of God is implied by the predominantly masculine gender images of the deity, but that maleness is hidden. God is a masculine deity whose maleness is repressed and avoided. People do think of God as a he *without* a male body.

The apparent absence of a divine phallus exalts God above male sexuality and renders it problematic in critical ways. That is, it is around matters of sexuality and the need to procreate that men experience their otherness from God. To be like God the creator they must procreate. But to be like God they should have no sex and no desire. It is a crucial question, then, to consider why divine masculinity is figured without desire and without its potent symbol, the phallus.

Indecent Exposures

Noah, the tiller of soil, was the first to plant a vineyard. He drank of the wine and became drunk and he uncovered himself within his tent. Ham, the father of Canaan, saw his father's nakedness and told his two brothers outside. But Shem and Japheth took a cloth, placed it against both their backs and walking backwards, they covered their father's nakedness; their faces were turned the other way, so that they did not see their father's nakedness. When Noah woke up from his wine and learned what his youngest son had done to him, he said, "Cursed be Canaan; the lowest of the slaves shall he be to his brothers." And he said, "Blessed be the Lord, the God of Shem; let Canaan be a slave to them" (Gen. 9:20–25).

In this myth, the waters of the Flood have subsided, and Noah, his wife, children, and their spouses have left the ark. Noah plants a vineyard and becomes drunk; during his drunken stupor, he lies naked in his tent. When Ham reports what he has seen to his virtuous brothers, they turn their backs and avert their gaze. This myth has many striking similarities with the story in which God turns his back to Moses (Ex. 33:12ff.). God turns away so that Moses will not see what should not be exposed, just as Shem and Japheth walk backward to avoid seeing their father's genitals.

The myth of Noah's exposure is crucial in making sense of why God's body must be veiled. The comparison of the two myths takes for granted and provides support for the conclusion that God is imagined as a father figure and that the veiling of God's body is necessary for the same reasons that a father's nakedness should be covered. That is not to say, of course, that God is always imagined as a father or even in masculine images. But the image of God the Father is one of the popular masculine images that Israelite literature employs to conceptualize the deity.

The cover-up of the divine father's body, then, is analogous to the hiding of the human father's nakedness in the story of Noah. What neither Israel nor Noah's virtuous sons dared imagine was the phallus of the father. But if we look to other religious traditions, we may see how the genitals of the deity have been considered a reasonable matter for speculation. Jesus' penis, for example, is depicted in a wide range of medieval art, as Leo Steinberg has shown, arguing that the emphasis on his penis is part of what expresses Jesus' humanness.[4] Furthermore, Jesus' foreskin became a sacred relic and an object of veneration in medieval Christianity.[5] Indeed, one medieval nun believed the foreskin of Jesus was used as a wedding ring in her marriage to Christ.[6] Early Buddhist sources describe the Buddha's body having seven marks, including a penis that is retractable like that of a horse.[7]

Nor should we assume that the Buddha and Jesus are exceptional cases because of their semihuman, semidivine status. Full-fledged gods, such as the Greek gods Poseidon, Apollo, and Zeus, are frequently sculpted in Greek art with their penises fully displayed. Greek myth tells how the god Ouranos, the god of the sky, was castrated by his son Kronos. Ouranos's manhood falls into the seas, and from it Aphrodite is born. Zeus's sexual exploits are the theme of many Greek myths as well.[8] The erection of Siva is also the subject of much Hindu mythology. The erect phallus of Siva, "the erotic ascetic" as Wendy Doniger calls him, is a symbol of the power to spill the seed as well as to retain it.[9] Hindu mythology tells of wives of Pine Forest sages who touch Siva's erect phallus. In another myth a woman finds an amputated phallus and, thinking it to be Siva's *linga,* takes it home and worships it.

The divine phallus is also of concern in ancient Near Eastern mythology.

Sumerian stories, for example, tell how the god Enki masturbates, ejaculates, and fills up the Tigris with flowing water and how he uses his penis to dig irrigation ditches, an important aspect of the Sumerian agricultural system. And perhaps most directly pertinent to the present discussion is the penis of the Canaanite god El, whose sexual exploits and erection are the subject of religious poetry.[10]

The Father's Nakedness

The myth of Noah's nakedness tells us nothing about why it is so problematic for sons to gaze on the father's genitals. It takes this prohibition as a given that needs no explanation. One reason for the prohibition was clearly the honor due to a father. It was disrespectful to see Noah naked, particularly in his vulnerable drunken state. To avert the gaze was to respect the father's honor. That exposure and shame are deeply entwined in Israelite culture is evident in another Israelite myth from the same source: the myth of Adam and Eve. As the familiar story goes, the first human couple become aware of their own nakedness after eating from the tree of knowledge against the express wishes of God. As some interpreters have pointed out, this story may be read as a kind of ascent of the human from the realm of the animal.[11] If it is read as a story about the move from animality to humanity, then Adam and Eve are not simply becoming differentiated from animals; they are becoming more like God. What characterizes this differentiation is an emerging awareness of their nakedness and a desire to cover their sexual organs.

Prior to their eating from the tree, Adam and Eve are in some sense like animals: "The two of them were naked . . . yet they felt no shame." Whether they are sexually active like animals is left unclear. After they eat of the fruit, their eyes are opened and they perceive that they are naked. They then sew together fig leaves and clothe themselves. The realization that they are naked and the desire to cover their genitals is meant to distinguish these first humans from animals.

Why is it the serpent who represents the animal realm from which Adam and Eve emerge? Freud has influenced many to see the snake as a symbol of the penis, but I suggest its significance lies elsewhere. One of the most striking features of serpents is the periodic shedding of their skins. Because it regularly sheds its covering, the serpent may be a symbol for both transformation and the lack of shame in the animal world. The serpent who periodically undresses becomes the vehicle by which Adam and Eve learn that they are naked and must clothe themselves.

To summarize, then, the myths of Noah and Adam and Eve regard shame about nakedness as a foundational moment in the emergence of human culture. The myth of Noah shows that this general human concern is regarded as particularly important for protecting the father's honor. Noah, as the only father to survive the Flood and, hence, the paradigmatic father of humankind, must have his dignity protected. To be uncovered is to reintroduce a state of disorder. Culture is preserved by the virtuous sons who cover their father's nakedness.

The link between nakedness and shame, between being human and being covered, suggests one reason why the divine father's body must be veiled. But the question remains as to why the father's nakedness is regarded as essential to human culture.

The Gaze and Homoeroticism

Within a culture that defines heterosexuality as norm, the male gaze is properly directed to women alone. Men should not look at men and boys should learn not to desire their fathers. The prohibition against a son's seeing his father's nakedness symbolically expresses and thereby institutionalizes heterosexual desire as a norm. The story of Noah is after all a second creation story, a telling of what human culture was and what it should be after its destruction in the Flood and rebirth in Noah's line. In this new beginning, heterosexual desire is reconstituted once more. In Gen. 2:23–24, a story from the same author as the myth of Noah (J), heterosexuality has already been presented as the norm. God decides that "the earthling should not be alone" and takes a piece of Adam's side to create a second creature. Thus emerges male-female complementarity. But in the refounding of culture after the Flood, another erotic relationship potentially disrupts male-female relations: that of sons and fathers. The prohibition against seeing Noah's nakedness deals with this potential disruption. The prohibition against a son's seeing his father's nakedness symbolically expresses and thereby institutionalizes heterosexual desire as a norm.

This interpretation of the Noah myth assumes that male-male sexual activity was considered problematic in Israelite culture, an assumption supported by the ancient text. The Holiness Code treats male-male sexual acts as an abomination (Lev. 18:22), punishable by death (Lev. 20:13). The language of the code is significant: "Do not lie with a man as one lies with a woman; it is an abhorrence." The description of the sin is consistent with Israelite attempts to keep the perceived natural order in place.

It is also significant that this list of prohibitions begins and ends with the injunction not to imitate the ways of the Egyptians or the Canaanites, both groups who are said to be descendants of Ham (Gen. 10:6). In ancient Israelite imagination, male-male sexual acts were considered something alien and hence were linked to the stereotyping of its proximate others, the Canaanites. The association of homosexual activity with

Canaanite practice in the Holiness Code thus lends support to my interpretation of the Noah story. In the cursing of Canaan for his father's sin,
the Canaanites are condemned as an immoral line.

Those who think Ham has committed a homosexual *act* with his father
are partially right. There is an element of homoeroticism in the Noah story.
Ham has looked upon his father's nakedness, but gazing is enough to generate desire. Thus the prohibition on Ham's seeing his father is intended to
direct the male gaze away from the male to the female body. Furthermore,
it is Noah's passivity, his taking of what was regarded as the female's position, that makes the viewing of his nakedness so problematic.

Conclusion:
Embracing Our Fathers

The image of a male God has clearly been one of the central problems
of feminist theology over the past twenty years. Many feminist theologians have explored the ways in which a male image of God validates male
experience at the expense of women. Like many other men and women
who have found the feminist critique persuasive, I either lapsed into silence or found other language to use to talk about God. Yet I have come
to think differently about images of male gods, about father gods, and
about human fathers as well.

I began to see that feminist analyses have not clearly distinguished between images of male deities and images of father deities. The two obviously overlap, but the maleness of God may have different implications
than the fatherliness of God. Indeed, it is striking to me that unlike feminist scholarship in general, feminist theology has reflected little on our
relationships to both our parents—our mothers and our fathers. I believe
these relationships are fundamental to our discussion, for if we agree with
nothing else from Freud, he was certainly right about the ways in which
divine and parental images are entangled. And the possibility of connecting to divine images, whether male or female, clearly is related to the relationships we have to our mothers and fathers. The experience of a fatherly figure reaching out to me has made me reflect on the need many
of us have for fatherly images that are nurturing and loving. I need to
imagine a God with a body, with fatherly arms, who does not turn his back
to me.

Because of the feminist critique, I had earlier rejected a fatherly image
of God, because to evoke such images participates in the oppression of
women by deifying masculinity. I remain worried by the problem. There
is a real danger that by celebrating fatherly images, we risk reinforcing
the symbolic structures that underlie women's oppression. But if we embrace such images with care, we may be able to help realize the goals of

the women's movement. "With care" means that fatherly images can be used only if equally powerful female images are also celebrated. And it means that only particular kinds of fatherly images should be used—not the incorporeal majestic God that helped to generate the hierarchical associations of masculinity and spirituality, with the corresponding association of femininity and embodiment, but an image of a tender loving father who faces and embraces the child. A loving and embodied God may support a different kind of masculinity, a masculinity that is capable of intimacy and tenderness. As a new generation of men emerges, men who have grown up with and take seriously feminist concerns—about parenting, about sharing household chores, about sharing the privileges of the religious life—a new generation of masculine images is needed as well.

Instead of feminizing men so they can have an intimate relationship with a male God, we might feminize this God, without always making him into a goddess. Indeed, I believe that in many ways the process by which we may now be creating new femininities and masculinities involves redistributing across the genders the traits that previously were thought to inhere in one or the other. As women have learned to be more assertive and powerful, men must learn to be more intimate, more related, more open. Ideally, this process will culminate in the dissociation between aggression and masculinity, on the one hand, and sensitivity and femininity, on the other. Obviously, we still have a long way to go. But I suggest that a different kind of masculinity requires a feminized image of a male God or what one day may simply be recognized as one version of God.

Our relationships to our images of the divine are not only those of child to parent but are entwined in eroticism, as this study and other feminist writings have suggested. As I have argued, I suspect that the image of a distant Father is deeply connected to the male fear of homoeroticism. In other words, as Freud suggested, the suppression of the erotic relationship between father and son is partly responsible for the creation of the authoritative father God. Embracing the Father involves a willingness to see male-male eroticism as an emotionally whole relationship. It does not mean that all men are homosexual, but it does mean that we recognize the part within ourselves that craves intimate bonds with fathers and other men, though those bonds do not take the form of sexual relationships.[12]

Homoeroticism, however, applies not just to men's relationship with male religious symbols. The same kind of process is at work between women and female images of deities. Thus far feminist analysis has tended to focus on the process of identification: how women's lives are deepened by being able to imagine themselves in the image of a female God. But if eroticism is part of our relationships with divine images, then women's relationships to goddesses potentially involve female homo-eroticism. The turn to goddess imagery does more than celebrate women's power and identity; it also celebrates female-female eroticism.

The use of both masculine and feminine images by both men and women opens up the possibility of various forms of intimate relations to the divine. I see this "polymorphously perverse theology" as *extremely liberating*. It will mean that all identities can find their rightful place in our contemporary theological expression and that we can celebrate all the craving for intimacy that we have and wish for. For all those reasons, it is time to re-embrace our fathers, to find a place for them in our contemporary pantheon, not as dominating or distant others, but as the loving, nurturing fathers we wish them to be.

NOTES

This chapter is adapted from *God's Phallus,* copyright © 1994 by Howard Eilberg-Schwartz (Boston: Beacon Press, 1994), by permission of the publisher.

1. Most influential for me were Rachel Adler, "'A Mother-Role in Israel': Aspects of the Mother Role in Jewish Myth," in *Beyond Androcentrism,* ed. Rita Gross, 237–59 (Missoula, Mont.: Scholars Press, 1977); Mary Daly, *Beyond God the Father* (Boston: Beacon Press, 1973); Carol Delaney, *The Seed and the Soil: Gender and Cosmology in a Turkish Village* (Berkeley: University of California Press, 1991); Rita Gross, "Steps toward Feminine Imagery of Deity in Jewish Theology," in *On Being a Jewish Feminist,* ed. Susannah Heschel, 234–47 (New York: Schocken Books, 1983); Rosemary Ruether, *Sexism and God-Talk* (Boston: Beacon Press, 1983); Judith Plaskow, *Standing Again at Sinai* (New York: Harper & Row, 1990). For a discussion of God's fatherhood and its implications in a broader perspective, see Johannes-Baptist Metz and Edward Schillebeeckx, eds., *God as Father?* (New York: Seabury Press, 1981).

2. I disagree with David M. Halperin, who argues in *One Hundred Years of Homosexuality* (New York: Routledge, 1990) that "heterosexual" and "homosexual" are strictly modern categories, the employment of which is limited to the past hundred years. It is true ancient Jews would not have used these terms. It is also true they would not have made sexual identities into essences that defined them as people. But the emphasis on procreation and fathering children was central to the definition of masculinity, as they construed it. And male-male sexual acts were considered an abomination. The best translation of this image of masculinity is the modern term "heterosexuality." Indeed, in many contexts both ancient and modern masculinity is constructed through a repression of male-male eroticism. See Gayle Rubin, "The Traffic in Women: Notes on the 'Political Economy' of Sex," in *Toward an Anthropology of Women,* ed. Rayna R. Reiter (New York: Monthly Review Press, 1975); Judith Butler, *Gender Trouble* (New York: Routledge, 1990);

and Eve Sedgwick, *Between Men: English Literature and Male Homosexual Desire* (New York: Columbia University Press, 1985). On the complementarity of men and women in Judaism, see also Rebecca Alpert, "In God's Image: Coming to Terms with Leviticus," in *Twice Blessed: On Being Lesbian, Gay, and Jewish,* ed. Christie Balka and Andy Rose, 61–70 (Boston: Beacon Press, 1989).

3. Raphael Patai, *Hebrew Goddess* (New York: Ktav, 1967), 21.

4. Leo Steinberg, *The Sexuality of Christ in Renaissance Art and Modern Oblivion* (New York: Pantheon, 1983).

5. Felix Bryk, *Sex and Circumcision* (North Hollywood, Calif.: Brandon House, 1970).

6. Caroline Walker Bynum, "The Female Body and Religious Practice in the Later Middle Ages," *Fragments for a History of the Human Body,* part 1, ed. Michel Feher, et al. (New York: Zone, 1989), 164.

7. Har Dayal, *The Bodhisattva Doctrine in Sanskrit Literature,* (Delhi: Motilal Banarsidass, 1975), 302.

8. Carl Kerényi, *The Gods of the Greeks* (London: Thames & Hudson, 1951).

9. Wendy Doniger O'Flaherty, *Asceticism and Eroticism in the Mythology of Siva* (London: Oxford University Press, 1973).

10. Frank Moore Cross, *Canaanite Myth and Hebrew Epic* (Cambridge, Mass.: Harvard University Press, 1973), 23.

11. Robert Oden, *The Bible without Theology* (San Francisco: Harper & Row, 1987), 92–105.

12. There is a danger, however, of exalting male-male connections. For it is precisely this "all boys club" to which women rightly object. Indeed, feminist criticism has pointed to the ways that patriarchy is a kind of "homosociality" in which women are exchanged for the creation of male-male bonds. But it is important not to let this legitimate critique of homosociality be conflated with homophobia. Homophobia should not be enlisted in the efforts to criticize male domination in the social order.

4

CHRISTIAN PIETY AND THE LEGACY OF MEDIEVAL MASCULINITY

Ulrike Wiethaus

In his essay "The Case for Men's Studies," Harry Brod argues for a demystification of past models of masculinity that have been used to create a false sense of immutable masculinity. To examine men's past identities can help us more easily to understand present gender roles as constructs and future definitions of gender as rich and open-ended.[1]

No doubt, masculine stereotypes that emerged during the Middle Ages still abound in contemporary culture. Sold as toys and expanded into "master stories" by movies and comic strips, figures such as the knight, the crusader, the alchemist, the feudal lord, or the wandering minstrel are still powerful enough to subtly shape gender norms and expectations. More ambiguous than knights and minstrels, however, are religious stereotypes of medieval masculinity. Images of monks, hermits, bishops, and popes have frequently been turned into symbols of power-hungry hypocrisy, well-hidden lechery, and worse.[2] And yet we are fascinated by the archetype of a monk as a symbol of unconditional surrender to a religious calling and of the radical rejection of materialism.

Yet when we have scraped off the patina of this idealization of religious devotion, the medieval religious men who emerge in full color can be reclaimed only in the critical spirit commended by Harry Brod. In the case of the Cistercian abbot Bernard of Clairvaux, what we find is a masculinity that is embodied and in its embodiment both powerful and stymied; a construction of masculinity that is fragile and tragic in its isolation and yet thoroughly committed to the rule of the fathers; a masculinity fascinating in its medieval "Otherness" and nevertheless very familiar in its androcentrism; attractive in its religious passion and love of the divine yet disturbing in its blindness to issues of gender justice.

Medieval Monastic Masculinity:
A Case Study

Bernard of Clairvaux, the son of noble parents, was born in 1090 in Fontaines near Dijon, France. In 1113, he entered the recently founded reform monastery Citeaux and was sent to build the daughter-house Clairvaux in 1115. He remained its abbot until his death in 1153. During those years, Bernard engaged in a tremendous range of activities as church politician, spiritual writer, and charismatic leader of the Cistercian order. He is regarded not only as one of the leading public figures who shaped the course of the twelfth century, but also as a monastic author who left a lasting imprint on the course of Western spirituality.[3] He is credited with the propagation of *bridal mysticism,* a particular type of devotion in which the human soul, envisioned as feminine, aspires to a union experience with her bridegroom, the human Christ. Bernard's masterly use of rhetoric, in particular his distinctly medieval pleasure in thinking in images, allows for multiple levels of meaning. It reflects a way of understanding reality that is reserved for only a select few in contemporary culture—poets and psychoanalysts. Especially noteworthy about the tradition of bridal mysticism is its emphasis on sexuality. Bernard's magnum opus, the homilies on the Song of Songs, as well as his homilies on Mary, *Homiliae in laudibus virginis matris,* brim with sexual imagery to describe spiritual ideas. Although references to masculinity are found throughout his texts, it is in his homilies on Mary that one of the most concentrated and intense expositions of Bernard's view of gender can be found. Here, a feminine "Other" is focused on without distraction, an exclusive and desirable female love object is presented that demands a relationship, and a meditative state of worship allows for the emergence of emotional dynamics that shape Bernard's understanding of monastic masculinity.

Bernard's biographical and historical context demanded the frequent use of gender categories for several reasons. To begin with, Western monasticism in general rests on a fundamental problematization of gender and gender relations. A male monastery is an exclusively homosocial institution that defines itself through the exclusion of female presence and the rejection of all physical, emotional, and social relations with women. It embodied an ideology that claimed, sometimes more sometimes less belligerently, that contact with women was the negation of monastic values.[4] To be a monk meant most of all not to be with women; women in turn were rhetorically associated with all that could defile a monk's existence—the pleasures of food and material goods, the hazards of a secular life and emotional attachments, and the responsibility for children and family obligations.

Throughout the centuries, monasticism has tolerated and even grown fat on the forbidden fruits of wealth, power, free movement in the world, and strong emotional ties, but it has never yielded to the one taboo underlying all others: contact with women. The claimed superiority of celibacy, the perceived danger of women as "polluters" of a "pure" all-male social group, and the evaluation of sexuality as grave violation of sacred vows—thus constituting a lack of will and control—survived the decline of monasticism and became a staple food for the Western psyche.[5]

A second reason for Bernard's pronounced concern with gender is more specific to the twelfth century. His literary production emerged during a far-reaching phase of historical transformation that has recently been interpreted as a "crisis in masculine identity".[6] According to this theory, the twelfth century represents a reorientation of masculine self-understanding, especially among members of the feudal nobility. This change has been traced to the erasure of the foundation of archaic early medieval aristocratic masculinity. Early medieval masculinity among the elites was defined by war, exclusive rights to rulership by the nobility, and a relatively unsophisticated economy without markets and money.[7] The twelfth century witnessed a pacification of Europe, with aggression directed outward toward the Middle East, and an increase in population numbers due to better nutrition and improved agrarian techniques. With the rise of the cities and the emergence of powerful new social classes (such as the administrative class, the *clerices*) competing cultural expressions proliferated. This resulted in a division between the religious and the secular spheres (expressed, for example, in the investiture controversies), with lay people developing a distinct culture of their own.[8] In order to control these tendencies toward lay autonomy, the church reacted with an increased repression and even criminalization of the sexual drive, thus reasserting its waning political influence through psychologically more effective means.[9] Over time, sexual repression became supplemented by inquisitorial procedures and the persecution of "heresies" and "witchcraft." Finally, through the stratification of society a greater consciousness of individuality and individual choice could emerge, at least among the religious and secular upper classes. This shift has led some scholars to credit the twelfth century with the "invention of the individual."

In coming to terms with these dramatic changes, an elite class of men created two novel practices, expressed both through cultural performance and literature: courtly love and bridal mysticism. Both focus male anxiety caused by these dramatic changes on an idealized female figure (the Lady, the Virgin Mary as bride) or a homoerotic male figure (Christ as beloved bridegroom). The adored love object is imagined as the sole source of satisfaction and frustration. Both courtly love and bridal mysticism reenact a drama of loss and desire, isolation and communion; both retreat into the personal and private realm of the imagination and leave behind the conflict-laden public scene. Men's worship of Woman as an idealized type and of Man as homoerotic gentle lover created a counter-world that eased upper-class men's anxiety-ridden transition into new roles and new social relations, without, however, upsetting the patriarchal imbalance between the sexes, be it at court or in the monastery.

In a provocative essay, Ulrich Müller claims that the ideology of courtly love constitutes a "collective neurosis" triggered by the religious elite's hostility toward sexuality.[10] Müller suggests that the church enforced standards of sexual repression so severe that asceticism became the ideal not just in the monastery, but also in the secular world. In the rhetoric of courtly love and bridal mysticism, however, repression could be lifted through language and ritual, and the repressed was allowed to manifest itself in socially acceptable forms.[11]

In order to keep the patriarchal system intact despite economic and social changes, new and rigid sexual norms were propagated by systematically persuading men of the inferiority and dangerous nature of "ordinary" women. That is, desire for women was turned into a matter of debasement, pollution, and a risk of losing status: hence, perhaps, the rise in misogynist literature in the twelfth and thirteenth centuries.[12]

The repressed sexual drive resurfaced in a setting that presented to men *one* exceptional Woman, the Lady, the Virgin Mary, the pure soul created in the image of God. This extraordinary female alone was "safe," that is, unpolluted and unpolluting, an object of male desire that would elevate a man during the sexual act rather than shame and degrade him. Given these dynamics of fear and fantasy, the Western split of women's sexual identity as either whores or virgins seems unavoidable. It is mirrored in a similar sexual polarization in the masculine self between "ascetic monk" and "wild animal." Yet this particular bipolarity is mitigated by numerous hybrid personas not available to women that allow for socially sanctioned sexual "conversions" (the admiration for male "sinners" who turn into saints), sexual "excursions" (the sanctioning of sexual contacts with lower-class women or women of other races, or of sexual acts during "loss of consciousness"), and sexual "inversions" (illegitimate and immoral sexual contacts approved as good when they prove and underscore masculinity; rape and adultery are the most notable examples).[13]

As persuasive as the theories of sexual repression, displacement of social conflict, and the reemergence of the forbidden in courtly love and bridal mysticism are, a crucial piece in the puzzle has still been left out. This missing piece is to be found, I propose, in Bernard's use of language and his distinctly medieval understanding of spirituality. Whereas the dilemma of repressed sexuality and a sense of masculine identity crisis establishes a certain affinity between ourselves and the twelfth century, Bernard's spirituality demarcates a historical rupture and difference that is easily overlooked.

The modern period is sometimes characterized as having lost the capacity to perceive physical reality as symbolic and bodily reality as metaphorical. The body as symbol has become more and more removed from our collective discourse, and its function as a means of expression has consequently significantly atrophied.[14] In the medieval period, however, the body, although of course already subject to civilisatory processes of alienation and taming, still functioned as a comparatively rich vehicle for communication. Especially in the religious realm, bodily phenomena such as levitation, voluntary starvation, miraculous bleeding, the healing power of saints' bone fragments, and so forth amply testify to the significance of the body as part of medieval religious "speech." It is only with the sixteenth-century "discovery" of the body as machine that the close relationships between body, culture, and nature became severed. The body began to lose its symbolic relevance in favor of a more abstract and "anti-body" form of cultural discourse.[15]

What we find in Bernard's spirituality is certainly a displacement of sexuality to the spiritual realm, a repression of the actual sexual body and its experience. But I think it is wrong to stop at this point. Bernard still embraced bodily reality as significant in ways that are thoroughly premodern. Instead of denying the body altogether, he metamorphosed the erotic body into his language and infused his spirituality with bodily experience. The highest imaginable realm of divine reality and the workings of the sexual body, in its capacity for sensual enjoyment and release, were for him identical in their *functioning*. This unity of bodily processes and psychological experience expresses a deep acceptance of erotic bodily reality as a truthful image of spiritual reality. Shifting so easily from one level of experienced reality to another without sensing a dichotomy can be labeled "archaic," "primitive," or "prelogical."[16] Although the proponents of *bridal mysticism* rejected physical sexuality as sinful or at least highly fraught with ambiguity, they accepted spiritual reality as fully sexual. Whereas the courtly lover is destined to remain eternally titillated yet sexually frustrated, the Cistercian follower of Bernard may, or is even expected to, revel in orgiastic abandon—spiritually. In courtly love, sexual desire is allowed and even encouraged, but the idealized Lady rarely grants sexual fulfillment; in addition, the social rules for choosing a suitable partner were rigid. Since union with the Divine is the explicit goal in bridal mysticism, however, sexual/spiritual desire *must* lead to sexual/ spiritual "intercourse"; the experience of sexual/spiritual fusion becomes a sign of distinction and accomplishment.

Since we have lost the body as a signifying reality, to "understand" spirituality in sexual terms seems possible today only if we use Freudian terms such as sublimation, repression, or sadomasochism. Bernard's mystical "body speech" thus represents an intermediary stage between a preverbal use of the body as means of communication and a postmedieval rejection of the body as symbol-system with a concomitant gradual "purging" of spirituality of any expression of physicality. This purging process has been more radical for men than for women, since women in patriarchy have always been identified with the body and nature and therefore were allotted "privileged" access to its significations (though they were, as a consequence, denounced as witches in the seventeenth century or hysterics in the early twentieth century).

Virgo ex Machina: Masculinity and Femininity as Patriarchal Constructs

In the following section, I will present a reading of Bernard's four homilies on the Virgin Mary, the *Homiliae in laudibus virginis matris,* that will illustrate the issues I have raised. The homilies are a mixture of devotional contemplation, exegetical and dogmatic interpretations, and thoughts about problems of monastic life based on a reading of parts of the first chapter in Luke. As we create holistic and just spiritualities for men and women today, the following analysis invites the reader to think more deeply about the relationship between embodiment, the construction of heterosexual masculinity, and our search for the divine beloved as male and female. We can embrace Bernard's acknowledgment of erotic spirituality; we can applaud him for honoring femininity as deeply expressive of divine truth; we must not, however, flinch from naming his violent misogyny and the crippling effect it has on his definition of spiritual masculinity.

The literature on the cult of the Virgin Mary is voluminous. In the past two decades there have been heated debates about her function in patriarchal Christianity. The post-Christian feminist Mary Daly interprets Mary as a symbol for the rape of the Goddess by patriarchy. Other feminists see her either as a slick tool to keep the virgin/whore split intact or as the prepatriarchal Goddess in powerful disguise.[17] Conservative theologians, on the other hand, credit Mary with keeping men from atrophying in the austerity of isolated masculinism; she becomes the necessary *anima* that protects the male *animus* from himself.[18]

For the purpose of this essay, I approach the image of Mary as a screen onto which men projected their understanding of gender—its functions, possibilities, and anxieties. Key issues in this examination are the notion of sexuality and the sexual act with its potential for crossing boundaries of body and self; the concept of childbirth and our fantasizing about our beginnings in relation to the mother; a replay of fantasies about parental powers, failures, and promises; and finally, our struggle with the unresolvable polarities of dependence and independence in our dealings with others, and the way in which we assign each category to either masculinity or femininity.

Bernard's homilies are focused on the annunciation scene in the first chapter of the Gospel of Luke (Luke 1:26–35). In Bernard's hands, the erotic undercurrents of the narrative are highlighted; the story subtly changes to a well-staged seduction of a literally man-made virgin, that is, a woman created by men for the male gaze, who is as far removed from flesh-and-blood women and their polluting influence as could possibly be imagined. True to the logic of bridal mysticism, the distant and majestic God of Luke's text is turned into an ardent lover. Mary becomes a highly prized object whose beauty and virtue are irresistible; the denial of union is impossible; the taboo at the heart of monastic life constitutes the narrative finale. Bernard's audience is both voyeur and apprentice. The monks are encouraged to identify with Mary and, through fostering her qualities in themselves, to aspire to the sexual/spiritual union with God for which Bernard provides the blueprint. Into this narrative flow are woven additional addresses to the audience, exegetical interpretations and references to relevant biblical texts, asides about Jews, and thoughts about Marian dogma.

Bernard's Virgin is a very young woman, accessible to the point of vulnerability. "It is usual for virgins—those who are really virgins—always to be timid and never to feel safe . . . because they know that they carry a precious treasure in an earthen vessel and that it is very difficult to live as an angel among men" (3:9). Bernard's only alternative (one wholly sanctioned by tradition) to such timidity is pain. Women who do engage in sexual activity must pay their dues: "Make haste, mothers and daughters, hasten all you who after Eve and because of Eve were born and do yourselves give birth in pain" (2:2). His Mary clarifies this point: "I . . . prefer to remain chaste [rather] than to conceive a child because of lust and then to bring him forth in pain deservedly" (3:7). Such recourse to a traditional patriarchal interpretation of childbirth is part of a larger strategy: in order to make plausible a sexually appealing virgin who successfully preserves her virginity, Bernard must divest real women of their spiritual appeal and distance himself from the danger of their polluting sexual entrapment. The Bernard as remembered in his biographies successfully fought off sexual seduction by jumping into an icy pond or making jokes, but Bernard the author takes recourse to standard misogynist opinion. "Solomon, . . . that wise man, was well acquainted with the weakness of this sex [women], frail in body and fickle in mind" (2:5). ". . . [W]oman, from whom evil had its beginning, you [Eve] whose reproach has been handed down to all womankind" (2:17). ". . . [T]he devil deceived the woman first and then overcame man through the woman" (2:13). Not accidentally perhaps, in one of the rare sections where Bernard refers to himself, the one male body zone that made the earliest intensive contact with a female body, the *mouth,* is described with negative sexual undertones. His mouth is "lewd," "foul," and he vomited "many vain, lying, and dirty words" (3:1). This ejaculatory self-pollution is juxtaposed to "those gracious and chaste words of the angel to the Virgin and of the Virgin to him" (ibid.)

Having deconstructed ordinary women as evil-bearing daughters of Eve, Bernard then engages in the construction of Mary. Being a man's woman like Athena, Mary, according to the inner logic of this scenario, cannot have been the creation of the enemy. The Christian paragon of masculinity, God, planned this transaction more smoothly than Zeus.

> This virgin [was not] discovered at the last minute, as if by chance. She was chosen ages ago. The Most High foreknew her and prepared her for himself. The holy hierarchy of men cheer on: "She was preserved by angels, prefigured by the patriarchs, promised by the prophets. Search the Scriptures and verify what I am saying" (2:4).

God worked hard on his new creation. "So it was that the Maker of mankind . . . had to choose one person out of all the living, or rather, he had to create someone who he knew would be worthy to be his mother, someone in whom he was sure he could delight" (2:1). What men produce is better than anything a female could give birth to; Mary's qualities are praised as "unique . . . extraordinary . . . wonderful . . . incomparable" (1:9). Her mind and her body are impeccable (read "holy," 2:2) to the male gaze, and as a consequence, the man-made creature inspires (incestual) lust even in the eyes of her father/creator.

This queenly maiden, adorned with the jewels of these virtues [virginity and humility], radiant with this perfect beauty of spirit and body, renowned in the assembly of the Most High for her loveliness and beauty, so ravished the eyes of all the heavenly citizens that the heart of the King himself desired her beauty (2:2). The troublesome real woman is successfully replaced: "Yes, he [God] gave woman for woman: a wise one for a foolish one; a humble one for an arrogant one. Instead of the tree of death, she offers you a taste of life; in place of the poisonous fruit of bitterness she holds out to you the sweetness of eternity's fruit" (2:3).

To what use can this *virgo ex machina* be put in the dreams of Bernard? She has two functions. First, she offers all the bliss a mother can give without threatening the vulnerable child. She nurses with a "gentle breast" and keeps the child "safe within her womb" (2:9). In sermon 2, Bernard contemplates more deeply the image that a woman "shall enclose a man" (2:8): "a woman enclosing a man, and a man folding up his limbs within a woman's frail little body. What can this miracle be? As Nicodemus asked, 'Can a man enter a second time into his mother's womb and be born anew?'" (ibid). For Bernard, and for medieval religious culture generally, the key issue is the contact between inferior (female) physical substance and superior (male) spiritual reality. "Who indeed . . . can grasp . . . not only the way in which the inaccessible splendor could pour itself out into a virginal womb but also how . . . it became a shade for the rest of this body, a small portion of which he had vivified and appropriated?" (4:4).

Mary's second function is sexual in nature, and here Bernard poses as seducer. His rhetoric dramatically turns into direct speech to the Virgin, whom he woos as a lover. Referring to the moment at which the Virgin accepts divine insemination, he cajoles her:

> You, I say, are the one we were promised, you are the one we are expecting, you are the one we have longed for. . . . Why do you delay? Why be afraid? . . . Let humility take courage, and shyness confidence. This is not the moment for virginal simplicity to forget prudence . . . open your heart to faith, your lips to consent and your womb to your creator. Behold, the long-desired of all nations is standing at the door and knocking (4:8). Virgin maid, open up your bosom, enlarge your womb, for he who is mighty is about to do great things for you (3:8).

And how is this great thing imagined? Lying on his couch and smelling the "Virgin's nard" (3:2; see Song of Songs 1:12), the king "rejoiced like a giant to run his course . . . he was moved by so great a desire that he sped ahead of his messenger and came to the virgin whom he loved, whom he had chosen for his own, whose beauty he ardently desired" (3:2). The sexual act itself, however, is more restrained due to the requirement to keep Mary's virginity intact: "This abundant rain which God had stored up for his inheritance fell with hushed silence into the virgin womb, penetrating her gently" (2:7).

Allowing his imagination free reign up to this point, Bernard erects barriers again to ensure that this spiritual/sexual experience is understood to be a privilege, difficult to obtain, and that knowledge about it is the secret of the monastic community. The sexual act is a corporeal dwelling within her (4:3), an inaccessible splendor that poured itself into a virginal womb (4:4), which ultimately can "only be taught by the giver, and learned only by the receiver" (4:4). Telling the story then becomes an act of initiation, the transition from the secular to the religious realm, the distinction between insiders and outsiders, the stellar reward for an other-wise difficult lifestyle, the privilege of an elite.

What ideals of masculinity—symbolized by God and Christ—supple-ment this vision of a perfect, that is, perfectly nonthreatening and unpol-luting—mother-*cum*-lover? The dreamed-of male child who belongs to the nurturing mother is incapable of being hurt or abandoned. "But as you gaze at this little one, think how great he is" (3:13), Mary is advised. "He was perfect from the beginning. From the very beginning, I tell you, he was filled with the spirit of wisdom and understanding, the spirit of counsel and fortitude, the spirit of knowledge and piety" (2:10). In order to alleviate anxiety, a child's frailty or fickleness of mind is projected upon real adult women, the daughters of Eve, as we have seen above. Already strong in childhood, the ideal adult male "is clearly great, he is as great as the Most High, for he himself is none other than the Most High" (3:12). He is truth, power, and wisdom (4:7), and he shows aggressiveness as a king (4:2).[19]

But Bernard was writing as a monk to monks, and so his image of the ideal male has to combine secular and monastic ideals. Not surprisingly, the feudal notion of a "great king" is fused with character traits that make him a monkish hermaphrodite. Like Mary, Christ is "meek and humble in heart" (3:14), and so should the monks be. "Let us learn his humility, imitate his gentleness, embrace his love, share his sufferings, be washed in his blood" (3:14). Also, Christ takes on the feminine function of nur-ture. He is "this good fruit [who] is both food and drink to the souls of those who hunger and thirst for righteousness" (3:6). He is beautiful and sweet-smelling (ibid.).

Feminizing the masculine at first glance appears to be a gesture of rec-onciliation with women, but Bernard offers only a fusion of ideal mascu-line traits with ideal feminine traits, which still keeps intact the original dichotomy between the "good" man-made Virgin and the "bad" women/mothers/lovers of flesh and blood. And as much as the monks are advised to identify with the one "good" feminine love object, Bernard creates im-ages of men identified with "bad" feminine love objects, that is, "ordi-nary" women. Foolish and arrogant like Eve (2:3), Jews deny Christ: "When Pilate asked, 'Shall I crucify your king?' did the frenzied house of Jacob not wickedly deny him and stupidly reject him, screaming back their answer as with one voice?" (4:2). Whereas Christians are credited with the spiritual understanding of scripture, the Jews, like women, are associated with the body, now a metaphor for a literal reading of the Bible. "If all flesh is grass, then the carnal people of Jewry were also grass. And while this people clung to the parched written code and were drained of spiritual sweetness, was the grass not withering? And when they boasted in the Law, after this had been done away with, did the flower not also fade?" (1:4).

His identification of body, women, and negative (read: nonhegemonic) male characteristics is clearly described in his Sermon on the Song of Songs 38:4. "I believe that by women he [Solomon] means people who are sensual and worldly, people devoid of manliness, whose conduct lacks both fortitude and constancy, people who are entirely superficial, soft and effeminate in their lives and behavior." Equally "bad women" were therefore all men who did not conform to his standards of monastic asceticism and Christian values.

A split between earthly and spiritual masculinity is upheld for men in ways that parallel the split of women's image, although it lacks the harshness of tone Bernard reserves for women. If the ideal monastic male is invulnerable, and has in addition absorbed useful "feminine" traits such as humility and obedience, the flesh-and-blood male is vulnerable, Bernard must admit. He is the representation of all of humanity, imagined to be completely cut off from what both Marian and earthly femininity symbolize, the creation of life, be it "pure" or "filthy." "We all have been made in the eternal Word of God, and look, we are dying . . . doleful Adam and his unhappy offspring, exiled from Paradise implore you [the Virgin] . . . David asks it, . . . your own fathers beg it of you, as do those now dwelling in the region of death . . . on your answer depends the comfort of the afflicted, the salvation of all the sons of Adam, your whole race" (4:8). To die and embrace death is the male salvific answer to the female act of giving birth: the Son washes his believers in his blood (3:14), he "freely poured out his soul in death" (ibid.). Death is unavoidable because the Father demands it: "Let us offer him the propitiation for our sins because for this he was born and given for us. Let us offer him up in the sight of the Father, offer him too to his own, for the Father did not spare his own Son but gave him up for us all" (ibid.).

At the core of elite male religious identity is the threat of death, and a return to the womb is the wished-for dream of renewed life. This dream can only be tolerated in its manifest form: in the disguises of a man-made virgin and her silent seduction.

Conclusion

Bernard of Clairvaux belonged to a small elite of male writers and preachers who shaped the course of society through the propagation of innovative religious imagery. Much like Western society at the close of the twentieth century, twelfth-century Europeans found themselves at a crossroads. Old gender systems fell apart, and men and women could choose to create egalitarian relationships among each other or to perpetuate patriarchal power inequities. Historian Jo Ann McNamara described the eventual resolution of the male identity crisis in the twelfth century poignantly in the form of a question: "How can men redefine manhood to prove women's incapacity to carry out public professional responsibilities?"[20] Times of transition cause identity anxieties, especially in regard to gender; Bernard tried to resolve such anxieties for men by reinforcing male hegemony with the help of religious symbols. A symbolic system that assigned women inferior roles supported women's oppression in the church at large. But men paid a price, too. Separation from women who symbolize nature and the creation of life forced men to confront death, and in the end to identify symbolically with mortality without the possibility of regeneration. Worship of the Virgin Mary as a "man-made" idol alleviates the death anxiety associated with the construct of hegemonic masculinity because it reconnects men with femininity, experienced as mothering, birthing, and providing sexual satisfaction. And since Bernard's vision of the Virgin Mary is that of a very young and helpless adolescent, men can be simultaneously assured of their superiority.

Does such reading of the four homilies leave any room for authentic religious meaning? Or is Bernard lost to us as an inspiring spiritual authority? Bernard acknowledged the erotic as power and let himself be guided by that insight. For that we can celebrate him. And for the rest, poet Audre Lorde should offer the guiding insight:

> Recognizing the power of the erotic within our lives can give us the energy to pursue genuine change within our world, rather than merely settling for a shift of characters in the same weary drama. For not only do we touch our most profoundly creative source, but we do that which is female and self-affirming in the face of a racist, patriarchal, and anti-erotic society.[21]

NOTES

The Latin text of the *Homiliae in laudibus virginis matris* is printed in the critical edition by Jean Leclerq and H. Rochais, *Sancti Bernardi Opera*, vol. 4 (Rome: Editiones cisterciences, 1966), 13–58. The English translation used in this chapter was prepared by Marie-Bernard Said and Grace Perigo, in *Magnificat: Homilies in Praise of the Blessed Virgin Mary* (Kalamazoo, Mich.: Cistercian Publications, 1979), 1–59.

1. Harry Brod, "The Case for Men's Studies," in *The Making of Masculinities: The New Men's Studies*, ed. Harry Brod, 39–62. (Boston: George Allen & Unwin, 1987).

2. E.g., Umberto Eco's novel *The Name of the Rose* (San Diego: Harcourt Brace Jovanovich, 1983) and the success of the movie based on the book.

3. Brian Patrick McGuire, *The Difficult Saint: Bernard of Clairvaux and His Tradition* (Kalamazoo, Mich.: Cistercian Publications,1991).

4. *Summa Cartae Caritatis*, XVII and XVIII; printed in *Les plus anciens*

Textes de Citeaux, ed. Jean de la Croix Bouton and Jean-Baptiste van Damme, 107–25 (Achel, France: Abbaye Cistercienne, 1974). See also Aaron W. Godfrey, "Rules and Regulation: Monasticism and Chastity," in *Homo Carnalis: The Carnal Aspects of Medieval Human Life,* ed. Helen Rodnite Lemay, 45–59 (Binghamton, N.Y.: Center for Medieval and Early Renaissance Studies, 1990).

5. Ute Ranke-Heinemann, *Eunuchs for the Kingdom of Heaven. Women, Sexuality, and the Catholic Church* (New York: Doubleday, 1990).

6. I am presenting an argument developed by Bernd Thum. See his "Geschlechterkultur und Minne: Ein Versuch zur Sozial-, Funktions- und Mentalitätsgeschichte des oberrheinischen Minnesangs im 12. Jahrhundert," in *Minne ist ein swaerez spil: Neue Untersuchungen zum Minnesang und zur Geschichte der Liebe im Mittelalter,* ed. Ulrich Müller, 3–75 (Göttingen: Kümmerle-Verlag, 1986).

7. Ibid., 4.

8. Peter Dinzelbacher, "Sozial- und Mentalitätsgeschichte der Liebe im Mittelalter," in *Minne ist ein swaerez spil,* ed. Müller, 75–111.

9. Thum, "Geschlechterkultur und Minne"; for a more cautious evaluation, see Allison Coudert, "Exemplary Biblical Couples and the Sacrament of Marriage," in *Homo Carnalis: The Carnal Aspects of Medieval Human Life,* ed. Lemay, 59–85. Pierre J. Payer offers the opposite view in: *The Bridling of Desire. Views of Sex in the Later Middle Ages* (Toronto: University of Toronto Press, 1993).

10. Ulrich Müller, "Die Ideologie der Hohen Minne: Eine ekklesiogene Kollektiveneurose? Überlegungen und Thesen zum Minnesang," in *Minne ist ein swaerez spil,* ed. Müller, 283–319.

11. Ibid., 292.

12. Howard Bloch, *Medieval Misogyny and the Invention of Western Romantic Love* (Chicago: University of Chicago Press, 1991).

13. The categories are mine.

14. Richard Sennett, *The Fall of Public Man* (New York: Alfred A. Knopf, 1977).

15. I am following here Burkhardt Krause in his "Hermeneutische Aspekte der Körpererfahrung im Mittelalter," in *Das Mittelalter—unsere fremde Vergangenheit,* ed. Joachim Kuolt et al., 71–117 (Stuttgart: Helfant Edition, 1990).

16. Ibid., 82.

17. Mary Daly, *Beyond God the Father* (Boston: Beacon Press, 1973); Marina Warner, *Alone of All Her Sex* (New York: Vintage Books, 1976); Elinor Gadon, *The Once and Future Goddess* (San Francisco: Harper & Row, 1989).

18. Romano Guardini, "Bernhard von Clairvaux in Dantes Göttlicher Komödie," in *Die Chimäre seines Jahrhunderts,* ed. Johannes Spoerl (Würzburg, Germany: Werkbund Verlag, 1953), 54–71.

19. It is remarkable that Bernard insists on the adulthood of Christ as he is in the womb, denying the vulnerability of infancy; the Cistercian monk twists christological dogma here to a certain extent by downplaying Christ's human nature.

20. Jo Ann McNamara, "The *Herrenfrage:* The Restructuring of the Gender System, 1050–1150," in *Medieval Masculinities. Regarding Men in the Middle Ages,* ed. Clare A. Lees, 3–31 (Minneapolis: University of Minnesota Press, 1994), p. 4. The essay is an excellent feminist survey of the gender issues at stake in Bernard's society.

21. Audre Lorde, "Uses of the Erotic: The Erotic as Power" in *Sexuality and the Sacred: Sources for Theological Reflection,* ed. James B. Nelson and Sandra P. Longfellow, 75–79 (Louisville, Ky.: Westminster/John Knox Press, 1994), 79.

5

MALCOLM X'S RELIGIOUS PILGRIMAGE: FROM BLACK SEPARATISM TO A UNIVERSAL WAY

Fareed Munir

The African American community has always struggled to find a coherent identity in the context of the religion and society in which it must exist. Its history of difficulty and pain necessitates that the question "Who are we?" be answered by reflection upon and interpretation of the past. Because, as Martha Lee has said, "their tie to Africa is undeniable, yet tenuous, and because their American origins are rooted in oppression,"[1] an answer to the above question is necessary in order to repair and restore the African American's spiritual life.

Many African Americans find the mainstream religion, Christianity, an adequate response. Others, however, find Christianity incompatible with their overall needs, for they are divided from mainstream society by language, politics, economic interests, and education. Such people reach beyond the boundaries of Christianity and embrace alternative religions that offer them a coherent value system.

Malcolm X was one successful individual who internalized and restructured his own identity with an alternative religious group's offering of a coherent value system. His religious pilgrimage began early in his life with his family of origin and early childhood; it continued with his early manhood as a streetwise hustler, pimp, and undisciplined secularist; and it extended to his joining Elijah Muhammad's Nation of Islam, in 1949, which began what is referred to as Malcolm's pre-Meccan period.[2]

Although they developed side by side, like father and son, Elijah and Malcolm parted ways in 1964. This began Malcolm's post-Meccan period, as he defected from the proto-Islamic black nationalist group to Sunni Islam—Islamic orthodoxy. Subsequently, he made a pilgrimage to Mecca, called hajj, which was the most important turning point in his evolution to Sunni Islam. The goal of this chapter, then, is primarily to examine and interpret the significance of religion throughout Malcolm's life and how it influenced his Nation of Islam experience and movement to Sunni Islam.

Malcolm's pilgrimage connected him with millions of Muslims throughout the world. Through it he evolved into something more than a proto-Islamic black nationalist leader, as he had been viewed by others, at odds with mainstream white society.[3] Moreover, it validated Malcolm's repudiation of Elijah's limited ideology of what it meant to be a man of order and discipline. Hajj expanded his knowledge and sensitized his heart to the importance of submission to Allah (one God) and the importance of emulating the Prophet Muhammad ibn Abdullah of the seventh century as the true example of a man, instead of Elijah Muhammad, whom he had regarded as the most honored and feared "black" man in his life.[4] Malcolm's thoughts, reordered by the notion of submission to Allah and emulation of his Prophet, provided him with a new set of guidelines to measure his own manhood.[5]

Sunni Islam shaped Malcolm's final identity and destiny. In his life, he embodied an African American male evolution. He was transformed from an angry reacting male, caught in the dominant racial and cultural belief systems,[6] to an optimistic one. Malcolm's religious pilgrimage was a journey that brought about in him an ideological change, a change that subsequently had a significant impact on Muslims and non-Muslims alike. Moreover, Malcolm's physical pilgrimage to Mecca was his completion of a lifelong journey that began with the love and closeness provided to him by his family of origin.

An African American Family

Malcolm Little, who subsequently assumed the names of Malcolm X and al-hajj Malik Shabazz, was born in Omaha, Nebraska, on May 19, 1925. His father, the Reverend Earl Little, was a large, dark-skinned man who had a third- or fourth-grade formal education.[7] An itinerant Baptist minister, Earl Little preached Christianity on the weekends. During the week, he was an active organizer for Marcus Garvey's Universal Negro Improvement Association (UNIA).

Earl Little believed, following Marcus Garvey, that an African American male could not truly be a man in America, because he could never accept the religious ideals or conceptualizations of whites. Earl implicitly accepted Garvey's rejection of a white God, because a white God could only benefit white people.[8] He preached a social gospel that personified Jesus as a black man, because, rationally, a black God benefited black people spiritually and socially.[9]

Earl Little used both Garveyism and Christianity to develop an interpretive metaphor, expressed in black popular religion. He used both of them as a foundation for true religious freedom.[10] He functioned outside of the realm of the typical "Negro" in America. With black popular religion fueling his self-identity, he was considered an "uppity nigger" by whites who recognized that his masculinity was expressed in a different way than that of other males of his kind.[11]

Earl Little married twice and had eight children. His seventh child, Malcolm, at an early age accompanied his father to the UNIA meetings held on Sunday nights or early Sunday mornings, before church services. The UNIA meetings possessed many of the characteristics of a Christian religious service, including enthusiasm, dedication, and outward fervor.[12]

Malcolm's involvement with the black popular religion of his father demonstrates that he had a close affiliation with religion as a child, with more than average contact with a religious setting. As an adult, his life reveals that he had received not just political but religious overtones from this experience.

When he provided Alex Haley with his description of the UNIA for the writing of his autobiography, however, before his pilgrimage (pre-Meccan days), he emphasized the importance of race and did not acknowledge the importance of religion in Garvey's movement. Because the Nation of Islam's doctrine centered on the black race, Malcolm played down the role of Christianity and the fact that his father was a Christian minister in the Garvey movement. By this time Malcolm was a leader in the Nation of Islam, and he had replaced Christianity with Islam. In addition, Malcolm's black popular religion went one step further than his father's version, as he espoused that a white God was degrading not only to African Americans but also to Christianity. Malcolm used Garvey's black nationalism and Islam to develop his interpretive metaphor.

Quite early, Malcolm realized that his father allowed only him but no other siblings to attend the UNIA meetings.[13] He was his father's favorite, because Earl believed the seventh son of his patrilineal line was special. On occasions Malcolm said, "I am my father's seventh son."[14] This idea, infused in Malcolm's psyche, contributed both to his self-esteem as a child and to his masculine identity as an adult. As a man, Malcolm came to believe that being the "seventh son" was a symbol of his specialness. The seventh son is a born hero; he is destined to be a man; and he is bound to do the will of God.[15]

It was during his Nation of Islam days, the pre-Meccan period, that Malcolm revisited and reinterpreted the number seven to represent the wisdom and strength of the black man; he is the maker, the owner of the planet Earth, and God of the universe. In other words, Malcolm confirmed from the Nation's symbolic, religious numerology that Allah (God) had guided him to follow in the footsteps of his father.[16]

In 1931, when Malcolm was six, his father was murdered.[17] Even after his father's death, Malcolm continued to experience the imagery left by the relationship he and his father shared through the influence of his

Grenadian mother, Louise Little, a remarkable woman. She was a fair-skinned woman, completely the opposite in complexion to her husband. Malcolm inherited not only the color of her skin but other aspects of her identity that he refused to acknowledge as a young man.[18]

Unfortunately, Malcolm's attitude toward his mother has allowed most biographers to depict her as a distraught, tragic figure who after her husband's murder succumbed to insanity and eventually had to be committed to the state mental hospital in Kalamazoo, Michigan, where she stayed for twenty-six years.[19] It is more important to remember that, prior to being committed, Louise Little continued on the same path as her husband, holding firmly to the liberation values of the Garvey movement.[20]

Even more remarkable, she maintained her religious affiliation as a Seventh-Day Adventist, for solace and strength. She fused Garveyism and Adventism and used them as an interpretive metaphor to help her deal with the stress and strain of holding the family together without a husband. Unlike some other traditions, in the Seventh-Day Adventist church the status of women had never been a subordinate one; strong-willed and high-spirited women held public positions.[21] Louise continued to express the ideals she had shared with her husband in the past. Clearly, Malcolm was the product of a family that practiced black popular religion of the time, a religion that attempted to address the spiritual and social needs of the African American family.

It is deplorable that such a strong and compassionate woman is usually portrayed as if her life had no impact upon Malcolm's manhood. Malcolm himself placed more importance on his father's than on his mother's role in his life. Malcolm was infused and socialized by an ultraconservative, patriarchal, traditional view of women, and the foundation for this view was laid by his father, who autocratically led his wife and children.[22] This way of viewing women was, for Malcolm, further built upon by the Nation of Islam. The Nation viewed all but the most extraordinary women only in domestic terms; they were to keep house, rear children, sew, cook, and take care of their husbands.[23]

Malcolm's limited view of women, then, was enhanced and legitimated by the paternally structured Nation of Islam. Its ideology focused upon "black male" superiority.[24] Implicit in its doctrine was the notion that the African American male was a provocative figure to all outside his own group. It molded a religio-cultural identity in African American males that made them always aware of their precarious role in American society.[25] Such powerful religious and social symbols operating in the life of young Malcolm reveal the wide range of religio-cultural experiences that he could draw upon. This is not to suggest that Malcolm was always conscious of them as driving forces in his life, but in order to appreciate Malcolm's growing up as a male in America, it is important to understand that his life's experiences included a compelling religio-cultural component that was continual and strong, beginning in childhood.

Urban Streets in Shaping Malcolm's Identity

Seduced by the excitement of Boston and subsequently New York, where he found employment, lost his job, and turned to stealing, selling, and using drugs, Malcolm, like many young African American men, took on an underground lifestyle.[26] He became uncouth and wild, with profanity as his everyday language.[27] He changed from a conservative young boy—following the values he had learned from his family of origin—to a young man practicing the tricks of the trade, acquired on the streets of two large cities. The streets of Boston and New York obscured like a veil everything decent he had learned earlier in life.[28]

In 1946, at the age of twenty, Malcolm was caught trying to pawn a stolen watch and was sentenced to ten years in the Charleston State Prison in Massachusetts. By this time, because of his past street life, he had identified himself as an atheist. He was so miserable and nasty that he was nicknamed Satan by the prison inmates.[29] Malcolm personified the aftermath of urban collapse and its impact on the African American male psyche, "the ravaging personal and social effects of underground drug economies, the sheer violence of everyday life in the ghetto, and the destruction of black male life."[30]

The Pre-Meccan Period

In prison, Malcolm felt for the first time since childhood a force larger than his own simply rationalized nihilism of the hustling code. Persuaded by his brothers Philbert and Reginald, who had become members of the Nation of Islam, Malcolm became a follower of Elijah Muhammad. Elijah's ideology brought Malcolm a new self-identity as man, an identity infinitely more impressive than his previous self-image as a hustler.[31]

Malcolm became now, as he understood it, Elijah Muhammad's "slave servant."[32] By accepting Elijah's version of Islam, Malcolm's earlier religious experience was restored, but in a more complex fashion. His new religious understanding built upon his parents' notions of black popular religion. Consequently, Malcolm accepted Elijah Muhammad as his mentor and legitimate heir to both his parents as he repaired and rebuilt his masculine identity in a hostile world.[33]

Irrefutably, the movement's doctrine reflected the knowledge and background of its current leader, Elijah Muhammad, and not Fard Muhammad, who had founded the movement in 1930 and disappeared in 1933.[34] Elijah had been a Baptist minister in the slums of Detroit, from 1923 to 1929, prior to joining the movement. Although Elijah and his Nation purported to shun Christianity, the religious eschatology taught in the name of Islam was actually a set of myths developed in large part from the Bible. Those myths were carefully meshed with communal-nationalistic themes that were a product of the time. Elijah advocated a religio-social ideology designed to "resurrect" African Americans by giving them a coherent system of identity.

Elijah taught that African Americans (blacks) were God's chosen people, and that the white man was the devil.[35] He taught his followers that man can evolve to a higher mental level until he becomes God. Elijah stated: "God is a man and we just cannot make Him other than man. . . . Let that one among you who believes God is other than man prove it!"[36]

Elijah carefully linked his movement to its founder, applying the orthodox Christian doctrine of God incarnated on earth to Fard Muhammad. Fard was alleged to be a member of a god-producing family, a family of the highest intelligence.[37] Elijah also taught that there had been several gods since the beginning of time. The first god created himself from and out of "total triple darkness." After dying, each god transferred his knowledge and divinity to the next god.

Fard Muhammad was a part of this process. He inherited the knowledge and the divinity from his father. This inheritable, special knowledge obligated the founder to save the African American people from the incarnate devil, the white man. In Elijah's book *Our Saviour Has Arrived*— a fitting title—he stated that "the [traditional] Muslims worship one God—Allah. . . . Yet 99% of the old world Muslims think that Allah is only a spirit and is not a man."[38] This demonstrated that Elijah talked about God and the devil only in corporeal terms. He taught his followers that mainstream Muslims were ignorant of the real truth.

It was crucial, according to Elijah, that African Americans understand the "knowledge of self," a coherent theory of identity. African Americans needed to learn more of their own history and destiny. This was the factor that would make way for the process of the resurrection of African Americans on earth. Elijah used the language of death and resurrection, but he did not believe in life after death. He believed that this present life was all-encompassing, so he used the term "resurrection" figuratively. African Americans were dead (i.e., ignorant) about their own history, so a mental resurrection had to take place.[39] They had to relinquish all theories of knowledge given to them by their white oppressors. But they could not do this until they submitted totally to Allah (Fard) and obeyed his messenger (Elijah). In other words, Elijah had connected his doctrine with an unorthodox version of the first pillar of mainstream

Islam, which focused upon Allah and his Messenger, Muhammad ibn Abdullah (d. 632 C.E.).

Elijah Muhammad maintained that Allah—the savior, or *messiah*—had appeared to him personally without a medium of any sort. Logically then, since Allah, who came in the "person of Fard Muhammad," had directly spoken to him, it was biblically, Islamically, and rationally fitting for Elijah to be divinely commissioned as the last and final Messenger of Allah.[40] African Americans needed to have their own prophet of Islam.[41] By the same sign, Elijah was convinced that the saving force and true religion of African Americans should be Islam, and not Christianity, the religion of his opponent and enemy, white people.

Elijah Muhammad published his own literature and, not surprisingly, these works had a greater impact on the lives of his Nation than the writings of mainstream Islam did. Elijah and his followers believed that the Quran was a holy book to be held in awe and placed on the highest shelf of the Muslim's home. However, they rarely read it.

In this context, although the proto-Islamic movement referred to itself as a religion, its religious values were of secondary importance to its nationalism.[42] Elijah extracted from mainstream Islam only what was needed to build a coherent system of pride and dignity for African Americans. For forty-two years, from 1933 to 1975, Elijah's mission, as he understood it, was to "cut the cloak to fit the cloth."[43]

In the spring of 1952 when Malcolm Little was paroled from prison, he went directly to the Detroit Temple and formally joined the Nation of Islam. It was then that he received his X, to become Malcolm X.[44] Malcolm's loyalty and dedication to Elijah over the next ten years moved him quite quickly up the ranks of the movement. He was appointed minister of the New York Temple. Subsequently, Malcolm was thrust forward by Elijah as the national representative of the Nation of Islam, which was interpreted by all as the second-highest position in the Nation, next to Elijah Muhammad. He met, recruited, and/or influenced several Muslim leaders, including Muhammad Ali (heavyweight champion of the world) and the current controversial minister, Louis Farrakhan. More importantly, his rise to prominence in the Nation of Islam made it possible for Malcolm to be recognized as a significant leader in wider circles, allowing him to have a profound impact on African American non-Muslim thought as well as on Muslim thought.

The Post-Meccan Period

As a matter of course, Malcolm grew beyond the boundaries established by his mentor Elijah Muhammad, and he began to dissent from certain policies that were fundamental to the movement. When President

John F. Kennedy was assassinated in Dallas, Elijah Muhammad issued a directive to all Muslim ministers to refrain from commenting on the death. In a speaking engagement in New York's Manhattan Center, however, when Malcolm was asked his opinion of the assassination, he defied Elijah and replied anyway.

In response, Elijah Muhammad restricted Malcolm's speaking for ninety days. At the end of the ninety-day period, Elijah extended the restriction to make it indefinite. Consequently, on March 8, 1964, Malcolm announced that he was leaving the Nation of Islam to lead his own organization, the Muslim Mosque, Inc. Later he added another component, the Organization of Afro-American Unity. Two elements distinguished Malcolm and his organizations from the Nation of Islam. The first was the introduction of Sunni Islam, which centered on belief in the egalitarianism and universalism of Allah, and the advocacy of the sunnah (i.e., the traditions) of Prophet Muhammad ibn Abdullah. This broadened Malcolm's notion of a religious role model by presenting an integrated, whole picture of Prophet Muhammad, the ideal man in Sunni Islam, negating the previously constrictive doctrine, held by the Nation of Islam, that Elijah Muhammad was the ideal man. The second was personal independence, which allowed Malcolm to lead his own organization and to appeal to all people, and not only to African Americans. Thus Malcolm began his declared Sunni phase and personal independence from Elijah Muhammad.

As Malcolm allowed himself to be influenced by Islamic orthodoxy, he questioned his own personal commitment to Elijah Muhammad's teachings. For example, he knew that Christians believed in a universal God, too. But Malcolm believed that God in the Western world, and in America in particular, had been appropriated by a Western culture that gave God a specific color and definite cultural attributes. Malcolm contended that Allah is free from human prejudices and false distinctions. He later acknowledged that Allah has no racial restrictions but welcomes people of all colors; God is universal in dimension.[45] Such a broad understanding of Allah demonstrated for him the egalitarianism of Allah and the need to submit to him, and not to a man.

This period of complex changes in Malcolm's life ended abruptly when he was assassinated on February 21, 1965—approximately nine months after he returned from hajj. Although Malcolm's hajj forms a clear boundary that makes it possible to distinguish between the pre-Meccan and the post-Meccan Malcolm, some observers claim that the post-Meccan Malcolm did not live long enough to develop his new American orthodox Islamic ideology totally: "His assassination put an abrupt halt to the process of redefining his perspective."[46]

This is true only in some sense. Malcolm's death stopped his complete expression of Sunni Islam. But his transformation to becoming a Sunni

Muslim had begun with a self-appraisal in prison, with his naive understanding of the Islamic religion. His transformation continued, despite shocks and setbacks. Malcolm's autobiography interprets this change in religio-cultural terms, resulting finally in his changing his name to one that reflected his internal evolution, al-hajj Malik Shabazz; al-hajj is an honorific title bestowed on one who has made the pilgrimage to Mecca, and whose total life is transformed by that experience. The Sunni Islamic religion's influence on Malcolm, then, cannot be adequately appreciated if it is not recognized as a guiding orientation that shaped his masculine identity.[47]

To understand how Sunni Islam enabled Malcolm to negotiate the last two years of his life, it is important to explore certain segments of his thought that are embodied in the pre-Meccan period. After all, Malcolm's pre-Meccan Islamic period in the Nation of Islam—referred to in Sunni Islam as al-Jahiliyya, the period of ignorance or limited definition of one's self identity—was the beginning of his change to Sunni Islam.

In retrospect Malcolm can be understood by going even further back to his conversion and his intellectual awakening in prison as the beginning of a dynamic growth process. It began when he, as a proud man, acted out ritualistic steps, such as the refusal to eat pork in prison[48] and the performance of ablution (washing)[49] and prayer.[50] Malcolm, bending his knees and praying extemporaneously, symbolically died and rose again. He knelt down as "Satan"—the nickname given him by fellow inmates—and got up a Muslim man. But he was a Muslim man only in the limited sense taught by Elijah Muhammad.

Elijah's ideology provided Malcolm with an idealistic, even visionary, frame of reference that liberated him from certain political, racial, and cultural assumptions he had learned from the world. His acceptance of Elijah's version of Islam filled the empty recesses of his life so that he himself was shocked by the suddenness of his transformation. He had opened himself to change. He could now reflect on the power of goodness. Subsequently, he used the post-Meccan period, particularly the last eleven months, to shine light on what he thought was a world of darkness, the earlier religio-nationalistic period of his life. Thus, upon reflection, Malcolm found that mercy had acted through various media: his family, who wrote and urged him to "turn to Allah," and Elijah Muhammad's Nation of Islam.[51]

This image of light penetrating darkness left an indelible impression on Malcolm. He later interpreted this image as the first visible manifestation of his progression toward Sunni Islam. The subtle contributions of unexpected blessings in his life acted powerfully also in the post-Meccan period, as Malcolm saw in retrospect. Concerning his refusal to eat pork in prison, he commented: "I had experienced, for the first time, the Muslim teaching, if you will take one step toward Allah—Allah will take two steps toward you [quote from the Quran]."[52] In other words, his break with Elijah Muhammad and the proto-Islamic movement was the necessary precondition to and impetus for Sunni Islam to shape his masculine identity. What Malcolm came to view as the dilemma of Elijah's pre-Meccan ideological "concoction of religion" was clarified by his acceptance of Sunni Islam. Malcolm's reflection on his total life empowered him to become a visionary who found idealistic tendencies within himself.[53]

An African American Pilgrimage

Malcolm's hajj dramatically underscores his vision. His trip, from April 13 to May 21 of 1964, was the crowning experience of his life. His experience in Mecca reaffirmed his faith in Islam as a religion that nurtured fraternity and fostered human worth and dignity. Malcolm was overwhelmed by the very gracious and generous reception he received from Muslim leaders and nonleaders in Jedda, Saudia Arabia. He stated:

> Never have I been so highly honored. Never have I been made to feel more humble and unworthy. Who would believe the blessings that have been heaped upon an American Negro? . . .
> The Deputy Chief of Protocol himself took me before the Hajj Court. His Holiness Sheikh Muhammad Harkon himself okayed my visit to Mecca. His Holiness gave me two books on Islam [Sunni Islam], with his personal seal and autograph, and he told me that he prayed that I would be a successful preacher of Islam in America. A car, a driver, and a guide have been placed at my disposal, making it possible for me to travel about this Holy Land almost at will. The government provides air-conditioned quarters and servants in each city that I visit. Never would I have thought of dreaming that I would ever be a recipient of such honors—honors that in America would be bestowed upon a King—not a Negro.[54]

In this passage, Malcolm emphasizes the manner in which he, as a Negro, had been treated. It was this respect that he received from the Muslim world that allowed him to "rearrange" his thoughts totally. Malcolm realized and abhorred the idea that he had submitted himself to a male deity (Fard), a god that was totally interpreted for him by Elijah Muhammad. Malcolm's journey to the holy city allowed him to witness men and women practicing submission to the one true Allah. Thus, Malcolm came to a point where complete submission to the divine alone yields a more humane and inclusive perspective on life.

It is important to mention here that, despite the profound impact hajj made on his life, there were limitations on Malcolm's influence over the

American public. The main limitation was that Malcolm was a product of the African American religio-cultural experience. Post-Meccan Malcolm was a Sunni Muslim. His use of Sunni Islam to explain ideas allowed him to move beyond those categories of knowledge identified by the American public. But people were not always comfortable with Malcolm's use of an Islamic rationale for cultivating identity, particularly African American male identity. Another factor that limited Malcolm's influence on America was his former pre-Meccan espousal of the religio-nationalism of the Nation. Some have even called this the revolutionary side of Malcolm, the side that remained more widely known in America than his post-Meccan Islamic side. The denial by the American public of Malcolm's change of thought restricted his ability to influence societal norms that govern what is acceptable and what is not. And, since norms of the culture define gender roles, Malcolm's shortened post-Meccan period limited the American public's interaction with, understanding of, and mastery of his discourse about his change of views.[55]

One can acknowledge, then, that there were limitations on what Malcolm imparted while he lived, as well as after he was killed. The limitations of his ideology after his death were more or less set by the time, as Sunni Islam had little influence in the African American community. Because Malcolm, even after hajj, was still known for his pre-Meccan activities, the American public had been influenced by an indelible negative image. While African American non-Muslims "were impressed with his change, the media took little notice of it and continued to project him as an angry man, a teacher of hate, and a promoter of violence."[56] They were not interested in the post-Meccan Malcolm. Malcolm acknowledged that his earlier public image, his so-called black Muslim image, kept blocking his influence for good in his community. He stated: ". . . My earlier public image, my old so-called 'Black Muslim' image, kept blocking me. I was trying to turn a corner, into a new regard by the public."[57]

Conclusion

Malcolm's personal changes, highlighted by his pilgrimage to Mecca, illustrate a transitional pattern of growth that succeeding African American Muslims and non-Muslims were able to grasp and to emulate. His growing and changing masculine identity matured within the African American experience, particularly through instruction in Sunni Islam. It continued to develop as part of the unique African American male experience.

Moreover, Malcolm's devotion to changing the dominant culture's negative perceptions of "black males" contributed to bringing about cohesiveness and coherence in the personal goals of African American males throughout America. His transformation served as an example. Additionally, it offered new global frames of reference from which to observe and analyze sociohistorical circumstances and conditions. Thus, Sunni Islam's impact on Malcolm's life contributed to the pilgrimage of African American males from narrower categories and boundaries of their historical experience to a broader expression of masculine identity.

NOTES

1. Martha F. Lee, *Nation of Islam: An American Millenarian Movement* (Lewiston, N.Y.: Edwin Mellen Press), 1.

2. Ibid., 2.

3. C. Eric Lincoln and Lawrence H. Mamiya, *The Black Church in the African American Experience* (Durham, N.C., and London: Duke University Press, 1990), 389.

4. Malcolm X, with the assistance of Alex Haley, *The Autobiography of Malcolm X* (New York: Grove Press, 1964), 196–98.

5. Ibid., 340.

6. Richard F. Lazur and Richard Majors, "Men of Color: Ethnocultural Variations of Male Gender Role Strain," in *A New Psychology of Men,* ed. Ronald F. Levant and William S. Pollack (New York: Basic Books, 1995), 337.

7. Eugene Victor Wolfenstein, *The Victims of Democracy: Malcolm X and the Black Revolution* (Berkeley: University of California Press, 1981), 42.

8. Randall K. Burkett, *Garveyism as a Religious Movement: The Institutionalization of a Black Civil Religion* (Metuchen, N.J., and London: Scarecrow Press, 1978), 46–47.

9. Ibid., 47, 184–85.

10. Wolfenstein, *Victims of Democracy,* 42; and see also Andrew Young, *Malcolm X: Another Side of the Movement* (Englewood Cliffs, N.J.: Silver Burdett Press, 1990), 8–9.

11. Ibid., 93.

12. Burkett, *Garveyism,* 18–25. Also see Randall K. Burkett, *Black Redemption: Churchmen Speak for the Garvey Movement* (Philadelphia: Temple University Press), 5, and Henry J. Young, *Major Black Religious Leaders: 1755–1940* (Nashville: Parthenon Press), 154. Burkett acknowledges that Garvey's movement can't be understood unless its religious dimension is taken seriously. The book consists of speeches and sermons by churchmen, which stand as testimonials to Garvey's ability to appeal to a wide spectrum of black church leaders who supported his program. Young points out that Garvey's movement was established in Jamaica with the assistance of a Catholic bishop. These are important points in that they reveal the place of religion in the Garvey movement. Most people who examine Garvey and his Universal Negro Improvement Association see it as a black nationalist movement only. The religious question is important, because it demonstrates that Malcolm had a greater exposure to and involvement in religion than has been

written and talked about. Such exposure could well have influenced the kind of major transitions made by Malcolm later in his life.

13. Bruce Perry, *Malcolm: The Life of a Man Who Changed Black America* (New York: Station Hill Press, 1991), 4–5.

14. Malcolm X, *Autobiography*, 2; also see Wolfenstein, *Victims of Democracy*, 97; and Perry, *Malcolm*, 2, 384.

15. Wolfenstein, *Victims of Democracy*, 97.

16. Malik El Shabazz, "Allah's Supreme Mathematics," [no date]. This refers to three pages from an original document of the movement called the "Supreme Wisdom" of the Nation of Islam. The information contained in these pages is esoteric and often makes no sense. Numbers are viewed in a symbolic way and interpreted as wisdom for the "Blackman's life." For example, the number *1* means "knowledge: The basic foundation of all things in existence." The black man is the basic foundation of his family. Another example is that *7* means "G.O.D. Gumar-Oz-Dubar, i.e., wisdom-strength-beauty. The most high most wise man which is the Asiatic Blackman." (The above transliteration is said to be from the Greek; it is not.) Also see "The Lessons of Elijah Muhammad," or "The Minister's Kit," which talks about the real identity and purpose of the "Blackman" in America. Such ideas are also discussed in "The Student Enrollment Lessons" that were given to people who joined the movement. For example, one of the questions in a student enrollment lesson is, "Who is the Original Man?" The response is, "The original man is the Asiatic Blackman, the maker, the owner, the Cream of the Planet Earth, God of the Universe."

17. Wolfenstein, *Victims of Democracy*, 112.

18. Perry, *Malcolm*, 4–5; see also Jan Carew, *Ghosts in Our Blood: With Malcolm X in Africa, England, and the Caribbean* (Chicago: Lawrence Hill Books, 1994), 112.

19. Carew, *Ghosts*, 109–10, 116.

20. Ibid., 130–33.

21. Arthur S. Maxwell, "What Is a Seventh-Day Adventist?" in *Religions of America: Ferment and Faith in an Age of Crisis*, ed. Leo Rosten (New York: Simon & Schuster), 251.

22. Malcolm X, *Autobiography*, 4; see also Perry, *Malcolm*, 6.

23. E. U. Essien-Udom, *Black Nationalism: A Search for an Identity in America* (Chicago: University of Chicago Press, 1962), 157–58.

24. Ibid., 135–36.

25. Elijah Anderson, *Streetwise: Race, Class, and Change in an Urban Community* (Chicago: University of Chicago Press, 1990), 164.

26. Ibid., 244.

27. Malcolm X, *Autobiography*, 77.

28. Ibid., 154.

29. Ibid., 152–53.

30. Michael Eric Dyson, *Making Malcolm: The Myth and Meaning of Malcolm X* (New York: Oxford University Press, 1995), 124.

31. Wolfenstein, *Victims of Democracy*, 213–15.

32. Perry, *Malcolm*, 238.

33. Ibid., 213; see also Wolfenstein, *Victims of Democracy,* 216.

34. Warith Deen Muhammad, *As the Light Shineth from the East* (Chicago: WDM Publishing Co., 1980), 11; see also Lee, *Nation of Islam,* 33; Clifton E. Marsh, *From Black Muslim to Muslims* (Metuchen, N.J.: Scarecrow Press, 1984), 53.

35. Elijah Muhammad, *Message to the Blackman in America* (Chicago: Muhammad's Temple No. 2., 1965), 103–22; see also W. Deen Muhammad, *Light Shineth,* 17; C. Eric Lincoln, *The Black Muslims in America,* 3d ed. (Grand Rapids: Wm. B. Eerdmans Publishing Co., 1994), 69.

36. Ibid., 6–7.

37. Akbar Muhammad, "Muslims in the United States: An Overview of Organizations, Doctrine and Problems," in *The Islamic Impact,* ed. Yvonne Haddad, Byron Haines, and Ellison Findly (Syracuse: Syracuse University Press, 1984), 201.

38. Elijah Muhammad, *Message,* 6–7.

39. Lee, *Nation of Islam,* 40–41; see also Elijah Muhammad, *Message,* 278.

40. Statements throughout Elijah Muhammad's text, entitled *Our Saviour Has Arrived* (Chicago: Muhammad's Temple of Islam No. 2., 1974), validate this statement. The title itself highlights the importance of the issue. The first-person "our" in the title refers to the idea that Fard came to and belongs to the African American people. Also, since Jesus is a white man, he is for whites. Logically then, African Americans have not had a savior. Therefore, it is the "Blackman's" turn. Also see Lee, *Nation of Islam,* 38–39.

41. Gayraud S. Wilmore, ed., *Religious Studies: An Interdisciplinary Anthology* (Durham, N.C.: Duke University Press, 1989), 293.

42. Lincoln, *Black Muslims,* 29.

43. C. Eric Lincoln, "The American Muslim Mission in the Context of American Social History," in *The Muslim Community in North America,* ed. Earle H. Waugh, et al. (Edmonton: University of Alberta Press, 1983), 223.

44. See original source letter of the Nation of Islam entitled "Acceptance Letter Instructions." This is a letter Malcolm received from the Nation's secretary on how to apply for his X. Although the X replaces the last name of the new person who joins the movement, it also means that a person is a registered Muslim. The instructions give the individual a format to follow. For example, line 2 states "You [candidate] must write your own letter. No one else can write it for you. If you cannot write or have other reasons why you cannot write this letter, please make it known to the Temple Secretary." In other words, the individual was required to write a letter of support for Elijah and the Nation and send it to the Chicago headquarters. The Chicago Temple was the only Temple that could approve someone's X.

45. Abdel Wehab M. Elmessiri, "Islam as a Pastoral in the Life of Malcolm X," in *Malcolm X: The Man and His Times,* ed. John Henrik Clark (New York: Macmillan, 1969), 74–75; also see Malcolm X, *Autobiography,* 190.

46. Marsh, *Black Muslim to Muslims,* 68.

47. Y. N. Kly, *The Black Book: The True Political Philosophy of Malcolm X (El Hajj Malik El Shabazz)* (Atlanta: Clarity Press, 1986), 22–23.

48. Malcolm X, *Autobiography,* 156.

49. Ibid., 193.

50. Ibid., 170; see also prayer instructions of the Nation of Islam. This is a page from a kit that served members, especially new members, as a form of orientation. The members of the Nation of Islam performed *sajdah* (i.e., bowing of the knees or prostration); they performed *dua* (i.e., supplication prayer), by saying whatever words came to mind. They bowed to the knees with hands extended, elbows slightly bent and palms up. They recited *al-Faatiha* in the English language only (opening chapter of the Holy Quran). Although members of the Nation called this *salat,* it is quite different from the formal *salat* in Sunni Islam.

51. Ibid., 163.

52. Ibid., 156.

53. Elmessiri, "Islam as a Pastoral," 70.

54. Malcolm X, *Autobiography,* 341.

55. Lazur and Majors, "Men of Color," 339.

56. James Cone, *Martin and Malcolm and America* (New York: Orbis Books, 1991), 266–67; see also Malcolm X, *Autobiography,* 366–67.

57. Malcolm X, *Autobiography,* 375.

PART III

THE ROLE OF MASCULINITY
IN SHAPING RELIGIONS

While particular religious traditions and forms of spirituality shape men's understanding of themselves as men, so too do definitions of masculinity and men's self-understandings influence the way they understand, appropriate, reject, and participate in religious institutions and spiritual traditions. The essays in this section deal with perceived crises of masculinity, or deep concerns about the roles and identities of men, in the late nineteenth and twentieth centuries. They focus on Christianity in America and Europe.

Evelyn Kirkley, a historian of American Christianity, examines two movements in the late Victorian period—the Freethinkers and the Men and Religion Forward Movement (M&RFM)—that gave contrasting answers to the question, "Is it manly to be Christian?" The Freethinkers, shaped by the positivistic scientism of the period, argued that authentic masculinity was characterized by "masterliness" and the bold exercise of reason, unfettered by superstition and a servile subjection to religious dogma. For them, Christian belief is antithetical to manhood; atheism, then, was the only manly option. The short-lived M&RFM took the opposite position. They contended that Christianity, in contrast to its feminized form in their day, was essentially "masculine, militant, [and] warlike." They believed that more of this kind of religion would produce more

77

true, Christian men, ready for "a heroic life of consecration and sacri-fice." In turn, they believed that these more authentically masculine men would save the church from effeminacy and have a better chance of win-ning the world to Christ.

Both groups viewed the relationship between masculinity and Chris-tianity as critical; the Freethinkers repudiated Christianity in the name of true manliness, while the M&RFM embraced it. However, both agreed that traditional masculine characteristics must be tempered with tradi-tionally feminine traits, such as sympathy, tenderness, and a rejection of competition. Kirkley begins and ends her essay by drawing parallels among these movements and two contemporary groups, the evangelical Promise Keepers and the interdisciplinary Men's Studies in Religion Group of the American Academy of Religion. The Promise Keepers, like the M&RFM men, see faith as integral to mature manhood; some in the AAR group find the sexism in Christianity too pervasive for it to be of much help in fostering healthy male humanness, while others find some Christian traditions that promote liberative, authentic manhood.

The theologian Mark Muesse explores twentieth-century American fundamentalism's understanding of men's and women's roles and its op-position to other forms of Christianity. He argues that fundamentalism exhibits a hypermasculinity characterized by fear of the body, competi-tiveness, aggressiveness, and a strong individualist ideology. Because re-ligious devotion and narrowly constrained sexuality are seen in the wider culture as unmanly, this exaggerated definition of masculinity compen-sates fundamentalist men for their own perceived sense of masculine de-ficiency. This sense of deficiency is further exacerbated by the funda-mentalist assertion of God's maleness. In a dualistic religious worldview characterized by a hierarchy of dominance and submission, in which God is imaged as exclusively male, fundamentalist men are feminized by their relation to God in faith. Muesse suggests that this feminization fuels anx-ieties about gender roles, homosexuality, and abortion and leads to rigid definitions of the family. In his view, these dynamics help explain funda-mentalism's militant rejection of other definitions of the family and other interpretations of Christianity.

Historian John C. Fout finds similarly rigid definitions of the family along the leaders of male Protestant moral purity organizations of early twentieth-century Germany. He argues that the growth of these organi-zations was fueled by male anxiety about the increasing public roles women played in society as a result of the gains of the women's move-ments of the period. Led by Protestant ministers and church officials, these organizations actively promoted an idealized notion of the Chris-tian family, "rooted in a biological and divine imperative" that rational-ized male dominance and strict adherence to polarized gender roles. Sin became, then, any "morally impure" behavior (e.g., abortion, female prostitution, homosexuality, and masturbation) that transgressed their definitions of proper gender roles. In the view of these Protestant leaders, the state had not only a right but an obligation to enforce the reigning gender order by punishing "sinful" aberrations. Fout believes this analysis helps explain the limited success of the women's movements, the religious basis for the persecution of dissenters from the gender order in the Nazi period, and some of the motivations and aims of the religious right in the contemporary United States. He closes by pointing out the toll these kinds of movements take on men, both heterosexual and homosexual, who do not fit narrow models of the "Christian family."

Several important issues and questions might be raised by the movements surveyed in this section. The fundamentalists are reacting, in part, to a perceived cultural prejudice that defines religious devotion as effeminate—the contention of the Freethinkers. This leaves their leaders the paradoxical, and perhaps impossible, task of explaining how it is that a "feminine" submission to God is, in fact, a masculine virtue. The Freethinkers, however, are also faced with the task of explaining how it is that "womanly" tenderness and sympathy are actually "gentlemanly." In other words, both groups seem to be involved in a relatively unconscious critique and redefinition of cultural definitions of masculinity.

While both the fundamentalists and M&RFM men affirm the centrality of Christian faith to authentic manhood, they have different visions of the implications of that faith for Christian discipleship. On the one hand, fundamentalism sees "the Christian gospel as directed toward the salvation of individual souls" and "allows no real place for the analysis of social or corporate structures that may contribute to human problems." On the other, the M&RFM men assert that any "red-blooded, high-minded" Christian man "of large vision and keen intelligence" will manifest a profound sense of responsibility for social service. For this reason, the M&RFM group drew praise from such advocates and sympathizers of the Social Gospel as Walter Rauschenbusch, Booker T. Washington, and Jane Addams. It is true, however, that American fundamentalists, like the leaders of the German moral purity organizations, can mobilize around social and political issues (e.g., abortion, homosexuality, and the Equal Rights Amendment) when those issues bear on their definition of the family and its role in their vision of God's ordering of the world.

6

IS IT MANLY TO BE CHRISTIAN? THE DEBATE IN VICTORIAN AND MODERN AMERICA

Evelyn A. Kirkley

Two events of 1990 epitomize the relationship of men to contemporary American Christianity. The Men's Studies in Religion Group was formed by the American Academy of Religion as a forum for scholarly discussion of masculinity and religion. And William McCartney, football coach at the University of Colorado, founded Promise Keepers, an evangelical men's group. Since 1990, the AAR Men's Studies in Religion Group has become a significant voice in the professional academic study of religion, while the membership of Promise Keepers has grown from 72 to 234,000.[1] Established independently of each other, these two groups proposed various answers to the question, "Is it manly to be Christian?"

The question is not new and neither are opposing responses to it.[2] In the late nineteenth and early twentieth centuries, some men rejected Christian belief as incompatible with strong, vital manhood, while others argued for an inextricable connection between Christianity and virility. The former position was most fully articulated in the Freethought movement. Between 1880 and 1920, thousands of middle-class, Euro-American, heterosexual men were attracted to organized atheism known as Freethought. Freethinkers championed freedom of thought against Christian superstition, clerical domination, and biblical tyranny. Believing that irrational, unscientific beliefs must be repudiated, they agitated for the complete separation of church and state. They formed local, state, and national groups, the most important of which were the Free Religious Association and the National Liberal League, later renamed the American Secular Union. They founded the town of Liberal, Missouri, in 1881, Liberal University in Silverton, Oregon, in 1898, and secular churches that met weekly for singing, lectures, and Sunday school. They published books and periodicals; *The Boston Investigator, The Index,* and *The Truth Seeker* had the highest circulation. They were spokespeople for a secular America.[3]

Men constituted 70 to 80 percent of the movement. They served as officers of Freethought organizations, edited the major periodicals, wrote most of the books, and contributed the bulk of the money. They argued that atheism attracted so many men because it was a more manly option than Christian belief. Long before contemporary historians did so, Freethinkers perceived the church as "feminized," numerically dominated by women and thereby weak, sentimental, and irrational.[4] To Freethinkers, that 70 to 80 percent of church attenders were women while the same percentage of atheists were men clearly demonstrated men's superior reasoning and intellectual capabilities. Relying on Comte, Fiske, Darwin, and Spencer, Freethinkers argued that man was evolving from superstitious belief to intellectual independence. According to lecturer B. F. Underwood, forward-thinking men have "outgrown belief in a personal, intelligent, anthropomorphic being"; the "time, money, devotion, and enthusiasm which in the past have been lavished on an imaginary being will in the future be given to the improvement and elevation of the human race."[5]

Men could realize authentic manhood only by rejecting Christianity. Christianity, according to a *Truth Seeker* editor, robs a man of "his manhood—his dearest possession; takes away his right to exercise his reason, his common sense, and makes of him a slave, a crawling, cringing, cowardly thing, a being who walks the earth with fear and trembling, who doubts his sense and denies his convictions."[6] The church created "a horde of mentally castrated little Willies, ready to hop into any prearranged or present hell that our political and religious priests may have prepared for us," wrote another.[7] To avert this hell, men "must reassert our individuality and throw off that hypnotic destroying force which is now sweeping everything to ruin. We must stop our ears to the delusive cadences of the Bethlehemic song, and sing the songs of Nature."[8]

Freethinkers sang "the songs of Nature" by reconstructing manhood scientifically and rationally. The first principle of atheist manhood was mental liberty. True men accepted no one's opinions as fact, but tried out every hypothesis and drew their own conclusions. Freethought editor Lemuel Washburn argued that "the only man who deserves the name of man is he who dares to think for himself and who respects his reason enough to follow it."[9] In contrast to cowering Christian men, atheists were "manly, self-reliant men, unafraid of the spectres which other men have raised up, able to look the sun in the face, sincere men who have faith in their own integrity, who will not bend the knee nor bow the head."[10]

Once he threw off the shackles of Christian belief, the Freethinking man fearlessly led others toward the truth. According to Austin Bierbower, atheist manhood meant "masterliness." "Standing at the head of nature," he declared, "we should, instead of deferring, make everything yield to us. Our march through the world should be a conquering one."[11] Man's refusal to be mollycoddled by feminine superstition and his brave leap into the rational unknown justified his domination of others, including but not limited to benighted Christians.

Held in tension with masterliness was gentlemanliness. The atheist man was noble, kind, pure, and unselfish. He lived by a moral code superior to that of other men. Moreover, he did not smoke, chew tobacco, use profanity, or drink alcohol to excess.[12] In 1885, Moncure Conway, Unitarian pastor and Freethinker, identified the atheist man with femininity: "The ideal manliness of our time is gentlemanliness. The man of our time is more womanly, more tender, more sympathetic, securing thus a happier home and a more beautiful society than were possible to the ages of strife and vengeance."[13]

When asked if these traits could be realized in a living man, Freethinkers answered unanimously: Robert G. Ingersoll. The most famous atheist of the nineteenth century, vilified as a blasphemer, Ingersoll lectured hundreds of thousands and wrote countless articles on Freethought.[14] Freethinkers spared no hyperbole in praise of Ingersoll's manly character, which united masterliness and gentlemanliness. He "has bravely stood for mental liberty, and has everywhere been as honest in act as in speech. He has done what hundreds of public men would do, were they not cowards—he has taken the fate of his opinions."[15] At the same time, he "was a man full of love—the love that makes home happy, the love that makes wife happy. He did not forget the vows he took when he made Eva his wife. His altar was erected in his home and that is the place to know a man—in his home."[16]

In 1890 Ingersoll himself defined atheist masculinity. The Freethinking man "will know that each man should be his own priest, and that the brain is the real cathedral. . . . The improved man will be self-poised, independent, candid, and free. He will be a scientist. He will observe, investigate, experiment, and demonstrate."[17] Simultaneously, he "will find his greatest joy in the happiness of others, and he will know that the home is the real temple. He will believe in the democracy of the fireside, and will reap his greatest reward in being loved by those whose lives he has enriched."[18] The atheist gentleman was a self-reliant individual, but his individualism was tempered by compassion for others.

While Freethinkers extolled atheist manhood, the Men and Religion Forward Movement of 1911–12 (hereafter M&RFM) sought to persuade men that they could only realize their full manhood by becoming Christians. The purpose of the M&RFM was simple: it was "a religious campaign for the men and boys of America, upon a magnitude and with a comprehensiveness of ideal never before attempted on this continent or on any other continent."[19] The first nationwide evangelistic campaign to target one gender explicitly and exclusively, it aimed to bring three million males into churches to balance the number of females. To that end, the M&RFM sponsored revivals and social service projects in more than sixty cities in the United States and Canada. It was financially supported by the YMCA and the brotherhood organizations of nine Protestant denominations.[20]

Armed with the slogan "More Men for Religion, More Religion for Men," M&RFM workers focused in six areas: Bible study, boys' work, evangelism, missions (home and foreign), social service, and community extension. They directed sophisticated marketing techniques at men, including advertisements on newspaper sports pages and electric signs on Broadway. During its seven-month life span, it captured the attention of the nation and the endorsement of prominent Protestants Walter Rauschenbusch, Washington Gladden, Harry Emerson Fosdick, John Mott, Josiah Strong, Booker T. Washington, and Jane Addams. Its "campaign leader" was Fred Smith, secretary of the International Committee of the YMCA. It was a self-conscious movement to masculinize Protestantism among Euro-American, middle-class, heterosexual men.[21]

M&RFM leaders believed that women's predominance in the church signified its decline; men had shirked their responsibility to Christianity. According to Fred Smith, "the general fact remains that in a very real sense this is a man's world, and if the Christian religion is to win the world, it must magnify a man's place in the task."[22] Christianity was "essentially masculine, militant, warlike, and if these elements are not made manifest, men and boys will not be found in increasing numbers as participants in the life and work of the Church."[23] To James Cannon, chair of the executive committee, the M&RFM sought "in a manly way, to bring the claims of Christ to the attention of these men who have permitted the things of this life to absorb their time and thought"; its objective was "overcoming indifference in the average man."[24]

God needed manly men to rescue an effeminate church. Christianity's future depended on a "harnessing of our manhood to the big problems of the Church of Jesus Christ—a putting of our strong manhood back of the program of Jesus Christ."[25] Men "are longing to be used, longing to serve, longing to feel that life is worth living; that God needs them as truly as they need God; that they may be co-workers with him in lifting and carrying the burdens of His heavy laden children."[26] Men were God's partners in a heavenly corporation.

Christian manliness was characterized by an active prayer life, an aggressive evangelistic witness, and a "real earnestness to the point of self-denial."[27] Men were exhorted to "sacrificial living," a call to which only the "ablest, the most worthy, the most efficient men . . . are quickest to respond."[28] True men answered the "call to a heroic life of consecration and sacrifice."[29] A father had a special role to play as "high priest" for his sons; "the father at home must illustrate daily his devotion to Christ."[30]

The embodiment of Christian manhood was undoubtedly Fred Smith: "virile, direct, pungent, fearless, unwearied, undismayed."[31] He possessed "great vision, steady persistence, remarkable executive ability and undaunted courage" such that "men think of a man's religion when they think of him, and they think of him as a striking exemplification of the message."[32] With "twenty-five years of devoted service, more than ten years of journeying in this and other lands, each year with its record of more than fifty thousand miles of travel and of well nigh ceaseless toil," Smith was the M&RFM's "prophet" of true manhood.[33]

The M&RFM explicitly eschewed competition between men in favor of cooperation. While the feminized church stressed individual conversion, men would revolutionize the church by putting evangelism into action. Social service was a uniquely masculine avenue of Christian service for men, one that appealed to man's intellect, love of challenges, and ability to solve problems. Christian men were responsible for social service, because "to the man who would live God's life in God's world, with the supreme purpose of ushering in His Kingdom, every act, every day, every talent, every capacity, every dollar, is sacred."[34] If social service was not emphasized, the church would remain enfeebled; "red-blooded, high-minded men, of large vision and keen intelligence, will not long be found in any church or other Christian organization which neglects the unlimited opportunities offered by social service in the name of our Lord and Master."[35]

Although Freethinkers argued that authentic masculinity was possible only if men repudiated Christian belief and the M&RFM urged real men to recommit themselves to the church, both agreed that a critical relationship existed between manhood and Christianity. Ironically, their visions of atheist and Christian manliness were strikingly similar: men were to be both masterful and nurturing. This vision was nearly impossible to achieve; who could be simultaneously aggressive and tender, overpowering and domestic, dominating and sympathetic? Ingersoll and Smith were mythologized more than realized visions of the ideal.

Freethinkers and M&RFM men forcefully articulated ideals of manhood because they believed it was endangered. In a rapidly industrializing and urbanizing society, Freethinkers believed that by abandoning the church, men would reclaim their natural role as leaders of American civilization. The M&RFM sought to masculinize Protestantism to empower men in a new corporate, consumer-oriented economy.[36] Their attempts to strengthen Euro-American, middle-class men's cultural dominance were unconscious. Feeling threatened, they sought to retain their power by means at their disposal.

Less than a century later, the Men's Studies in Religion Group of the American Academy of Religion and Promise Keepers echoed the responses of Freethinkers and the M&RFM regarding the relationship of manliness and Christianity. The Men's Studies Group has sponsored sessions on the study of masculinity and religion at annual meetings of the AAR, the largest national organization of religion scholars. Sessions have addressed historical, social, and psychological constructions of masculinity; sexuality and male identity; fathering and faith; iconography; and biblical understandings of manhood. In this interdisciplinary and interfaith group, which eschews heterosexism, racism, and sexism, participants have included gay and heterosexual men, men of color, and women. Topics of papers presented have ranged from "Gay Men, Straight Men, and Child Care" and "'The Call of the Wild': Remembering John the Baptist" to "The Ties That Bind: Blood, War, Women, and Men" and "Male Identity and Masturbation."[37]

In exploring the intersections between masculinity and religion, some scholars presenting papers in the Men's Studies in Religion Group have claimed that Christianity has distorted authentic manhood. Downplaying the impact of religious ideas and institutions in shaping manhood, some participants have emphasized psychology, biology, and culture. Like Freethinkers, some seek a rational, scientific, and empirical analysis of manhood. And like Freethinkers, some question whether authentic men can be Christian; these argue that, as a patriarchal tradition, Christianity oppresses men, and they encourage men to seek sources beyond Christianity to nurture dynamic masculine spirituality. See, for example, Seth Mirsky's essay in this volume, in which he heralds the promise of Goddess spirituality for men's efforts to discover and create nonoppressive (read nonpatriarchal) ways of living in the world.[38]

Other scholars in the group, unlike Freethinkers, conclude that certain expressions of Christianity promote liberative manhood. See, for example, the chapters in this volume by Steve Smith, Stephen Boyd, Mikeal Parsons, Alton Pollard, Merle Longwood, and James Nelson.

In contrast to the AAR Men's Studies Group, Promise Keepers assert a necessary connection between a patriarchal reading of Christianity and authentic manhood. Since 1990, this organization of evangelical Catholics and Protestants, 90 percent of whom are Euro-American and married, has spawned cell groups in local congregations and huge annual rallies. Held in sports arenas across the country, rallies include worship, singing, prayer, and inspirational speakers such as Charles Swindoll and James Dobson. A march on Washington, D.C., is planned for 1996 for more than a million men.[39] Like the M&RFM, Promise Keepers is a grassroots movement that has received widespread media attention.

Using sports and military imagery, Promise Keepers, like the M&RFM, preach a simple message: real men love Jesus. Members pledge to keep seven commandments: to honor Jesus Christ, form spiritual friendships with other men, practice purity, build strong marriages and families, support their local church, forge interdenominational and interracial relationships, and evangelize.[40] They commit themselves to be better Christians, husbands, and fathers, in that order. According to founder Bill McCartney, "A real man, a man's man, is a Godly man, . . . a man of substance, a man that's vulnerable, a man who loves his wife, a man that has a passion for God, and is willing to lay down his life for Him."[41]

While first and foremost an evangelistic organization, Promise Keepers, like the M&RFM, has a deeper concern than men's individual souls. Men's emotional repression, sexual promiscuity, and spiritual malaise indicate the need for a men's revival. However, according to Promise Keepers, the feminized church, decline in family values, and moral decay of U.S. society are also due to men shirking their responsibilities to themselves and their families. If men reclaimed their rightful place as leaders in their homes, churches, and society, they would not only discover authentic masculinity but foment national revolution. Like the M&RFM, Promise Keepers seek to restore male headship as a remedy for national moral and spiritual crisis.

Weaknesses exist in both the AAR group's and Promise Keepers' constructions of authentic manhood. The Men's Studies group, a wide-ranging forum for academic discussion, offers few practical suggestions for men seeking a nurturing liberative manliness and Christian spirituality. Promise Keepers have the opposite problem: they prescribe a rigid, God-given plan for men that presumes all men are heterosexual, married fathers. In preaching that men must be heads of their households, it validates male hierarchy and supremacy. It suffers from almost no input from women about Christian manhood.

The Freethought movement, M&RFM, the AAR Men's Studies in Religion Group, and the Promise Keepers responded variously to the question, "Is it manly to be Christian?" All agreed that Christianity is critical to empowering men personally, interpersonally, and societally. To Freethinkers and to some within the Men's Studies group, rejection of Christianity was central to achieving authentic manhood, while to others within the Men's Studies group, to M&RFM men, and to Promise Keepers, true manliness could not be realized without it. These responses reveal a similar perception that masculinity was and is in crisis and that there is a need for a spiritual solution to those crises. In the late twentieth century as in the late nineteenth, men (and women) are challenged to create liberative masculine spirituality and spiritual masculinity.

NOTES

1. Edward Gilbreath, "Great Awakening," *Christianity Today* 39 (Feb. 6, 1995): 22.
2. Three theoretical considerations inform my analysis of historical constructions of masculinity. First, since men negotiated gender boundaries with varying degrees of self-consciousness, conceptions of masculinity must be coaxed from documents that use "manhood" and "men" generically. Second, at least three overlapping contexts of masculinity must be examined: religious, sociocultural, and psychosexual. Third, analyses of masculinity cannot proceed apart from studies of race, class, sexual orientation, and womanhood. The study of masculinities must be rooted in the context of other social factors.
3. Marshall G. Brown and Gordon Stein, *Freethought in the United States: A Descriptive Bibliography* (Westport, Conn.: Greenwood, 1978); Sidney Warren, *American Freethought, 1860–1914* (New York: Columbia University Press, 1943); Samuel Putnam, *Four Hundred Years of Freethought* (New York: Truth Seeker, 1894); Stow Persons, *Free Religion: An American Faith* (New Haven, Conn.: Yale University Press, 1947); Patricia Brandt, "Organized Free Thought in Oregon: The Oregon State Secular Union," *Oregon Historical Quarterly* 87 (1986): 167–204; James P. Moore, *This Strange Town—Liberal, Missouri* (Liberal, Mo.: Liberal News, 1963); Evelyn A. Kirkley, "'The Female Peril': The Construction of Gender in American Freethought, 1865–1915," Ph.D. diss., Duke University, Durham, N.C., 1993.
4. Barbara Welter, "The Feminization of American Religion, 1800–1860," in her *Dimity Convictions* (Athens: Ohio University Press, 1976); Ann Douglas, *The Feminization of American Culture* (New York: Alfred A. Knopf, 1977).
5. Benjamin F. Underwood, "Will the Coming Man Worship God?" *The Truth Seeker*, April 17, 1880: 242–43.
6. Lemuel K. Washburn, "The Crime against Man," *The Truth Seeker*, July 20, 1912: 453.
7. John T. Craps, "How to Regain Manhood," *The Truth Seeker*, Jan. 25, 1913: 58.
8. Ibid.
9. Lemuel K. Washburn, "Freethoughts," *The Truth Seeker*, July 22, 1911: 449.
10. Henry White, "The Superior Man—VI," *The Truth Seeker*, June 23, 1906: 390.
11. Austin Bierbower, "Is Worship Demoralizing?" *The Truth Seeker*, July 30, 1898: 488.
12. Susan H. Wixon, "Can Man Be an Angel?" *The Boston Investigator*, June 18, 1879: 2.
13. Moncure Conway, "A Minister's Parting Charge," *The Index*, July 2, 1885: 8.
14. Warren, *American Freethought*, 89–95. Many biographies of Ingersoll have been written; among the best are Clarence H. Cramer, *Royal Bob*

(Indianapolis: Bobbs-Merrill, 1952), and Orvin Larson, *American Infidel: Robert G. Ingersoll* (New York: Citadel, 1962). For a full bibliography, see Gordon Stein, *Robert G. Ingersoll: A Checklist* (Kent, Ohio: Kent State University Press, 1969).

15. Lemuel K. Washburn, "Be Thyself!" *The Boston Investigator*, Jan. 19, 1887: 1.

16. Hannah Luce, "A Woman's Reminiscence of Ingersoll," *The Truth Seeker*, Sept. 2, 1911: 546.

17. Robert G. Ingersoll, "The Improved Man," *Freethought*, March 15, 1890: 167.

18. Ibid.

19. Fayette L. Thompson, ed., *Men and Religion* (New York: Young Men's Christian Association, 1911), 1.

20. Fred B. Smith, *A Man's Religion* (New York: Association, 1913), 67; *Messages of the Men and Religion Movement*, 7 vols. (New York: Association, 1912), 1:23–27; Thompson, *Men and Religion*, 168.

21. Clarence A. Barbour, ed., *Making Religion Efficient* (New York: Association, 1912), 18; Gail Bederman, "'The Women Have Had Charge of the Church Work Long Enough': The Men and Religion Forward Movement of 1911–1912 and the Masculinization of Middle-Class Protestantism," *American Quarterly* 41 (Summer, 1989): 442–45; Thompson, *Men and Religion*, vii.

22. Smith, *Man's Religion*, 71.

23. Ibid., 70.

24. Thompson, *Men and Religion*, 85.

25. Ibid., 6.

26. Smith, *Man's Religion*, 266–67.

27. Thompson, *Men and Religion*, 99.

28. Smith, *Man's Religion*, 133.

29. Ibid., 137.

30. Thompson, *Men and Religion*, 84.

31. Smith, *Man's Religion*, 5–6.

32. Ibid., 6.

33. Ibid., 5–6.

34. Ibid., 171.

35. Ibid., 175.

36. Bederman, "'Women Have Had Charge,'" 432–65.

37. American Academy of Religion/Society of Biblical Literature, *Annual Meeting Program*, 1993 (Washington, D.C.), 68; 1994 (Chicago), 116; 1990 (New Orleans), 104; 1992 (San Francisco), 44.

38. Seth Mirsky, "Men and the Promise of Goddess Spirituality: Reflections along the Way," chap. 15 in this volume.

39. Gilbreath, "Great Awakening," 28.

40. Ibid., 22.

41. Laurie Goodstein, "Men Pack RFK on Promise of Religious Renewal," *The Washington Post*, May 28, 1995, A6.

7

RELIGIOUS MACHISMO: MASCULINITY AND FUNDAMENTALISM

Mark W. Muesse

Fundamentalism provides an especially instructive case for analyzing the dynamics of religion and gender. Since fundamentalism is an extreme version of Christianity,[1] it reveals with great clarity many tensions, contradictions, and conflicts that operate more covertly in Christianity's more moderate forms. "Fundamentalists," observes Karen McCarthy Brown, "are just extreme examples of the rest of us."[2] Particularly in matters of gender and sexuality, the study of fundamentalism illumines problems that plague the whole of Christianity and, to a large degree, the cultures shaped by Christian influence.

The American academic community has only recently acknowledged fundamentalism as a religious perspective worthy of scholarly consideration. The study of the fundamentalist construction of gender, therefore, has remained largely uncharted territory. Studies that have ventured into this domain focus on fundamentalist views of women, precisely because such analysis reveals the latent dynamics of Christianity's sexism. But much is to be gained by also viewing the fundamentalist perspective from the point of view offered by the study of men as a gendered group. When the critical eye is directed toward the experience of male fundamentalists and the fundamentalist construction of masculinity, a new light is cast on fundamentalism itself.

Scholars have never had an easy time defining the "fundamentalist phenomenon." Especially in recent years, the term *fundamentalism* has come to be used in both academic and popular circles in such an imprecise manner as to render the category virtually meaningless. All manner of religious phenomena from Appalachian snake handling to Shi'ite Islam are often assimilated into this rubric. For this reason, it is crucial to be clear about how one uses the term. In this chapter, fundamentalism refers to a particular manifestation of twentieth-century American Protestantism that upholds certain formulations of Christian doctrine as essential for salvation *and* militantly opposes variant interpretations of

Christianity and the perspectives of non-Christian worldviews. Among these doctrines are: the deity and virgin birth of Jesus Christ; his literal, bodily resurrection and second coming; the vicarious sacrifice of Jesus for the atonement of sin; and the divine inspiration of the Bible as the inerrant word of God.

What distinguishes fundamentalism from worldviews that affirm similar tenets, such as evangelicalism and pentecostalism, is its aggressive opposition to alternate understandings of the Christian traditions. Evangelicalism, for instance, holds to the truth of fundamentalist doctrine but acknowledges the possibility of other versions. Genuine fundamentalism, however, categorically denies the legitimacy of any theology claiming to be Christian that refuses to hallow creedal statements expressed precisely in these terms.

In this chapter, I offer an interpretation of fundamentalism's militant opposition to alternate versions of the Christian tradition and demonstrate its relationship to the fundamentalist understanding of male and female roles. I will develop and defend the thesis that fundamentalism enshrines a hypermasculine theology animated largely by insecurities about the masculine role as defined by the wider culture. Fundamentalism champions many traditional masculine virtues in part because fundamentalist men measure themselves against a cultural standard that considers them effeminate by virtue of their religiousness and controlled sexuality. The exaggerated masculine qualities of the fundamentalist worldview, including its militancy, help fundamentalist men compensate for a perceived sense of deficient masculinity. One of the significant ironies of fundamentalism, consequently, is that while it expressly challenges the secularizing influences of modernity, it tacitly and uncritically accepts modern secular conceptions of appropriate maleness.

Fundamentalist Theology as Hypermasculinity

The careful observer cannot help but notice the close parallels between the dominant qualities of fundamentalism and the elements of hegemonic masculinity as defined by twentieth-century European-American culture. Numerous studies characterize the modern construction of masculinity in these terms: a predilection for linear rationality and a suspicion of affective and nonrational modes of thinking, a perceived need for power as control, an instrumentalist view of the body, competitiveness and aggression, and the perception of the self as an individual entity separated from other individuals (see Merlyn Mowrey's "The Accommodating Other," chap. 9 in this volume). So prominent are these masculine elements in fundamentalism that it can be appropriately characterized as a hypermasculine religion. A consideration of the more important correlations between modern masculinity and fundamentalism will make this contention clearer.

Contemporary hegemonic masculinity displays a marked preference for reason over emotion; the same is true of fundamentalism. Although it has often been popularly portrayed as a religion given to emotional excess, fundamentalism prides itself on its rational, hardheaded foundations. Images of sweat-drenched preachers and tearful conversions belie a religious outlook that aspires to cold, scientific objectivity and clear, linear thinking. If anything, most fundamentalists are suspicious of the intuitive and affective dimensions of human experience. Especially in matters of salvation—the experience of determining one's eternal destiny—the emotions are not to be trusted. Although the moment of salvation may offer the convert an emotional catharsis, faith, according to fundamentalism, is never *based* on feeling or any other subjective experience.

As heirs of Enlightenment rationalism, fundamentalists insist that belief must be founded squarely on facts available to public scrutiny. Fundamentalists expend much intellectual energy, therefore, trying to prove that the claims of the tradition are consistent with the canons of accepted rational thinking. The sentiments expressed by W. A. Criswell are typical of the fundamentalist reverence of reason:

> It is an amazing and marvelous thing when you look carefully, not superstitiously, sneeringly, or with ridicule, at the Word of God to see that our blessed Lord addresses His message to the intelligence of the man. Look, see, handle, judge for yourself. It is an intelligent and reasonable gospel, and it is reasonable to be a Christian.[3]

This obsession with clearly formulated statements of truth rather than affective pietism, which fundamentalists regard as characteristic of liberal theology, funds a hypervigilance concerning right doctrine. Because salvation depends in great measure on the apprehension of correct doctrinal truths, whole church bodies frequently split over theological issues that may appear insignificant or inconsequential to the outside observer.

The fundamentalist enchantment with rationality means that emotionality is reserved for particular contexts and situations. Emotion must be contained within certain boundaries, and unspoken rules of propriety govern emotional expression in church. Fervent conversion experiences, for example, are common, but by no means definitive or necessary.[4]

Another characteristic of dominant masculinity is a perceived need and quest for control. Fundamentalism strives for a sense of control in its yearning for well-defined boundaries to demarcate and order human experience. The fundamentalist mind has a low tolerance for ambiguity. Binary oppositions are commonplace in the fundamentalist way of dividing up reality: God and man, the saved and the unsaved, Christianity and humanism, democracy and communism, the church and the world, male and female. Underlying the concern for sharp distinctions is a tremendous anxiety about the loss of order. Without absolute boundaries, chaos threatens to engulf the whole world in anarchy.

In a revealing statement, Francis Schaeffer explains the consequences of a world in which the lines between male and female become fuzzy:

> To deny the truth of what it means to be male and female as taught in the Scriptures is to deny something essential about the nature of man and about the character of God and his relationship to man. But this denial has equally tragic consequences for society and human life. If we accept the idea of equality with distinction, we logically must accept the ideas of abortion and homosexuality. For if there are no significant distinctions between men and women, then certainly we cannot condemn homosexual relationships. . . . The idea of absolute autonomous freedom from God's boundaries flows into the idea of equality without distinction, which flows into the denial of what it means to be male and female, which flows into abortion and homosexuality, and the destruction of the home and family, and ultimately to the destruction of our culture.[5]

Schaeffer's logic discloses how fundamentalism binds together issues of gender, homosexuality, and abortion with anxieties concerning the well-being of family and civilization. Each of these issues, as well as other planks in the fundamentalist political platform, is integrated with a particular understanding of order bequeathed to modernity by Newtonian science. In both the fundamentalist and Newtonian worlds, reality is pre-eminently knowable and rational because it follows absolute laws predicated on sharp distinctions. To the fundamentalist way of perceiving reality, this is the only order possible. Setting up the world in terms of binary oppositions locks fundamentalism into a perspective that negates competing or alternate visions of order by relegating them to the category of disorder.

A world that can be understood, that follows predictable, reliable patterns, is a world that can be managed and divested of its fearsomeness. Religious folk are often accused by others of being too devoted to the category of mystery, but this is not true of fundamentalists. The fundamentalist spirit drives toward finding a reason for everything. The certitude that is a hallmark of fundamentalism derives in part from the sense that mystery has been dispelled. Mystery, the fundamentalist spirit seems to say, is tantamount to chaos. To disperse mystery is thus to keep chaos at bay and to maintain a feeling of control over life. Fundamentalism, says Karen McCarthy Brown,

> is the religion of those at once seduced and betrayed by the promise that we human beings can comprehend and control our world. Bitterly disappointed by the politics of rationalized bureaucracies, the limitations of science, and the perversions of industrialization, fundamentalists seek to reject the modern world, while nevertheless holding onto its habits of mind: clarity, certitude, and control.[6]

But life has a nasty way of not respecting the longing for rational control and clarity. Fundamentalism, like other Christian traditions, deals with this fact by repressing or suppressing those aspects of existence that are not always amenable to conscious understanding or control. "Unconscious motives, deep longings, and fears are denied, and responsibility for them is abandoned, as fundamentalism makes a pretense of being all about cut-and-dried truth and clear and recognizable feelings."[7]

The body and its sexuality are particularly troubling. Fundamentalist attitudes toward the body and sex are of course not unique in the history of Christianity. But whereas some other Christian traditions have attempted to reclaim a more open approach to embodiment, fundamentalism has remained firmly committed to keeping sexuality and the body under careful regulation. Fundamentalism thus reveals an instrumentalist view of the body, a trait also shared by hegemonic masculinity.[8] On this view, the body is regarded as less an integral part of the self and more an instrument or machine that must be vigilantly governed.

One expression of this perspective is fundamentalism's concern with dress and cosmetics, especially for women. John R. Rice waged a lifelong campaign to keep the female appearance plain and unprovocative:

> What is wrong with the miniskirt? It is not modest. What is wrong with a woman wearing shorts? It is not modest apparel. What is wrong with a halter and shorts in the summertime and the bikini bathing suits? All this is a deliberate playing up of a woman's sex in order to attract men and that is wicked. You know we don't have to argue about that, not to decent, honorable people.[9]

Rice detects a sinister motive in "immodest" apparel for women: inciting the lust of men, thus making it more difficult for males to keep their sexual impulses under control. More recent liberalizing trends within fundamentalism, however, have produced a whole genre of Christian sex manuals, with the express intent of enabling the faithful to enjoy their sexual lives more fully.[10]

But common to both the prudishness of Rice and the more affirmative outlooks is the restriction of sexual expression to marriage. Indeed, a significant part of the entire fundamentalist movement, especially major aspects of politicized fundamentalism, can be interpreted as an effort to keep sex—as both sexuality and sex-defined roles—within the traditional norms prescribed by the institution of marriage. Sex-related and marriage-related concerns make up a generous portion of both the fundamentalist catalogue of sins and the religious right's moral-political agenda. Driving the fervency of this agenda seems to be a pervasive fear of the body, its sexuality, and ultimately its mortality. As numerous researchers have shown, these qualities, while not limited exclusively to men, are especially manifest in contemporary constructions of masculinity.[11]

The masculine qualities of competitiveness and aggressiveness also play prominent roles in fundamentalist life. Always looking to outdo other churches, fundamentalists are preoccupied with church statistics and are incessantly concerned with increasing Sunday school enrollments, attendance at worship services, and conversions to Christ. Fundamentalists also exhibit a preference for military metaphors, clearly seen in church hymnody and rhetoric about Christianity's relation to the secular world. Tim LaHaye's influential series on the threat of secular humanism includes such titles as *The Battle for the Mind* and *The Battle for the Family*.[12] American nationalism plays a significant role in the fundamentalist worldview. Even a cursory glance at the religious right's political agenda reveals the intense concern with American military and economic superiority.[13] Finally, aggressiveness is quite evident in the fundamentalist evangelistic impulse. Most fundamentalists feel compelled to share the good news of the gospel with the unsaved and to sponsor missionary activities among the "heathen masses." While fundamentalists interpret evangelistic "crusades" as an expression of compassion and soulful concern, nonfundamentalists often interpret this style of evangelism as intrusive and arrogant.

A final element of modern masculinity found in fundamentalism is the ideology of the individual, or what Catherine Keller calls the "separative self."[14] This ideology holds that the self is an entity that exists essentially in isolation from other individuals. Such a view of the self comes to expression in the hypermasculine virtues of self-sufficiency and independence. In American culture, the ideal of the "self-made man," an individual whose success is attributable to no one but himself, has given mythic expression to these values. In fundamentalism, the ideology of the individual is expressed in two interrelated ways. First, fundamentalism understands the Christian gospel as directed toward the salvation of individual souls: Jesus Christ is one's *personal* Lord and Savior. Second, the fundamentalist perspective allows no real place for the analysis of so-cial or corporate structures that may contribute to human problems: Sin is always a failure of the individual will. Thus, fundamentalism perceives the church as a collection of individuals, a confederacy, so to speak, of saved souls. Again, fundamentalism is not especially unique in its em-phasis on the value of the individual, but it insists on this value with an unusual passion.

In one very important area, fundamentalism is not traditionally mas-culine: its persistent demand for controlled male sexuality. In this area, fundamentalism radically departs from twentieth-century ideals of mas-culine behavior. Traditional hegemonic masculinity generally allows for—and often insists on—the notorious "double standard": virginity or monogamy for females and relative sexual freedom for males. But in fun-damentalism, no double standard for male and female sexuality exists. Both women and men are expected to remain celibate until marriage and sexually exclusive within marriage. This deviation from the standards of hegemonic masculinity generates anxiety about male sexuality and man-liness for fundamentalist men. This anxiety in tandem with the anxieties raised by male religiousness helps stimulate the hypermasculine qualities of the fundamentalist worldview.

The Idealization of Women and the Debasement of Men: Gender Roles in Fundamentalism

According to fundamentalism, the anxieties and conflicts associated with human sexuality are generally more problematic for males than fe-males. By nature, males have more difficulty keeping their sexual im-pulses and activities under the strict control demanded by the will of God. "It is usually agreed that the male in all species of living creatures has the stronger sex drive. . . . God designed the man to be the aggressor, provider, and leader of his family. Somehow that is tied to his sex drive."[15]

Undergirding this view are beliefs about the inherent qualities of each sex. Women, says fundamentalism, are naturally superior to men in mat-ters moral and spiritual. "The highest form of God's creation," claims Bailey Smith, the former president of the Southern Baptist Convention, "is womankind."[16] Women are intrinsically more loving, more faithful, and more tender. Consequently, they are less subject to raging demands of the sexual self. According to Tim and Beverly LaHaye, "Women have their own brand of spiritual problems, but mental-attitude lust is seldom one of them."[17] Fundamentalists thus claim a heightened appreciation for the female: "God has a very high view of women. They are to be exalted, honored, and lifted up."[18] Randall Balmer has observed how this perspective derives from a widespread nineteenth-century belief in female superiority. As a result, males "came to be characterized as aggressive and indifferent to godliness, whereas women became the lifeblood of the churches."[19]

Yet despite the perceived natural supremacy of females, fundamentalism prescribes a strident gender hierarchy that requires the submission of women to men. According to Elizabeth Rice Handford, God has established an order of authority in the universe, set up in this fashion:

God
Christ
Man
Woman.[20]

At each level, God requires submission and obedience to the higher authority. Just as Christ submitted to the will of God the Father, so too the wife is expected to submit to and obey her husband, for "God makes the husband the saviour of his wife's body."[21] Woman's obedience and deference to man, argue fundamentalists, should not be taken to mean that women are inferior to men: "not inferior—different."[22] God has decreed, however, that ultimately man is in authority over woman, not to rule as a tyrant but to maintain harmony, security, and stability in the home and in the nation. To challenge this authority, just as to rebel against the authority of God, is to court chaos. Obedience to authority is so important in the fundamentalist view that women are encouraged to submit to their husbands even if the husband is unsaved or asks her to disobey what she feels is God's will. "The Scriptures say a woman must ignore her 'feelings' about the will of God, and do what her husband says. She is to obey her husband as if he were God Himself."[23] If the husband leads his wife to contradict the will of God, he—not she—is responsible, and God will hold him accountable.

Within this hierarchy, the roles for each sex are clearly prescribed, Handford explains:

God made the man to be the achiever, the doer, to provide for the home and protect it, to be high priest and intercessor for the home. His body carries the seed of life, and he is responsible for the children that will be born, to guide them, nurture them, direct them.

God made the woman to be keeper of the home, to make a haven within its walls, a retreat from the stress of battle, the nourisher of the children. A woman's body is fashioned primarily for being a wife and mother.[24]

Despite the spiritual superiority of women, men are directed to fulfill the leadership roles in government, family, and church. F. LaGard Smith explains:

> The man's typically greater physical strength has historically dictated his role as the family's protector and provider. Even though modern social relationships and employment circumstances have greatly diminished the importance of man's physical strength, his role as provider and protector is commensurate with his responsibility for the spiritual guidance and protection of the family. It is an obligation which he bears, not because of a spiritual superiority, but because it is a God-imposed duty. Galatians 3:28 changes neither the natural distinctions between male and female nor their commensurate spiritual roles.[25]

Smith is not unaware of the apparent contradiction between the spiritual inferiority of men and the requirement that they exercise spiritual and public leadership. Speculating on the divine rationale for such an odd arrangement, he argues that the spiritual weakness of men is precisely the reason God imposes the obligation of male leadership. Without a sense of duty, males are likely to lapse into absolute moral and spiritual complacency.

It is the language of duty, obligation, and responsibility, not the language of privilege, that characterizes the fundamentalist understanding of the male role. Such rhetoric, and the gender dynamics that inform it, disclose a rather base view of maleness. Men are essentially lustful creatures whose sexual impulses and spiritual slothfulness must be governed by the clear regulations pronounced by divine command. Balmer's analysis is illuminating on this point:

> The Victorian myth of feminine spiritual superiority is so entrenched in twentieth-century fundamentalism that many preachers have felt obliged to shake men out of their spiritual complacency. Consider, for instance, the machismo posturings of evangelist Billy Sunday, who insisted that in Jesus we find "the definition of manhood." "God is a masculine God," the fundamentalist firebrand John R. Rice insisted to a male audience in 1947. "God bless women, but He never intended any preacher to be run by a bunch of women." But the intensity of Rice's protestations merely verifies the pervasiveness of the myth. Presbyterian preacher Donald Grey Barnhouse confirmed this in his characterization of a typical Christian household. "The husband is not interested in the things of God, so the family drifts along without any spiritual cohesion," he wrote. "Perhaps they go to church together on Sunday morning, and the wife goes to all the activities of the week, but the husband seems uninterested." Barnhouse then offered a familiar, albeit paradoxical, prescription for this malaise: feminine submission. "With delight she learns the joy of knowing it is her husband's house, his

home; the children are his; she is his wife," he wrote. "When a woman realizes and acknowledges this, the life of the home can be transformed, and the life of her husband also."[26]

Balmer's study not only elucidates the dynamics of dominance and submission in fundamentalism; it also points to an often overlooked element of male experience within fundamentalist churches: profound discomfort.

The Feminization of Fundamentalist Men: Male Discomfort in the Church

Virtually all analyses of contemporary masculinity simply ignore the role of religion and spirituality in the lives of men. This omission, I suspect, is due in part to the secular outlook of most sociological and psychological researchers, whose academic framework traditionally overlooks the importance of religion in human life. But the neglect of the religion factor also derives from the traditional association of spirituality with femininity. According to traditional conceptions of masculinity, religiousness is not manly (see Evelyn Kirkley's analysis of the debate surrounding this issue, chap. 6 in this volume). How does the association of religiousness with femininity affect the experience of males in fundamentalist churches and in turn the particular emphases of fundamentalist theology and practice?

The Christian apologist C. S. Lewis once wrote without the least touch of irony, "God is so masculine that in relation to Him we are all feminine." This declaration intimates that on some level men who submit to worshiping a male God must in some sense regard themselves as feminine, at least as contemporary culture defines femininity, masculinity, and their complementarity. In this volume (chap. 3) and elsewhere, Howard Eilberg-Schwartz has developed a compelling analysis of this dynamic in ancient Judaism.[27] Eilberg-Schwartz argues that the maleness of God must have evoked, albeit for the most part subconsciously, homoerotic anxieties among ancient Jewish men. These anxieties in turn supported a male dominance/female submission hierarchy.[28] If Eilberg-Schwartz is correct, similar dynamics probably operate in contemporary fundamentalism, which is recalcitrant in its insistence on the maleness of God and human submissiveness. The fundamentalist demand for gender hierarchy and its obsession with homosexuality (particularly male homosexuality) may be partially associated with male discomfort with an exclusively male God.

Although the insistence on the maleness of God is not peculiar to fundamentalism in the Christian tradition, other distinctive features of fundamentalism may contribute to the male experience of discomfort with religion. Consider, for example, the fundamentalist requirement of being "born again." Carol Flake aptly describes the nature of this event for nineteenth-century evangelical men and how ministers dealt with it:

> The central evangelical experience of yielding to a superior being was a humbling experience for a man; how could he surrender himself emotionally without losing his manhood? It was the genius of evangelical preachers to make the born-again experience seem a masculine rite of passage. Christianity was like a team, an army, into which one was initiated, with Jesus as the commander. That was a kind of subordination men could understand.[29]

But despite clerical attempts to masculinize Christianity, evangelical and fundamentalist men must have still harbored doubts about the manliness of religion, as evidenced by the energetic debate over "muscular" Christianity. The fact that conservative clergy even felt compelled to make Christianity seem more masculine attests to the association of spirituality with femininity and to the need to compensate men for being religious.

Male shame and guilt tend to be exacerbated by some fundamentalist values, further compounding the male sense of discomfort.

> Traditionally, most of the vices put on parade from the pulpit were those that tended to lure husbands rather than wives away from respectability: drinking, gambling, whoring, cursing, immoral conduct. If a man didn't feel the watchful eye of God upon him as he struggled against temptation, he could certainly sense the accusing eyes and hear the wagging tongues of his fellow church members.[30]

To be clear, I am not arguing that the factors of male discomfort in fundamentalism are usually or ever brought to consciousness. More likely, this experience is masked or repressed by the emphasis on emotional reticence embraced by fundamentalism and reinforced by the hegemonic construction of masculinity. Indeed, the overt machismo of fundamentalism *depends* on the submerged anxieties about masculinity generated by fundamentalist religiousness.

Conclusion:
Fundamentalism as Compensation

Fundamentalist men who take seriously the ideals of hegemonic masculinity experience themselves as at least partially emasculated. Fundamentalist theology in particular, and Christian theology more generally, requires them to assume a traditionally feminine posture in relation to God and to the principal experience of salvation. The condemnation of certain hegemonic masculine practices as sinful and the emphasis on control of male sexuality engenders mostly subconscious anxieties and conflicts about appropriate manliness. As compensation for these emasculating dynamics, fundamentalism offers men a hypermasculine world-view, with a rationalistic theology, a universe of clearly demarcated boundaries and order, a sense of control, and a militant outlook. In short, fundamentalism provides men with a religious machismo to mask deeper masculine conflicts.[31]

The study of gender, and the study of men in particular, thus adds an important element to the analysis of fundamentalism. Any complete understanding of the fundamentalist phenomenon must, I believe, take into account these gender dynamics and their influence on the characteristic aspects of the religion. At the same time, studying fundamentalism through the lens of gender reminds us that any complete analysis of cultural masculinities must not neglect the role of religion and spirituality in the lives of men.

NOTES

1. I am reluctant to use the term *fundamentalism* to describe cross-cultural religious phenomena. *Fundamentalism* is a term indigenous to North American Protestantism, and in this chapter I use it exclusively to refer to this specific Christian phenomenon.

2. Karen McCarthy Brown, "Fundamentalism and the Control of Women," in *Fundamentalism and Gender,* ed. John Stratton Hawley (New York: Oxford University Press, 1994), 197.

3. W. A. Criswell, *Great Doctrines of the Bible,* vol. 2, *Theology Proper/ Christology* (Grand Rapids: Zondervan Publishing House, 1982), 17.

4. Consequently, most fundamentalists are suspicious of their first cousins, the pentecostalists and charismatics, and seek to distinguish themselves as sharply as possible. See John R. Rice, *I Am a Fundamentalist* (Murfreesboro, Tenn.: Sword of the Lord Publishers, 1975), 191–92, 216. Although these groups share a basic doctrinal theology, fundamentalists are generally opposed to *glossolalia* (speaking in tongues) and other ecstatic religious experiences. Interestingly, pentecostalists and charismatics display a higher degree of gender equality than fundamentalists; women have long been accepted as pastors and evangelists by pentecostalists and holiness groups.

5. Francis A. Schaeffer, *The Great Evangelical Disaster* (Westchester, Ill.: Crossway Books, 1984), 136.

6. Brown, "Fundamentalism," 176.

7. Ibid., 182, 183.

8. On the idea of the instrumentalist view of the body and its history, see James B. Nelson, *Embodiment: An Approach to Sexuality and Christian Theology* (Minneapolis: Augsburg Publishing House, 1978), 37–47.

9. Rice, *I Am a Fundamentalist,* 184.

10. Tim and Beverly LaHaye, authors of several books on the subject and popular fundamentalist leaders, even conclude that "Christians generally experience a higher degree of sexual enjoyment than non-Christians." See Tim LaHaye and Beverly LaHaye, *The Act of Marriage: The Beauty of Sexual Love* (Grand Rapids: Zondervan Publishing House, 1976), 9.

11. James B. Nelson, *The Intimate Connection: Male Sexuality, Masculine Spirituality* (Philadelphia: Westminster Press, 1988), 67–76.

12. Tim LaHaye, *The Battle for the Mind* (Old Tappan, N.J.: Fleming H. Revell Company, 1980); *The Battle for the Family* (Old Tappan, N.J.: Fleming H. Revell, Company, 1982); *The Battle for the Public Schools: Humanism's Threat to Our Children* (Old Tappan, N.J.: Fleming H. Revell Company, 1983).

13. Edward Dobson and Edward Hindson, *The Fundamentalist Phenomenon: The Resurgence of Conservative Christianity,* ed. Jerry Falwell (Garden City, N.Y.: Doubleday & Co., 1981), 186–223.

14. Catherine Keller, *From a Broken Web: Separation, Sexism, and Self* (Boston: Beacon Press, 1986), 1–6.

15. LaHaye and LaHaye, *Act of Marriage,* 23.

16. Bailey Smith on *Larry King Live,* March 21, 1989, cited in Randall Balmer, "American Fundamentalism: The Ideal of Femininity," in *Fundamentalism and Gender,* ed. John Stratton Hawley (New York: Oxford University Press, 1994), 47.

17. LaHaye and LaHaye, *Act of Marriage,* 33.

18. John MacArthur Jr., "Husbands, Love Your Wives," *Fundamentalist Journal,* vol. 4, no. 6 (June, 1985): 36.

19. Balmer, "American Fundamentalism," 51.

20. Elizabeth R. Handford, *Me? Obey Him? The Obedient Wife and God's Way of Happiness and Blessing in the Home* (Murfreesboro, Tenn.: Sword of the Lord, 1972), 13.

21. Handford, *Me? Obey Him?* 21; see also Schaeffer, *Great Evangelical Disaster,* 135.

22. Handford, *Me? Obey Him?* 16.

23. Ibid., 16.

24. Ibid., 15; see also MacArthur, "Husbands," 36; LaHaye and LaHaye, *Act of Marriage,* 37–38.

25. F. LaGard Smith, *Men of Strength for Women of God* (Eugene, Oreg.: Harvest House Publishers, 1989), 206, 207.

26. Balmer, "American Fundamentalism," 53–54.

27. Howard Eilberg-Schwartz, *God's Phallus and Other Problems for Men and Monotheism* (Boston: Beacon Press, 1994).

28. Eilberg-Schwartz's argument follows these lines: On some level, the men of Israel must have been aware that God's "natural"(given the prevailing heterosexual norms of Israelite culture) human partner ought to have been the *women* of Israel. Yet the patriarchal assumptions of Hebrew society could not allow for that possibility. Hence, the misogynist elements of the biblical tradition must derive in part from the masculinist desire to disrupt the natural

complementarity between YHWH and human females. If women can be viewed as impure and inferior, then they no longer serve as suitable partners for God.

29. Carol Flake, *Redemptorama: Culture, Politics, and the New Evangelicalism* (New York: Penguin Books, 1984), 92, 93.

30. Ibid., p. 92.

31. Comparing Christian fundamentalism to similar militant groups such as the Gush Emunim in Israel may clarify the point. John S. Hawley and Wayne Proudfoot observe that men of the Gush Emunim "take particular pleasure in using their dress and language to contradict the 'wimp' image of religious Jews that is often held by secular Israelis. They wear commando boots and flight jackets as a complement to skullcaps and long fringed garments, and they talk about how 'an AK-47 assault rifle and hamar make a perfect match with a book of Talmud and tefillin.'" John S. Hawley and Wayne Proudfoot, "Introduction," in *Fundamentalism and Gender,* ed. John Stratton Hawley (New York: Oxford University Press, 1994), 33.

8

POLICING GENDER: MORAL PURITY MOVEMENTS IN PRE-NAZI GERMANY AND CONTEMPORARY AMERICA

John C. Fout

This chapter focuses on the male Protestant moral purity organizations in Wilhelmine Germany, and the growing anxiety about "appropriate male behavior" that was reflected in many of their publications. It also discusses at some length their educational aims, a major component of which was the regulation of male behavior according to the standards they sought to impose on all heterosexual men.

Male-dominated moral purity movements appeared in the late nineteenth century across the Western industrial world, including the United States. In Germany an ever-expanding network of moral purity organizations was established in the prewar years, and that growth continued through the Weimar era. (Then in the Nazi period the sexual and gender politics of moral purity were realized.) These men, it will be shown, thundered and railed against the sins of the flesh, from the threat of venereal diseases to female prostitution, from nudism to pornography, from homosexuality to abortion, from the use of prophylactics and the concern about the decline in the birth rate, to fears about the evil effects of masturbation. Because of the broad and complex array of the movement's concerns, this chapter addresses one central component of moral purity's agenda in Wilhelmine Germany, its apprehensions about male behavior in a society experiencing rapid industrialization and urbanization. A second goal is to make connections between the ideas expressed by the German moral purity movement and the concerns of the radical religious right in contemporary America.[1]

In a typical pamphlet from 1913, entitled "How Should We Educate Our Sons in Moral Purity?" Johannes Levsen, the general secretary of the German branch of the Young Men's Christian Association, one of the many moral purity organizations, spoke of the terrible danger threatening young German men. "There has always been this special threat to young people," he emphasized, "but never so much as in our time. It is immorality with its consequences for body, soul, and intellect."[2] Of course, the moral purity movements have traditionally been associated with their attacks on what they postulated was the growing malignancy of sin and vice. One of the questions to be answered here is: How was "vice" understood by these moral purity activists and what was the purpose of their campaign for moral purity? To be sure, they located their discourse explicitly in a broad range of "sexual sins" in their diatribes against what they perceived was a rapidly changing pattern of public morality. For them it was in a state of precipitous decline, symbolized by the programs of the sexual reformers—principally sexologists, feminists, and homosexual rights activists, who sought, among other demands, to decriminalize sexual activities between consenting adults outside of marriage. Ultimately, it will be shown that moral purity's concerns went far beyond the question of sexual mores. The debate was only on the surface about "sexual vice"; in reality it reflected a very tangible crisis in gender relations, primarily burgeoning heterosexual male concern about eroding gender boundaries and the increasingly public role for women outside the traditional domestic sphere.

There had been a dramatic increase of women in the workplace due to the rapid tempo of industrialization, and though the increases came primarily in working-class occupations, from the 1890s some real gains were also being made in employment for middle-class women. There was also a mobilization of women in large numbers in the middle-class and working-class (or socialist) women's movements, which experienced brisk expansion from the 1890s onward. The Federation of German Women's Associations had been established in 1894 as an umbrella group for mostly middle-class women's organizations, and by 1913 the federation claimed a total membership of 470,000. The federation could rightfully assert some substantial achievements for women. These included expanded educational opportunities and increased access to a wider range of occupations.[3]

Given such developments, it is not surprising that a sizable segment of the middle-class male population and many working-class men, skilled workers in the main, became increasingly alarmed about the public role of women in society. The disquiet of moral purity men was perhaps representative of the majority of men in Wilhelmine society. The ultimate aim of these moral purity organizations, I believe, was to regulate male behavior with the specific intent of countering the endeavors made by women to carve out a public role that was something other than that of wife and mother in the private or domestic sphere. I would also posit that the emergence of these German "men's" organizations reflected a dramatic increase in male anxiety and represented the advent of an "organized men's movement," a development that has largely gone unnoticed by scholars of gender relations and women's history.

For moral purity men, then, to "sin," I would argue, was to exhibit behavior that transgressed traditional gender roles and the permissible sexual behavior associated with those roles. The women's movements and women's activities, especially the changing patterns of women's employment, as well as the male homosexual rights movement, had now called those roles into question. Dr. Magnus Hirschfeld, a physician and sexologist, had founded the world's first homosexual rights movement in 1897 with the establishment of the Scientific Humanitarian Committee in Berlin; its goal was to reform Article 175 of the German criminal code. That law criminalized sexual acts between males and bestiality.[4] It should also be recognized that standards of sexual behavior in general—such as increased use of birth control—were undergoing transformation in late Imperial Germany, and these changes were disturbing to many in Wilhelmine society. The fact that the women's movement was now beginning to challenge Article 218, the law that criminalized abortion, was equally seen as a threat.

These male moral purity groups, then, evolved out of a context where the gains made by women brought into question the roles played by men in the public sphere or even in the privacy of the family. In manifestos, petitions to local, state, and national governments, articles, pamphlets, and books published in the generation preceding the outbreak of World War I, moral purity authors sought to educate boys and men about their proper male role and duties. They endeavored to teach other men how to behave and accept their assigned and obligatory functions as heterosexual males—standards, naturally, defined by the moralists themselves and ones that would have limited women to traditional roles as wives and mothers. As a group these moral purity men were mostly middle-class, university-educated, and employed in occupations in government, the church, teaching, and medicine and other professions, positions that were either exclusively male or employed relatively few women. The men's movement sought to restore the centrality of the heterosexual male in society and subvert any further gains for women.

Many of these middle-class occupations represented by the rank-and-file of moral purity organizations were the target of the middle-class women's organizations noted earlier, which sought to expand the existing but still very limited positions in professional careers available to women, and to open new employment opportunities, such as positions in teaching, social work, medicine, or local government. Therefore, there was a direct relationship between the social and occupational status of moral purity men and the movement's aims as a men's crusade. While many of their diatribes against sin were directed specifically at working-class women, it was probably women of their own class that were the source of their greatest anxiety. Nonetheless, the situation was most complex because class and gender issues were intertwined. Given the sex and gender system then dominant, many middle-class men turned to working-class prostitutes for sexual satisfaction, but they became concerned that this class of women was increasingly a source of venereal disease for them and their families—these women too had become a source of male anxiety. Male dominance was being threatened on many levels, and the moral purity movement sought to prevent further slippage in men's presumed public and private roles, including control of women's productive and reproductive capacities.

It must be underscored that the primary leadership role in moral purity was played by Protestant ministers and church officials at the national and local levels, and the moral purity movement was vigorously supported by the Protestant state churches across Germany at every level from the local parish to the national church leadership. Once again the church was serving its traditional function as the upholder of the gender order. Thus the alliance between moral purity and the church served to maintain male domination of religious and other existing institutions and to create new organizations where male dominance could be firmly institutionalized. Thus the moralists had the strong backing of organized religion, and not just its "fringe" members; ministers and prominent churchmen from all levels within the Protestant church hierarchy were active supporters of moral purity.

In seeking the further criminalization of sexual acts that violated "traditional sexual norms," moral purity organizations sought the aid of the state in preserving the gender order. The state, it was hoped, would use the power of the law to perpetuate conventional standards of behavior that were male-defined. Moral purity leaders associated male control of the state with male domination of the family, and they argued that the state had the right and the obligation to intervene, even in family life, when the sexual activities of individuals might threaten the gender order or even the political and social order. Sexual vice and gender disorder, they believed, could threaten the stability of the state in a variety of ways. As one moral purity authority put it, this natural order was God-ordained and "any deviation, any breach in this order has always led to irrefutable calamity; it destroys the happiness of the individual, it disrupts family life, and it undermines the welfare of the nation."[5]

These moral purity men had developed a kind of siege mentality in the matter of gender relations, and they were obsessively concerned about the growing presence of women in the male sphere and the possibility of the breakdown of a world that was gender-segregated. There was also broad anxiety about the emergence of a homosexual role for some males, which was characterized by moral purity as weak, effeminate, sickly, and sexually out of control, characteristics these "perverse men" supposedly shared with females—at least that was the way the moral purity advocates saw it. Together, all these threats implied a change in the way men and women related to each other and a weakening of the traditional dominance of "masculine men" in a patriarchal society. Therefore, the moral purity movement sought to shape a restatement of what appropriate male behavior should be in the family and in society at large.

We turn now to a discussion of my central thesis that their emphasis on the evils of sin and the value of moral purity—that is, sexual chastity outside marriage—was in reality a discussion about appropriate gender roles and acceptable sexual behavior for men. These men's groups created an innovative counter strategy that weakened the possibilities of institutionalizing the social changes advocated by the women's movement. The moral purity understanding of dominant males and passive females was reflective of the dominant paradigm of the sex and gender system of modernism. Despite feminist and other reformers' efforts, that paradigm was restated by the men's movement with cultural assumptions about male dominance largely intact. In the period from the late 1880s to the outbreak of World War I, moral purity advocates discussed in explicit detail the sexual sins of contemporary society, which they argued could lead—and, in their minds, were leading—to the moral decay of the German nation. In reality, what the male moral purity movement represented was an attempt to become the only arbiter of sexuality. Men, they posited, were naturally meant to control that domain of life; issues around men's and women's sexual and reproductive bodies should be decided by men, not women.

One of the earliest moral purity pamphlets that addressed the issue of sin, sexuality, and men, *The Morality of Man's Honor: A Word to German Men and Youth,* was written by a Protestant superintendent, G. Weitbrecht. This pamphlet was often reprinted and generally appeared on the movement's list of important publications. It was placed in small shops, factories, offices, military posts, and public meetings, places frequented by males, and was illustrative of how the campaign to dominate the discourse was waged by moral purity. Weitbrecht explained that he would be one of the first to admit that "thank God there are thousands upon thousands of young men who keep themselves pure and chaste, and are thereby healthy, clean, and strong." Conversely, too many men, he feared, failed to control their sexual drives and succumbed to sin and illness. Similarly there were too many women who had no morality or honor; they had merely become the paid playthings of lust and had joined the ranks of the fallen—a condition that was generally accepted by moral purity as permanent for women, since virginity could never be restored. For the chaste male, the question of male honor was significant for more than just himself; he had to consider "the honor of the female sex" as well.

"The immoral rake who misuses a female being as a means to satisfy his lust," Weitbrecht thundered, "dishonors through her the female gender, the gender to which his mother and his sister belong."[6]

What were the implications of these remarks? Men, not women, according to Weitbrecht were the deciding factor in sexual relations, and men's actions should determine what was appropriate for both genders (moral purity men as a whole, it must be emphasized, held such assumptions). All women should be thought of in the category of mothers, nothing else. Moreover, he asked, how could an unchaste young man consider becoming the head of a family one day? "How can you give orders, if you cannot command yourself? How can you govern and rule, if you cannot govern and rule yourself?"[7] Men needed to be socialized for their role as leader in the public sphere and as father and head of the family in the private. Though men and women should exist primarily in separate spheres, men were to be the dominant gender in both, if moral purity had its way. Traditional Western extremes of the female gender embodied by the Virgin Mary and Eve were reincarnated in the modern era by moral purity as the good mother and the venereally diseased working-class prostitute. For the middle-class men of the moral purity movement, women of their own class were not perceived as entertaining sexual desires and were to be excluded from any control over sexual behavior and sexual politics. Conversely, working-class women were viewed as leading sexually illicit lives and being responsible for luring decent men into sins of the flesh and contaminating them with their filthy diseases.

The relationship between appropriate gender roles, acceptable forms of sexual behavior, and the regulation of sexuality is essential to an understanding of the debate over morality issues. One of the most articulate statements of the dominant mentality was provided by Richard von Krafft-Ebing in his 1886 study, *Psychopathia Sexualis.* That is ironic since Krafft-Ebing, professor of psychiatry and neurology at the University of Vienna and one of the leading European sexologists of the late nineteenth century, was also anathema to the moral purity movement for his advocacy of the decriminalization of various sexual acts, including sodomy. Krafft-Ebing began with the assumption that heterosexual marital monogamy and sexual activity within the confines of marriage, naturally for procreative purposes, was the basis for determining what defined "normal sexuality" in higher civilizations. In his mind, "episodes of moral decay always coincide with the progress of effeminacy, lewdness and luxuriance of the nations." He too believed that the moral ruin of a nation was brought on by debauchery and adultery. Moreover, like his contemporaries in the moral purity movement, he saw the big industrial cities as the hotbeds of immorality in his own time.[8]

Krafft-Ebing delineated what, according to his logic, were the substan-

tial connections between normal gender roles and acceptable sexual behavior. He argued that "since love implies the presence of sexual desire it
can only exist between persons of different sex capable of sexual intercourse." "Manliness and self-reliance," as he put it, were certainly not the
qualities of an "impotent onanist." Men had stronger sexual needs than
women, since, after all, women who are "physically and mentally normal
and properly educated" have all but no sexual desires. Nature makes men
aggressive and women naturally passive. Nonetheless men can easily become enslaved by their passions for women, and a man "becomes more
and more dependent upon her as he grows weaker, and the more he yields
to sensuality."[9]

Krafft-Ebing's views on male homosexuality, despite his support for the
decriminalization of sodomy, found resonance within the parameters of
acceptable male behavior as validated by moral purity. While Krafft-Ebing
characterized homosexuals as men who experienced sexual desires for individuals of their own sex exclusively, and though he admitted that homosexuals can love their own kind as passionately as "normal" heterosexuals, he went on to describe that love as "the exact opposite of natural
feelings" and one that was only a caricature. Moreover, homosexuals, he
sought to convince his readers, were individuals who were subject to "excessive sexual desire" and often they were "sexually neurasthenic," or
suffering from a psychic and emotional disorder that, as he put it, was either the result of a congenital disorder, was brought on by excessive masturbation, or came about as a product of enforced abstinence. The homosexual was also inclined by his nature, according to Krafft-Ebing, to
the passive role in sexual intercourse and thus shared those desires in
common with women rather than with normal males—only the homosexual inclined to pederasty was likely to engage in the active role but
even then, according to Krafft-Ebing, "only in cases of moral defect and
by reason of excessive desire."[10]

The homosexual role, then, even for Krafft-Ebing (and especially the
moral purity movement) was not a "normal" male mode of behavior—
heterosexual men were not like homosexuals. While he expressed his sympathy for those who suffered from this "abnormality," he ultimately
viewed their behavior as an anomaly. Homosexuality or the homosexual
role mirrored, according to this interpretation, what most males in Western society would consider were the attributes of the female gender, and
those modes of behavior were to be avoided at all costs. The homosexual
male was considered the polar opposite of the heterosexual male. Likewise, the sexual activity in which the former engaged accordingly reflected
his effeminate nature and was a product of his congenital degeneration.
Homosexuality, for Krafft-Ebing, could only represent a contradictory relationship to the "natural" characteristics of the male and female genders.

In a pamphlet entitled *The Man as Father of a Family* other key characteristics in the moral purity's arsenal of male traits were established. The virtues of becoming the father of a family, the schoolteacher author pointed out, were "the natural rights of a man." Just as girls play with dolls and anticipate motherhood as their natural role, boys must understand their future position as head of the family. As a man, he argued, one must have an occupation, and all of these go together, "man, career, fatherhood." Of course, it was the occupation that made the man. If a young man refused to acquire the necessary training for his future career, then he denied his right to be called a man. In turn, man's work provided the necessary support for the family. Conversely, the right of the family is denied to the onanists and self-abusers, all child molesters and sodomites, and all whores and those who carry on with whores. It is in one's youth that the future possibility for a family is shaped or lost. In adulthood man's responsibilities to the family, his central role in it, and his support of it were the distinct features of the male heterosexual role.[11] Moral purity men, therefore, sought to convince men—and women as well—that being a male meant being a father and head of the family. Moreover, being a male meant having a profession. These responsibilities demanded qualities that were by their logic male rather than female attributes.

Given the context of Wilhelmine society, these views are significant if one sets them against the backdrop of the increasing demands of middle-class women for access to professional occupations and the demands of working-class women for better pay for the unskilled jobs they held. Women were systematically closed out of most skilled occupations and various arguments were used to rationalize that exclusion; women did not have careers because if they worked at all, it was argued, it was merely to supplement the efforts of their men. It was often reiterated that it was wrong for women to want access to men's work. By claiming the rewards of work as the sole domain of men, the moral purity movement sought to limit any new opportunities for women to expand areas of women's work. The moralists wanted to maintain the strict gender polarization and gender-specific features of paid employment. The male moral purity movement understood the power that came with the male role.

It is also essential to recognize why the idealization of the "Christian family" was a central component in moral purity ideology. The family was not only the wellspring of heterosexual marriage where sex was only for procreative purposes and where traditional gender roles were sustained, but it also now became for moral purity the institution where male dominance over the two genders was ultimately to be rationalized. Though men and women were supposedly equal in God's eyes, nonetheless men should rule over the family just as they did in society at large. Therefore, when moral purity men (and women) spoke of traditional family values, they articulated a view of the family that was entirely male-defined. In this metaphor of the "Christian family," moral purity also reiterated its belief that the gender order was divinely ordained, a claim the churches supported. Within that framework, men's dominant position inside and outside the sphere of the family had to be preserved at all cost. Building from those sets of assumptions about gender and sexuality, the male moral purity movement sought to restate what that traditional role for men should be, in the family and in society at large, according to a "Christian" viewpoint they claimed to represent. To assert that role, men had to maintain their position as the dominant arbiters of sexuality, which would in turn continue the gender dominance of men over women. It had to be established, moral purity advocates believed, that the characteristic feature of the two genders was their immutability, since they were rooted in a biological and divine imperative.

These efforts by the moral purity movement also reflected intense male gender anxiety. Men were not only increasingly distressed about the changing role for women in the public sphere, but they were concerned about what those changes would mean for men. They sought to counter if not reverse the gains made by women, and they sought to regulate male behavior to meet this challenge by educating young boys, youths, and mature men to abide by the assumed standards of male behavior that clearly differentiated the strong aggressive male from the biologically passive female. Assumptions about appropriate gender behavior, they wished men to understand, were based in the biology of maleness. To behave in any other way was to threaten loss of strength and virility and that would lead normal males to succumb to effeminacy or, worse, to take on the alarming homosexual role.

I have also argued that the male moral purity movement was in reality an organized men's movement. By failing to recognize this crucial development, scholars have not been able to adequately explain the failure of the women's movement to achieve many of its goals. Moreover, the emergence of both women's and men's movements makes it eminently clear that the modern era should be characterized as a period of intense crisis in gender relations. While the women's movement was in the main geared to improving circumstances for women, the men's movement was largely reactionary, and though it had as its goal the education of men about suitable male behavior, the ultimate aim of this education, I would posit, was to subvert the women's movement. By moving to establish the male-dominated family as a site for traditional Christian values and acceptable gender roles and sexual behavior, moral purity, with the ardent support of the churches, adopted a compelling argument against changes in the

111

gender order. The new men's organizations that the moral purity movement created were to serve as locations where such male behavior and power could be continually institutionalized.

The Religious Right in Contemporary America: The Continuity of Moral Purity Ideas

Despite the fact that much has changed in modern society in the past one hundred years, the religious right in our own time continues to preach about gender, sexuality, and female and male roles as if the clock has stood still. It still seeks to dominate the contemporary debate over sexual politics, from abortion to homosexuality, from birth control to sexuality, and condemn all sexuality outside of the realm of monogamous, heterosexual marriage. While antibiotics are now readily available to cure many venereal diseases, AIDS is a new nightmarish specter in our society, which the religious right uses and abuses to condemn homosexuality and all forms of extramarital sexuality. But just as the old moral purity movement mistakenly blamed just the female prostitute for the spread of venereal disease, it now blames the homosexual for the spread of AIDS. Equally importantly, the new religious right holds up the specter of disease as yet another rationale for the condemnation of any form of sexuality that does not fit its own narrow standards. Moreover, just as the moral purity movement preached abstinence in the face of incurable venereal diseases, the religious right preaches abstinence in our time and condemns the use of condoms, which would save people's lives and prevent the spread of AIDS. At the same time, the condom does not just represent protection against disease, it, like all other forms of birth control, gives all people, and women especially, sexual freedom, while it controls the population, now developing at a totally unrestrained rate. Yet neither a better life for all people nor the population explosion is the concern of the religious right.

Another central continuity from the late nineteenth century in the United States is that the religious right in our time is led all but overwhelmingly by white male Protestants, although the voice of white Catholics is also strong. At a time when the United States is increasingly becoming a multiracial and multicultural society, the religious right reflects both the anxiety over the ongoing reorganization of our culture and the declining dominance of white male patriarchy. It is a patriarchy that is racist and heterosexist. The new right represents the view that white men must maintain control. And that the majority of women now also work outside the home and the homosexual rights movement has achieved many gains are yet other sources of white male anxiety.

The religious right goes beyond its attempt to control the productive and reproductive capacities of women. There has been a devastating impact of its creeds on all men, heterosexual and homosexual. It seeks to impose on all men one gender role and one form of sexuality, while it castigates all other sexual behavior and gender roles. In its view the only acceptable society is one in which heterosexual males are organized within the framework of the traditional "Christian family." This family should exist to the exclusion of all others, and in this family white, heterosexual males should engage in reproductive, monogamous sexuality and the male should reign supreme. The religious right continues to play the role of gender police in our society. It still thinks American society should be organized as if an older rural agrarian order still exists and it still believes that organized religion must condemn all people who do not fit into a family structure as defined by their values. Many Christians have forgotten some of the most basic tenets of Christianity and have turned some churches into bastions of discrimination against those men and women who do not believe and live as they do. It is taking a terrible toll on men in our society who do not wish to live by these standards, or who believe that these standards are not applicable to all people.

NOTES

Reprinted by permission from John C. Fout, "The Male Gender Crisis in Wilhelmine Germany and the Attempt to Regulate Male Behavior," *Journal of Men's Studies,* vol. 1, no. 1 (August 1992), pp. 5–31.

1. This is a much shorter and somewhat revised version of my "The Moral Purity Movement in Wilhelmine Germany and the Attempt to Regulate Male Behavior," *The Journal of Men's Studies* 1 (1992): 5–31, which contains a lengthy bibliography. See also my "Sexual Politics in Wilhelmine Germany: The Male Gender Crisis, Moral Purity, and Homophobia," *Journal of the History of Sexuality* 2 (1992): 388–421.

2. Johannes Levsen, *Wie Erziehen Wir unsere Söhne zur sittlichen Reinheit?* (Nowawes: Verlag des Weisskreuzhauses, c. 1913), 5.

3. For the women's movement, see, e.g., Richard J. Evans, *The Feminist Movement in Germany* (Beverly Hills, Calif.: Sage Publications, 1976), or Ute Frevert, *Women in German History: From Bourgeois Emancipation to Sexual Liberation* (New York: Berg, 1989).

4. For a brief history of the German gay rights movement, see James Steakley, *The Homosexual Emancipation Movement in Germany* (New York: Arno Press, 1975).

5. Adolf Henning, *Die öffentliche Sittenlosigkeit und die Arbeit der Sittlichkeitsvereine: Eine Denkschrift,* 2d rev. ed. (Berlin: Verlag der Geschäftstelle der deutschen Sittlichkeitsvereine, 1897), 4.

6. G. Weitbrecht, *Die Sittlichkeit des Mannes Ehre: Ein Wort an die*

deutschen Männer und Jünglinge (Stuttgart: Verein zur Hebung der Sittlichkeit, 1889), 4–6.

7. Ibid., 7.

8. Richard von Krafft-Ebing, *Psychopathia Sexualis,* trans. F. Klaf from the 12th German ed. (New York: Stein & Day, 1965 [1886]), 3–4.

9. Ibid., 8–9.

10. Ibid., 240–41.

11. G. Közle, *Der Mann als Familienvater* (Berlin: Verlag der deutschen Sittlichkeitsvereine, 1899), 60–61.

PART IV

THE EFFECTS
OF MASCULINITY

We have emphasized that there is not one masculinity; there are many. So when we discuss the effects of masculinity we are not referring to a universal category that is experienced the same way by every man. But we did acknowledge that there is a "hegemonic masculinity" that functions as a kind of ideal against which many men measure themselves. All four of the authors in this part view masculinity as a social construct, though they differ regarding the extent to which they view this construction as infinitely malleable or determined by one's given biological makeup.

In chapter 9 Merlyn Mowrey focuses upon femininity, but she sees this construct as integrally related to masculinity, as both accommodate each other. She claims, however, that only women are viewed as "other" in a fundamental way. The masculinity that forms the backdrop for her discussion is that which is experienced by men in North America as members of dominant classes whose assumptions about masculinity and femininity are rooted in an ancient patriarchy that has been supported in Western culture particularly by Christianity. Within Christianity, Mowrey believes there is an abiding sexist dualism that subordinates women to men. She argues that this dualism has been understood in classical Christianity to have existed even before the Fall, though after the Fall the distinction was increased as women were regarded as those especially responsible for the entrance of sin into the world. (Other interpreters of the Christian tradition view the pre-Fall and post-Fall relationships between men and women differently. See, for example, Stephen Boyd's chapter in part 1 of this volume, in which he describes one strand of Christianity, including Luther, that views men and women as equal prior to the Fall.)

Mowrey believes this definition of femininity, emphasizing the accommodating other, has been internalized by women, and that it has had profound implications for how women view themselves, including how they sexually objectify their own bodies. She challenges us to pursue right relationships that express justice and equality, based on a model of mutual friendship.

The three other authors in this part examine masculinities that are not a part of the hegemonic ideal against which Mowrey has developed her interpretation of femininity. Christopher Ronwaniente Jocks examines masculinity as it has been expressed in the history and culture of one group of Native American men, the Kahnawà:ke (Mohawk) men, of which he is both a descendant and a scholar. Recalling his childhood visits with his grandfather, who was an ironworking man, Jocks describes a way of life in which Native American men often performed work, ceremonies, and other activities primarily with other men, and yet maintained close ties with the women in their lives. He does not go so far as some scholars who describe the physical separation of men and women in the Mohawk tradition as "a cultural imperative," in which each sex group possesses "a distinct kind of power." But Jocks does acknowledge that a basic tenet for Mohawks and other Native American traditions is that men and women are different. He argues that among the Native Americans of the Long House traditions, including the Mohawks, there was an emphasis on "a good mind," in which reason and emotion, thought and action are not separated. In contrast to the culture Mowrey describes, the Mohawks have no sharp dualism in which men represent reason, masculinity, and culture while women represent emotion, femininity, and nature.

Jocks suggests that there may be important contributions the Mohawk tradition can make to a broader discussion of masculinity, but he cautions Euro-American men against attempting to borrow, use, or otherwise appropriate knowledge from this culture without becoming a part of the living communities that embody it. In fact, he closes with a warning—stop the oppression first, and only then might it be possible to discover what American Indian men might be able to contribute to modern North American men's quest for a new masculinity.

In chapter 11 Harry Brod examines the experience of masculinity within still another group of men who do not fit the hegemonic masculine ideal. He explores two contrasting images of Jewish male identity by using the symbols of "mice" and "supermen." Noting that the comic book hero Superman was created by two young Jewish men, he proposes that we consider Superman as a prototypical Jewish superhero, despite the counterintuitiveness of such thinking. He explores the ambivalence of masculinity—including the dynamics of power and powerlessness (experienced in the extreme in the Holocaust) and sexuality (Jewish men as effeminate)—experienced by Jewish men by contrasting the images of Superman (hypermasculinity) and his alter ego Clark Kent (wimp). To overcome this dichomotized portrayal of masculinity, Brod proposes the idea of a "testicular," as distinguished from a "phallic," image of what it means to be a man. (Compare James Nelson's chapter in part 6 of this volume; Nelson proposes this imagery for men in general, and not only for Jewish men.)

Timothy Nonn explores the meaning of the lives of another group of men who have suffered from oppression in his study of a selected sample of poor men in the Tenderloin District of San Francisco. Though the poor men he interviewed varied in color, ethnicity, and sexual orientation, Nonn suggests that all of them experience the stigma of failure for not living up to the dominant masculine role of "breadwinner." They respond to this failure, says Nonn, in three ways. The "predator" responds by reformulating masculine values through hypermasculine aggressiveness and violence; the "victim" responds by accepting the dominant masculine values, viewing himself as a failed man; and the "survivor" responds by affirming his own self-worth and human dignity, creating opportunities that reform the stigma of failure. Nonn clearly wants to encourage strategies that will enable more of these men to live as survivors, and he calls upon the church to rethink its ways of relating to poor men. Just as Jocks suggests that Euro-American men may learn something important from Native American men by joining in solidarity with them, after they stop the practices that oppress them, Nonn believes that the church can enable privileged men to learn from poor men, if it adopts a totally new pastoral approach based on solidarity, social justice, and equality, rather than charity alone.

The essays in this part together raise some interesting questions. What is the role of oppression in helping men to recognize and address the negative aspects of masculine roles? What might motivate men who do not feel they are oppressed to consider changing their self-understanding of what it means to be a man? What options are available for men to respond to the limitations of the masculine roles that are part of the hegemonic ideal? What role can religion play in helping men construct and maintain healthy alternatives to the gender roles that are harmful to both men and women?

9

THE ACCOMMODATING OTHER: MASCULINITY AND THE CONSTRUCTION OF FEMININE IDENTITY

Merlyn E. Mowrey

This chapter is about socialization and the stereotype of femininity as it relates to masculinity in contemporary North America.[1] That means it is about processes that shape our gender assumptions and our gendered identities, experiences, and relationships. From the generality of this topic, you might infer that it relates equally to all of us, but it does not. Socialization reflects the ideals of the status quo, and the privileged of society are its models.[2] Although our definitions of femininity and masculinity reverberate through the lives and identities of all who are socialized to take on their meanings, those definitions are not usually modeled on lesbians or gay men, people of color, or marginalized people. In fact, they often function to exclude them.[3] Other real people are missing in this discussion. Stereotypes of femininity and masculinity are at best generalizations and at worst caricatures. They may tell some of the truth about all of us because they *are* our stereotypes, but they do not tell all the truth about any of us because *we* are not stereotypes, not even those of us who most epitomize their ideals. Femininity and masculinity are defined in terms of each other, socializing us to take on reciprocal identities and roles that can limit and distort the potential of men as well as women. In a sense, then, each stereotype functions to accommodate the other. The masculine and feminine modes of accommodation are different, however, and that difference and the legitimations given for it render only women as "other" in a fundamental, not merely comparative, way. This chapter examines the dominant stereotype that presents the feminine as the "accommodating other," the historical roots and modern sources for that stereotype, the processes to which it subjects us when we take it on, and the priorities it reflects in its most recent formulations. The conclusion challenges us to reconsider and resist the impact of gendered stereotypes on our identities and relationships, for the benefit of both women and men.

Background

Our assumptions about the meanings of masculinity and femininity are rooted in the emergence of patriarchy more than five thousand years ago.[4] They achieved their most influential expression, however, in the Bible and classical Greek thought, the foundational symbol systems of Western culture.[5] Despite significant differences in these two systems, they shared assumptions about the meanings of the world of nature, gender, relationship, and order. Theirs was a new stage of consciousness, according to Rosemary Ruether, in which men imagined that they could free themselves from their dependency on nature and from mortality itself by naming a transcendent power that was their true source and home and that was free of all of the limitations of the physical world. Nature lost its meaning as the organic unity of reality, and its component parts—earth and sky, life and death, matter and spirit, female and male—were rearranged into a hierarchical structure. A transcendent, spiritual power represented by the sky and the father became the original and eternal force that had created the physical, immanent, finite world of nature represented by the subordinated mother earth. In both biblical religion and Greek philosophy, "patriarchal reversal myths" gave over the power of creation and procreation to a spiritual realm or potential which was identified with males and maleness. Females, associated with created matter, were secondary, auxiliary beings, depicted as biologically and morally defective males, or as ontologically dependent and inferior to males. For a time, these two symbol systems followed separate but parallel tracks, but those tracks merged in the Hellenistic era. Christianity, at times quite self-consciously, fused the two into its own perspective and was the vehicle through which these symbol systems pervaded the West.[6]

In the period of classical orthodoxy, Christianity developed its own anthropology to explain the patriarchal assumptions it had inherited, reformulating but not significantly changing the meanings of nature, gender, relationship, and order. It asserted, not a shared human nature, but an essentially different nature for males and females. Even prior to the Fall, according to Christian theology, woman in her originally created state would have been subordinate and deferent to man because she represents bodiliness, emotionality, and sensuality, which are prone to disorder and sin, while he represents "headship," mind, and reason, requiring that he dominate and control her. The "fallen" situation is far worse than original creation, and thus, "woman's suppression must be redoubled . . . as a reflection of her inferior nature and punishment for her responsibility for sin."[7] Of course, the rationale for the subjugation of woman required also that man subjugate all aspects of his own humanity associated with femininity and so, through repression and denial, masculinity was elevated and purified. Woman, however, could not escape her own essential nature. So great a suspicion did this cast on her that Christian theologians often pondered the problematic implications of woman's true nature and redeemability. Augustine, for one, conceded her redeemability, but not her equal participation in the image of God. In *De Trinitate* (7.7.10) he explained that "woman, together with her own husband, is the image of God, . . . but when she is referred to separately . . . she is not the image of God, but as regards the man alone, he is the image of God as fully and completely as when the woman too is joined with him in one."

This dualized patriarchal anthropology has endured in Western Christianity, along with Augustine's unique importance as the "font of orthodoxy."[8] As the West became increasingly secularized and new fields of knowledge emerged, many were pressed into service to provide "scientific" legitimations that confirmed these core meanings of gender: male and female as two different kinds of human beings, males superior and dominant, females inferior and subordinate. These assumptions became embedded in every major explanatory system, in the language and thought of Western civilization until *gender itself became a metaphor defining power relations of dominance and subordination in such a way as to mystify them and render them invisible.*[9]

Modern Discourses on the Human Being and the "Accommodating Other"

Modern assumptions about human nature have been shaped by the liberal humanist tradition and the priority it has given to the capacities for reason and autonomy. Despite the critiques to which that tradition is now subject, it has informed our dominant discourses, producing what counts as "common knowledge" or "common sense," that is, what we all "know" to be true about human nature. This kind of "knowing" is not based on reasoned analysis; rather it "accrues" almost unconsciously in response to the explicit and implicit assumptions embedded in language, institutions, common practices, role models, stereotypes, expectations, opportunities, and meanings that are widely produced and reproduced within a society. Through this "discursive authority,"[10] what counts as truth and reality in a given environment comes to seem natural, normal, and inevitable to the individuals formed in and by that environment. While these meanings are not monolithic, or even necessarily coherent, they profoundly influence our deepest feelings about what is real and true.

According to Linda LeMoncheck, we most value and define ourselves in terms of those capacities that distinguish us as human beings from objects and animals: the capacities for sentient life, self-awareness, abstract thought, moral judgment, aesthetic discernment, and, perhaps most importantly, the capacity for self-determination.[11] Yet, are these assumptions about what makes us human equally applicable to men and to women? To treat a woman as "fully human" would require that she be viewed as having the same capacities and rights to self-development and autonomy as any other person—that is, any man—and that she be treated in ways that do not violate those rights.[12] Is this what we learn that it means to be a woman? The dominant discourses shaping our assumptions about gendered identities commonly presuppose a dualism in which masculine and feminine traits are contrasted:[13]

MASCULINE/FEMININE
active/passive
mind/body
rational/emotional
independent/dependent
dominant/subordinate
objective/subjective
judging/nurturing
strong/weak
logical/intuitive
competitive/cooperative
risk-taking/safety seeking
self-interested/self-sacrificing
controlling/supporting
assertive/deferential
achievement oriented/relationship oriented
culture/nature

According to this familiar dualism, the human characteristics we most value we attribute to masculinity, and we define femininity as its opposite. The male is the paradigmatic human, the generic human, and masculinity is the norm. The female is the deviant human, the specific human, and femininity is whatever masculinity is not. This negative mode of defining femininity prompts Sarah Hoagland's wry observation that the male/female dualism isn't a dualism at all. It is a monism.[14] The male is human. The female is "other."

But the female is a particular kind of other, an "accommodating" other whose very difference is required to compliment and complement what it means to be a male. Femininity is an agreement that the female will absent herself from the world of male prerogatives, power, and freedom. Hers is a "constitutive absence."[15] Of course, any identity as rigidly formulated as our familiar male/female dualism injures those upon whom it is imposed, simply because it represses individuality and authenticity by limiting the acceptable ways a person can be. The feminine stereotype poses further threats, however, because it discourages women from developing the most valued human potentials, and because femininity undermines autonomy. Feminine socialization is in the direction of childishness, passivity, and acquiescence. Sandra Bartky likens the outcome for women to cultural domination, but women are not an overthrown culture with another culture of their own with which they might identify. The culture of men is women's only culture.[16] While we might challenge Bartky, pointing out ingenious ways that women have developed women-centered subcultures,[17] they have had limited influence on the dominant discourses through which our subjectivities are formed, and so they have not subverted our dominant images of femininity. Our socialization, therefore, encourages identification with the male culture[18] that has defined the feminine—with women's "enforced absence"—to serve itself.[19] To be feminine might vary in specific content, but throughout patriarchy it has been defined in terms of what men want women to be.

Socialization and the Formation of Feminine Identity

It is important to note, however, that empirical research does *not* support our assumption that these stereotypical masculine and feminine differences are natural, that is, innate, biologically based characteristics or tendencies determined by sex.[20] Nevertheless, the dominant discourses shape our assumptions, leading us to accept such stereotypical gender differences as true and meaningful, to notice what counts as evidence, to discount or ignore counterevidence, and to conform our own attitudes and behaviors to them to a considerable degree.[21] Of course, we all experience ourselves in ways that differ from the dominant discourses. Yet because we often interpret such experiences as idiosyncratic and exceptional, they seldom undermine the power or pervasiveness of our shared gender assumptions. Such experiences, however, can serve as evidence for the artificiality of our gender stereotypes and a resource for alternative conceptions of the self.

The dominant discourses exert considerable ideological power because we internalize them and because the sanctions attached to them suggest that masculine and feminine are not negotiable. The meanings of femininity in the dominant discourses are the meanings given to females with which to make sense of ourselves and our experiences.[22] These meanings are continually reaffirmed because they pervade our culture, reinforcing the discourses and re-creating us in their image through our participation. The discourses offer us ways of being and modes of psychic and emotional satisfaction we learn to enjoy. They are effective because they are made real in the satisfactions available to us as women in marriage, family life, law, religion, educational institutions, the workplace, and the stereotypical representations of our selves and our lives that are on constant display.[23] We are affirmed and rewarded for conformity to the dominant discourses, and rejected, punished, or treated as suspect for deviation, shaping our desire in pursuit of the modes of satisfaction that are made available to us. What counts as meaningful in our shared definitions of feminine, then, comes to feel good to us as women (e.g., we enjoy adorning ourselves decoratively in order to attract men), and those things that are not feminine fill us with anxiety and threat (e.g., we fear success, or at least we are told that we do). The point is that *the power of discourses must be understood in terms of the power to shape our own desire. This is the meaning of internalization, and this is the power of reward, felt as pleasure.*

Thus all women, to some extent, internalize society's definitions of femininity and judge themselves according to those definitions, definitions designed to accommodate men and to earn male approval. But women do not experience this standard of judgment to be anything other than their own, since it has been internalized, and its yearnings speak to each woman in her own voice. A perusal of women's fashion magazines provides revealing evidence. These magazines are about women and for women, and they self-consciously intend to sell women femininity. And what does femininity look like in women's magazines? Examine the photographs and ask: Whose gaze is presupposed here? Why are these models so flirty, so seductive, so naughty, so orgasmic, so . . . well, so nude so much of the time? For whose eye do these models dress up . . . dress down . . . dress off? The answer is obvious—for the male connoisseur that we women have internalized as our own standard of judgment. The publishers know something about us that we seldom realize about ourselves: we see ourselves, not from our own point of view, but from our understanding of what men want us to be. Those male standards have become our own opinions about what it means to be a woman. The female model speaks to the female reader about being feminine in a single shared vocabulary: the language of male desire. Still skeptical? Consider this: according to a recent CBS news report, more than 80 percent of all models in women's fashion magazines—not *Playboy*, but women's fashion magazines—have breast implants. Why?

The Accommodating Other as Sexual Object

Throughout patriarchal history, the accommodating role most valued for women was that of legitimate wife and mother, which necessitated men's control of women's bodies to assure paternity and the shaping of women's identities and desires to live within and serve the patriarchal family. This remains a powerful core meaning of femininity, but a new mode of accommodation has emerged idealizing the feminine as sex object. This explains the ease with which Madonna single-handedly turned the bra into outerwear. Female beauty is now defined primarily in terms of sexual attractiveness and availability. The current fashion of wearing underwear in public does the job nicely, encouraging women to present themselves as already almost undressed. Today, cultural presentations of feminine beauty are dominated by images of sexual display, especially in popular entertainment and other discourses aimed at young women (and men). Female desire, then, is formed to serve male desire.[24] So now I know whose gaze is presupposed in those women's magazines: those models are flirting with me, they take off their clothes for me, they have breast implants for me . . . so that I can identify with them and feel beautiful, that is, sexually attractive to men.

Since sexuality has often been socially repressed, some view this new sexuality permitted to women as a sign of their increased freedom and self-expression. Biddy Martin, however, warns that feminine sexuality is not being "permitted" at all. It is being produced and expanded, used to gain access to women and exert control, not through prohibition, which we would surely notice, but through "normalization," which is invisible. It is control nonetheless, exerted by equating our social value with our sexual attractiveness. Our own cooperation with the increasing sexualization of ourselves allows for a regulation of desire toward particular social and political ends.[25] What looks like sexual freedom, then, functions primarily to increase men's access to women's bodies. Without analysis of what sexuality means, how it came to have those meanings, and whom it serves, more sexuality is not a radical departure from the status quo. It may be a new mode of accommodation, but it is accommodation all the same. As Mariana Valverde observes, "Sexual objectification . . . brings into graphic relief a woman's social status as subordinated, other-defined object for man, the defining subject."[26] The sexualized feminine ideal does not present woman as a subject who is sexual; rather it presents women's sexuality as an object for men. It reduces a woman to a body, a body part, a thing that willingly makes itself available to be used by another, thereby demeaning, diminishing, and fragmenting the female self.

There is a double bind emerging here that needs to be acknowledged: the feminine ideal that women are encouraged to pursue is also an ideal that elicits disdain. Certainly no single word more immediately evokes that feminine ideal than the word "blonde." She's beautiful, right? (How do you drown a blonde? Put a mirror at the bottom of the pool.) Well, yes, she is a little dumb. (What do you call an intelligent blonde? A golden retriever.) But boy, is she sexy. (What's a blonde's favorite pair of earrings? Her shoes.) Man, is she SEXY! (What's the mating call of a blonde? Boy, am I drunk.) She's so sexy, it's disgusting! (What's the difference between a bowling ball and a blonde? You can only get three fingers in a bowling ball.) Yes, she's so sexy, *she's* disgusting . . . and stupid, and vain, and irresistibly exploitable.

Blonde jokes reveal a sad truth. The ideally feminine sexual object is often, even to men, perhaps especially to men, laughable. It is an ideal that we are told men chase, reward, and fantasize about. We, as women, are told to chase her too. But the joke is on us. This ideal of femininity encourages us to be childish, vain, witless, sexually available, and vulnerable, unable to distinguish between rape and a good time. It is an ideal women are rewarded for pursuing and disdained for attaining. It is an ideal that accommodates male power, expands men's access to women, and legitimates their contempt for women.

Of course, the new image of masculinity that such femininity accommodates is also disparaging, depicting men as sexual predators, opportunists, exploiters. This reflects no better on men than sexual objectification reflects on women, but there is a difference. While such an image of men is problematic, it does not make them seem pitiful or laughable. In fact, such behavior often elicits envy and respect. Even when it is criticized, it seldom brings down on men as a group the contempt often expressed toward women.

Such contempt is not new. As Beverly Harrison has noted, "the practice of male supremacy over time breeds real hostility to women."[27] Blonde jokes are just a current way to express that hostility, a far more trivial way than the increased violence against women that is socially accepted and even eroticized as entertainment. Hostility is also expressed in romanticizing and rewarding passive, unassertive women and in labeling as "unfeminine" assertive, competent women. And it is not only men who express hostility toward women. Women, too, cooperate with misogyny in their lack of value for themselves or other women.[28] Our assumptions about femininity deprive women of the qualities we value as most fully human, and often reduce them to usable objects. It should not surprise us to discover that men and women alike display contempt, even when they endorse feminine stereotypes.

A Challenge

My point here is *not* that women are formed absolutely by the dominant discourses that define femininity, nor am I arguing that there are no alternatives to femininity as the "accommodating other." I am making the following argument: (1) The dominant discourses in our culture have attributed to masculinity the human potentials that we most value. Femininity has been defined as the dualized other, functioning to accommodate prerogatives of masculinity. (2) Because of the formative power of those discourses, some degree of internalization of those shared assumptions is inevitable for all of us, whether or not we consciously choose them. (3) In addition to what we learn from our culture about masculinity and femininity, we each experience ourselves in ways that refute those definitions and challenge their discursive authority, offering grounds for resistance and resources for alternative definitions and satisfactions. (4) The rewards for complicity are seductive and can make conformity pleasurable, even seemingly irresistible. Likewise, the punishments for deviation can be cruel and dangerous, making resistance difficult, even seemingly impossible.

Yet we all, male and female, have both responsibilities and opportunities to resist the dominant discourses that define femininity as the "accommodating other," making it possible to conceive of and experience ourselves more broadly, respectfully, and fairly. Why and how should we respond to this challenge?

We should reject the dominant stereotype for femininity, first, because it does not tell the truth about women any more than masculinity tells the truth about men. Empirical research refutes those stereotypes, as do our own subjectivities, which seldom conform as nearly as we assume or pretend. Further, the "truth" that the stereotype of femininity tells deprives women of full humanity and then makes that fact neutral. With the help of patriarchal religion, that fact is made sacred. James Poling points to the complicity of Christianity in maintaining dualistic definitions of women, perpetuating the exclusion of women, and legitimating male authority over women. A moralistic preoccupation with sexual fidelity (primarily of women) and heterosexuality has obscured Christianity's impotent critique of sexism and sexual violence as well as racism and homophobia.[29] Carter Heyward describes sexual justice as the most trivialized, feared, and postponed dimension of social justice.[30] Men, too, are affected. For all the social power and value that masculinity can bestow upon men, it cannot make them "whole" as long as dualized gender definitions lead them to disparage and reject in their own selves all human characteristics tainted with feminine associations. They, too, suffer from brokenness and have much to gain.

How might we initiate such a challenge? First, through the willingness to acknowledge our own complicity in endorsing stereotypical meanings of femininity (and masculinity). The question of blame usually arises about now, effectively subverting further constructive efforts. But, hey, there's plenty of blame to go around. Let's share it. Whether it is comfortable to acknowledge or not, it is obvious that men benefit from the socialization of women to be feminine. Training in masculinity prepares men to assume their power and privilege, to "dominate women and men of lower classes or races in a 'natural' way without self-reflection or guilt."[31] And privileged women, who have access to the most resources with which to resist feminine stereotypes, often succumb the quickest, unable to turn away from the rewards of sharing in the privileges of the men of their class. For these, and smaller rewards of even momentary male approval, women can be shockingly eager to identify with men and affirm the dynamics and rewards of masculinity/femininity. Rather than arguing over guilt, let's simply acknowledge that the individual is never innocent.[32]

Reflecting on complicity requires us to turn our attention to the ways we invest our time, energy, and money in the dominant discourses of masculine/feminine. These are so numerous, so subtle, so unconscious, that awareness itself takes both critical and creative efforts. We need to recognize the rewards for our complicity. We need to acknowledge the damage it does to us. Most importantly, we need to name its pleasures. The goal, according to Valverde, is to "transform desire itself, by seizing the social and cultural forces which create and shape our innermost passions."[33] We must begin exploring the pleasures we have learned to feel through domination, if we are men, through subordination, if we are women, and realize that such pleasures, though really felt—in the body, in the heart—are as constricting as the stereotypes that eroticize them. This is why the attraction with which traditional heterosexual relationships begin tends to increase inequality, enhancing men's power and diminishing women's.[34] What is felt as attraction is the pleasure we have learned to feel in male power and female accommodation. And the love that grows there is constricted too, as Letty Pogrebin's distinction between love and friendship reveals: "Gender hierarchies are not conducive to friendship. Sex can flourish between unequals, and love can thrive . . . but friendship requires equality. Unlike love, it cannot be unilateral. . . . Unlike sex it cannot be imposed. Friendship must be mutual."[35] It is disturbing to acknowledge that our stereotypical gender identities make friendship difficult between men and women. This does sound like our notion of heterosexual love, but it doesn't sound like intimacy, and we must finally ask, is it adequate as pleasure?

Just as our own lives and subjectivities reveal selves that are not limited to masculine and feminine stereotypes, our capacity for passion is not limited to the pleasures made available for us in masculine and feminine roles. It is these more whole and authentic selves and their passions we must explore in search of alternatives. But how to begin?

In this time of "deferred" sexual justice, we should not assume that the customary gender inequalities are neutral or inevitable.[36] Nor should we assume that the excesses of our current definitions of masculine/feminine are the only problem and that the solution lies in retreating to more traditional (less sexualized) definitions. *Whatever veneer femininity has been given in particular times and places, it is the consistent practice of defining only the male as the fully human and the female as the accommodating other that we must resist.*

Perhaps any definitions of masculinity and femininity are vulnerable to being used in ways that distort and restrict our humanity. Perhaps the problem must be solved in terms of the underlying meanings of "right order" that have informed masculine/feminine. The Western tradition, relying heavily upon Christianity for religious legitimation, has envisioned gender relationships in terms of dominance/subordination. The sacred model of right relationship between God and humanity became the obligatory model of relationship between man and woman. But for many, the assumption that man is to woman as God is to humanity has become increasingly uncomfortable, and the consequences for ascribing unequal nature, power, and value to men and women, increasingly indefensible.

How might right relationship be reenvisioned to affirm the full humanity of women and men alike, and avoid assuming or imposing stereotypical assumptions about the meaning of maleness and femaleness? What kind of a model of relatedness can we believe in and learn to desire? What kind of a model can make a safe and comfortable place for all of us; nurture our responsibilities to our partners, our children, ourselves; cultivate our capacities for trust, intimacy, and pleasure; sustain us through suffering?

To reenvision right order in a way that assures we resist our often unconscious tendencies toward dominance/subordination, Mary Hunt argues that our priority must be justice until equality is reached.[37] But can justice in pursuit of equality be felt as a passion? Can we learn to feel desire in mutuality? In contrast to heterosexual relationships that begin in attraction and increase inequality, Hunt offers as a model women's friendships, which begin in equality and move toward deeper unity.[38] Equality as a goal can help us resist dynamics of dominance and subordination as well as dualistic assumptions about gender identities and roles. And friendship as a standard can help us redefine right relationship. Hunt defines friendship as "voluntary human relationships that are entered into by people who intend one another's well-being and who intend that their love relationship is part of a justice seeking community."[39]

Rather than modeling all relationships on the heterosexual pattern of dominance/subordination, Hunt's model could dignify and enrich heterosexual relationships by cultivating in partners the commitments of friendship toward each other and toward their children and their communities. While Hunt acknowledges that historically the Christian tradition has had little to say about friendship, it is an appropriate subject for theological and ethical reflection in a tradition based upon the imperative to love one another.[40] And surely the ideal of love is more meaningfully evoked by partnership of equals seeking ever greater unity than by the dynamic of dominance and subordination justified by and maintaining inequality. Unity as an ideal is appropriate in all kinds of friendships and can expand our understanding of heterosexual relationships to include the richness of them all. Such unity is experienced as affirmation between friends, empowerment between compatriots, comfort and safety between parent and child, rapture between lovers. Surely here is a starting place to reshape our innermost passions in service of not only more honest and humane selves and relationships, but more just selves and relationships.

NOTES

1. Although our stereotypes for femininity vary (from voluptuous Marilyn Monroe to waiflike Kate Moss to athletic Cindy Crawford), they all present femininity to accommodate male desire. Male pleasure and ideals of femininity are manipulated and changed over time, but the construction of femininity as "accommodating other" is the consistent feature of our ideals. To focus on that, I refer to the feminine stereotype in the singular.

2. See bell hooks, *Feminist Theory* (Boston: South End Press, 1984) and Alison Jaggar, *Gender/Body/Knowledge* (New Brunswick, N.J.: Rutgers University Press, 1989), 145–71.

3. This is not to suggest that stereotypes impact all "excluded" people similarly. Sometimes those least represented in stereotypes conform to them in exaggerated ways, while others reject them and struggle to be self-defining, as both hooks and Jaggar note.

4. See Gerda Lerner, *The Creation of Patriarchy* (New York: Oxford University Press, 1986), or Marilyn French, *Beyond Power* (New York: Ballantine, 1986).

5. Lerner, *Creation of Patriarchy,* 199.

6. Rosemary Ruether, *New Women, New Earth* (San Francisco: Harper & Row, 1975), 13–15.

7. Rosemary Ruether, *Sexism and God-Talk* (Boston: Beacon Press, 1983), 95.

8. Ruether, *Sexism,* 94–99.

9. Lerner, *Creation of Patriarchy,* 211.

10. Chris Weedon, *Feminist Practice and Poststructuralist Theory* (New York: Basil Blackwell Publisher, 1987), 98.

11. Linda LeMoncheck, *Dehumanizing Women* (Totowa, N.J.: Rowman & Allanheld, 1985), 16–24.

12. Ibid., 24.

13. See Bernice Lott, "Dual Natures of Learned Behavior," in *Making a*

Difference, ed. Rachel Hare-Mustin and Jeanne Marecek, 65–102 (New Haven, Conn.: Yale University Press, 1990).

14. Sarah Hoagland, "Introduction," in Julia Penelope's, *Call Me Lesbian* (Freedom, Calif.: The Crossing Press, 1992), xii. See also Penelope, *Call Me Lesbian,* 78–88.

15. Biddy Martin, "Feminism, Criticism, and Foucault," in *Feminism and Foucault,* ed. Irene Diamond and Lee Quinby (Boston: Northeastern University Press, 1988), 16.

16. Sandra L. Bartky, *Femininity and Domination,* 22–32 (New York: Routledge Press, 1990).

17. See Sarah Hoagland, *Lesbian Ethics* (Palo Alto, Calif.: Institute of Lesbian Studies, 1988), and Patricia Collins, *Black Feminist Thought* (London: Harper Collins Academic, 1990).

18. Bartky, *Femininity and Domination,* 561ff.

19. Winnifred Tomm, "Sexuality, Rationality and Spirituality," *Zygon* 25, no. 2 (June, 1990): 225–26.

20. See Carol Tavris, *The Mismeasure of Woman* (New York: Simon & Schuster, 1993).

21. E.g., we all "know" that females can't compete with males in math, right? Wrong. Other than the few gifted math students—among whom males out-perform females—females are slightly better in math than males at every grade level (including college). This research made *CBS News* and was reported by Dan Rather. But whom do you believe? Those researchers, or the first talking Barbie who whined in despair that math was too hard for her? Right!

22. Weedon, *Feminist Practice,* 30–31.

23. Ibid., 100.

24. Mariana Valverde, *Sex, Power and Pleasure* (Philadelphia: New Society Publishers, 1987), 158.

25. Martin, "Feminism," 8–11.

26. Valverde, *Sex, Power and Pleasure,* 138.

27. Beverly Harrison, *Making the Connections* (Boston: Beacon Press, 1985), 137.

28. Ibid., 137–38.

29. James Poling, *The Abuse of Power* (Nashville: Abingdon Press, 1991), 134–46.

30. Carter Heyward, *Touching Our Strength* (San Francisco: Harper & Row, 1989), 4.

31. Valverde, *Sex, Power and Pleasure,* 165.

32. Weedon, *Feminist Practice,* 92–97.

33. Valverde, *Sex, Power and Pleasure,* 176.

34. Mary Hunt, *Fierce Tenderness* (New York: Crossroad Press, 1992), 147.

35. Letty Cottin Pogrebin, "Hers," *New York Times,* Oct. 6, 1983, quoted by Hunt, *Fierce Tenderness,* 92.

36. Hunt, *Fierce Tenderness,* 170.

37. Ibid., 170.
38. Ibid., 100. Hunt's model is based on women's friendships, both sexual and nonsexual, but it is intended to apply to male-male and male-female relationships as well, and to extend beyond individual relationships to structure more just and committed communities.
39. Ibid., 29.
40. Ibid., 9.

10

DEFENDING THEIR PEOPLE AND THEIR EARTH: NATIVE AMERICAN MEN AND THE CONSTRUCTION OF MASCULINITY

Christopher Ronwaniente Jocks

High steel was my grandfather's way of life. For many years he was a foreman, well known and respected by other Mohawk ironworking men, judging from the stories I still hear about him. His name was Joseph Jocks, and he led crews that built bridges and skyscrapers from New York City to San Francisco to Alaska. In one of my earliest memories of him we are driving at week's end on old Route 9, from his and my grandmother's home in Brooklyn back to Kahnawà:ke, "at the rapids," our homeland on the St. Lawrence River, near Montreal. It is 1961, the trip takes ten or twelve hours, and I am seven years old. The two of us ride together in his two-seated Jaguar roadster. Bada, as my cousins called him, or Big Daddy, as my brothers and I did, was everything a young boy could want to emulate: physically strong, opinionated, but fun-loving too, with an air of recklessness and freedom. I cannot remember him ever diminishing himself to gain someone else's approval; he demanded, and invariably got, respect. His confidence and sense of self seemed impregnable. His life was full of adventures and conquests, faraway places, and dangerous work done with skill. At the same time on any matter involving family or future he sought out and heeded the advice of Margaret, his wife, whom we called Ista, "mother." This, when I was young, was my image of Mohawk men.

Sociologist Morris Freilich in 1958, and anthropologist David Blanchard in 1983, pointed out the direct descent of the ironworking way of life from that of Mohawk warriors and hunters even before the European invasion: in both cases men spend long months away from the home village; in the company of other men; led by temporary, self-chosen leaders; pursuing work that defied the inertia of comfort and security, and whose danger demanded alertness, mental and emotional conditioning, and of course, physical strength and agility.[1] Other similarities can be discerned as well. Since their travels took them to cities across the continent and abroad where they often lived for months or years at a time, Iroquois ironworkers developed a certain cosmopolitanism just as their wide-ranging forebears did, not only long ago as warriors, but in the interim as voyageurs for the French fur trade, riverboat pilots, and even as entertainers in turn-of-the-century Indian shows—although this last occupation often involved women and children as well. They were not easily intimidated. Beneath the bravado and independence, however, most of these men maintained strong ties with Kahnawà:ke, usually sending the bulk of their pay back to the homeland, and returning home themselves whenever they could. Thus the proud defiance by which the outside world most often knew them was actually employed in support of and in service to the wives and clan mothers back home.

This dynamic mix of independence and relationship is the subject of this chapter. It is a distinctive characteristic of Kahnawà:ke culture and history, and especially, the culture and history of Kahnawà:ke *men.* In the next section I will trace the roots of a few key ideas drawn from Longhouse cultural expression—"Longhouse" referring to the system of traditional knowledge and practice out of which Kahnawà:ke arose, and which it shares to a greater or lesser extent not only with the handful of other Mohawk communities, but with all the modern Iroquois people: the Mohawks, Oneidas, Onondagas, Cayugas, Senecas, and Tuscaroras. (I describe the Longhouse as a "system of traditional knowledge and practice," rather than simply "religion," even though it includes ceremonial, mythological, and other elements clearly religious in nature, because it so thoroughly integrates religious concerns with political, social, economic, and even scientific ones. Thus the Longhouse is indeed a religious tradition, but not in the same sense as most modern religions are.)

Next I will briefly describe and assess recent changes in the territory that have followed the decline of ironwork since the 1980s. Finally, I will discuss the significance of these and other Native North American struggles for all of us as men and women seeking to bring new life to the spiritual roots of masculine identity everywhere. From time to time I may refer to the experiences and expression and histories of other First Peoples, because there is much that American Indian people share, but I will deal primarily with Kahnawà:ke for the simple reason that I know it best, being a descendant and a student of its way of life.

This study has led me to conclude that of all that might be distinctive about the Native North American approach to the working or reworking of masculinity, one crucial moment is to be found in its confrontation with exclusionary dualism, that habit of thought and perception that reduces infinite gradations and complex relations into binary states. This confrontation provides a compelling illustration of a Longhouse understanding of the relationship between knowledge, action, community, and history—a complex of religious insights that can perform at least two functions: first, it may further explain American Indian rebukes of attempts to borrow, use, and otherwise appropriate their religious knowledge outside of its living context; and second, it makes an important contribution to the global discussion of what masculinity is, and ought to be, about.

Longhouse Roots

Euro-American intellectual history conditions academicians to distinguish religious "phenomena" from those of other cultural and historical domains such as politics, economics, or more recently, ecology, gender, and health. Longhouse tradition makes no such distinctions, or does so only on the surface and temporarily—for example, for reasons of diplomatic necessity. In all their internal deliberations and collective actions, the tradition teaches Longhouse people to work toward *ka'nikonhrí:io,* "a good mind," whose achievement demands the maintenance of peaceful, productive relations in all aspects of life. The repeated reference to *ka'nikonhrí:io* is found everywhere, throughout the several layers of Longhouse tradition, from the Creation cycle and the organizing work of Okwiráse, to the Kaianeren'kó:wa, sometimes known as the "Great Law" or the "Great Peace," the epic of the origin of the Iroquois confederation.[2] In all the doings of the Longhouse, whether for religious ceremony, political deliberation, or just to visit and enjoy one another's company, people are reminded to put on "a good mind."

"Mind," it is crucial to note, in the Longhouse world is definitely *not* the mind of Plato or Descartes. It does not distinguish between what Euro-American thought knows as cognitive and affective faculties; thought and emotion are not separated. Thus one dictionary of Mohawk translates the noun root *o'nikòn:ra* as "spirit, character, thought, opinion, mind, belief, intention, expectation, consciousness" and cites this root in the composition of words that translate into such diverse English concepts as "I am careful," "I am patient," "it is funny," "I am sad," "I worry about something," and "I console someone."[3] Therefore, when Longhouse people speak of "the good mind," they conceive not only of true or wholesome or edifying *thoughts,* but of an entire state of health that seamlessly encompasses spiritual, mental, and emotional dispositions.

This is readily and movingly apparent in the narrative of the grief of Aionwà:tha (more popularly known as "Hiawatha"), which relates the origin of the Condolence Ritual, an integral part of Longhouse political and religious culture. While Tekanawí:ta, the Peacemaker (also known as Deganawidah), is beginning to gather the nations under the Kaianeren'kó:wa, the Great Peace, Aionwà:tha suffers the death of all his children. No longer able to endure human company, he wanders alone in the forest, his mind covered in darkness. This is how a modern version of the story tells what happens next:

> The next morning, he found a place where the joined rushes grew. He made three strings out of the joined rush plant. He called this plant "Oseweneste." As he strung them, he put some words together saying, "If I found or met anyone burdened with grief as I am, I would console them. I would lift the words of condolence with these strands of beads, and these beads would become words with which I would address them."[4]

These three strung twigs become the prototype and the heart of the ritual known in English as "Wiping Their Tears," or "The Requickening." They serve to clear the obstructions of grief from the eyes, the ears, and the throat, respectively, of the person or the group in mourning, and are first used by the Peacemaker, according to the narrative, to remove the sorrow of Aionwà:tha. The importance of soothing distraught emotions is vividly illustrated in Gibson's version of the Condolence Ritual, which includes traditional speeches such as the following:

> Thus it happens, and it is dreadful what will happen to one: repeatedly it may fail, one's life, for repeatedly it gets clogged up, ones [*sic*] throat, with grief; that is what happened to you, it got clogged, your throat, with grief. . . . Now we will remove the grief-caused obstruction from your throats, our uncles, you chiefs of the Four Brothers, and then you will rejoice again, then it will improve, your breathing; your bodies will get strong again and also your mind. Thereupon you shall speak calmly. Thereupon we will thank one another. Moreover, in the time ahead, for at least one day, you shall think peacefully again.[5]

The dramatic climax of the Kaianeren'kó:wa occurs soon after the grief of Aionwà:tha is assuaged, enabling him to become "clear-minded" and thus to assist in the transformation of Atotárho, the last holdout against the Great Peace. Deformed by his alienation from humanity, Atotárho is portrayed as a cannibal, resisting and threatening all who would pacify him, yet all the while bellowing from the woods in a thunderous voice, "Is it not time yet?"[6] Finally, in one of the most moving passages in all of religious literature, Tekanawí:ta and the complete delegation gather around Atotárho with one mind proclaiming, "Now you are looking at all of the ones who will be standing with you."[7] He relents, the snakes are combed out of his hair, his thoughts are calmed, and his body is restored to human form. The lesson is clear: all effort should be made to bring back the alienated, employing solidarity and "a good mind." At times the Longhouse may even be extended—new positions created, as was done for Atotárho—to encourage and facilitate the return of such a one.

One further lesson: Atotárho's cry, "Is it not time yet?" seems to reveal that he already knows what is to happen, and in fact is impatient and eager for it to take place. He has the information, but information alone cannot effect his cure. Only the concerted *action* of the delegation can do that. It may sound almost blasphemous in this "information age," but information—knowledge in the sense of the accumulation of objectified "facts"—is not highly valued in the Longhouse world. Rather, what is valued is the ability, the skill and good-mindedness, to put knowledge into effect. "Walk your talk," I was told repeatedly by Longhouse men. "Knowing" the elements of a ceremony is useless unless one can enact that knowledge—rekindle it, in Longhouse metaphor. To extend the idea further, my present theory is that in the Longhouse world, knowledge becomes full only when it is enacted by an individual, who is always a member of some kind of community, and whose actions are thus always historically situated.

In summary, even this briefest glimpse of a small piece of traditional Longhouse narrative and practice reveals the following set of proposals:[8]

1. Longhouse life aims at cultivating "a good mind": a conjunction of individual and collective well-being characterized by a complete array of healthy relationships. These posit a community that extends kinship, in principle, not only to all *onkwehón:we* ("real human beings"), but beyond, to other-than-human beings, including those beings of extraordinary power whose deeds are told in mythic narrative.

2. Longhouse thought does not separate mind and emotions. It does not typify the former as rational, exalted, and male; nor the latter as irrational, problematic, and female. It understands the phenomenal or natural world as organically and relationally ordered, and thus, the original seedbed of human understanding.

3. When conflict and alienation occur, it is better to persuade, to heal, and if possible to accommodate, than to attack and excise.

4. Knowledge is not valued for its own sake, but only insofar as one has the skill to enact it, and to direct it toward good-mindedness.

5. Knowledge is enacted by individuals, but individuals act necessarily in a matrix of community and history.

Details of the Longhouse way of life at the time the Kaianeren'kó:wa originated are only partially known. The European invasion, missionization, modernity, and the intrusion of various U.S. and Canadian policies have taken their toll. I have not even mentioned the nineteenth-century reworking of Longhouse tradition known as the Handsome Lake Code. It is my contention, however, that the key tenets listed above continue to exert strong influence at Kahnawà:ke and other Longhouse communities—even among those who have embraced Catholicism or for other reasons no longer identify themselves as Longhouse traditionalists or participate in Longhouse "doings."

Return to Kahnawà:ke

As it turns out, there was little chance for me to follow my grandfather's example of Mohawk manhood. My father spent more than twenty years in the U.S. military, and in the days of that Jaguar summer of 1961, when perhaps two-thirds of the men of Kahnawà:ke were ironworkers, my family was only visiting, stopping off between his former assignment in Alaska and his new one in Southern California. I came to maturity in the Southwest, shaped by a very different environment, and although I returned to Kahnawà:ke for brief visits once I was on my own, it would be thirty years before I started going back more often and staying longer, needing to learn more about the place, its people, and my connections to them. By then much had changed. In a tight and overbuilt economy most ironworking jobs simply vanished. My grandfather had retired, but like many of his generation, he was ill equipped for the small world of village life after a life of high steel work. He settled into leisure awkwardly for a few years, then followed Ista up to the Sky World.

For Kahnawa'kehró:non today, the decline of ironwork has merely intensified pressure that has been building for more than a hundred years, since the Canadian government began intruding in and dictating their affairs: pressure to give up their distinct identity and ways. Surrounded by a larger Quebecois population and culture with which they had a long history of mutual antagonism and alienation; surrounded even more vividly and concretely by the St. Lawrence Seaway, for the construction of which they had been unable to block Canada from taking one-tenth of their small territory (now about twelve thousand acres), they have more reason than ever to look primarily to their own resourcefulness to find solutions to these new difficulties.

It will not be easy. The community continues to suffer old divisions between Catholics, Protestants, and Longhouse followers, and between those who support and those who reject the imposed Band Council government. Now there are deep divisions even among those who identify themselves as traditional, or Longhouse. Three separate Longhouse groups meet at Kahnawà:ke, each with a different understanding of the tradition. One of these groups, by far the largest, is allied with the

Warrior Society, whose men and women showed such defiance in defense of their relatives and territories during the 1990 "Oka Crisis."[9] A strong proportion of Kahnawà:ke's young people readily identify with them, yet the *rotiiáner,* the "chiefs" of the traditional Longhouse confederation, along with portions of the community at Kahnawà:ke, have repudiated the Warriors for their promotion of gaming and other controversial enterprises, their reliance on intimidation even against members of their own communities who oppose them, and their rejection of the chiefs' authority. So there is argument as men and women strive to understand their common identity even while fending off antagonistic external political and economic initiatives.

At the same time, any study of Iroquois history will demonstrate that such conflict is not new. Like all traditions of peace, this one may always have been more an ideal than a reality. The tension between warriors and "peace chiefs" has been especially endemic, forming the backdrop of the Kaianeren'kó:wa, thus predating the invasion from Europe. But this conflict especially implicates men, and so the distinct features of the response framed in the Kaianeren'kó:wa and elsewhere in Longhouse tradition, some of which I have tried to outline, should call it to our attention.

Thunder and Drums

Fifty years ago Ira Hays, Pima warrior, helped raise the flag of the United States over Iwo Jima. Back home he returned to an older war. Traditionally his people, living across the continent from the Iroquois, made a gentle brew from the century plant, which they drank together with song and ceremony to bring down the rain, joking together, happy and quiet under the gathering clouds. Now the interstate traffic roars by, and it is easy to think the clouds might not hear very well. When they do bring the rain, far off over the mountains, the men with investments to protect, golf courses and swimming pools and suits to pay off, are there with big elbows to make sure they have enough. Ira Hays tried harder to bring down the rain, but all that drinking burned him up inside, a warrior till the end. *Every American Indian man is a warrior.* When he gives to his relations rather than saving up for that new techno-toy; when he jokes in his Native language and refuses to mimic the market-tested phrases of movies and sitcoms and commercials; when he gazes lovingly at the land that claims him, tending and protecting the Ones who tend and protect him; and yes, even sometimes when he drinks himself to death, he is doing what he can to defend himself, and through himself, his people. Whatever he manages to heave into the hungry maw of consumerism—old hulks of Indian cars, dead juniper trees, washing machines, and sometimes himself—to block it up, hoping to weaken it and so keep some of his nephews and nieces and children and grandchildren from falling defenselessly into it, all of this makes him a warrior. It also makes him, in the noninstitutional sense of the word, religious.

On the other side of the river, in the suburbs of Phoenix and other urban centers, some men pursue a different kind of religious work. From the safety of their armchairs and retreat centers, modern Euro-American men hunt down completeness lost or damaged. They seek to uncover the "warrior within"—a knight, perhaps an Indian. For what is missing some blame their mothers or wives, or themselves for cleaving too closely to them, but perhaps their need includes something simpler: a longing for a time when the world was not so *safe*—or rather, when the dangers of life were visceral and immediate, met in a field between thundering sky and thundering hooves, rather than by accountants in fluorescent-lit conference rooms. Perhaps they long, too, for work with a sacred charge: the knight's divine pledge, the Dog Soldier's sacrifice, staked to the ground, for "all my relations." At the end of the twentieth century, modern men seek to be "EarthKnights," to protect and heal a stricken planet. Books such as Sam Keen's *Fire in the Belly: On Being a Man,* and the series by Robert Moore and Douglas Gillette, including such titles as *The Warrior Within: Accessing the Knight in the Male Psyche,* attempt to chart this complex transition into new, and their promoters hope healthier, forms of masculinity.

As it turns out, these two movements, of modern North American men working toward a new masculinity and American Indian men working to keep their communities alive, are intimately related. In their quest for a new masculinity Euro-American men search for models outside the modern intellectual tradition, sometimes looking back to pre-Enlightenment Europe, sometimes looking beyond Europe to Africa, Asia, or Native America. From an American Indian's perspective, the results rarely seem to go beyond either wistful gestures of belated but fatuous respect, or worse, profoundly disrespectful and haphazard appropriations of Native American ceremonial procedures and instruments. All the while, the same masculinity Euro-American men seek to revise is deeply implicated in the *ongoing* five-hundred-year campaign against which First Peoples continue to struggle, yet to which they have also had necessarily to adapt. Indian men are thus engaged on two fronts: redefining or revitalizing a traditional masculine identity within besieged communities on the one hand, while fighting off relentless pressures to assimilate, to be swallowed up by postmodernity, on the other.

If this man of half Kanien'kehá:ka ("people of the flint place," the name by which "Mohawk" people designate themselves in their own language, thus rooting themselves in their original homeland in the flinty lands from the Adirondacks south to the Mohawk River) and half Irish-German-American descent could offer anything to the project of Euro-American men to refashion masculinity, it would be to urge consideration of the following, drawn from my understanding of a small portion of Longhouse tradition, abstracted above, as well as what I have learned and experienced of other Indigenous North American ways of life.

Reject All Forms of Appropriation

Native North American spiritual knowledge or practice that can be bought and sold by strangers is inauthenticated by its very alienation from the originating community. To copy or imitate it is to reject the beliefs that underlie it. The *only* way to participate legitimately in American Indian ceremonial life is to become a member of an American Indian community. That's the only way it works. Not surprisingly, this usually means being related by blood or marriage, but the point has to do with kinship, shared history, and shared ecology—not biology. Every Indian community I know of has full-bloods who have forgotten the meaning of kinship, and at least one or two non-Indians who have achieved and maintained it.

Reconsider Epistemology

In his 1994 book *Unreasonable Men*, Victor J. Seidler exhaustively analyzes the Enlightenment formulation of reason, its association with masculinity and hegemony, and the consequent alienation of men from nature, emotion, and women. Seidler writes that as long as this formulation has been around, it has been met with the rebellion of romanticism, yet its most fundamental premise often remains unchallenged:

> If we are to escape from the terms of discussion as they were set by the Enlightenment, namely between rationalist objectivism on the one hand and a pluralistic relativism on the other, then we have to look more carefully at the ways reason was conceptualized. This questions the terms in which the discussions about modernity and post-modernity are usually set. Rather than focusing upon a distinction between a unified Cartesian conception of reason and a fragmented pluralistic vision of diverse reasons and rationalities, we begin to investigate some of the implications of reason being set in opposition to nature.[10]

The Longhouse tradition provides but one example of an alternative, drawn from a North American context. In it, as I have tried to show, there is no opposition between reason, masculinity, and culture, on the one hand, and emotion, femininity, and nature, on the other. In fact nature is the primary ground for human knowledge, since it is understood as organically and relationally ordered. But this is not enough, for knowledge itself is conceived differently. Rather than a disembodied object unaffected and unchanged by any means or intention under which it is encoded, transmitted, used, bought, or sold, in the Longhouse world knowledge is comprehended holistically. It is fully knowledge only when it is acted out in a full context of intention, history, and thus, responsibility. The transmission of knowledge inescapably creates ethical valence, which is why traditional knowledge is understood as a sacred trust. It is also why offhand or recreational appropriation of such knowledge, as if it were merely another trendy meditation fad, is so deeply offensive to traditional people.

Retrain Judgment and Perception

We assume that the training of a warrior requires him quickly and unambiguously to distinguish enemy from ally, and to ignore the infinite gradations of culpability within all of us—the unmeasurable complexity of associations and motivations that inform our every act. This ability to reduce overwhelming complexity to a binary judgment, essential in small ways to everyday life, seems to have taken deep root in postmodern Euro-American culture. As trivial details proliferate and dominate our lives, we habitually simplify; we learn to avoid complexity. Business, politics, science, even recreation and personal relationships, take on the rhetoric of war. But the more we look for binary solutions to complex situations, the less we are able to think creatively, to reformulate the question. Atotárho simply becomes an obstacle. Eradicate him. Under such habits of thought the "Great Peace" stagnates.

Emphasize Kinship

Both Keen's *Fire in the Belly* and Moore and Gillette's *The Warrior Within* propose that the new Warrior dedicate himself not to tribe or nation but to the healing of the planet. He is to be an "EarthKnight," channeling ardor and aggression into the defense of nature. But from my perspective as an American Indian man, a word of caution ought to be sounded. Defense of an abstract Earth, devoid of living kinship relations, might easily become a foil for all manner of ugliness. Keen reveals as much in his profound misunderstanding of small-scale societies:

> When living within the seasons of nature, hunters, gatherers, and farmers were compulsively conservative. Their myths had a single subtext: Do everything the way it has always been done; don't innovate; repeat the patterns of nature. Early tribal and agricultural societies were relatively harmonious because of their emphasis on conformity and continuity.

Within tribal societies everyone knew his place, but individuality was not encouraged. It took the notion of a God who transcended the order of nature, whose power created and controlled nature, to provide the social sanction for the development of individualism.[11]

Moore and Gillette, too, write of defending our "ecological habitat," and "global networking" to preserve "a viable and humane planetary community" without a word about kinship.[12] By contrast, I would assert that Longhouse thought and practice, and that of other First Peoples as well, begins by observing and understanding relationships among other-than-human beings as embodying the original patterns for our kinship community. Through ceremony, we continue to extend and maintain these kinship relations. *We learn from them.* Without their help and inspiration we would be lost. I doubt that Indian people have any use for "Earth-Knights" who wall themselves off from these relations, who think they know or will soon know everything, including how to "save the planet." In the long run this is probably the greatest difference between the training of modern or postmodern Warriors, as envisioned by these authors, and the training of traditional warriors among First Peoples.

The kinship imperative applies equally to men's relationships with women. An important subtext within much of today's men's movement involves achieving a warrior's ferocity and masculinity by *defying Mother.* Jungian psychology lauds this sentiment, much of romantic European literature typifies it, and, since Robert Bly, an entire workshop industry has proliferated based on it. Postmodern men are told that we have all become too mixed up with our mothers, lovers, wives—too compromised and entangled by postmodern socialization that teaches us to feel guilty for the abuses of patriarchy.

On first glance gender relations in Longhouse and other Native American traditions seem to support this sentiment further, because they do cultivate a strong sense of gendered identity. Although certain individuals may cross gender lines or embody other gender alternatives, the basic tenet is that men and women are not the same. In his study of Kahnawà:ke ironworking, David Blanchard describes entrance into that profession as a male initiation ritual in which a young man usually must indeed defy the objections of his mother or aunts. Blanchard further asserts that men choose such a life not in spite of the fact that it keeps them away from their families for months at a time, but because of it. He describes physical separation of men and women as an Iroquois cultural imperative, writing that "for the Mohawk, men and women each possess a distinct kind of power," and that "when this power is active, that is to say, during the years of fertility and sexual potency, men and women must not spend a great deal of time together, or their powers will become 'mixed up.'"[13]

As attractive and satisfying as such an idea might be to some men, I would counter that it is only partially accurate. Longhouse men indeed value work and other activities they do as men, with other men, and in most Longhouse ceremonies men and women sit separately. But traditionally raised Longhouse men also value occasions set aside for exchange with their female relations. They maintain these kinship relations with women throughout their lives.

In the end, however, to ask American Indian men to provide answers or even suggestions for Euro-American men who continue to benefit materially from the exploitation of Indian land and people, yet in the process find themselves diminished in spirit or psyche, is surely asking too much. Let the destruction stop first. Begin to dismantle some of these devouring machines. Then we can clear the air—burn sage, cedar, and sweet grass—and sit down to smoke.

NOTES

1. Morris Freilich, "Cultural Persistence among the Modern Iroquois," *Anthropos* 53 (1958): 473–83; "Scientific Possibilities in Iroquoian Studies: An Example of Mohawks Past and Present," *Anthropologica* 5 (1963): 171–86; David Blanchard, "High Steel! The Kahnawake Mohawk and the High Construction Trade," *Journal of Ethnic Studies* 11 (1983): 41–60; Richard Hill, *Skywalkers: A History of Indian Ironworkers* (Brantford, Ontario: Woodland Indian Cultural Centre, 1987).

2. The most extensive written versions of the Longhouse Creation cycle are those collected by J.N.B. Hewitt, and published in two parts under the title *Iroquoian Cosmology* (Twenty-first and Forty-third Annual Reports of the United States Bureau of American Ethnology, published in 1903 and 1928, respectively). Although the two versions of the Kaianeren'kó:wa published by Arthur C. Parker in 1916 are still the most widely quoted—the so-called "Newhouse Version" long having been considered traditional by many at Kahnawà:ke—neither can compare in richness or breadth to the Onondaga text recited by John Arthur Gibson to the anthropologist Alexander A. Goldenweiser in 1912, now published in an outstanding translation by Hanni Woodbury, with her excellent introduction under the title, *Concerning the League: The Iroquois League Tradition as Dictated by John Arthur Gibson*, Memoir 9, Algonquian and Iroquoian Linguistics (Syracuse: Syracuse University Press, distributed for Algonquian and Iroquoian Linguistics, University of Manitoba, 1912/1993).

3. David R. Maracle, *Iontewennaweienhstáhkwa': Mohawk Language Dictionary* (Belleville, Ontario: Mika Publishing Co., 1990), 224.

4. *Traditional Teachings* (Cornwall, Ontario: North American Indian Traveling College, 1984), 24.

5. Gibson, *Concerning the League,* 616–17.

6. This is Woodbury's translation of Gibson's Onondaga phrase "áhson khén nén:."

7. Gibson, *Concerning the League,* 233.

8. Drawing on my recent dissertation, "Relationship Structures in Longhouse Tradition at Kahnawà:ke" (Santa Barbara: University of California at Santa Barbara, 1994), I have extended some of these items beyond the brief discussion above. A more detailed treatment awaits further publication.

9. For vastly different accounts of that conflict, see Bruce Johansen, *Life and Death in Mohawk Country* (Golden, Colo.: North American Press, 1993), on the one hand, and Geoffrey York and Loreen Pindera, *People of the Pines: The Warriors and the Legacy of Oka* (Toronto: Little, Brown & Co., 1991), or Rick Hornung, *One Nation under the Gun: Inside the Mohawk Civil War* (Toronto: Stoddart, 1991), on the other.

10. Victor J. Seidler, *Unreasonable Men: Masculinity and Social Theory* (London: Routledge, 1994), 4.

11. Sam Keen, *Fire in the Belly: On Being a Man* (New York: Bantam, 1991), 96.

12. Robert Moore and Douglas Gillette, *The Warrior Within: Accessing the Knight in the Male Psyche* (New York: William Morrow & Co., 1992), 210.

13. Blanchard, "High Steel!" 56–57. Blanchard went so far as to assert that "men who spend more than an occasional weekend with their wives are not considered 'right in the head,'" despite the fact that many Kahnawà:ke ironworkers, including my grandfather, went to great lengths to take their families with them whenever possible to the cities where they worked.

11

OF MICE AND SUPERMEN:
IMAGES OF JEWISH MASCULINITY

Harry Brod

In this chapter I want to explore certain cultural images of Jewish men, focusing particularly on the dynamics of power and powerlessness and, closely related to this, of heroism and victimization. As one would expect in any analysis of masculinities, issues of violence and sexuality come to play pivotal roles here. I shall begin by examining some well-known images in popular culture, some of them not usually associated with Jewish themes, before turning to incorporate into the discussion depictions of Jewish men within the Jewish tradition. The first popular culture icon I shall discuss is paradigmatically non-Jewish, and one of the questions I shall pose is that of the relationship between representations of the quintessentially non-Jewish and the quintessentially Jewish man.

Heroism and Survival

My discussion starts with the work of two young Jewish men who lived in Cleveland, Ohio, during the Depression. They enjoyed reading the Sunday comic strips and decided to create a character of their own. Jerry Siegel and Joe Shuster tried to market this character but found no takers. Finally, somebody decided to accept this character and introduce him in a comic book. The character these two Jews created eventually made his debut on the cover of the first issue of *Action Comics* in June 1938, heralding the first appearance of Superman.[1]

We do not usually think of Superman, the first and still prototypical superhero, as a Jewish character. Nonetheless, I will argue that we should do so, the counterintuitiveness of such an idea notwithstanding. In fact, much of what I wish to explore is the question why it goes so much against the grain to imagine Superman as Jewish.

I am hardly the first to raise such a question. The cover of the August 4, 1992, issue of the *Village Voice* highlights a picture of Superman in his traditional pose leaping into the air, above which, in large red letters, is written "SuperJew!" The cover article's title is "Is Superman Jewish? The Chosen Heroes from the Golem to Alan Dershowitz's Book" (this being shortly after the publication of Dershowitz's *Chutzpah*). The title inside is "Up, Up and Oy Vey!"[2]

The author, Jeff Salamon, notes some stereotypically Jewish things about Superman. Kryptonians are superintelligent, and Superman's father, Jor-El, was a scientist. (I would add that in the Superman canon one never learns what his mother, Lara, actually did. Her role seems to be tearfully to watch baby Kal-El fly off to Earth in his rocket as the planet Krypton explodes around him.) As the sole survivor of his race, he lives in a permanent diaspora. Henry Louis Gates Jr. stresses this theme of Superman as an immigrant when he writes of "Superman, the hero from Ellis Island, personified as an (undocumented) alien who had been naturalized by the ultimate American couple, Eben and Sarah Kent."[3]

A striking puzzle arises regarding the relationship between Superman and his alter ego, Clark Kent. Perhaps the best way to explain the puzzle is to contrast Superman with another comic book hero, Batman. Batman's secret identity is Bruce Wayne, a real person who predates and grounds the Batman identity, which is a fictional creation. But with Superman, the matter is reversed. Superman is the real person. He really is a being from another planet. Clark Kent is the fiction. (Although he was raised by the Kents, he left his hometown and went to the big city where nobody knew him, so it is not clear why he needed to maintain this identity when he left Smallville for Metropolis.)[4] While Bruce Wayne certainly has to maintain fictitious elements of his character and prevaricate in order to preserve his secret identity, he does not create out of whole cloth a persona completely opposite to his real nature, as Clark's personality is to Superman's. The problem, then, is why Superman goes to such great lengths to preserve the Clark persona. And especially, why does he want Lois Lane to fall in love with Clark rather than with Superman? Why does he want Lois to fall in love with a lie?

An enlightening answer is given by another cartoonist in the Jewish tradition. In the Introduction to *The Great Comic Book Heroes,* Jules Feiffer writes that this is Superman's joke on the rest of us.[5] Clark is Superman's vision of what other men are really like. We are scared, incompetent, and powerless, particularly around women. Though Feiffer took the joke good-naturedly, a more cynical response would see here the Kryptonian's misanthropy: his misandry embodied in Clark and his misogyny in his wish that Lois be enamored of Clark (much as Oberon takes out his hostility toward Titania by having her fall in love with an ass in Shakespeare's *A Midsummer-Night's Dream*).

I wish at this point to call to mind some contemporary villains faced by popular heroes, villains who at first glance appear to be unconnected to Jewish issues, and then relate them to what I have already said. Shortly after the film *Batman Returns* appeared, an article in the *New York Times* called attention to the anti-Semitic stereotypes embedded in the film's villain, the Penguin.[6] He is an evil, ugly, greedy, conspiratorial, smelly, unkempt, ill-mannered, hook-nosed, claw-handed fishmonger out to rule the world and destroy Christmas. Consider this alongside other villainous characters from the *Star Wars* films. I quote from Paul Hoch's *White Hero, Black Beast: Racism, Sexism and the Mask of Masculinity:*

> Two other stereotypical dark beasts appear. The first, the 'filthy jawa' is a short, 'extraordinarily ugly,' 'rodent-like' and 'shrouded' being who 'scurries' about 'collecting and selling scrap . . . jabbering in low, gut-teral croaks and hisses' and giving off offensive odors. Such 'vermin' are 'disgusting creatures,' cringing 'hereditary cowards,' wandering 'mi-grants' whose 'covetous hands' produce nothing but try to pawn off inferior merchandise on the hard-working farmers who are their cus-tomers, while these underhand operators 'bow and whine with impa-tient greed.' Significantly, 'hygiene was unknown among the jawas,' for these 'travesties of men . . . had long since degenerated past anything resembling the human race.' The jawa is the only race in the entire book whose name is not capitalized throughout. Moreover, the chance of a two consonant name having just the two consonants "j" and "w" of the word Jew in precisely that order is only 21×20 (in fact less than one in a million if the extreme infrequency of these particular conso-nants in English usage is taken into account). The jawa is an anti-Semite's dream! The novel's other dark desert beasts are the Tuscan Raiders or Sandpeople: 'outrageous mahouts' who 'pursue a nomadic existence,' 'vicious desert bandits' who 'make sudden raids on local set-tlers.' These 'marginally-human' murderers 'wrapped themselves mum-mylike in endless swathings and bandages' and emitted 'terrifying grunts of fury and pleasure.' In short, the usual stereotype of the ma-rauding Arab. Lest we be in any doubt about these two sets of desert sub-men who squabble so bitterly among themselves, we are told that some scientists believe 'they must be related' and 'the jawas are actu-ally the mature form.'[7]

We have, then, these two negative images of Jews, and in particular Jewish men: the evil, dark image of the Penguin and the jawas, and the also negative, but not evil Clark Kent type of character. Clark is a sort of quintessential characterization of the Jewish man. He is a quasi-intellec-tual. He is a writer, wears glasses, he is inept, timid, cowardly, and de-scribed as mouselike.

And speaking of mice, one of the reasons I have begun and remained with the theme of comic books is that one of the most extraordinary Jew-ish books of recent years—indeed one of the most extraordinary books of recent years—is the comic book *Maus* by Art Spiegelman, about Holocaust victims and survivors and their families in the postwar United States.[8] In *Maus*, the Jews of the Holocaust are drawn as mice, the Germans are cats, the Poles are pigs, and, when the tale moves to the contemporary scene, non-Jewish Americans are dogs, and American Jews are drawn with masks of mice on their faces. Spiegelman usually draws himself as a mouse, but occasionally as wearing the mask of a mouse; so his own identity is ambivalent.

This is a very effective symbolization of the ambivalence of post-Holocaust American Jewish male identity. Spiegelman's self-portrait is particularly striking in that it embraces ambiguity, precisely what most depictions of Jewish men in popular culture avoid, engaging in the sort of rigid dichotomous polarization evident in Superman/Clark Kent. On the one hand, Superman is *so* super that the principal problem his writers have is coming up with a threat to him credible enough to add any suspense to the plot. On the other hand, Clark Kent is such a complete nebbish that he too is an unbelievable character. As to the effectiveness of his "disguise," here is an explanation offered by one of the editors of Superman's comic book appearances, E. Nelson Bridwell: "It may surprise the sophisticate of today that she [Lois Lane] took so long to penetrate the simple disguise of a pair of glasses. But in a day when people accepted the chestnut about the girl whose attractions are never noticed until she is seen without her glasses, Superman's camouflage worked."[9] The principle behind the disguise, then, is the old saw that men don't make passes at girls who wear glasses. To the extent that the disguise works, it thus marks Clark as feminized.

It is precisely the extremism of the polarization between Superman and Clark that makes him such a paradigmatically Jewish American male character. In *Tough Jews: Political Fantasies and the Moral Dilemma of American Jewry,* Paul Breines argues that the image of the Jewish male as a super-schlemiel is so accepted—even by Jews who want to counter it—that when Jews create a Jewish hero, a tough Jew, he turns out not to have Jewish characteristics at all.[10] Hence, I believe this Superman was created out of the depths of powerlessness felt by Siegel and Shuster, and hence many other characters cast in the same mold. Herein lies the dilemma: to create a heroic Jewish male image one must abandon the Jewish component and rely on the dominant culture's version of the heroic male. Jewish male heroes must be non-Jewish Jews, to borrow Isaac Deutscher's phrase. This is why it is so difficult to see Superman as a Jewish character. My purpose here is not to answer the question of under what circumstances Jewish men may have been said to be either mice or Supermen, but rather to criticize the dichotomized way in which the question is posed, and furthermore to look for alternatives to this inadequate approach to Jewish masculinity.

In *Tough Jews,* Breines discusses Leon Uris's *Exodus,* especially the film version, which defined Jewish heroism for a generation of American non-Jews. Its hero is Ari ben Canaan, whose name tells us that he is a lion, but also a Canaanite, played in the film by Paul Newman, complete with blue eyes. Since the ethos of heroism has changed in recent years, and we now make heroes out of gangsters, instead of Ari ben Canaan played by Paul Newman we now have Bugsy Siegel played by Warren Beatty. But the principle, of course, remains the same. Jews have to out-Gentile the Gentiles in order to make it. The point is made in Breines's book by Arthur Koestler, who was a member of a *Burschenschaft,* a Jewish fraternity, in Vienna in the early part of this century. Koestler writes that the member was to demonstrate that "Jews could hold their own in dueling, brawling, drinking and singing just like other people. According to the laws of inferiority and overcompensation," Koestler adds, "they were soon out-Heroding Herod once more"—practicing dueling for hours each day, eventually becoming the "most feared and aggressive swordsmen at the University."[11]

Breines, in *Tough Jews,* examines the dichotomization of Jewish masculinity, using a passage from Philip Roth's *The Counterlife.* A male, Jewish, "not altogether disillusioned, left-leaning, Zionist intellectual" says of American Jews in Israel:[12]

The American Jews get a big thrill from the guns. They see Jews walking around with guns and they think they're in paradise. Reasonable people with a civilized repugnance for violence and blood, they come on tour from America, and they see the guns and they see the beards and they take leave of their senses. The beards to remind them of saintly Yiddish weaknesses and the guns to reassure them of heroic Hebrew force.[13]

Note the counterpoint of a feminized Yiddish culture and language against a masculinized Hebrew and Israeli language and culture, and the need for American Jews to achieve a clear, positive Jewish identity through vicarious identification with Jews elsewhere, whether they be Israeli Jews as above or the Jews of the Holocaust, as in *Maus.*

The difficulty of coming to terms with the question of what constitutes heroism and courage in Israel and in the Holocaust emerges again in a *New York Times* book review by Lawrence Langer of Tom Segev's recent *The Seventh Million: The Israelis and the Holocaust,* in which Langer writes:

Segev offers an illuminating account of how 'Holocaust' and 'heroism' came to be associated in the public imagination, especially through the naming of the Yad Vashem Holocaust Martyrs' and Heroes Remembrance Authority and the Ghetto Fighters' Museum (kibbutz). He observes provocatively that because of this association, many surviving victims 'agonized over the fact that they had merely survived the Holocaust but had not rebelled. The myth of heroism was a heavy burden, at odds with their memories and experiences.'[14]

It seems to me that in speaking of the Holocaust, to put the word "merely" in front of the word "survived" is itself a crime against humanity. But according to this book, at least some of the survivors have come to feel this about themselves. The slander of having gone like lambs to the slaughter weighs particularly heavily on Jewish men because of the history of male heroism. We very much need a more nuanced understanding of the relationship between victimization and heroism, able to overcome the dichotomy between being either a total victim or a total hero. Discussions of survival in the Holocaust have been distorted by the exaggerated dichotomies between heroism and victimization, which I have argued are endemic to discussions of Jewish men.[15]

Sexualities and Their Discontents

When Jewish men are viewed as powerless, as victims, they are seen as effeminate in our culture. And effeminacy here signals homosexuality. There are indeed important historical structural parallels between anti-Semitism and the oppression of lesbians and gays. For example, unlike forms of oppression such as racism and sexism, one cannot by and large tell by just looking who is or is not Jewish or lesbian or gay. In both anti-Semitism and lesbian and gay oppression, however, there are stereotypes that suggest one can tell who is just by appearance and behavior. These two forms of oppression are therefore uniquely suited to terrorize the population as a whole, to have everyone policing themselves lest they appear to be "one of them." Heterosexism has accordingly played the role in the United States in the 1980s that anti-Semitism played in Europe in the 1930s, functioning as pivotal in "law and order" campaigns to intimidate and isolate the population as a whole. The connections between these two phenomena come further into view when one realizes how much of the current wave of Jewish feminism has been Jewish lesbian feminism. In accordance with the Jewish practice of paying one's intellectual debts and honoring one's teachers, we must keep at the forefront of our consciousness how impoverished Jewish feminism would be without those very important contributions.

The common or analogous marginalization of Jews and other "Others" is also discussed in Michael Kimmel's "Judaism, Masculinity, and Feminism." Kimmel talks about walking down the streets of New York City in an anti–Vietnam War parade when someone yells from the sidewalk, "Drop dead, you commie Jew fag!"[16] Kimmel wonders why that combination of epithets rolls so trippingly off the tongue. What do they have in common? His answer is that all three are perceived as being less than real men, as threatening the nation's national and sexual security.

The issue of Jewish men regarded as effeminate within the Jewish tradition itself is discussed by Lori Lefkovitz in "Coats and Tales: Joseph Stories and Myths of Jewish Masculinity," in which Lefkovitz examines the history of the interpretation of the story of Joseph.[17] Of Joseph's appearance the text says little more than that he is beautiful. But at a certain historical moment this becomes an interpretive problem for the rabbis. Perhaps he is too beautiful. Why did he resist the sexual advances of Potiphar's wife anyway? Maybe something's wrong, maybe he is not sufficiently masculine. The story becomes problematic, and various midrashic solutions emerge to try to solve the problem, some arguing that Potiphar's wife was unattractive, while others alternatively marvel at Joseph's ability to control his manly lusts. Joseph also partakes of the pattern in which, as Lefkovitz points out,

> It is the younger son, often the child of the more beloved but less fertile wife, the physically smaller, more delicate, more domestic son, the son closer to the mother, a hero of intellect rather than of brawn, who will be chosen by God over his brothers. . . . An awareness of this pattern may have contributed to an image of the Jews as a feminized people ruled by their women.[18]

Feeling themselves under continual threat of feminization, many Jewish men bristle at any suggestions of homosexuality, as shown by the recent uproar when Labor Party Israeli Knesset member Yael Dayan began speaking of David's love for Jonathan as homosexual in the context of a debate over the rights of gays and lesbians in Israel's military.[19] The dominant contemporary image of Jewish male heterosexuality in our culture is of sexual incompetence, like Clark Kent or the early Woody Allen. In stark contrast to this contemporary American image, Andrea Dworkin in "The Sexual Mythology of Anti-Semitism" very usefully reminds us that in Nazi ideology the Jewish male was the rapist, cast in images very similar to the myths of African American men in the United States.[20]

Conclusion

I shall close by returning to Superman, now as discussed in a recent essay by Arthur Flannigan-Saint-Aubin, "The Male Body and Literary

Metaphors for Masculinity," in which he cites an interview with Superman's creators to the effect that they "were never able to imagine the Man
of Steel with a penis."[21] Flannigan-Saint-Aubin believes this is because
Superman's whole body is phallic, and one cannot very well have one penis atop another. He argues further that the Freudian model of masculinity has conceptualized the male genitals as synonymous with the phallus,
thereby ignoring the testicles and constituting a massive displacement
and denial. Freudians have spoken for generations about castration anxiety as being anxiety about the loss of the phallus. Actual castration, however, involves the testicles, not the penis. This misidentification goes re-
markably unremarked upon.

Flannigan-Saint-Aubin sees a model for a desirable masculinity in the
new character of Clark Kent. The once-familiar characters have under-
gone major revisions of late in the comic books and even more recently
in the new ABC television series *Lois and Clark: The New Adventures of
Superman.* Superman now has his share of existential anxieties—he is a
stranger in a strange land, worried about adjusting to terrestrial culture.[22]
And Clark is no longer the timid mouse of old. He now has adventures in
his own right. Both Superman and Clark are now more complete, integrated personalities. Seeing Clark as a model of masculinity is thus not to
adopt a completely passive stance. Rather, this endorses a mode of masculinity designed to overcome the dichotomous polarizations I earlier argued were endemic to portrayals of Jewish men. In his search for a new
embodied metaphor to symbolize this new masculinity, Flannigan-Saint-
Aubin comes to envisage testicular as opposed to phallic imagery. As opposed to the phallus—understood as hard, aggressive, and linear—the testicles just sort of "hang loose." They are vulnerable, sensitive, plural
rather than singular, and generative of life, as the source at which semen
is produced.[23]

Flannigan-Saint-Aubin's image for a more positive masculinity of
course refers to men in general, not specifically to Jewish men. I close
with a cautionary note about contemporary culture's use of images of
Jewish men to embody changes in men along these lines. Some have seen
as a sign of progress the presence of a number of positive Jewish male
characters on U.S. network television in recent years, including Michael
on *thirtysomething,* Stuart on *L.A. Law,* Joel on *Northern Exposure,* and
Jerry on *Seinfeld.* (Now that he is a comedy writer for a TV show, Seinfeld should be seen as a successor to Buddy on the old *Dick Van Dyke
Show.* This is the same Buddy whose ambivalent Jewishness can be seen
in the facts that while he appeared on the "Alan Brady Christmas Show"
without comment, he also had his Bar Mitzvah in one episode.)

The choice of Jewish men to represent such nice, sensitive, "new" men
might therefore be seen as an occasion for Jewish pride, especially since

they are so identified as Jews, in contrast to what Donna Perlmutter called the "blatant de-Jewification" carried out when such works as Nora Ephron's *Heartburn* and Neil Simon's *Brighton Beach Memoirs* made their transitions to the screen in the eighties.[24] I would argue, however, that the choice of Jewish men to embody this type represents a strategy whereby the producers of these shows minimize their risks. Since Jewish men are already seen as feminized by the culture, using them to embody the more "sensitive" traits stereotypically associated with women is therefore both less threatening and more plausible to the audience than if these characters were blond, blue-eyed WASPs. In the same vein a generation ago, the first commercial film released by a major studio to focus on a gay relationship, John Schlesinger's 1971 *Sunday Bloody Sunday,* starred Peter Finch as the bisexual Jewish doctor. While these characterizations certainly do contain positive traits, the common use of Jewish male characters to embody characteristics usually considered "softer" thus presupposes the culture's negative valuation of Jewish men as already feminized, and is thus implicated in this characterization constructed by the culture to be disparaging. Thus, despite what may be initial appearance to the contrary, images of Jewish men continue to incorporate the ambiguities present in such images.

NOTES

This chapter has been adapted from Harry Brod, "Of Mice and Superman," in *Gender and Judaism,* edited by Tamar M. Rudavsky (New York: New York University Press, 1994) and is reprinted by permission of the publisher.

I wish to express my thanks to the organizers of the Melton Center's "Gender and Judaism" Conference for inviting me to speak and thus giving me the opportunity to develop the ideas herein expressed, and to the reviewers for this volume for helping me to refine them. Since I am acutely aware of how it has been women's struggles that have made possible the discussion of gender within Judaism, I greatly appreciate the generosity of spirit shown by devoting a plenary session to the subject of Jewish masculinity.

1. *Action Comics,* no. 1, June 1938, Detective Comics, Inc.

2. *The Village Voice,* New York, Aug. 4, 1992, pp. 1, 86.

3. Henry Louis Gates Jr., "A Big Brother from Another Planet," *The New York Times,* Sept. 12, 1993, section H, p. 51.

4. The writers and editors of Superman comics were aware of the problem. Among several stories exploring the issue, the cover story of the October, 1963, issue of *Action Comics,* no. 305, is "Why Superman Needs a Secret Identity," told as "An Imaginary Story" picturing various catastrophes that would befall Superman and those closest to him were he to lose his secret identity (ed. Mort Weisinger, Sparta, Ill.: National Periodical Publications, 1–14). The last panel of the story carries an invitation: "Readers, can

you figure out some more reasons why a secret identity is so vital to Superman? We'll print the best letters."

5. Jules Feiffer, ed., *The Great Comic Book Heroes* (New York: Dial Press, 1965), 18–21.

6. The film *Batman Returns* was directed by Tim Burton (Warner Bros., 1992).

7. Paul Hoch, *White Hero, Black Beast: Racism, Sexism, and the Mask of Masculinity* (London: Pluto Press, 1979), 49–50. Hoch is quoting from the novelization of the film.

8. Art Spiegelman, *Maus: A Survivor's Tale,* vols. 1 and 2 (New York, Pantheon, 1986 and 1991).

9. E. Nelson Bridwell, ed., *Superman: From the Thirties to the Seventies* (New York: Crown, 1971), 13.

10. Paul Breines, *Tough Jews: Political Fantasies and the Moral Dilemma of American Jewry* (New York: Basic Books, 1990).

11. Breines, *Tough Jews,* 141.

12. On the conflict between the "Jewboy" vs. the "nice Jewish boy" in Roth, see Barbara Gottfried, "What *Do* Men Want, Dr. Roth?" in *A Mensch among Men: Explorations in Jewish Masculinity,* ed. Harry Brod (Freedom, Calif.: Crossing Press, 1988). In citing this and other essays from a book I edited, I do not wish to engage in self-promotion but rather to acknowledge those whose work has influenced my own.

13. Philip Roth, *The Counterlife* (New York: Farrar, Straus & Giroux, 1986).

14. Lawrence L. Langer, "Zion's Response to the Holocaust," *The New York Times Book Review,* April 18, 1993, 37.

15. One of the possible sources of a more nuanced understanding of the dialectic of victimization and resistance is recent scholarship on Jewish women's resistance in the Holocaust. I do not wish to assert here that women's actual behavior was necessarily different from men's but merely that our understanding of the dynamics of survival has greatly benefited from a particularly sophisticated understanding of the dialectic of victimization and heroism provided by feminist scholars working on this subject. See, e.g., Marlene E. Heinemann, *Gender and Destiny: Women Writers and the Holocaust* (New York: Greenwood Press, 1986), and Carol Rittner and John K. Roth, eds., *Different Voices: Women and the Holocaust* (New York: Parago House, 1993).

16. Michael Kimmel, "Judaism, Masculinity, and Feminism," in Brod, *Mensch among Men,* 153–56.

17. Lori Lefkovitz, "Coats and Tales: Joseph Stories and Myths of Jewish Masculinity," in Brod, *Mensch Among Men,* 19–29.

18. Lefkovitz, "Coats and Tales," 20–21; see Arthur Waskow, *Godwrestling* (New York: Schocken, 1978).

19. Michael Parks, "A New View of David Stirs Goliath-Size Roar," *New York Times,* Feb. 11, 1993, A2, cols. 1–2.

20. Andrea Dworkin, "The Sexual Mythology of Anti-Semitism," in Brod, *Mensch among Men,* 118–23.

21. Arthur Flannigan-Saint-Aubin, "The Male Body and Literary Metaphors for Masculinity," in *Theorizing Masculinities,* ed. Harry Brod and Michael Kaufman (Newbury Park, Calif.: Sage Publications, 1994), quoting R. Greenberger, J. Byrne, and M. Gold, eds., *The Greatest Superman Stories Ever Told* (New York: D.C. Comics, 1987).

22. The anxiety-ridden comic book superhero was created by Stan Lee (born Stanley Lieber) at Marvel Comics in the 1960s. Spiderman, secretly Peter Parker, was guilt-laden over failing to stop the criminal who then murdered his Uncle Ben, with whom he and his Aunt May lived in Forest Hills (where I grew up) in New York City. Peter's personality was that of a teenage Clark. The role of Jewish men in the comic book industry is a subject worthy of discussion in its own right. (Spiderman, the first anxious superhero, was the precursor of the revised, anxious Superman.)

23. Flannigan-Saint-Aubin's approach may perhaps best be understood as an application to men of the sort of approach taken by Luce Irigaray in *This Sex Which Is Not One,* trans. C. Porter (Ithaca, N.Y.: Cornell University Press, 1985).

24. Donna Perlmutter, "Jewishness Goes Back in Closet on the Screen," *Los Angeles Times,* April 12, 1987, Calendar Section, pp. 20–24.

12

"I Took It like a Man": Survival and Hope among Poor Men

Timothy Nonn

The Reproduction of Failure

The Tenderloin District of San Francisco is an urban poverty ghetto noted for drug and sex trades, cultural diversity, and violence. Poor men who live there are stigmatized as failures. The church, a central institution in the Tenderloin, reinforces this image through charity. As objects of charity, poor men are imprisoned in a shame-based identity that denies their moral agency *as men*. Failure, in which poor men are stereotyped as outcasts and derelicts, is commonly interpreted as moral weakness or turpitude. In fact, failure is socially reproduced through hegemonic relations that privilege a certain class of men. A central aspect of these hegemonic relations is the dominant standard of masculinity—typified by the role of "breadwinner"—by which poor men are judged as failures. The church, by functioning as a conduit for culturally dominant values as well as material resources, plays an important role in the reproduction of failure through its ministry among poor men. Thus, the masculine identity of poor men is part of a social structure that is reproduced through social practices. Anthony Giddens explains the centrality of social practices: "It is fundamental to affirm that *social systems are not constituted of roles but of (reproduced) practices;* and it is practices, not roles, which (via the duality of structure) have to be regarded as the 'points of articulation' between actors and structure."[1] By examining the reproduction of failure among poor men, it is possible to comprehend a social system that both limits opportunities for solidarity among men and offers possibilities for resistance and social change.

The theory of the social construction of masculinity indicates that gender is a site for historically contested relations of power. Masculinity is not a fixed essence but an arena of conflicting values between social groups. Dominant masculine values include self-reliance, aggressiveness, career-mindedness, and independence. Contemporary social theory on gender employs the language of warfare (e.g., "tactics and strategies") in analyzing the relationship of identity and social structure. R. W. Connell writes that "hegemonic masculinity is constructed in relation to women and to subordinated masculinities."[2] He defines hegemonic masculinity primarily as men's dominance over women and secondarily as some men's dominance over other men. Social scientists challenge apparent changes in gender roles among a privileged class of men who possess little interest in fundamental change. Also, while individuals may change, men's collective power remains embedded in social and cultural institutions. Michael Messner claims that changes in gender roles among white, middle-class men are more a matter of personal lifestyle than a restructuring of power and politics.[3] Hegemonic masculinity is the basis by which Tenderloin men are stigmatized as failures. Forced to live amid poverty, drugs, and violence, they are stripped of or denied access to a masculine identity constructed around the role of "the good provider."[4] As white heterosexuals, poor men are stripped of an identity associated with privilege and power; as gay men or men of color, they are denied access to a masculine ideal associated with white middle-class heterosexual men.

Poor men alternately comply with and resist institutional practices that reproduce failure. The responses of Tenderloin men to the stigma of failure may be framed in a topology of masculinities in which they assume the role of predator, victim, or survivor. Thomas J. Gerschick and Adam S. Miller characterize disabled men's responses to the dominant standard of masculinity as reformulation, reliance, and rejection.[5] Similarly, in the Tenderloin, a "predator" exhibits a *reformulation* of dominant masculine values through the exercise of hypermasculine aggressiveness and violence; a "victim," in a downward slide of self-destructive behavior, exhibits *reliance* on dominant masculine values through an acceptance of his failure as a man; finally, a "survivor" exhibits a *rejection* of dominant masculine values by reconstructing masculinity around the value of endurance. The struggle for survival creates opportunities for change in which the stigma of "failure" is supplanted by the status of "survivor." Tenderloin men are active moral agents who participate in the denial or affirmation of their human dignity and self-worth.[6] Survivors exercise resistance to hegemonic masculinity and the institutionalized reproduction of failure perpetuated, in part, by churches that often fail to recognize and affirm the moral agency of poor men. Using interview data, this study explores the social construction of masculinity among poor men in the Tenderloin by examining: (1) the tension between the dual identities of "failure" and "survivor"; (2) resistance to the debilitating effects of religious charity that categorize Tenderloin men as failures; and (3) the development of a masculine persona based on the value of endurance in a struggle for survival.[7]

Tenderloin men alternately perceive the church as an adversary, contributing to their sense of failure, and an ally, reinforcing their capacity for endurance. The goal of many Tenderloin churches is solidarity with the poor. But the church's ministry among the poor is flawed by a failure to relate gender to class identity. Further, critical analyses of the church's stance on poverty only employ the category of class in arguing for recognition of the moral agency of the poor. For instance, Thomas Schubeck says the Catholic bishops "fail to encourage the poor to act as agents of their own [economic] development."[8] Werner Levi says the church's traditional "restriction to alms giving automatically limited the category of the poor, reflecting a paternalistic attitude, ignoring the possibility of self-help by the poor."[9] Lacking a perspective on poor men that utilizes the category of gender, the church is incapable of fully affirming them as moral agents in their struggle for survival and justice.

The Mask of Failure

The charitable work of Tenderloin churches has greatly alleviated the suffering of the poor. But their own literature reveals an interpretation of poor men as individual failures. Little has changed since a 1950s brochure for St. Anthony's Dining Room described poor men as "tragic failures" who must be rescued from "a pitiable and precarious existence at the bottom rung of life's ladder." Submissiveness and gratitude are anticipated responses in a pastoral strategy of charity that stresses middle-class values and benevolence. The same brochure assured donors that each man must remove his hat to denote politeness: "It is a courtly little gesture of appreciation by men who have no other way of showing their gratitude—and some of those men have been strangers to politeness for a long, long time."[10]

A man with his hand out is an object of pity and scorn, and society expects poor men to wear the mask of failure.[11] Martin says that poor men waiting for food at Glide Church "stand there and they wait however long is necessary and they take whatever abuse is necessary because they don't have the skills necessary to do any better." Burdened with the shameful stigma of failure, existence becomes an alienating experience that drives many Tenderloin men deeper into a downward spiral of addiction, depression, and withdrawal. Erving Goffman notes that "we believe the person with the stigma is not quite human."[12] The masculinity of poor men is suspect. Albert, a fifty-year-old white man, says: "You have to say to yourself, 'Yeah, look at me, here I am a grown man and I'm waiting in the soup line.'" In the Tenderloin, St. Anthony's (operated by St. Boniface Catholic Church) and Glide Memorial Church (United Methodist) provide food and other services to the poor. The lines are long and the wait seems endless. Men think about their problems in line while people pass by and stare. Thomas, a forty-one-year-old black man, says he gets depressed in line. "When you lower people to the level that they have to stand in line for hours for food, then you've stripped them of their pride and dignity already. And so people don't really care. You've taken everything when you make them stand in line like that."

There are few choices when you are hungry and broke, so each day the poor line up around the churches. It is a dehumanizing experience. Men describe feeling like "animals" or "cattle." Albert, who barely survives on disability insurance, wishes he could eat in a restaurant instead of being humiliated by waiting in a food line.

> At St. Anthony's, even after you're waiting in line for an hour, you get downstairs and they put you through the cattle car thing. You gotta go through the maze. That, to me, is humiliating. . . . That's one of the things that I like about being able to buy your own food. When you walk into a restaurant, even if you walk into MacDonalds, you don't have to walk through no maze to get to your food. You can just walk up to the counter and get served.

Tenderloin men are trapped in a maze of shame and "compassion" in which charity often sustains an unequal relationship between giver and receiver. They become increasingly dependent and consequently "develop feelings of impotency in the face of domination and exploitation" by service providers.[13] Subordination, often associated with a loss of manhood, breeds anger. Carl I. Cohen and Jay Sokolovsky note "the general antipathy toward religious institutions" that poor men feel when they are treated with condescension or antagonism.[14] Tenderloin men complain bitterly about workers in soup kitchens: Thomas says, "They're bossy, pushy, disrespectful, inconsiderate. In some cases, [they have a] very nasty tone. And they herd you in and herd you out like prisoners." Most of the soup kitchen workers are themselves either homeless, and live in shelters, or only recently off the streets, and live in single-occupancy residential hotel rooms. They have little authority but are resented by men in line for giving instructions or for expelling disorderly persons. George Orwell notes that "a man receiving charity practically always hates his benefactors."[15] Thomas imagines how soup kitchen workers might plan a meal: "They'd probably say, 'These scumbags! Do we have enough here for all these scumbags? Well, it's okay. Whatever we throw together, they'll eat. Maybe we can throw together some leftover dog food.'"

Albert claims that most soup kitchen workers are ex-cons and substance abusers who are accustomed to rigid institutional procedures and abusive behavior. He says they make eating a distressing experience.

A lot of times because of the people that they use as workers—this is not a note to bring them down—but they are institutionalized. They treat you like you're in prison. They yell at you. . . . They tell you, "Hey, speed it up. Go up these stairs. Go down those stairs. Get up against the wall. Do this, do that, do the other thing." Like I really need that when, you know, when I'm hungry and I got three cents in my pocket and I'm totally depressed. I don't need that kind of stuff.

Life in the Tenderloin is a contest for survival that demands street skills and fortitude. Men usually attempt to avoid confrontations with soup kitchen workers or others in line. They display a studied detachment. Albert says, "It's a game-playing atmosphere where a person, number one, is interested in survival." But confrontations are easily provoked when men are thrown together in an atmosphere of desperate need. Thomas explains why fights often break out in food lines.

A lot of people take it personal because a lot of people have struggled their whole lives, and they're in a struggle for survival. And they have built up a chip on their shoulder. And they take everything as a personal attack on them. So if you say, "Move this way!"—and your tone of voice is stern—they take it as a personal attack. And that causes them to lash out. *That's because they've been beaten down all their lives, and they've been virtually demasculated,* if you will. So my manhood is still intact. Nobody can demasculate me. But a lot of people out there have been worn down by society to the point where they've been virtually demasculated. So the last thing they have—or the last thing they feel they have—is their manhood. And if they feel like you're stepping on their toe, then you got yourself in a fight.

Most poor men avoid violence; instead, they view survival as a game that involves playing the role of a failure. Some play the role of victim to elicit the compassion of church workers who dispense food, clothing, and beds. Ricardo, a fifty-one-year-old Puerto Rican, learned to fight as a young gang member in Brooklyn. He says that fighting comes easily, but it is more effective to play the role of a man down on his luck to get services. He contrasts his method for getting into a homeless shelter with a less successful approach.

If I can't get into a shelter—there's more shelters. I'll go up to the next one. I don't care if I get there wet. The wetter I get, in my mind, the faster they'll take me because they see, 'Damn! This guy, he's been out there for a while.' Here comes a guy, he's dry, and he's talking crap. This guy don't want to hear that, 'No. We're full up.' You see, I'm going to make myself look like I need your services. I don't go no place without a full load. It's a role. You're an actor.

Goffman argues that an act—depending on whether or not an actor believes in the "performance"—may be either sincere or insincere.[16] In the Tenderloin, performance of masculine roles is central to survival. Playing the role of failure requires considerable skill. Ricardo sometimes acts the part of a lost puppy. At other times, he and other men will use the threat of violence—a threatening glare or menacing silence—to obtain resources. They play the role of a prowling wolf. Father Louis Vitale of St. Boniface Church relates a story about a man who regularly attends Bible study.

> One of the guys—kind of a tough guy. He has a room. But he's on and off the streets. He eats at St. Anthony's. He even said to me, 'I'm a thief.' It's kind of like he's ashamed of it but, on the other hand, he's tough enough to do it. . . . He started telling me how he survived. There was a little bit of bravado. He referred to himself as a wolf. 'You've got to be tough. You've got to be out there and survive.'[17]

Performance of different masculine roles aids poor men in their struggle to survive, but there is little hope of their escaping the extreme poverty. Poverty peels away all traces of masculinity until a man's soul is laid bare. Tenderloin men are afflicted by failure. Rev. Cecil Williams of Glide Church says a Tenderloin man feels like a "powerless, impotent nobody."[18] Although the church provides basic provisions for existence, even compassion, Tenderloin men crave something else. They need an understanding of themselves as men. As objects of charity, their masculine identity is suspect. Only through enduring suffering do Tenderloin men regain a sense of worth as men and overcome failure.

The Hope of a Survivor

Tenderloin churches struggle with the tension that exists between the pastoral strategies of charity and solidarity. A current brochure from St. Anthony's relates its charitable work to a commitment to social justice: "We seek to create not only a community of care but one of conscience, one willing to risk the changes that will put an end to poverty."[19] A brochure from Glide Church claims that Pastor Williams "has mobilized the poor and disenfranchised to demand their rights."[20] Williams says, "Everybody has to have hope that things are getting better. In the old churches they called it saving people. We call it liberating." He says, "We're taking lonely, alienated, starving, craving people and we're trying to free them to be full human beings."[21] Charity often establishes an unequal relationship between giver and receiver that maintains unjust social relations between the poor and privileged. Solidarity requires a recognition of the moral agency of the poor in their struggle for survival and justice. Solidarity with poor men must begin with an understanding of their struggle *as men* to resist the stigma of failure and attain the status of survivor.

Survival is no easy task. Hope is a rare commodity in the Tenderloin. The sidewalks are littered with old condoms, broken bottles, empty syringes, and crumpled lottery tickets. It is difficult to endure, and many men give up. Robert, a homeless forty-six-year-old black man, loves to play chess near the cable car turnaround at Powell and Market. It keeps him going. But many lose hope. The hotels are haunted by reclusive alcoholics and the streets are crowded with emaciated addicts. Robert says that homeless people give up after they have lost their self-esteem: "They been down for so long. And the system has played this game of chess with them for so long. They have just said, 'Hey, forget it.'"

Whether Tenderloin men are waiting for a winning lottery ticket or for the next drink or fix, they need something to keep them going. William, a fifty-one-year-old white man, spends most of his time alone in a small residential hotel room. He eats at the "Good Soups" cafe. The cafe is favored by single elderly white men. William will talk about his dream of starting a pet store with anyone who listens. He knows he may not attain his dream but refuses to give up.

> If a person really cares about working, he's going to find a way of working one way or the other. I'm still working at it. And before I'm done— I may not get a job or may not get a place of my own to work—but still in all, it's something that I'm not going to look at and just say, 'Oh, forget it. You're not going to make it.'

Giving up signals a retreat into meaninglessness and decay from which few return. Mark, a thirty-seven-year-old white man, has struggled with alcoholism and homelessness. He is now a member of St. Boniface Church. It was a long road back. During his drinking days, when he had a bowel movement, he would scoop out the feces from inside his pants, then continue drinking. While it is difficult for poor men to maintain a sense of dignity, Albert says that they always have a choice between despair and hope.

> Your *human dignity* is always going to prevail. At least, you're waiting in line. You're not saying, 'The hell with waiting in line. I'm going to go look what's in the garbage pail.' Dignity—it's only a certain amount of dignity that you can maintain. And, *as hard as it is, you have to realize that things could either be worse and hope that they'll get better,* or whatever.

Thomas claims that giving up is morally wrong. He has thought often of suicide but ultimately believes all life is sacred—even at the bottom of society.

> I don't believe that people should give up on themselves because that's almost *sacrilegious* to give up on life, to give up on yourself, and just say, 'Well, I'm just ready to go out,' or, 'I'm just ready to give up.' I don't believe that people should do that. *That's the wrong attitude to take because as long as you have life there's always a chance.*

The daily choice between giving up or living with adversity leads to an interpretation of masculinity as the capacity to endure suffering. Eddie, a fifty-five-year-old white Vietnam veteran, says simply: "A man is a survivor." John, a forty-one-year-old black man with AIDS, relates poverty to his illness. His serene humor almost obliterates the gathering shadows. He says that he will never give up.

> Since I've been here, I've entertained the thought of killing myself for the first time in my life. This is like a kid who's had every obstacle thrown in front of him from age thirteen on. Abandoned in the streets. I succeeded. Why? because I wasn't going to let it take me. I'm a survivor. You get out there. Self-pity is going to get you nowhere.

Suicide is common in the Tenderloin. Sometimes it happens quickly—they leap from a window or hang themselves in a lonely apartment. Other times it happens slowly—with drugs or alcohol. Tenderloin men must work up courage each day to wait in line for food. They must learn to accept the endless minor indignities of poverty: disdainful glances, harsh words, routine snubs. They must discover inner resources to survive in a climate of public ostracism. Masculinity—the ability "to take it like a man"—is a thin barrier separating life from death. Thomas says:

> I just made up my mind, 'Look here. I'm going to do my best each and every day. I'm going to do my best.' And if I don't make it in society, then I can go to God and say, 'Look, Lord. I did the best I could. I didn't take the cheap way out. I didn't take the short cut. *I took it like a man.'*

A Tenderloin man who endures is a survivor. Survival—more than physical prowess or even material success—is a badge of honor.[22] A common expression heard on the streets, "It makes or breaks you," encapsulates an identity that unites men across lines of race, class background, and sexual orientation. James, a thirty-one-year-old gay black man, says: "You learn the hard way. You learn through trial and error under the most extreme conditions. This is almost hell." Father Louis says that formerly homeless men feel pride in surviving street life. They tell him: "I used to be on the streets. I know what it's like. But I made it. And I was determined that I was going to get through it. And I did."

Survival is full-time work. There are countless dangers on the streets, and residents recognize three basic social groups: survivors, predators, and "vics," or victims. Survival requires an attitude in which Tenderloin men resign themselves to uncertainty and deprivation. Ricardo moves from place to place because of a violent temper and a talent for avoiding landlords. He says that survival requires a certain toughness that not all men achieve.

> It's a job trying to survive. It's a job trying to eat. If you got kids, it's a job trying to keep that 'cause society wants to take the kids from you. They got BCW [Bureau of Child Welfare]. They'll take the kids. It gets to the point—the ones that you see out there that looks really terrible, is the ones that just gave up. There is but so much you can take. Your mind has to be strong. You see, I grew up with thirteen brothers. I had to fight. I knew how to fight automatically. I grew up feeding myself. Then I had kids. Then I grew up doing that. Then I learned how to really fight in the service. So, you see, these are people that they just gave up because they—some people can't take a challenge. There is a limit to how much you can take—pressures of society that'll make you snap. And, some people, like myself—at least, I like to think of myself as one—that have been through so much pressure that we know how to respond to pressure.

Tenderloin men support one another in their struggle to survive. A central aspect to the identity of survivor is the development of a norm of reciprocity by which poor men learn the value of relating as equals. James says, "You kind of have to take care of each other here just so everybody survives." There are extrinsic factors that contribute to their sense of solidarity. The police term the Tenderloin a "containment area," in reference to large numbers of criminals, addicts, and prostitutes. One day, a resident who was watching several drug transactions near his apartment building asked a nearby police officer why he did not arrest the dealers and addicts. The officer casually replied, "They're already in jail." There are also intrinsic factors for men's solidarity in the Tenderloin—specifically, their understanding of masculinity as the capacity to endure suffering. Noting their capacity for mutual assistance under extreme conditions, Father Louis compares Tenderloin residents to survivors of Nazi concentration camps. "It's akin to the experience of people who are prisoners-of-war or people that are in situations where they're captive or living in very oppressed circumstances. [One can see] the power of the people in sticking together and building their own reinforcement system."

Through their capacity to endure adversity and suffering, some Tenderloin men overcome the stigma of failure and create a masculine identity based upon survival. Endurance is a viable form of resistance to the values and standard of hegemonic masculinity that perpetuate the reproduction of failure. As survivors, they retain hope in the future. The image of masculinity as endurance also serves as a buffer against the damaging effects of receiving religious charity and governmental assistance. Instead of feeling subordinate and dependent on others for survival, Tenderloin men discover inner resources that allow dignity and self-esteem to develop. Through endurance, Tenderloin men transform the daily experience of emasculation, powerlessness, and isolation into a tenacious awareness of their worth as men.

The Origin of Solidarity

Tenderloin men present the church with new opportunities for solidarity that arise from traditional works of charity. Jon Sobrino writes: "In authentic solidarity the first effort to give aid commits a person at a deeper level than that of mere giving and becomes an ongoing process, not a contribution."[23] Solidarity is a process of dialogue and mutual awareness by which both service-providers and the poor are transformed. Most importantly, solidarity represents a fundamental shift in social relations that undermines an unjust social order. It is difficult for the church to make the shift from charitable compassion to passionate solidarity when it functions mainly as a conduit for social resources. The church is invested in perceiving poor men as failures when its interests lie in transmitting middle-class values to the poor. To participate in the struggle of poor men for survival the church must discard the assumption that poor men are failures and affirm them as survivors who demand dignity and justice. The moral agency of Tenderloin men—demonstrated in their capacity to endure suffering—provides the foundation for developing a pastoral strategy of solidarity among men in poverty. The origin of solidarity is the point of engagement where the marginalized make their claim known and the privileged hear and respond. When poor men remove the mask of failure, privileged men are invited to remove the mask of success and stand with the poor as brothers.

The church's presence among the poor may serve as a site for the transformation of gender relations if a shift occurs from the reproduction of failure to solidarity with poor men in their struggle for survival and justice. The challenge for the churches, and for privileged men, is to find a way to support poor men in their struggle to turn the value of endurance into a resource for change. This requires a new interpretation of the relationship between suffering and compassion. In a context of privilege, men understand endurance of suffering as a brief test of manhood that establishes their right to compete with other men. In a context of poverty and marginalization, men understand endurance of suffering as a routine task that establishes their right to coexist with other men. In a context of privilege, men understand the capacity for compassion as a voluntary humanitarian gesture that sets them apart from other men. The term "compassion fatigue" reflects popular distrust in the power of the poor to shape their own lives. A reporter writes, "I can't give to them all. There's just not enough of me—or my money."[24] In a context of poverty and marginalization, men understand the capacity for compassion as a requirement that emerges out of a recognition of interdependence. Suffering and compassion are not options for poor men; they are conditions of survival. The statement, "I took it like a man," assumes different meanings in the minds of poor men and privileged men. For privileged men, suffering and compassion often reinforce a system of inequality, competition, and hierarchy. For poor men, suffering and compassion form a basis for fraternity, cooperation, and egalitarianism. For privileged men, suffering and compassion are easily divided by the fear of subordination. For poor men, suffering and compassion are united by the need to give and receive support on a daily basis.

The church can serve as an effective agent for social change by addressing the issue of failure among men. First, the church must work *to eliminate the stigma of failure* that condemns poor men to lives of marginalization and isolation. Poor men are not better or worse than other men, but they live in extreme conditions that generate innovative responses. Stereotypes are based upon an unfamiliarity that is only overcome through understanding and friendship. Second, the church must work *to transform a practice of charity* that often functions to maintain inequitable social relations. As a mediator of middle-class values the church remains blind to or even denigrates values that emerge from extreme conditions of poverty. The benevolence of charity needs to be balanced with a commitment to justice that stresses the full and equal participation of the poor in society. Third, the church must work *to achieve solidarity between all men* by addressing men's oppression of other men. The reproduction of failure is partly based upon the fear of failure felt by all men. Healing social divisions that doom some men to lives of desperation and want requires that all men confront the inward split that leads them to hide their own failures. Manhood, Michael Kimmel argues, is founded upon men's fear of each other. He says that masculinity "is more about the fear of being dominated than it is the drive to dominate, the fear of being conquered by another man than it is the drive to conquer women, the terror of another man having power or dominion over us than it is the drive to have power or dominion over others."[25] The role and function of poor men as failures is a social issue that must be addressed by all men since it is men who gain the world and lose their souls from the reproduction of failure.

NOTES

1. Anthony Giddens, *Central Problems in Social Theory* (Berkeley: University of California 1990), 117.

2. R. W. Connell, *Gender and Power* (Berkeley: University of California 1987), 186.

3. Michael A. Messner, "'Changing Men' and Feminist Politics in the United States," *Theory and Society* 22 (1993): 723–37.

4. Jessie Bernard, "The Good-Provider Role: Its Rise and Fall," in *Men's Lives*, 2d ed., ed. Michael S. Kimmel and Michael A. Messner (New York: Macmillan, 1992).

5. Thomas J. Gerschick and Adam S. Miller, "Gender Identities at the Crossroads of Masculinity and Physical Disability," *masculinities* 2 (1994): 34–55.

6. Models of moral agency—the capacity to choose and act according to a set of values—develop in relation to gender; models of masculinity focus on autonomy while models of femininity emphasize relationality. See Sarah Lucia Hoagland, "Some Thoughts about 'Caring,'" in *Feminist Ethics,* ed. Claudia Card (Lawrence, Kans.: University of Kansas Press, 1991), 246–47.

7. The interviews were conducted over a one-year period, from May 1993 to May 1994, with eight men who live in the Tenderloin. The names used are fictitious.

8. Thomas Schubeck, *Liberation Ethics: Sources, Models, and Norms* (Minneapolis: Fortress Press, 1993), 98.

9. Werner Levi, *From Alms to Liberation* (New York: Praeger Publishers, 1989), 62.

10. Gene Mugnier, "The Miracle of Jones Street," St. Anthony's Dining Room (operated by the Franciscan Friars of St. Boniface Catholic Church), San Francisco, CA, 1952. For a discussion of the church's characterization of poor men as "failures," see also James F. Rooney, "Organizational Success through Program Failure: Skid Row Rescue Missions," *Social Forces* 58 (1980): 904–24.

11. See Timothy Nonn, "Hitting Bottom: Masculinity, Poverty and Homelessness," in *Men's Lives,* 3d ed., ed. Michael S. Kimmel and Michael A. Messner (Boston: Allyn & Bacon, 1995).

12. Erving Goffman, *Stigma: Notes on the Management of a Spoiled Identity* (New York: Touchstone, 1963), 5.

13. Carl I. Cohen and Jay Sokolovsky, *Old Men of the Bowery* (New York: Guilford Press, 1989), 197.

14. Ibid., 100.

15. George Orwell, *Down and Out in Paris and London* (New York: Harcourt Brace Jovanovich, 1933), 184.

16. Erving Goffman, *The Presentation of Self in Everyday Life* (New York: Doubleday & Co. 1959), 17.

17. Father Louis Vitale, in a personal communication to the author.

18. Cecil Williams, *No Hiding Place* (San Francisco: HarperCollins, 1992), 190.

19. Brochure produced for St. Anthony's Foundation by Marcus Associates, San Francisco, Calif., 1990.

20. Sydney Atkinson, "The Glide Mystique," in *Glide In-Out* (San Francisco: n.p., 1974). Glide is a United Methodist church.

21. Gerald Adams, "Glide Memorial's Special Karma," *San Francisco Examiner California Living,* April 25, 1971, pp. 11–14.

22. The valorization of suffering in the construction of masculine identity is examined by Timothy Beneke in "Notes on Compulsive Masculinity, Psychoanalytic Feminism, and Existentialism," in *Sexism and the Pains of Manhood* (Berkeley: University of California Press, forthcoming).

23. Jon Sobrino, *Theology of Christian Solidarity* (Maryknoll, N.Y.: Orbis Books, 1985), 3.

24. Jim Herron Zamora, "Invisible People and Compassion Fatigue," *San Francisco Examiner,* June 20, 1994, p. 15.

25. Michael S. Kimmel, "Should/Can/Will Men Support Feminism?" Keynote address at conference "Test the West" held in Vienna, Austria, in 1992.

RESOURCES FOR RECONSTRUCTING MANHOOD

PART V

MYTH, RITUAL, SPIRITUAL DISCIPLINE, AND COMMUNITY

One major component of the contemporary men's movement identifies the malaise of masculinity as fundamentally spiritual or religious in nature. The problems of masculinity, these men of the movement argue, relate to the modern world's disparagement of tradition, myth, ritual, and spirituality. But the issue involves more than just the lack of depth in secularity. As some of the authors in this volume have observed, religious and spiritual dimensions of existence are often associated primarily with women and femininity. Masculinities based on the rejection of the feminine therefore incorporate the spiritual dimension only with great difficulty and discomfort.

In the chapters in this part the authors endeavor to recover or strengthen the spiritual dimension in men's lives. Some write from the perspective of traditional religious communities. Others have rejected or partially rejected traditional religious expression, finding it to be hopelessly patriarchal or insufficient to address the issues men now face. While the writers in this latter category believe in the value of myth, ritual, and community, they are not convinced the major religious traditions of the West can guide men to construct a more wholesome manhood. They look, therefore, to submerged traditions within or to traditions outside the modern West.

Mikeal Parsons's "Re-membering John the Baptist" is the work of an author who wants to remain faithful to his Christian roots and who believes important mythic strands within Christianity, when carefully reconstructed, offer valuable guidance for contemporary men seeking transformation. Parsons's chapter focuses on the enigmatic figure of John the Baptist and the fate of his image in the early church. In a suggestive analysis, Parsons contends that in the Christian community's earliest memory, John was recalled as a man of great vitality, sensual and earthy, prophetic and full of conviction. In the hands of the subsequent tradition, the image of John is gradually tamed and divested of what was later considered its more dangerous elements. Parsons believes this earliest image of the Baptist provides an evocative mythic resource for contemporary men.

Robert Moore and Douglas Gillette, in "Initiation and the Male Spiritual Quest," are critical of the dominant religious institutions in the West. Contemporary religion, they say, has failed to facilitate the development of authentic manhood, in part because modern religious practitioners have neglected to appreciate the deep human need for myth and ritual. Thus they implicitly criticize religious institutions for surrendering too much to secular culture. What contemporary men need, argue Moore and Gillette, is to appreciate the importance of rites of passage in their lives. Authentic maleness, which they call "true" or "deep" masculinity, is fostered by communal rituals that enable males to die to their immature selves and awaken to self- and other-affirming lives. While they do not wholly repudiate the central religious traditions of the West, Moore and Gillette find the greatest aids to reflection in premodern and non-Western traditions.

In "Men and the Promise of Goddess Spirituality," Seth Mirsky delineates what he sees as the great value for men of ancient Goddess traditions. Inspired by the work of feminist thealogians and theologians, Mirsky believes Goddess mythology serves to help contemporary men achieve a right relation with other men, women, children, and the wider world of nature. No doubt some men (and women) will be taken aback and perhaps offended by the suggestion of a female deity as the focus of religious devotion. Some might flinch at the idea of stepping out of our inherited mainstream traditions to embrace a divine figure who is not part of those traditions. Or perhaps they will recoil from Mirsky's frank acknowledgment that the Goddess is an imaginative construct. Others might argue that given a male proclivity to idealize and idolize women, the last thing men need is a female deity. But Mirsky believes these potential pitfalls are precisely the virtues of Goddess spirituality. To make the Goddess the center of one's spiritual practice serves to challenge and uproot problematic aspects of traditional masculinity: a conservatism that is slavishly devoted to tradition and rationality, the fear of a loss of absolutes that might ensue when one recognizes that conceptions of the divine are constructions of the imagination, and the tendency to androcentrism.

Moore and Gillette's and Mirsky's recommendations about the recovery of myths and practices outside the dominant Western traditions raise several interesting issues. First, one might ask why the Western religions, which have been dominated by men, are viewed by some as insufficiently able to promote male well-being and happiness. If the perception that these male-dominated traditions are unwholesome for men is true, what specific factors account for this? Is modern religion's flirtation with secularity partly responsible? Perhaps the responsibility lies in the fact that these traditions are not dominated by men, per se, but elite groups of men, whose self-interests are not coterminous with those of other men and women.

Second, Moore and Gillette and Mirsky's work invites the revisitation of an earlier question explicitly raised by Christopher Jocks. What are the problems connected to appropriating myths and practices not indigenous to one's own traditional heritages? Jocks, for example, is critical of attempts within the mythopoetic men's movement to utilize Native American rituals and traditions without a full appreciation of and solidarity with the native communities out of which they come. In what ways, therefore, do myths and rituals change when they are taken out of their embeddedness in the communities that produced them? And where should communities turn when they find their practices and stories inadequate to serve their needs?

A final issue pertains to a matter of language. What guiding interests animate men's search of religious traditions, whether those of their own heritage or those outside that heritage? Should men be looking for a "true" masculinity or for something that takes them beyond masculinity altogether? Parsons and Moore and Gillette seem to favor the recovery of what they might call genuine masculinity. Mirsky avoids using this terminology and elsewhere has expressly argued against it.[1] One might contend that since "masculinity," whatever that might mean, is constructed over against "femininity," whatever that might mean, any search for an "authentic" masculinity is bound to be problematic since it includes less than the fully human. Thus it is important to ask what characteristics and qualities a true masculinity manifests. Those authors in this volume who advocate a true masculinity clearly recommend something that expresses more than the traditionally masculine. Is it legitimate to say, then, that what unites the visions of Parsons, Moore and Gillette, and Mirsky is at bottom the same reality, in spite of their use of different languages to name it and advocacy of different avenues to reach it? Or are they in fact advocating fundamentally different versions of what it should mean to be male?

"The Thunder of New Wings: AIDS—a Journey beyond Belief," by William F. Brantley, presents yet another perspective on male spirituality. Brantley, a gay man living with AIDS, poignantly recounts his struggle with the heterosexist aspects of contemporary American culture and most churches as he comes to accept first his homosexuality and then his infection with HIV. Like the other authors in this part, Brantley is critical of the dominant religious traditions of the West, even as he strives to remain loyal to his Christian faith. In Brantley's work, however, we are offered not just the story of a man who has felt the pain of being rejected by church and culture; ultimately, he also speaks movingly of the lessons of embracing his sexuality and his disease. For Brantley, AIDS has been a spiritual teacher, not just a curse but also a blessing. It is clear that for Brantley accepting his sexuality and his illness has meant refashioning for himself the significance of being male. Among those who live with AIDS, the imperatives of traditional masculinity flounder because the disease necessitates the growth of nurturant communities of support, genuine friendship, compassion, and the embrace of mortality, all of which contemporary dominant masculinity makes difficult to achieve.

Brantley's story can in some senses be read through the lens furnished by Moore and Gillette's chapter. Moore and Gillette speak of the importance of moments of crisis as the occasion for personal growth and wisdom. These moments, when appropriately negotiated, are transformative and enriching. Often they entail new insight and new directions for living. For Brantley, the journey to accept his sexuality and to learn to live with AIDS illustrates Moore and Gillette's contentions. Moore and Gillette maintain that the "initiated" man, the one who has successfully negotiated the moments of crisis, will struggle against the "antisocial and unjust political and economic interests that are the enemies of an inclusive human future." For Brantley, the struggle is now not with himself but with the structures of a world that privileges the few at the expense of many. He issues to religious communities everywhere the challenge to respond in a humane way to the cultural crisis facing a world in which AIDS is a reality.

The final offering in this part is Alton Pollard's "Magnificent Manhood: The Transcendent Witness of Howard Thurman." As in the life of Brantley, we glimpse in Howard Thurman the dialectical movement between personal spirituality and social activism, between the journey inward and the journey outward. But unlike Brantley, Thurman suffered no crises of identity. Firmly rooted in the African American community and the Christian faith, Thurman was able, Pollard argues, to negotiate the perils of a racist society because he never lost sight of who he was. Thurman's rich spiritual life, nurtured by mystical experience, generated a radically inclusive vision for society and enlivened a bold search for its embodiment. For us today, Thurman stands as a shining example of the possibilities of prophetic manhood, grounded in community, tradition, and spiritual experience.

NOTE

1. Seth Mirsky, "Three Arguments for the Elimination of Masculinity," in Björn Krondorfer, ed., *Men's Bodies, Men's Gods: Male Identities in a (Post-) Christian Culture* (New York and London: New York University Press, 1996), 27–39.

13

RE-MEMBERING
JOHN THE BAPTIST

Mikeal C. Parsons

In a circle of men beside the South Bosque River, I sit chanting to the beat of a drum:

> Do you know
> what I have done to you?
> You call me Teacher and Lord;
> and you are right, for so I am.
> If I then, your Lord and Teacher,
> have washed your feet,
> you also ought to wash one another's feet.
> John 13:12–14

The twenty-five men then wash one another's feet with water from the river after having shared the Eucharist. It is eleven o'clock on Sunday morning, and this is a worship service at a Baptist men's retreat. The service concludes with the men embracing and offering the peace of Christ to one another.

The night before, these same men had participated in an Ngoma ceremony, a drumming ritual taken from traditional African religion. We drummed our prayers to God and for each other, focusing mind and body on the needs, pains, and desires of our brothers. The drum served as the vehicle of prayer, and our prayers took the form of image and feeling rather than reason and thinking. In a sense, it was our hands that prayed. So some of us drummed, some of us danced around the fire, some of us sang, and all of us prayed.

I share with these men a deep longing for religious rituals and experiences that are both sensual and spiritual. For many men, the church has failed to provide such rituals and experiences, and for some men, this search for an integrated spirituality has led them to abandon institutionalized religion and to seek refuge within one of the mythopoetic men's movements.[1] The men with whom I am intimate are increasingly dissatisfied with the traditional mode of Christian worship and liturgy, though we continue to identify with the Christian tradition. With them, I belong to a predominantly white, "progressive" Protestant church for whom worship is almost exclusively a left-brain experience, grounded in what Edward Farley has called rationalistic epistemology.[2] The intimate connection between male sensuality and spirituality has been severed.[3] I, and other men like me, are rarely challenged by the theology and liturgical habits of the traditional church to integrate our imagination, intuition, emotions, and sensuality into a holistic spirituality, and so we are open to whatever lessons the mythopoetic men's movement can teach us about recovering sacred images that empower men to grasp and reclaim the deeper aspects of their bodies and souls.

Why are men so spiritually schizophrenic? James Nelson has helpfully articulated two distinct but interrelated forms of dualistic thinking historically prevalent in the Christian community. One is a "spiritualistic dualism" in which the "spirit" (or "mind" or "soul") is essentially different from and superior to the "body" (or "matter"). Nelson has observed that one consequence of this dualistic division of body-spirit has been a certain perception of Christian spirituality, which came to dominate the church for many centuries. It meant a life controlled by disciplines of prayer and meditation whereby one was enabled to rise to higher, often mystical, communion with God. Such spirituality still persists for many Christians. Holiness is tantamount to bodilessness, and saints are sexless people, mystically attuned to a life transcending earthly matter.[4] The other is a "sexist dualism" which absolutizes the differences between masculine and feminine gender roles and systematically subordinates women (identified with inferior body and matter) to men (identified in essence with spirit and mind).

Nelson notes that these two dualisms "often coalesced into one powerful composite dualism,"[5] a dualism still current within much organized religion. The effort of this essay is to contend with spiritualistic dualism by seeking to reconnect the male body and mind, sensuality and spirituality, and thus also to challenge the sexist dualism that argues for the hierarchical and inherent superiority of men over women.

I am working within the Christian tradition and therefore seek to draw on the Christian scriptures for constructing an authentic spirituality for men. I am interested in exploring what, if anything, the mythopoetic men's movement might contribute to men interested in constructing a spirituality within the Christian tradition, and conversely what, if anything, the Christian tradition has to contribute to the struggle of the mythopoetic men's movement to redefine male spirituality.[6]

The split between body and spirit and the hierarchical positioning of men to women that Nelson observes occurred very early in the Christian era. Despite strong, sporadic impulses toward anti-dualism (e.g., Gal. 3:28), the dichotomy is evident even within the New Testament writings themselves. One such example is to be found in the New Testament's treatment of the character of John the Baptist. My thesis is that John the Baptist challenged both the "spiritualistic dualism" and "sexist dualism" of Mediterranean antiquity and that very early in the Christian tradition efforts to silence him are evident not only in his beheading but also in the Gospel writers' treatment of him.

My goal is to present a "plausible" interpretation via a twofold exploration of the text, one literary, one historical.[7] First, I will examine the story of John the Baptist in Mark 6, focusing on the treatment of John by Herod and using gender as an analytic category.[8] Since most scholars accept that Mark is the first Gospel written, followed by Matthew and Luke, and then John, I will then "excavate" the character of John the Baptist by looking at his portrayal in the Gospels in rough chronological order, focusing on each evangelist's treatment of John.

Beheading of John the Baptist in Mark 6

The story of John the Baptist in Mark 6:14–29 is told in the context of the spreading reputation of Jesus (Mark 6:13–14). Herod, upon hearing of Jesus, is reminded of John the Baptist and asserts that John whom he had beheaded has risen from the dead (6:16). Mark then goes on to recount John's beheading in a literary flashback, an event that had occurred at some earlier, unspecified time but is only now narrated. Read through the lens of gender analysis, John's beheading is a horrible example of the extent to which an oppressive gender system collaborates to remove those persons who rise up in protest against it. In this story, a person, in this case a man, is punished by death for challenging the sexist dualism of his patriarchal culture.

Herod had arrested John the Baptist and thrown him in prison "on account of Herodias, his brother Philip's wife, for he had married her" (6:17), angry with John because he had challenged the legality of Herod's marriage: "It is not appropriate for you to have your brother's wife" (6:18). The issue here is more about sexual politics than sexual purity. The charge leveled by John is evidently against endogamy, marriage within one's extended family, a practice intended to preserve or advance the wealth, status, and power of a family.[9] In a culture of limited goods, this practice had the devastating effect of keeping power in the hands of a very few. In this sexist system, women were possessions to be acquired. Herod's marriage to Herodias amounted to keeping his brother's wealth (including Herodias) in the family.

Both men and women collaborated in the system, as Herodias' plot against John attests.[10] In the patriarchal system reflected in Mark, women are denied positions of official authority and the "only powerful woman in Mark is also, after Judas, one of its most reviled villains."[11] Of course,

Herodias' options are severely limited. What would happen to her if John's challenge to the practice of endogamy were successful? Even Herod, who by virtue of his position near the top of the patriarchal pyramid, has the greatest opportunity to benefit from the system, is manipulated by it. Herod fears that John the Baptist has been raised from the dead (for revenge?). And he is forced by his need to demonstrate his power before his (male) guests to grant the bizarre request of his daughter.

Herod's power stands in sharp contrast with the power of John the Baptist. Of the characters who populate the New Testament writings, John the Baptist is the only one whose physical appearance is given any attention at all.[12] We are told in Mark 1:8 that John the Baptist wore a garment of camel's hair, a leather belt around his waist, and ate locusts and wild honey. In many cultures, hair is closely associated with physicality, sexual energy, an intimacy with nature, and nonconformity. Hair certainly functions this way throughout the biblical tradition. The focus on Esau's physicality is noted from his birth when "all his body [was] like a hairy mantle" (Gen. 25:25). Samson's hair is the secret to his strength and prowess, and its loss renders him impotent to resist the plot concocted between Delilah and the Philistines (Judges 16). Explicit instructions are given in both Old and New Testaments on how the hair should be kept or worn in order to maintain cultic purity (cf. Lev. 10:6; 1 Cor. 11:6, 14). Disheveled hair (according to Leviticus) or long hair (according to Paul) dishonors a man, pollutes his community, and ultimately threatens the political power structures that undergird the society.

The hairy garment of John the Baptist, then, is itself emblematic of the source of his power, a power that derives not from the dominant patriarchal structures (to which Herod is enslaved), but rather a power which originates in his own physical/spiritual energy, his defiance of cultural boundaries, and his grounding in a marginalized community, outside society. In other words, the power of John the Baptist derives from sources outside the power structures of the dominant patriarchal society.[13] John's dress also links him most closely to Elijah (cf. 2 Kings 1:8), the character who arguably in the Old Testament best reflects this integration of the sensual and spiritual.

This stance outside society is reinforced by his diet of "locusts and wild honey" and his location "in the wilderness." This closeness to the natural world gives further clues to the source of his spirituality and power. He draws his strength to challenge and resist Herod's world from a divine but earth-based source (cf. Ps. 24:1). John's role as initiator also underscores his rejection of the power structures of the dominant society. Jesus, through his baptism, is also initiated into John's marginalized community's struggle against the oppressive status quo. Jesus' apparent submission to John the Baptist and his community was evidently a constant source of embarrassment, if not an outright threat, to the early church.

His physicality, diet, locale, and initiating role, then, intimately link John's sensual and spiritual selves and challenge the spirit-body dichotomy. Herod, representing the status quo gender system, recognizes that John's challenge to the sexist dualism of endogamy is grounded in his defiance of spiritualistic dualism. The particular form of John's execution, then, is also instructive. Severing John's physicality from his spirituality, literally splitting apart mind and body, is certainly a fitting punishment against one who disrupts the prevailing dualisms of the culture. The removal of John the Baptist is no little relief to those committed to preserving the status quo gender system of the dominant culture.[14]

Excavating the Remains of John the Baptist in Matthew, Luke, and John

Noted New Testament scholar Raymond Brown has contended that "we find no tendency in the Christian records to excise the memory of [John the Baptist]."[15] While this is true in the sense that John the Baptist is never completely removed from the Gospel narrative, there is an increasingly intensified effort to diminish the role of John the Baptist (and his followers) in the story of Jesus and the early Christian movement. These efforts to remove certain aspects of John the Baptist from the Gospel narratives are more subtle than his dramatic beheading and therefore perhaps more insidious. John's spiritual/sensual connectedness (depicted through his dress, diet, locale, and role) and his challenge to the sexist practice of endogamy (conveyed through the account of his beheading) are diminished in Matthew and Luke and finally removed in John.

Matthew

Matthew, though preserving the references to dress and diet, clearly subordinates John's role to Jesus: "Then Jesus came from Galilee to John at the Jordan, to be baptized by him. John would have prevented him, saying, 'I need to be baptized by you, and do you come to me?' But Jesus answered him, 'Let it be so now; for it is proper for us in this way to fulfill all righteousness.' Then he consented" (Matt. 3:13–15). John's role as initiator of Jesus is "explained away" as fulfilling "righteousness."

Matthew also records the narrative of John's beheading with one or two subtle changes that obscure John's challenge to sexist dualism. In Mark, we are told that Herod arrested John, "for the sake of Herodias, his brother Philip's wife, *because he had married her*" (Mark 6:17; my emphasis), while Matthew simply reports that Herod arrested John, "for the sake of Herodias, his brother Philip's wife" (Matt. 14:3), omitting the reference to Herod's marriage to her. Likewise in Mark, John the Baptist emphasizes the sin of endogamy in his accusation against Herod with his words, "It is not lawful for you to have *your brother's wife*" (Mark 6:18, my emphasis), while in Matthew he says simply, "It is not lawful for you to have her" (Matt. 14:4).[16] The cumulative effect of these nuances is to muffle John's prophetic role in challenging the sexual politics of Herod.

Luke

Though Matthew modifies Mark's presentation of John with a light touch, Luke is much more severe in limiting the role of John the Baptist in his narrative. On the surface, it would appear that Luke gives much more attention to John than any of the other evangelists give. After all, the rhetorical pattern of Luke 1—2 suggests a comparison and contrast between Jesus and John in terms of the two annunciations (Luke 1:8–23; 1:26–38), the births and circumcisions (Luke 1:57–66; 2:1–21), the prophetic oracles (1:67–79; 2:22–38), and the childhood summaries (Luke 1:80; 2:40, 52).

Closer examination, however, demonstrates that Luke gives all this attention to John so that John can be "carefully played off against Jesus, and in each case . . . shown to be the lesser of the two."[17] In this regard, the titles given to the two in the Infancy Narrative are illuminating: John is called the "prophet of the Most High" while Jesus is given the clearly more exalted title of the "son of the Most High." This subordination continues throughout the narrative. In Luke 7, Jesus gives the double-edged verdict on John: he is both the "greatest among those born of women" (7:28), but at the same time, "the least in the kingdom of God is greater than he." John belongs to the age of the prophets or at most is the transitional figure to the preaching of "the kingdom of God" which is inaugurated in Jesus' ministry (Luke 16:16).

This subordination is extended also to John's followers in Luke's sequel, the Acts of the Apostles. The faith of John's disciples is judged inadequate because they had only received John's baptism (Acts 19:1–7). The bestowal of the Holy Spirit through the hands of Paul reveals the "spiritual" defect of John's baptism and the inferiority of his movement. In typical patriarchal logic, there can be only one leader of this movement, and, in Luke, John the Baptist and his followers are consistently confined to second-class citizenship in the kingdom of God.

Luke says nothing about the dress or diet of John, and the connection between John's physicality and spirituality is lost (cf. Luke 3:1ff.). Further, John's role of initiating Jesus is rendered highly ambiguous by Luke's rhetoric; while Jesus is certainly baptized in Luke's account, it is very unclear from the text who performs the act (cf. 3:21–22).[18] Not only is John's challenge to spiritualistic dualism muted, but his challenge to Herod's practice of sexist dualism, so prominent in Mark, is also diminished. In fact, the entire narrative of John's beheading is reduced to Herod's statement in Luke: "John I beheaded" (Luke 9:9).[19] Gone, then, is John's refutation of Herod's sexual politics in the practice of endogamy. Though John the Baptist is certainly an important figure for Luke, in the Third Gospel he no longer represents a challenge to the spiritualistic and sexist dualisms permeating ancient Mediterranean culture and perhaps by now also the church!

John

In the Fourth Gospel, John the Baptist is no longer given a physical depiction but rather is a "man sent from God" whose purpose is to bear witness to the Light, the Lamb of God (John 1:8, 29). Nor is any mention made of John baptizing Jesus. Nor, more importantly, is there any mention in the Fourth Gospel of John's beheading, not even Herod's terse statement recorded in Luke, "John I beheaded." From the narrative neglect of the Baptist in the Fourth Gospel, it appears that the Fourth Evangelist has made John the Baptist's assertion into a self-fulfilling prophecy: "He [Jesus] must increase, and I must decrease" (John 3:30). All that is left of John the Baptist by the time the Fourth Evangelist finishes with him is a disembodied "voice crying in the wilderness"!

Summary

Why does John the Baptist receive such harsh treatment? One might argue from the evidence of Matthew and Mark that early Christians blame the oppressive gender system of Herod and Herodias for this dismembering of John the Baptist, while the church preserves the integrity of John's spirituality and sensuality (after all, John's disciples in Mark seek to give him proper burial). Luke and John themselves, however, emasculate the very features that demonstrate the Baptist's challenge to spiritualistic and sexist dualisms.

Karen Jo Torjesen has suggested that as the church shifted from the private space of the household to the public space of basilicas and temples in the third and fourth centuries, there was also a shift from the position of shared and egalitarian leadership among men and women to a patriarchal perspective that privileged the male over the female. Women, identified with sensuality, were limited to the private sphere, and men, identified with the "spiritual," took over exclusive leadership of the church in its newly found public sphere.[20] The results were scandalous for both sexes.

Perhaps as the church moved from private to public space and became increasingly institutionalized (and therefore patriarchal) there was also less room for a character like John the Baptist, whose story was so out of step with the social conventions of masculinity. Men filled the public space as leaders of the church (so the Pastoral Epistles) but were forced to renounce their sensual/sexual selves. This ascetic tradition, culminating in a celibate order of male priests, was finally successful in co-opting John the Baptist as one of its "founders"—the same John the Baptist whose earliest traces in the Christian tradition linked him more to the integrated sensual/spiritual tradition of Elijah than to the asceticism of the later Desert Fathers!

Thus, in the end, both culture and church sustain the spirit/body split that leads to the problematic for modern man of how to be both spiritual and sensual and also of how to create a coherent vision of sexual equality. The scalpel of the evangelists is no less effective than the henchman's ax in severing John's sensual self from his spirituality. Nor have we, as modern men, been spared the sharp edge of that sword!

Conclusion:
Remembering John the Baptist

How do men reintegrate sensuality and spirituality, body and mind? How do Christian men, in particular, remember John the Baptist? Christian men seeking authentic spirituality will have to come to grips with the fact that they must move in two communities, the mainstream church and whatever group vitalizes their interest in men's issues. Feminists who still choose to identify with the Christian tradition have had to struggle with this issue. Men committed to being authentically male and authentically Christian will find ways to allow each of those communities to inform the other. This may mean taking our place in the "wilderness" between organized Christianity and a grassroots men's movement, moving back and forth between the two.

The Christian tradition provides for the mythopoetic men's movement a rich resource of stories and myths that contribute to the "reservoir" upon which we draw when "the conventional and current ways wear out."[21] One advantage to incorporating the biblical stories is their cultural familiarity. But the mythopoetic men's movement provides new ways of looking at these stories, critically and at times suspiciously, ways that are sensitive to what these images do and how they deeply shape the identities of Christian men. It means becoming aware of both the positive and harmful effects on gender identity of these stories for both women and men.

Further, by taking seriously that these stories and images emerge from our physicality and contingent, historical experiences, men can begin the process of healing the split between male sensuality and male spirituality.

The loss of the sensual from the Christian tradition has truncated especially white, Western male spirituality. Remembering John the Baptist in this context is an opportunity for men to learn to honor the male body, and thus begin to heal the spirit/body split that cripples so many men today.[22] Through the recovered image of John the Baptist, among others, men can learn to challenge the sexist dualism of our culture, and thus participate in the vital issues of gender justice. The tragic story of John the Baptist, however, also serves to remind us how dangerous these pursuits really are!

The mythopoetic men's movement with its characteristic emphasis on earth-based spirituality and ritual (like the Sweat Lodge, where the physical and spiritual are intimately integrated) may provide the context for Christian men to remember John the Baptist and thus contribute to the healing of the self, relationships, and the earth and to develop a clear, embodied vision of justice. Wherever such a vision takes shape, women and men will be found working together, whether within or outside the liturgical and didactic habits of the institutional church, to dismantle an oppressive gender system that many in our society continue to conspire together to maintain. The mythopoetic men's movement, despite its obvious problems, at its best is a hopeful sign that some men, now searching for a holistic and authentic spirituality, are also now joining the struggle for gender equity.

NOTES

1. The so-called mythopoetic men's movements are grassroots phenomena with no national organization but many local men's councils, workshop leaders, and writers to which men are responding in enthusiastic ways. The mythopoetic men's movement, as I have experienced it, is not to be identified with the backlash movement, the Promise Keepers, founded by the head coach of the University of Colorado football team, whose goal is to reassert male dominance in the nuclear family. Still, many have noted a tendency toward misogynism, even among the more prominent leaders of the mythopoetic men's movement. On this, see especially Susan Faludi, *Backlash: The Undeclared War against American Women* (New York: Crown, 1991), 312, and Philip Culbertson's critique of the men's movement and attempt to reform from within in "Men Dreaming of Men: Using Mitch Walerk's 'Double Animus' in Pastoral Care," *Harvard Theological Review* 86 (1993): 219–32. On the mythopoetic men's movement as but one perspective on men's issues, see Kenneth Clatterbaugh, *Contemporary Perspectives on Masculinity: Men, Women, and Politics in Modern Society* (Boulder, Colo.: Westview Press, 1990).

2. See Edward Farley's insightful critique of the four modes of knowing in *The Fragility of Knowledge: Theological Education in the Church and the University* (Philadelphia: Fortress Press, 1988).

3. A major point made by James Nelson, in *The Intimate Connection: Male Sexuality, Masculine Spirituality.* (Philadelphia: Westminster Press, 1988).

4. Ibid., 23.

5. Ibid., 22.

6. Though I am employing the mythopoetic strategy of exploring stories as a reservoir for shaping an authentic male spirituality, I do not employ the Jungian language of archetypes. For a critique of Jungian archetypes as a perpetuation of the soul/body dichotomy, see Naomi R. Goldenberg, *Returning Words to Flesh: Feminism, Psychoanalysis, and the Resurrection of the Body* (Boston: Beacon Press, 1990). By employing universalizing archetypes, some within the mythopoetic men's movement (see, e.g., Robert Bly, *Iron John: A Book about Men* [New York: Vintage Books, 1990]) have inadvertently employed a theory of disembodied, universal ideas to connect men with their physicality. The effect is once again to cut men off from their physical, sensual selves.

7. On a "plausible interpretation," see Mieke Bal, *Death and Dissymmetry: The Politics of Coherence in the Book of Judges* (Chicago: University of Chicago Press, 1988), 240–41.

8. For a feminist critique of this story in Mark, see Janice Capel Anderson, "Feminist Criticism: The Dancing Daughter," in *Mark and Method,* ed. Janice Capel Anderson and Stephen Moore, (Minneapolis: Augsburg Fortress, 1992), 103–34.

9. This reading would make sense especially if the reader is aware of Josephus's description of Herod and Herodias (see *Antiquities,* vol. 18, no. 5, pp. 1–4).

10. Of course, blaming Herodias for John's death may itself be a move motivated by a patriarchal perspective; see Anderson, "Dancing Daughter," 131ff.; also Mary Ann Tolbert, "Mark," in *The Women's Bible Commentary,* ed. Carol A. Newsom and Sharon H. Ringe (Louisville: Westminster/John Knox Press, 1992), 272.

11. Anderson, "Dancing Daughter," 131.

12. We know next to nothing from the canonical Gospels of the physical attributes or dress, for example, of Jesus, Peter, or Paul.

13. This defiance may be best seen in his searing challenge to the leaders of the religio-political establishment who come to be baptized by him: "You brood of vipers! Who warned you to flee from the wrath to come?" (Matt. 3:7/Luke 3:7). This saying is found in the other earliest document from the early church, a sayings Gospel known as "Q" comprising material shared by Luke and Matthew (but not in Mark) and coming from a period slightly earlier than Mark (probably the decade of the 50s in the first century). For more on Q, and its depiction of John the Baptist, see Walter Wink, *John the Baptist in the Gospel Tradition* (Cambridge: Cambridge University Press, 1968), and more recently Robert L. Webb, *John the Baptizer and Prophet: A Socio-Historical Study,* Journal for the Study of the New Testament—Supplement Series 62 (Sheffield: JSOT Press, 1992).

14. John's disciples continue this dissenting posture by valuing John's

body enough to seek to give it an honorable burial (Mark 6:29—unlike Jesus' disciples, who leave that task to women and outsiders like Joseph of Arimathea; cf. Mark 15:43–16:1). Compare this reading with Anderson's rendering ("Dancing Daughter," 127ff.) of John's beheading as a "symbolic castration."

15. Raymond E. Brown, *The Birth of the Messiah: A Commentary on the Infancy Narratives in Matthew and Luke* (New York: Doubleday & Co., 1977) 283.

16. It is also interesting that Matthew's account seems to exonerate Herodias. In Matthew, Herod, not Herodias, wishes to put John to death (Matt. 14:5; cf. Mark 6:19), though she is not completely vindicated since she is still responsible for prompting her daughter to ask for John's head on a platter (even here, however, Herodias speaks in indirect discourse as opposed to her direct speech in Mark 6:24).

17. John Darr, *On Character Building: The Reader and the Rhetoric of Characterization in Luke-Acts* (Louisville: Westminster/John Knox Press, 1992), 84. The title of this chapter was suggested to me by Darr's chapter title on John the Baptist, "Recapitating John the Baptist: Holism, Rhetoric, and Characterization."

18. Many scholars read this ambiguous text as Luke's way of removing the embarrassment in the early church of Jesus' submitting to John's baptism; see Wink, *John the Baptist,* 83.

19. This is also another instance of the subordination of John to Jesus: only Jesus' confrontation with Herod is fully dramatized in Luke (cf. Luke 13:31–35; 23:6–12); see Darr, *On Character Building,* 78–79.

20. Karen Jo Torjesen, *When Women Were Priests* (San Francisco: Harper San Francisco, 1993). I am in basic agreement with Torjesen's argument but would suggest from my analysis here that the process of exclusion for males who defied the accepted gender roles of the dominant culture began as early as the end of the first century C.E.

21. Bly, *Iron John,* xi.

22. Though little has been said in this chapter about the environment, healing the mind/body schism may also empower men to honor the earth and participate in the vital issues of ecology. On this topic, see further, Sam Keen, *Fire in the Belly: On Being a Man* (New York: Bantam Books, 1991), 91–93, 177–85; 230–32, and passim.

14

INITIATION AND THE
MALE SPIRITUAL QUEST

Robert Moore and Douglas Gillette

Increasingly today, men and women are struggling to live in a twilight world of gender confusion. Anxiously they wonder what, if anything, constitutes their own unique sexual identity. Women don business suits and become bankers and lawyers. Men clean house and learn to change diapers. These shifts in traditional work roles may be all to the good. But are there any real differences between men and women? If not, what joy is left us in sexual union? Have we become interchangeable parts, androgynous to the core?

Some teach us to feel ashamed of our sex-specific differences. Supporters of radical androgyny go so far as to discourage research into the dissimilarities in brain structure, or in the chemical, hormonal, or instinctual configurations that may influence some culturally exaggerated scripts. Some theorists offer stereotyped ideals of "feminine" psychological characteristics, now alone deemed fully human. Boys are said to be developmentally inferior to girls. Men are held to be biologically and emotionally inferior to women. Some radical feminists assert women would be better off without men entirely—or that male children should be genetically or socially engineered to eliminate "masculine aggressiveness."

This is not to say that all feminist criticism is invalid. The feminist critique of patriarchal societies makes a great deal of sense. Patriarchy *does* tend to institutionalize a particular kind of masculinity, prone to exploiting and oppressing other human beings, other species, and the environment. But oppressive, "macho" societies deny *men* their mature masculinity as certainly as they degrade women and feminine attributes. Typically a small minority of underdeveloped males at the top of the social pyramid will control power and wealth to the exclusion of all others, male and female. They rank these others in a descending order of usefulness to themselves and defend against them with all the force of their inflated self-regard. Patriarchy is therefore a manifestation of the infantile grandiosity suffered by its leaders.

Patriarchy is set up and run not for men as a gender or for masculinity in its fullness or in its mature expressions but rather by men who are fundamentally immature. It is really the rule of boys, often cruel and abusive boys. For the most part, we believe human societies have always consisted of boys and girls more or less unconsciously acting out their immature and grandiose fantasies. Our planetary home more often than not has resembled the island world in William Golding's *Lord of the Flies.* Thus our societies have, on the whole, opposed the realization and expression of *both* mature feminine and masculine psyches.

We feel it is wrong to view patriarchy as the expression of mature masculinity or of masculinity in its essence. Patriarchal societies are out of balance partly because at their helm are unbalanced men. And while we abhor the often horrific abuses of patriarchal systems, we also remember that males helped generate, from earlier urban neolithic cultures, all the higher civilizations we know from recorded history. The efforts of dynamic, life-engendering men have left an astounding record of discovery and achievement. Clearly the energies of men, in partnership with women and their feminine energies, have fueled (and will continue to fuel) the significant advances of imagination and social organization that characterize our species. Men of the past, in every tribe and nation, have struggled to learn how to use their power to bless the human community. We continue to struggle today.

Defining masculine and feminine characteristics has led to much discussion. After years of research, depth psychologists and others argue that each sex carries both the psychological and physical traits of the other. No man is purely masculine, just as there is no purely feminine woman. Jungian psychologists call the feminine characteristics of the male psyche the Anima; the female psyche's masculine characteristics they call the Animus.

Both the Animus and the Anima develop in complex fashion as the personality grows to maturity. Neither men nor women can reach psychological maturity without integrating the respective contra-sexual other. A man's female elements enhance his manhood, just as a woman's male aspects enhance her womanhood. Typically masculine characteristics are dominant in a man, as are feminine characteristics in a woman, although there are of course exceptions. Central to all these discussions is the question of whether masculinity is in its *essence* more coercive, more abusive of power, more compulsively dominance-seeking than femininity. Many have implied or argued that biological gender differences *necessitate* rigid sex-role differentiation and make masculine dominance *inevitable.*

Even if it could be proved, however, that some traditionally masculine or feminine *tendencies* may be inherited, this would not be a basis for justifying the usual caricatures of these traits. Above all, it does not justify the assumption that men are inherently violent, inordinately aggressive, insensitive, and uninterested in intimate relationships, nor that women have a monopoly on gentle nurturing, emotional, and intuitive behaviors. Probably the most accurate argument is that men are more "hard-wired" for some psychological tendencies and women for others. Unfortunately, historical cultures nearly always have amplified rather than helped us compensate for these tendencies.

We intend rather to advance understanding of the deep masculine and the challenge of stewarding masculine power. *For whatever the source of masculine abuse of power, it is our responsibility as contemporary men to understand it and to develop the emotional and spiritual resources to end it.* We want to help men express what psychoanalyst Erik Erikson termed the "generative man" within themselves.

Contrary to those thinkers who, with Reinhold Niebuhr, regard power itself as inevitably leading to evil, we believe it is possible to steward power responsibly. The drive toward attaining personal and corporate empowerment is as much a part of our instinctual makeup as eating, sleeping, and procreating. We cannot wish away what Friedrich Nietzsche called the "will to power," the desire to overcome. We cannot and should not raise our children to eschew this primal and ultimately life-enhancing instinct. The issue should never be how to get rid of the urge for power, masculine or feminine. The real issue is how to steward it, and how to channel our other instincts along with it into life-giving and world-building activities.

The creative use of instinctual male energies, like the good use of any energy source, requires maturity. Human maturity has probably always been a rare commodity. But we believe it was, at least in some respects, more available even in patriarchal states, with all of their drawbacks, than it is in our modern societies. In the past there were powerful rites of initiation presided over by ritual elders to help boys and girls remake themselves into men and women capable of assuming their social responsibilities. The scope of these premodern initiation rituals was often limited by inflexible cultural norms. But they did provide boys and girls with workable blueprints for achieving gender-specific maturity and were based on mythic visions of the tribe's view of the best in human nature—their normative vision of the possible human.

All human beings need to be initiated into the wise and life-enhancing uses of human psychological resources. Where misunderstood, the energies of our psyches can wreak havoc upon our lives. Despite the elaborate training our modern society provides an individual mastering a trade, we do not think to offer anything similar to the man who wishes to master his own psyche. But our lack of teachers does not change our need to learn how to access the powerful energies of our deep souls.

Essentially, the process of initiation removes our ego from the center of the universe. When a society abandons initiation rituals, individual egos lose an appropriate means of learning this valuable lesson. Life circumstances will urge the same lesson upon the ego eventually, but perhaps in a very painful, inopportune manner. But by far the most serious consequence of ceasing initiatory practices is the loss of a periodic social forum for considering the nature of maturity. A society has to know what maturity is before it can pass the knowledge on. When people bemoan our culture's loss of values, in part they are missing the old transformative rituals—for rituals provide a structure within which social values can be recalled and reconsidered.

As a complete cultural system, modernity has largely turned its back on God, on effective processes of initiation, on ritual elders, and even on family, tribe, and nation. Consequently, an individual ego can no longer reach the sober but joyous realization of its *non*central position in the psyche and in the wider universe. Nature fills the vacuum modernity has created with our modern egos, which expand terrifically to fill the empty space. Where a powerful Transpersonal Other is missing, God is replaced by unconscious pretensions to godhood.

An individual psyche, bloated by dangerously distorted assessments of self and of others around it—family, friends, lovers, company, nation, and perhaps the entire globe—must pay the price for its infantilism. Corrupt politicians, money-hungry yuppies, drug dealers, wife (and husband) abusers, and new racists are but a few examples of infantilism run amok. Petty dictators, self-styled fundamentalist "messiahs" and their terrorist henchmen, Khmer Rouge genocidal murderers, Chinese Communist Party bullies, and irresponsible international oil company executives, among many others, cause the social and environmental devastation that always accompanies the ego inflation of the human psyche unchecked by a sense of limits grounded in a Transpersonal Other. These would-be men and women have failed to grasp a sufficiently wide and deep vision of the archetypal realities upon which our psyche is founded. It is time we look again to these deep structures and draw from them the psychic support our modern era so desperately needs.

The Importance of Initiation

Initiation into a richer, deeper, more mature way of being human always occurs in sacred time and space. Mircea Eliade noted that premodern peoples all recognized the heterogeneous, multidimensional nature of reality. According to him, these peoples experienced two basic forms of reality. The day-to-day form Eliade called "profane," hence the other—the mind-bending, gut-wrenching form—was termed "sacred."

Sacred space and time always carry a charge of libido. Bearing an up-rush of unconscious archetypal material, sacred reality can devastate an ego if not adequately contained and managed. Before it becomes heal-ing—which it does only under optimal conditions, when stewarded by a magician—it makes a person crazy. We all know the craziness of contact with the sacred dimension, from the death of a loved one, the loss of an important job, or a separation or divorce.

The three stages that follow the constellation of the magician arche-type have been described by all the scholars of initiation. Eliade speaks of a wearing down of profane time, the entrance into sacred time, and then the reenactment of archetypal cosmogonic processes. Joseph Camp-bell speaks in parallel of the call, the belly of the whale, and the return. Using more technical language, Victor Turner describes structure, limi-nality, and the reconstruction of structure (or status enhancement).

Stage One:
The Call

The call to initiation can come at any time. Jungians believe the ar-chetypal self is always trying to get our attention. The self engineers all sorts of attempts to call us into initiation. The urgency of the call in-creases at certain phases of our lives when our ego structures are partic-ularly inadequate to face our changing circumstances. The self's methods of calling us send us into crisis, and we are forced to attend to the mes-sage. Of course we may be (and most frequently are) completely uncon-scious of being led by this process. *But to the archetypal self, life is quite simply a continuous process of initiation, a series of deaths and re-births.*

There are two basic kinds of call into the initiatory process. The first is directly linked to our life cycles. In adolescence, the call comes to boys and girls in part because of the suddenly accelerated release of sex-specific hormones. This call is to accept adult feelings, interests, and re-sponsibilities. In premodern societies, the initiatory call is celebrated and embraced by well-known puberty rites, Arnold van Gennep's original *rites de passage*. Boys were separated from their mothers and isolated in special structures created for the purpose. They were then initiated into manhood by the tribe's ritual elders.

The use of terror and physical mutilation, either scarring or circumci-sion, was one important aspect of a boy's initiation. The inculcation of wonder and awe through the teaching of the tribe's sacred myths was an-other. Alternatively, the boys were driven out into the wilderness on vi-sion quests. They faced physical danger and even the possibility of death. A girl's initiation occurs differently; at the time of her first menstruation, she will often be set apart and instructed by the wise old women in the mysteries of womanhood. A girl's passage is easier to place, since it occurs with a definite physical event; perhaps the ceremonies making a boy's passage into maturity are more elaborate because the event needed to be created. The primitive tribes who hold these initiation ceremonies realize that human beings need to die to their old selves before they can be born anew.

Life-cycle changes can be gut-wrenching and mind-bending. But when the call to initiation comes to us through *trauma,* the second form of the call to become fulfilled, it can be emotionally and cognitively even more difficult to handle. Often the self will initiate a life crisis without the ego even being aware of the fact. A man is going along with his life, things seem to be going pretty well—he has a loving wife, a middle-class lifestyle, kids who are thriving in school, and there looks to be a promotion on the horizon. And then, pow! He comes home one day to find a note on the refrigerator that his wife has left him and has taken the kids and the checkbook.

After experiencing a tear in the seamless fabric of his consciousness, a man realizes that everything that had seemed so certain is not certain at all. He begins to challenge his assumptions. As one by one they are stripped away, he tumbles head over heels into crazy time.

Grief over a loss sheds a whole new light on everything. We find depths within ourselves that had previously remained hidden and repressed. A forbidding new world shatters our illusions of omnipotence. We are forced to submit to a radical realization of our helplessness and our finitude. Suddenly our plans and dreams are crushed as irrevocably as houses are tumbled in earthquakes and farmlands are smothered in toxic volcanic ash.

Every time we reach a crisis of real proportions, we go over the first threshold. This stage parallels what ritual scholars call "stripping" or "ritual humiliation." This is where the first ordeals are faced, and where the ego realizes the forces it is up against are far greater than expected. The fears faced by the Greek initiates into Demeter's mysteries were engineered to bring about this realization.

There are people who seem not to be unnerved by their major life crises. They manage them with hardly a whimper, and never with the odd look in the eyes that signals the onset of crazy time. Maybe a man does handle things well when the crisis is upon him and then falls apart privately later. Or perhaps he never does fall apart. His life rigidifies. His speech becomes clipped and short, as if choked off. His eyes lose their luster. When we see a neighbor deal with a loss as if nothing has happened, it may be precisely because nothing has happened. He may be so locked out of his emotional soul that he was able to feel nothing at all. A crisis demands change and suffering, and a rigid response does no one any good.

If a man comes upon an initiatory phase in his life, perhaps a midlife crisis, and he doesn't recognize it as potentially initiatory, he can end up less of a man than he was to begin with. The crisis can cripple him. If he gets the right guidance during the crisis, he can become much larger than before. But to accomplish this he must die to certain aspects of himself. If he is unwilling to let those aspects go, he reduces himself—by rigidifying the old myths of his life, and not accepting the new ones offered him by his unconscious.

A man moving into extraordinary space and time often begins acting out his sexual impulses. The ancients kept temple prostitutes in recognition of this. A man may have grown comfortable and complacent with his wife, when suddenly he meets someone new. He pursues his new affair at all costs, putting his job, his status, and his marriage in jeopardy. His old structures are unexpectedly dissolved, and he finds himself floundering in deep water. Most often what he is trying to do is hold on to his youth and deny the reality of his approaching death. And so he finds himself suddenly abandoning the social expectations his old persona has led everyone to expect.

There is an important truth to recognize concerning the acting out of sexual impulses. At bottom an extramarital affair is a spiritual quest. A misdirected quest perhaps, but a quest nonetheless. A man who starts sleeping around is looking for spiritual renewal. He is looking in the wrong place, but that is probably because there are no ritual elders available in his life to guide him.

Social norms and expectations are dissolved in sacred space and time. With this dissolution comes a rapid rise in anxiety. The escalation of anxiety levels indicates that previously unlived material from the deep unconscious is pressing up against the repression barrier, and threatening to erupt. When a man feels the pressure of a call from the unconscious building up, he needs to find a safe and contained way of being in extraordinary reality. He needs boundaries and someone to help him steward these boundaries and insulate his ego against the powerful instincts, needs, and memories that threaten to overwhelm him.

If a man is not to become a tyrant holdfast, he must acquire true humility. Humility helps him to submit his ego to the liquefying and deconstructing effects of his own unleashed unconscious. In traditional societies it was the older men who ritually humbled a boy, showing him, at times with brute psychological and physical force, that his ego was not in fact the center of the universe. While humiliation doesn't always allow for a state of true humility, it is sometimes regrettably necessary to humiliate an arrogant ego. A basic psychological rule is that an ego that cannot learn humility on its own will, in fact, find some means of humiliating itself.

People often sense their own need for humiliation and go off unconsciously looking for humiliating experiences. They may turn to alcohol or drugs in a primitive attempt at self-abasement. In the absence of the rituals ancient peoples used to confront the greatest modulator of grandiosity there is—death—modern men often only flirt with their own mortality. Men who cover their bodies in tattoos, cut themselves with knives, or burn themselves with cigarettes are involved in this same search for submission. Men who torture others are unconsciously mutilating their own grandiose selves, projected onto their victims.

Stage Two:
The Belly of the Whale

The belly of the whale is equivalent to what Saint John of the Cross called "the dark night of the soul," and Turner called *liminality.*

There is no escaping the largely unpleasant material now brought to our attention. Our shortcomings, repressed desires, and shadow sides are exposed. At this fateful time we may withdraw our projections from others, and admit our own less-than-ideal attributes. In this liminal space we experience what psychologists call "the return of the repressed." Painful memories, unresolved childhood developmental issues, unfinished business with our hidden grandiosity—all rise to the surface in painful succession.

Unresolved childhood rage can burst forth with an almost cosmic intensity. The passion for life that we deny ourselves can emerge in a murderous frenzy. Those talents, hatreds, enthusiasms, and potentials we have never lived out, but have projected onto others, come pounding on the doors of our repression barriers. Smoldering neuroses become psychoses. Pervasive suspiciousness becomes florid paranoia. Naive tenderness becomes pathetic dependence and maudlin sentimentality.

Sacred space and time look very crazy to the structured ego. And structure is something human beings need, because it reinforces the ego, not to mention the orderly functioning of society. To an outside observer, someone undergoing deconstruction and regeneration is a loose cannon, dangerous and definitely to be avoided. We all have experienced watching someone at a painful crisis, a divorce perhaps, turning to his friends and being met by subtle avoidance behaviors and disapproval. The friends who give him a cold shoulder do not wish to be reminded of the weaknesses in their marriages. The fear is that even proximity to someone in the belly of the whale marks the friend to be swallowed next. Extraordinary states bear a "psychic contagion," and this is why ancient people used boundaries and taboos to contain them. Extraordinary reality threatens to undo us.

Containment is an important part of the optimal experience in the belly of the whale. A marriage partner can offer containment, though this is rarely successful. A relationship as intimate as that may not necessarily be strong enough to withstand the eruptions of rage and other archetypal material that occurs in crazy time. And sometimes the rage is directed specifically against the marriage partner.

Religious communities can provide ritual containment, but because most establishment religions have been thoroughly modernized, even this possibility is unlikely now. A modernized religion either does not acknowledge that extraordinary space and time exist, or does not think them vital to the process of human psychological growth. Many modern clergymen look askance at parishioners who are in the midst of life transitions. And few have any understanding of themselves as ritual leaders; they have forsaken the call to be true initiatory guides. Most modern ministers have virtually no understanding of the power of ritual and symbol. True to their iconoclastic Protestant heritage, they reject such things as "superstitious devices." But ritual prepares and orients the psyche that has been called to enter crazy space. Without it, and without some means of understanding the symbols and images that occur there, the psyche can only lose its beginnings.

In short, many religious leaders no longer understand or accept their roles as ritual elders and spirit guides. They believe a little training in a pastoral counseling technique qualifies them to heal. They have little sense of the depth and power of the human soul.

But if our desire for guidance is keen enough, we will find it. It may not be from the expected, or even the ideal, direction; still it seems to be true that the self always finds some way to carry out its agendas. Nonetheless we must make every effort in this society to offer some means of initiation, and the containment it requires.

While extraordinary reality can be terrifying, it is also regenerative and transforming. As the dark night of the soul begins to lift, and the heavy weight of sorrow and fear begins to dissipate, we may feel a kind of ecstasy.

Stage Three:
The Return

As Joseph Campbell reminds us, we face enormous difficulties getting back out of sacred reality. A man's initiation must be reflected in a number of positive qualities, values, and achievements that influence the way he lives and his attitudes and involvements in the wider human community. We present a few keys that may be used to recognize maturation along the line of development.

An initiated man will develop his capacities for self-understanding—for knowing himself, his patterns, his "shadow" tendencies, his strengths and weaknesses, the primary agendas for struggle in his movement toward wholeness and full empowerment as a man. He will do what is necessary and pay the price of moving toward mature awareness of the psychosocial dynamics manifest in himself and others.

An initiated man will not be easy prey for the simplistic, totalistic, and tribal visions offered by the spiritual, political, or ideological charlatans of his day. He will not allow "true believers" of any totalistic pietism to narrow his view of either the human past or the human future. He will find other means to manage his anxiety without surrendering the freedom of his mind to ideologues.

An initiated man will not allow himself to ignore his moral and spiritual responsibility for the stewardship of his cognitive, intellectual, and academic achievements. He will struggle resolutely against the prostitution of his mind by antisocial and unjust political and economic interests that are the enemies of an inclusive human future.

What is certain is that he will provide liberating, empowering, and healing ritual leadership for his people. He will steward his shamanic potential for the earth community.

The best way to negotiate a successful return to the world is to be helped with establishing, while still in the belly of the whale, new structures and behaviors.

NOTES

This chapter is adapted from Robert Moore and Douglas Gillette, *The Magician Within* (New York: William Morrow & Co., 1993), by permission of the publisher.

15

MEN AND THE PROMISE
OF GODDESS SPIRITUALITY:
REFLECTIONS ALONG THE WAY

Seth Mirsky

Men generally are not accustomed to considering feminism in its constructive aspect: as a path (or variety of paths) toward a positively transformed self and world. Usually—and necessarily in a male-dominated society—it is feminism's critical character that takes precedence, for there is so much in our lives that demands critique. Yet what I find most promising in the more visionary feminist perspectives is precisely their insistence on the possibility of different lives for both men and women: lives not determined by patriarchal values, taking form in ways we have yet to discover. For me, feminist Goddess spirituality carries such promise. Its far-reaching potential to change men's lives motivates the reflections that follow.

In the great blossoming of feminist work in constructive theology and thealogy[1] over the past quarter century, men, for all practical purposes, have yet to be heard from (other than as opponents). With few exceptions, male students and practitioners of contemporary religion have not responded seriously to the profound reenvisioning of the divine effected particularly by those feminists working to re-create Goddess traditions.[2] These traditions carry challenging and disorienting messages for men, but messages that I believe ultimately hold the promise of healing—both for men and for a world that has suffered too long under men's rule. If men wish to understand the implications of these messages for our lives, we must begin our own explorations of the Goddess and of all that she evokes.

I come to Goddess spirituality by the varied routes through which I attempt to make sense of my life in the world: politics, study, feeling, meditation, ritual, and theology. My reflections here arise in response to a simple-sounding question I originally set for myself—a question that consciously echoes the title of a groundbreaking essay by feminist thealogian Carol P. Christ[3]—namely, do men need the Goddess? I now realize that I am not in a position to answer this question in any more than a suggestive way, for I have not answered it decisively in my own life. Nor can I answer for all men, since I know that the particular conditions of my life have much to do with how I experience Goddess spirituality: what is powerful for me, what is scary, what is comfortable, and what I may miss entirely. There are many ways to the Goddess, and indeed many Goddesses to encounter.

The sources for my reflections encompass both written word and lived personal experience. As thealogian Emily Erwin Culpepper notes, "The primary source, the continuing referent, for thealogical inspiration is one's Self, understood as the consciously reflective Self in communication with others."[4] Thus my own deepest intuitions and feelings, experienced alone or shared with others, motivate my engagement with Goddess thealogy and animate its expression here.

Added to these, as partners in critical and constructive ongoing conversation, are the voices of those who have written, often bravely and movingly, of their own encounters with the Goddess and of the messages she brings for contemporary women and men. In particular, I have found nourishment and encouragement in the ideas and practices of feminist Witchcraft and other Pagan, nature-oriented traditions.[5] The character of my account of Goddess spirituality inevitably reflects my choice of sources, but this choice in turn bears witness to what I have found most important and enlivening in the varied thealogical approaches that have arisen in recent years.

What I offer here is a consideration of issues I find important when I think of the Goddess, and particularly those that concern men's position in Goddess spirituality. From questions of religious symbolization to insights into the political dimensions of spiritual practice, the Goddess challenges the habitual patriarchal understandings of the world with which I and other men have grown up. In seeking to change those understandings (and the actions to which they give rise), men may find much of value in Goddess spirituality, including alternative models of maleness and a renewed sense of participation in the natural world. What is perhaps more important, through an appreciation of the deeply life-affirming message of the Goddess, men ultimately may render ourselves safe for, and thereby fit to live on, a fragile and beautiful planet.

On Creating Religion:
The Goddess in Question

My reflections on Goddess spirituality begin with the matter of just who or what the Goddess *is*. Here already the transforming character of feminist thealogy becomes evident, for this single term—*Goddess*—is imagined and engaged with in a multitude of creative ways, by writers and activists in vital conversation. Feminists involved with the Goddess realize that, in many respects, they are participating in the creation of religion to supplant the moribund and oppressive patriarchal traditions that still hold sway at the end of the twentieth century.[6] For them no religious concept is a given, and even "the Goddess" is a contested term. This conscious acceptance of the responsibility for symbol creation means that the Goddess who is honored and evoked by feminists is likely to remain a Goddess in question.

A brief survey of contemporary Goddess thealogy reveals a striking lack of unanimity, although certain elements—among them the Goddess's strong association with embodied, earthly life—do remain constant. For Nelle Morton, the Goddess functions as a revelatory "metaphoric image";[7] for Carol Christ, as a living symbol affirming the value of women's lives and of human connection to nature.[8] Naomi R. Goldenberg understands the Goddesses (and Gods) as "inner psychic forces,"[9] while Culpepper identifies the Goddess as (among other things) "an organizing principle for meditation, ritual and action."[10] In her description of the Goddess of Witchcraft, Margot Adler highlights "the fact that one can *worship* the Goddess without *believing* in Her."[11] And finally, in what I find a particularly intriguing and evocative conceptualization, Starhawk defines the Goddess in the terms of sublime paradox, as simultaneously "psychological symbol" and "manifest reality": "She is both. She exists, *and* we create Her."[12]

What are we to make of such a jumble of varying and even conflicting interpretations? Either it indicates a distressing lack of clarity about as central a thealogical term as the Goddess, or it illustrates the great creative potential of the Goddess as occasion for the free play of religious imagination. I suspect the latter. For I believe that the Goddess, as she is being currently remembered and created, provides worlds of religious meaning and experience for those who invoke her. Although I myself am never quite at home with personifications of the divine of any sort, I find that contemplation of the Goddess elicits in me an intuition of a kind of power that feels deep and authentic, connecting me to a larger reality that usually remains locked out of my consciousness.

If Goddess spirituality thus allows for both profound individual spiritual experience and a creative proliferation of religious meanings, it also incorporates a constant questioning of its own premises. For example, serious objections to a tendency toward rigid monotheism have been raised by a number of writers within Goddess feminism. Adler, drawing on the polytheistic perspective of Neo-Paganism, suggests, "The problem of Goddess monotheism will have to be resolved if the feminist Craft [Witchcraft] is not to become just another One True Right and Only Way."[13] And

Culpepper sharpens and expands on this criticism by focusing on the political effects of what she calls "Mother Goddess Monotheism," a phenomenon that, she argues, results in the "*generic erasure*" of the multiplicity of different women's lives.[14] Pointing out the dangers of a falsely assumed unity, she writes: "Distortions in thealogy occur when a monotheistic focus on The Goddess allows imagery of this Goddess to remain predominantly envisioned by privileged groups."[15]

What is instructive about this sort of questioning of the Goddess is the space that feminist thealogy provides for it. Indeed, the political logic of feminist spirituality *requires* it: if an emerging religious conceptualization serves to hinder rather than further liberation, then the conceptualization itself needs to be reassessed and perhaps revised, in a context of community participation. As long as Goddess thealogy and practice can maintain this kind of critical flexibility and suppleness, while continuing to honor the deep roots they have sunk into the powers of earth-based spirituality, I believe they can provide the transforming insights and experiences that their followers—both female and male—seek.

Political and Spiritual Dynamics: The Goddess in Practice

> . . . Before we can bring to birth the vision of an integrated culture, we have to see it. We have to see new images in the mind's eye, venture forth into a changed landscape, tell new stories. . . . So our vision-seeking lands us inevitably in the realm of religion, however unwilling we are to go there, because what we term religion is the soil of culture, in which the belief systems, the stories, the thought-forms upon which all other institutions are based are consciously or unconsciously grown.[16]

This observation by Starhawk points up the powerful political motivation behind much of contemporary Goddess spirituality, and indicates feminists' realization that significant social change must reach to the sources of our value systems to have any lasting effect. Such a redefinition of the political and spiritual realms as common territory is for me one of the major accomplishments of activist-thealogians like Starhawk, as they seek to build on and deepen the impact of the women's movement in transforming patriarchal society. Similarly, Carol Christ draws on the work of anthropologist Clifford Geertz to describe important connections between social and symbolic worlds: "Symbols have both psychological and political effects, because they create the inner conditions (deep-seated attitudes and feelings) that lead people to feel comfortable with or to accept social and political arrangements that correspond to the symbol system."[17]

It follows, then, that changing society requires (among other things) changing the symbols through which society lives. For Christ, Starhawk, and others, Goddess spirituality can be a vehicle for such change, since in a fundamental sense it is a spirituality in, of, and for the world.

As evoked by many thealogians, the Goddess expresses the outlook of "immanence": the idea that, as Starhawk puts it, "the world itself is the content of the world, its true value, its heart, and its soul."[18] In other words, whatever we mean by "divinity," "the sacred," "the ultimate," and other such terms is to be found in this world, the one in which we live. Rather than diminishing our conception of the divine, this perspective heightens the value we place on our actual lives and on the world as we know it. Starhawk describes this change in orientation as "choosing an attitude: choosing to take this living world, the people and creatures on it, as the ultimate meaning and purpose of life, to see the world, the earth, and our lives as sacred."[19] Such a stance encourages an ethical and political involvement with the needs of life on earth, rather than a personal escape into the imagined consolations of a "transcendent" spiritual realm "beyond" the cares and struggles of finite human existence.[20]

Before going on to explore what I see as issues of particular relevance to men in Goddess spirituality, I wish to bring up one additional aspect of the politics of religion that I find important in considering the Goddess. It is a point that has been made repeatedly by feminist thealogians (and theologians), perhaps never more dramatically than by Nelle Morton: ". . . To substitute Goddess, an exclusively female image, and one classed as pagan, in the place of God immediately confronts the maleness in God, which produces a shock, a shattering, and opens the way for exorcising the old image."[21]

In other words, "gender-neutral" terminology and imagery or "equal-time" theology (e.g., "God . . . he" alternating with "God . . . she") are not strong enough alternatives to displace the traditional patriarchal images of divine authority that persist in our minds (even if we are not religious).

This is a controversial point but a crucial one for me, in that I do not consider myself to have an allegiance to a patriarchal God—or any God— to begin with. Even so, when I reflect on the Goddess, "a power comes who is different from what comes when we say 'he' or 'it.'"[22] For me, it is a power strong enough to clear some space in my consciousness and allow me to sense the possibility of a vitality in the universe that has not been defined, domesticated, and eradicated by the patriarchal order. Usually it is just a possibility that I sense, but enough of one to encourage me to use the word "Goddess": as a political act, and because of the particular kind of mystery she brings.

The God: Maleness in the Realm of the Goddess

Within some varieties of Goddess spirituality there is a recognized and defined place for men and for conceptions of "maleness." The prominence of this male aspect depends on which tradition, thealogian, or practitioner is involved, but where a male facet exists at all, it is usually embodied in the figure of the Horned God, or simply the God.[23] A central characteristic of the God is that he is always understood to be in relationship with the Goddess.[24] Like the Goddess, the God is a divine figure immanent in nature, but unlike her, he undergoes death and rebirth (usually in relation to the yearly agricultural cycle). Whereas the Goddess is the primary reality—the overall continuity and renewal of life—the God expresses the truth of mortality: all that is born dies, and all that dies is reborn, in the continuing cycles of nature.

Although the God is not invoked in simple fashion as a "role model" for men in Goddess spirituality, he does convey certain ideas of what maleness might mean in a nonpatriarchal context. The God refers to a complex of qualities that can be associated with maleness, which Starhawk defines simply (and adequately, to my mind) as "the power of being at home—strong, potent, and awake to feeling in a male body."[25] These qualities do not oppose the attributes associated with the Goddess, but rather share in the same life-oriented outlook she reflects. They do, however, contrast sharply with the imperatives of patriarchal manhood, for which the feeling of being at home—in one's body, within relationship, on the earth—is virtually inconceivable.

Like the Goddess, the God has many names and aspects, all of which connect him intimately with the earth, with life, with the sensual and the sexual. Starhawk gives a sense of the kind of vital power the God can convey to men when she writes: "If man had been created in the Horned God's image, he would be free to be wild without being cruel, angry without being violent, sexual without being coercive, spiritual without being unsexed, and able to truly love."[26]

Other male attributes commonly represented in the figure of the God include playfulness, vulnerability, gentleness, concentration, and a willingness to deal with death—both as a hunter killing what is needed to nourish other life, and as a voluntary sacrificer willing to undergo psychic and/or physical death in service to the life force. Always there is a connection to nature; always there is a relationship to the Goddess.

This link to the Goddess expresses the God's ultimate allegiance to life, despite his involvement with death. He neither glories in nor seeks to overcome death, but rather recognizes death—including his own—as essential to the continuation of life, and thus embraces mortality: "The God chooses to sacrifice in order to remain within the orbit of the Goddess, within the cycle of the natural world, and within the ecstatic, primal union that creates the world."[27] This sacrifice can also be interpreted as the willingness to give up the false strength of a consciousness that has not explored and come to terms with its own underside, its own hidden and scary depths. In the great cycle of the year, the God goes down into his darkness and arises once again with the gift of new life, and so can we in our own lives. In the words of John Rowan, who has written at length of men's passage to the Goddess:

> Once we see the richness and value of the downward path, accepting that what is down there can be positive, everything changes. We lose our fear, carefully instilled by the patriarchy, of what is underneath, behind and below. The vortex becomes positive, the blood becomes positive, the darkness and silence become positive.[28]

A man (or a woman) in touch with that realm, the God seems to tell us, is one who is truly at home in this world, alive to the mystery at the heart of human existence. In this and other ways, the God provides men with an opening into the realm of the Goddess and with teachings about where to search for a male identity other than that dictated by patriarchal norms.

Sons and Lovers—and Fathers?

In the area of human relationships, Goddess spirituality envisions men primarily as sons and lovers. "Our sons, our Sacred Children, were not raised as traitors, but as lovers of life, lovers of women, brothers or lovers to each other, helpers of the Goddess in the most essential skill of nurturing."[29] Just as the Goddess as mother gives birth to the God and later takes him as consort in the course of the yearly mythological cycle, so are men understood to be the sons and (possibly) lovers of women in the earthly, social realm. Fatherhood is not a prominent part of this conception. Although this arrangement has much to recommend it and is vastly preferable to a patriarchal preoccupation with fatherhood, I suspect it may be inadequate as a paradigm of men's development over a lifetime. In making this observation, I am concerned particularly with what kind of religious model might best encourage men to take responsibility for life: both for its creation and for its nurturance in the world.

The psychological and political advantages of a thealogical understanding of men as sons and lovers are considerable. By defining men primarily in terms of their relationship to women—or at least to the female creative power of the world as represented by the Goddess—it reverses the emphasis on men's ostensible self-sufficiency that has undergirded (and been reinforced by) the long history of "rule by fathers," or patriarchy. Such a perspective once again recognizes the primordial power of women's ability to bear life and rightfully places life-giving at the heart of a system of human values.[30] For men, this understanding provides a strong connection to the renewing powers of natural life embodied by the Goddess, and allows for the elaboration of a range of models of manhood that do not depend for their strength on the denial of the female.[31] To me, these are all positive effects of the conceptions of male identity put forward by Goddess spirituality, and I agree with Rowan when he writes, "Unless and until both men and women genuinely believe that the female can be powerful, men are going to hang on to their power."[32]

But if men can be sons and lovers of the Goddess, can we be fathers as well? Or, in other words, can there be fatherhood without patriarchy? I want to answer yes to these questions, even while recognizing that recent history—that is, the past several thousand years—might suggest otherwise. For although the models of son and lover provide men with many rich patterns for living lives of integrity that honor the Goddess, I believe they are lacking in one serious dimension: that of taking responsibility for life.

At his best, a father (not unlike a mother) is deeply involved with and concerned for the life he helps engender, and his involvement takes the form of nurturance, not control. This is a kind of fatherhood that can be compatible with the Goddess. We need men who can competently and conscientiously share with women in taking responsibility for meeting the needs of life on earth. Such men do not seek to rule the world but rather to nourish it, in partnership with the Goddess. By contrast, men who feel that their involvement with life begins and ends at the point of fertilization cannot be counted on to care what happens to that life once it is out in the world.[33]

What can prevent fathers from becoming patriarchs? Although I am not inclined to offer any guarantees, it is clear to me that a strong connection to the Goddess (however she is named) is essential. With it, a man may be a son, a lover, and perhaps a father in his life and thereby honor the Goddess who *is* life. But without it, fatherhood can become a desperate attempt to overthrow the mother, to steal the inexhaustible power of the source of life. The effects of such miserable attempts are all around us, in the form of the myriad systems of control—political, economic, scientific, ideological, and spiritual—erected by would-be fathers, who are not really fathers at all in any life-serving sense.

Men and Nature:
Reclaiming Connection

Feminist theologian Christ suggests Goddess spirituality has the potential to bring people—not only women but men as well—into a sacred relationship with the rest of nature. "For me Goddess has always been more than a symbol of female power. Goddess symbolizes my profound conviction that this earth, our source and ground, is holy. I have always known this. I will never know anything with stronger conviction."[34] Here, where personal intuition and conviction open up to a deeper connection with the world as a whole, I find the most far-reaching and nourishing implications of Goddess spirituality for men. If, as I believe, patriarchal manhood is founded on the notion of separation—from women, from non-human nature, from everything considered "other" by a self-contained male identity—then reclaiming connection with the earth and all other "others" is crucial to men's search for more life-affirming ways to live. In response to a question I sometimes cannot avoid—What can make men safe for the earth?—Goddess spirituality provides at least the beginning of an answer.

Men, no less than women, are creatures of this world, all of us arising out of the earth, depending on it for sustenance, and returning to it at death. The immanent thealogy of the Goddess recognizes this process as sacred and identifies it as the realm where divinity is to be found. If men choose to deny our part in these cycles of natural life, we only create the conditions for our own alienation but do not in any way alter the fact of our participation in them. How we respond to our embeddedness in nature is, finally, up to us.[35] Goddess spirituality urges men to embrace and find meaning in the whole of life of which we are an integral part, thereby offering us a chance to rejoin, on intimate terms, the world from which patriarchal modes of living have divided us.

On a symbolic level, Goddess spirituality (like much of the culture it seeks to challenge) tends to imagine nature mainly in female terms: "Mother Earth," "Mother Nature," the Earth Goddess Gaia, and so on. These are undeniably powerful and lasting images, and for some men as well as many women they bear strong positive associations that bring a sense of personal connection with the mysteries of life.

Yet I question whether men ever can identify completely with a nature personified in exclusively female terms. Although Goldenberg suggests, "In our present situation, in which women are the ones who nurture us, natural life can probably only be imagined with female symbols,"[36] Starhawk appreciates the value of images such as "Father Earth" and the "Green Man" within Goddess religion: "The image says, 'Experience this:

you are rooted in earth, know the force that twines upward—how it is to flower, to swell into fruit, to ripen in the sun, to drop leaves, to ferment, to be intoxicating. Know the cycle, over and over; you are not apart from it. It is the source of your life.'"[37]

I believe what is at stake in these differing views is of great importance to men interested in the Goddess. For if men are to abandon the delusions of alienated grandeur that patriarchy entertains, we must effectively rein-scribe ourselves in nature by reinhabiting it symbolically. If nature is fe-male, so also is it male.

However, such a return of male symbolism and meaning to the natural world must take place on the terms of the Goddess. I am convinced that any attempt to retrieve men's selfhood from the patriarchal structures that now define it must include an honoring of women and of the earth, and an affirmation of men's vital connection to both. We are all of us bound to one another on this planet, situated in a complex interplay of relationships, in ways we can barely imagine. At the very least, Goddess spirituality challenges men to rethink our identities in light of this real-ity, and holds out the possibility of remaking ourselves for the good of the world—which is, of course, our own good in the end. Surely this is a promise to live for.

NOTES

1. This term, indicating theory concerned with the Goddess or with fem-inist religion in general, derives from Naomi R. Goldenberg. See her *Chang-ing of the Gods: Feminism and the End of Traditional Religions* (Boston: Beacon Press, 1979), 96.

2. Exceptions include Jungian theorists such as David L. Miller, *The New Polytheism* (New York: Harper & Row, 1974) and Edward C. Whitmont, *Re-turn of the Goddess,* (New York: Crossroad, 1982), as well as poets Robert Graves, *The White Goddess* (New York: Farrar, Straus & Giroux, 1966) and Robert Bly, *Iron John: A Book about Men,* (Reading, Mass.: Addison-Wesley, 1990). These men's explorations of the Goddess exhibit varying degrees of sympathy for feminist perspectives.

3. Carol P. Christ, "Why Women Need the Goddess: Phenomenological, Psychological, and Political Reflections," in *Womanspirit Rising: A Feminist Reader in Religion,* ed. Carol P. Christ and Judith Plaskow (San Francisco: Harper & Row, 1979).

4. Emily Erwin Culpepper, "Contemporary Goddess Thealogy: A Sympa-thetic Critique," in Clarissa W. Atkinson, Constance H. Buchanan, and Mar-garet R. Miles, eds., *Shaping New Vision: Gender and Value in American Culture* (Ann Arbor, Mich.: UMI Research Press, 1987).

5. See especially Starhawk, *Dreaming the Dark: Magic, Sex & Politics,* (Boston: Beacon Press, 1982), *The Fifth Sacred Thing* (New York: Bantam,

1993), *The Spiral Dance: A Rebirth of the Ancient Religion of the Great God-dess,* (San Francisco: Harper & Row, 1979), *Truth or Dare: Encounters with Power, Authority, and Mystery* (San Francisco: Harper & Row, 1987); Carol P. Christ, *Laughter of Aphrodite: Reflections on a Journey to the Goddess,* (San Francisco: Harper & Row, 1987); Margot Adler, *Drawing Down the Moon: Witches, Druids, Goddess-Worshippers, and Other Pagans in Amer-ica Today* (Boston: Beacon Press, 1986); Naomi R. Goldenberg, *Changing of the Gods: Feminism and the End of Traditional Religions,* (Boston: Beacon Press, 1979); Zsuzsanna Emese Budapest, *The Holy Book of Women's Mys-teries Part One* (Los Angeles: Susan B. Anthony Coven No. 1, 1979), *The Holy Book of Women's Mysteries Part Two* (Los Angeles: Susan B. Anthony Coven No. 1, 1980).

6. See for example Christ, "Why Women Need the Goddess," 274–75, and Starhawk, *The Spiral Dance: A Rebirth of the Ancient Religion of the Great Goddess* (San Francisco: Harper & Row, 1979), chap. 13.

7. Nelle Morton, "The Goddess as Metaphoric Image," in *The Journey Is Home* (Boston: Beacon Press, 1985).

8. Christ, "Why Women Need the Goddess," 276–85.

9. Goldenberg, *Changing of the Gods,* 41.

10. Culpepper, "Contemporary Goddess Thealogy," 59.

11. Margot Adler, *Drawing Down the Moon: Witches, Druids, Goddess-Worshippers, and Other Pagans in America Today,* revised and expanded edition (Boston: Beacon Press, 1986), 173.

12. Starhawk, *Spiral Dance,* 81.

13. Adler, *Drawing Down the Moon,* 226.

14. Culpepper, "Contemporary Goddess Thealogy," 60–62.

15. Ibid., 66.

16. Starhawk, *Dreaming the Dark: Magic, Sex and Politics* (Boston: Bea-con Press, 1982), 72.

17. Christ, "Why Women Need the Goddess," 274.

18. Starhawk, *Dreaming the Dark,* 10.

19. Ibid., 11.

20. Both Starhawk and Christ have argued this point eloquently in their writings. See especially Starhawk, *Dreaming the Dark,* chap. 3, and Carol P. Christ, "The Meaning of the Journey" and "Finitude, Death, and Reverence for Life," both in *Laughter of Aphrodite.*

21. Morton, "The Goddess as Metaphoric Image," 151.

22. Starhawk, *Truth or Dare: Encounters with Power, Authority, and Mystery* (San Francisco: Harper & Row, 1987), 21.

23. The most developed exposition I have seen of maleness within God-dess cosmology and practice is that of feminist Witchcraft. Therefore, my un-derstanding of the Horned God leans heavily on the writings of Starhawk, Bu-dapest, Goldenberg, and Adler.

24. This is one area of marked contrast with the figure of the "Wild Man" popularized by Robert Bly. Bly's perspective emphasizes the Wild Man's es-sential separateness (which would seem to correspond, on a psychological level, to the isolated autonomy of what Bly calls the "deep masculine"). See

Robert Bly, *Iron John: A Book about Men* (Reading, Mass.: Addison-Wesley Publishing Co., 1990).

25. Starhawk, *Dreaming the Dark*, 85.

26. Starhawk, *Spiral Dance*, 95.

27. Ibid., 30.

28. John Rowan, *The Horned God: Feminism and Men as Wounding and Healing* (London: Routledge & Kegan Paul, 1987), 78.

29. Zsuzsanna Emese Budapest, *The Holy Book of Women's Mysteries, Part Two*, 118.

30. Of course, honoring the power of motherhood in women is only one step toward fully respecting women as whole persons, but a necessary one.

31. Besides much in the writings of Starhawk already cited, I find attractive images of "maleness" in several of the versions of Tarot cards depicted by Vicki Noble in *Motherpeace: A Way to the Goddess through Myth, Art, and Tarot* (San Francisco: Harper & Row, 1983)—in particular, the Sons of Wands, Cups, and Discs, and the Shaman of Wands. See pp. 204–7, 220–21.

32. Rowan, *Horned God*, 85.

33. The male-led antiabortion movement exemplifies this attitude, exhibiting great concern for life from the moment of conception until the moment of birth, and little concern for life thereafter.

34. Christ, "Meaning of the Journey," 209.

35. Christ makes this point in "Rethinking Theology and Nature," in Judith Plaskow and Carol P. Christ, ed., *Weaving the Visions: New Patterns in Feminist Spirituality,* ed. Judith Plaskow and Carol P. Christ (San Francisco: Harper & Row, 1989), 316.

36. Goldenberg, *Changing of the Gods*, 109.

37. Starhawk, *Dreaming the Dark*, 87.

16

THE THUNDER OF NEW WINGS:
AIDS—A JOURNEY BEYOND BELIEF

William F. Brantley

Thank God our time is now when wrong
Comes up to meet us everywhere
Never to leave us till we take
The longest stride of soul humans ever took—
Affairs are now soul size.
The enterprise
Is exploration into God.
    —Christopher Fry, "A Sleep of Prisoners"

Before we speak of these mysteries, let us call on God Himself, not with loud and clamoring words, but with our soul yearning toward Him in silent prayer, praying as we always may, alone in communion with the Alone.
    —Plotinus, *Ennead* V.I.6

I believed what society and the church had taught me, overriding my own most basic thoughts. Believing, I lived in a highly sophisticated prison. But after many years, I found an entrance to freedom. I came out from my hiding place—the "gay closet." To preserve that part of the self known as the mind, I had to tell. To protect that part of the self known as the body, I had to tell. To find and free that part of the self we call the soul, I had to tell. I had to tell my family and friends. "I'm gay . . . and I have the AIDS virus."

And 205 of my friends have died. Many more are infected and are going to die. I am going to die.

In the first minutes after discovering I was HIV positive, thoughts of suicide flooded my mind. From then until now, some one hundred months, those thoughts have been a constant companion—a real presence that is profoundly troubling and profoundly comforting.

HIV disease is a progressive disease—running in many stages with myriad responses from infection to death. No one can predict how long the progression might take. Some die a few years after infection; others have lived fourteen and more years. But this *is* a fatal disease—no cure, no magic elixir, no exit from the dark corridor leading from infection to death. There is no exit, but the corridor need not remain dark. I, and others, have found illumination, light for the journey. Some time after I found out I was going to die, I also found out how to live—for the first time.

Living with HIV is a wildly daunting challenge, much like starting life all over again—except without almost every support system. Most of us have lost jobs, insurance, homes, cars, possessions, families, and friends. Our lives—already on the margin—are often lived in poverty and fear, stuck on fast-forward. Our lives are tortured and twisted by church, state, society, sometimes in hospitals, and in a surprising number of homes. Like a baby from the womb, we are expelled from home—naked, frightened, hungry strangers in an alien land.

A friend of mine who worked with people with AIDS for more than a decade and who herself lived and died with cancer, suggested that 98 percent of us eventually find some way to go "gentle into that good night"— usually without help from churches or much assistance from the mind-healing arts and sciences. Too many exit prematurely by our own hands, goaded by conventional wisdom and conditional love. Perhaps 5 percent find a fair degree of peace and fulfillment early in the diagnosis. But for as many as 90 percent, this great and necessary work is confined to the final months of life.

Why this denial? My observations lead me to believe that church and state, society, and families in North America not only keep silent about AIDS but actively discourage all Americans from dealing realistically with sex and death. Given our masculine socialization, men, including gay men, have a very difficult time dealing with issues centering on our sexuality and mortality.

However, for me and for the seventy gay men I interviewed in great depth, AIDS has served as a catalyst to break us out of the prison of our own homophobia, to find peace with the One who created and sustains us, and to activate us to right some of the wrongs we and others face. In this chapter, I want to recount aspects of my own journey out of darkness into light and share some profound stories of other gay men I have known. Along the way, I will share some of the lessons I have learned about long-term survival, offer some advice to non-gay allies, and touch on the role—negative and positive—institutional religion plays in our journeys.

"Odd" Beginnings: Childhood

Seven months after Franklin Roosevelt's first inaugural, in 1933, I was born in a poor community now called Daddysville, North Carolina. Believing myself from age four to be different, strange, odd (and even being told that later), I had trouble with what everyone said about God. Mostly I was not sure whether God was, as Mama said, related to Jesus, or whether God was more related to President Roosevelt, as my Dad believed. I was something like a secular Baptist or a religious Democrat.

When I was eight years old, my parents moved to Detroit, leaving me behind with my grandparents, to make room for my newborn sister. At age twelve, I was crushed to find out that my parents had divorced. The next year, I ran away from home and traveled alone on trains across the country to California to live with my father and stepmother. I left behind all of my family, the matrix of my life until then.

Gypsy-natured as my father was, we moved the next year to Detroit. Shortly thereafter, my father and his new wife went to visit his parents in North Carolina, and I was on my own. I enrolled myself in the tenth grade. And on Labor Day, I went down to Cadillac Square and met President Truman. A day later, as I stood looking in the window of a downtown stamp store, I let myself get picked up by a twenty-five-year-old gay man. I didn't even know the language he used to describe what he wanted to do.

Somewhere inside, I knew I did not measure up to my father's rampant and promiscuous heterosexual example of manhood. I felt guilty and sinful. A lifetime of hard work to prove my manhood had begun.

Partly to compensate for that sense of inadequacy and guilt, and partly to avoid undressing in the gym class locker room, I took ROTC in high school. I became city commander of sixteen schools and presided at the federal inspection as cadet colonel.

While still in high school, I found that I enjoyed writing and newspaper work. I won *Scholastic* magazine's national first prize for news writing: a little scholarship and my first typewriter. That night I tried to tell my father about the honor—he hadn't wanted to go to a "school thing" with me. He told me not to bother him; he needed his sleep. Two days later, after my picture was in the paper, a work friend mentioned it to him. When he came home, he was mad that I hadn't told him.

Temptation to Sin:
The College Years

College scholarships soon came along, only briefly displacing my thoughts of guilt and sin about who I was. I chose the smallest college in the smallest city, hoping that I might be able to avoid lust-powered temptation.

Still I had four different partners during college—two at school, one in New York, and one in San Francisco where I worked one summer on the *San Francisco Chronicle*. The other sexual encounters were single events. But the third time with the same man in San Francisco's City Hall, I discovered he was a policeman. Fortunately for me, he had more to hide than I could even realize.

But it scared me. I promised myself never to do such a thing again. I felt guilty, perverse, sick. I had to shut the door on that terror-filled portion of my life. So I turned to celibacy again; my closet was nice and sophisticated. And I nailed the door shut!

During those years, what passed for faith was strongly shaped by the example of good people around me who called themselves "believers." While in college, I joined an American Baptist church in Indiana. I also flirted with the Unitarians because I admired A. Powell Davies, the pastor of the All Souls Unitarian Church in Washington and the strongest anti-McCarthy voice in the nation. Later my heart discovered the majesty and comfort of the Episcopal liturgy. And I even toyed with the idea of attending seminary.

Marriage Is the Answer:
Beginning a Family

Immediately after college, I went to work on a newspaper in Muncie, Indiana. I worked hard and loved my job. After several years, I had responsibility for the editorial staff and news content of the paper.

One day at the office in 1959, the society editor casually asked how old I was. After my reply, she said, "Well, if you don't get married soon, people are going to talk." I muttered a response and turned to walk the forty feet (or was it a million miles?) back to my desk with my face flushed. I put my head down and began to work feverishly.

I knew she was right, and that realization was a major turning point in my life. I believed that if I married there would be no talk. I could keep my job there or at least work somewhere on a newspaper. Someday I might even be able to go to seminary. I wouldn't be a social outcast shunned by family and friends. I wouldn't be the butt of jokes and innuendo.

Marriage was the answer. "Get married, have kids, and put all that childish stuff behind you." The message was universal, emphatic, dogmatic, and reassuring. Marriage would save me.

The society editor introduced me to someone, and we were married some eight months later.

It actually worked for a while. The three sons we had are proof that I could function heterosexually. And I played the roles as well as anyone could. I was husband, son, and father.

And I was dying inside. I slammed the door on who I was, cutting off access to my soul. For twenty-eight years, I played the role I and society cast me in. However, it became significantly more difficult in the last dozen years. During the first years, I had been celibate outside my marriage. During those last years, I was celibate inside my marriage.

Seeing the World:
Career and Travel

My career took off and became a fast-paced, exhilarating adventure. Just before our third son was born, I was enticed by another paper, and we left Muncie. I became city editor of a Dayton, Ohio, newspaper. During the 1960s, I covered every major political personality in the United States—Kennedy, Nixon, Wallace, Rockefeller, and others. I had been in the presence of David Ben-Gurion and the great religious philosopher Martin Buber. I knew the "big guns" in most major Christian denominations.

For about twenty-two months, I was active in Republican politics in Ohio. I worked some with Murray Chotiner, then White House counsel to the president, who had been Nixon's campaign manager back in the early California days. From this connection, I was offered, but turned down, a White House job in 1971. From politics, I turned to public relations and found work with a company in St. Louis, where I specialized in financial reporting and investor contact.

My wife was unhappy so far from her home base, so when the opportunity arose, I joined Ball, a company back in Muncie that needed a financial and investor relations practitioner. I was quickly on Wall Street where I became something of a lion in my field. I traveled indefatigably, visiting 125 cities in less than two years to talk to investors and stockbrokers. Ball's visibility, share price, and trading volume all increased, making lots of people very happy.

Along the way, I became an expert in antique Ball jars, created a fine museum of antique glass food containers, and wrote the definitive book on the subject, which eventually sold fifty thousand copies. Then for a brief sojourn, I became the editor and publisher of *The Saturday Evening Post.* When that ended abruptly, I was out of a job for the first time in my life.

Soon thereafter, I began working for a high-visibility public company in North Carolina. The next several years, I worked hard and traveled without respite—weekly to New York and bimonthly to Europe. I became well known in the world's financial centers such as London, Zurich, and Amsterdam.

And I steadily began to—or maybe continued to—lose my family. But the travel and big cities offered many opportunities. In my off hours, I haunted the great museums. I enjoyed the varied local cuisines as well as a full array of churches—architecture, music, and messages.

And the big cities offered something more fundamental to my existence: a chance to live, to be as complete as I knew how.

Dual Life:
The Closet

But I had to stay in the closet, for after all, I did not want to become another tragic newspaper story. From my days in Muncie, I still remembered the story about a fine Episcopal layman from a nearby diocese who stepped out of his ninth-floor office window; there were rumors about his sexuality. And besides, divorce was out of the question. I still remembered the pain I felt when I learned that Daddy had divorced Mama. I had vowed that I would never do such a thing.

Around the age of fifty, the crises of mind, soul, and body were becoming terrifying, destructive, mean. I decided to play the "second half of my ball game," as I put it to myself, according to my needs and my own rules. I quit my job—exiting the pettiness and corruption, as well as the glory and money, inside corporate life. I struck out on my own, and within a few weeks I had more clients than I could handle. I expanded, took on employees, got a partner, sold part of the practice to a British firm, and then the business collapsed. All of this time, I was waffling between wanting to commit suicide and constant agony. I opted for the agony as I began to rebuild my business.

I began to lead a moderately active gay life—always outside my home state. I had known something about this new disease in the gay community as early as the first mention in June, 1981. But of course, that didn't apply to me. Friends said it came from the showers in gay bathhouses, so we stayed away from bathhouses in our small, tightly knit group. Little did we know that four years later, the disease would be identified as HIV—the virus that causes AIDS. My friends began to die.

Diagnosis:
HIV

On October 19, 1988, in Winston-Salem, North Carolina, I learned by registered letter that I had HIV/AIDS. From the post office, I mentally stumbled toward my therapist's office—the year before he had helped me find an alternative to divorce or suicide—separation. I showed him my letter, and then hugged him as *he* began to cry.

Numbness gripped me. I was going to die—and probably pretty soon. I drove past Forsyth Hospital and thought that would be where I would die. Somehow I got through the week, and with the help of a gay friend in Durham, I got through the weekend.

I plunged immediately into the work of getting an infectious disease doctor. He told me I would be dead by January—such was the state of medical knowledge of this disease even then. I found an AIDS support group, and met a young man who was HIV positive and was willing to counsel with me. Selden became one of my most solid, saintly, and enduring friends until he died in 1990.

I had my will drawn, along with a durable power of attorney and a living will. I paid for my funeral, bought my tombstone—an upright triangle of marble—had it engraved and put up in the family cemetery. I told my oldest son and his wife about my status and, to my amazement, they said they were not surprised.

As the months passed, I lost my home, car, insurance, and some erstwhile friends. I was shunned by my sister, brother, sister-in-law, and two sons. HIV came to affect my short-term memory, and my business was ruined. Clients, sensing something was wrong, dropped me. My professional life was over.

So I moved near my boyhood home, next door to my aunt, where I found acceptance and support. I joined the only church in the world I thought would accept me. I plunged into support groups and joined the board of the AIDS Service Agency as the board's only openly gay, infected person. I spoke to church groups, seminary classes, college seminars, philanthropic foundations, service clubs, public housing officials, and reporters.

The Soul in the Abyss

As I outlived that first doctor's diagnosis, the fighting became discouraging, and the old tapes began playing once more. It was like watching reruns while my life was stuck on fast-forward. "Get it over with," I counseled myself. I made my suicide plan, prepared supplies, and sank into a place unknown before—the deepest, darkest recesses of my soul. I agonized in that abyss for days. It was my Gethsemane.

I was paralyzed. My world was coming apart. Yet somehow I found the strength to face myself honestly, and I discovered my greatest sin. Through all those years of guilt and self-hatred, I had unknowingly held firmly to one sinful belief: *God was wrong when He created me as I am.*

I began to write and read and paint and wrestle and think my way out of the abyss. I read Viktor Frankl, Carl Jung, Scott Peck, Evelyn Underhill, and Joseph Campbell. I wrote thousands of words chronicling my days and nights, my hopes and fears.

And then, I finally began to emerge from my dark night. And I was reborn into the light of day. I came out of the depths as an anagoge—I'm too shy to call myself a mystic. I have seen beyond the glass into the blinding darkness of Love's Light. I have experienced That whose center is everywhere and whose boundaries are nowhere. Beyond belief, I had come to know that love, nourished in hope, is life's ultimate essential. After all, what else could HIV mean besides Hope Is Vital?

Transformation

Michel Foucault, in the last of his lectures in the early 1980s shortly before his own death of AIDS, talked about the value of *parrhesia:* truthtelling without fear of personal consequences.[1] Twenty years earlier in *The New Man,* Thomas Merton had called it "free speech" and said it became important after the Fall, "that self-alienation which resulted from man's refusal to accept himself as he actually is." *Parrhesia* "expresses the union and cohesion of all the . . . gifts which made man *what God intended him to be*" (emphasis mine). It "symbolizes the perfect communication of man's intelligence with God by knowledge (*gnosis*) and contemplation (*theoria*) . . . also the perfect communion of his will with God by charity."[2] Truth telling became a significant cause and result of my theological metamorphosis (e.g., this definition of sin was nearly identical to my "greatest" sin). Indeed, *parrhesia* turned my introspection outward to action.

And my new-found knowledge and hope energized me. I found that I could live quite happily in a mobile home and on $1,000 a month. Duke University Medical Center and Medicare helped with medical treatment (AZT was $1,000 a month and another drug I now take costs $4,500 a month). When I could qualify, I volunteered for drug studies and experiments. I had lymph nodes removed for a viral load experiment, had needles driven into muscles and along bone in neurological studies, and took drugs of hope which later disappeared into the black hole of pharmaceutical research.

My volunteer work came at a fever pitch—thirty to fifty hours a week. I trained to learn to facilitate a support group, the only one in the state for infected gay men only. I volunteered in the Infectious Disease Clinic at Duke University. I visited HIV patients in the hospital and made cakes for clients and staff each time I went. I was a peer counselor. I started the AIDS Service Agency's art auction, much to the consternation of some board members. Three years ago, I was recognized with the award for the year's greatest contribution to the North Carolina gay community for AIDS work, an award affectionately known as "Queer of the Year."

Other Life Journeys: Interviews

After climbing out of my abyss, I discovered a few other gay men were using this HIV diagnosis as something other than a good excuse to roll over and die. Something was happening to these guys. There was an awakening, the leaping of life-affirming spirit.

I conceived an idea: find them, hear them—listen as they told their stories. I used $1,200 I had earned from an experimental drug study, wrote letters to AIDS service groups around the country, and got in the little car I had purchased with Social Security Disability payments. I found seventy men: black, white; old, young; rich, poor; highly educated and not; open, shy; militant, gentle; churched, alienated; accepted, rejected. Most of them had never been asked to tell their stories. Over fifty days and nights, I traveled 12,625 miles through thirty-one states and ran my tape recorder for 196 hours.

Dozens of times, my gay brothers who share this virus said words like "AIDS is a blessing," or "AIDS is a gift from God," or "Being HIV positive is the most important thing to ever happen to me."

Their stories were and are the most moving and stirring stories; more exhilarating to know and more difficult to bear than most any I've ever found.

A young man from Kansas was sent away by his parents who told him, "We never want to see you again. You are an abomination. We wish you had died when you were born." They printed his obituary in the town newspaper and placed his tombstone in the church cemetery. Twenty years later, he returned to his parents' house to try to reconcile. Those twenty years were distilled in a flash of pain, and he found a way to deny their death-dealing lie: he committed suicide in their front yard.

One gentle young man from North Carolina seemed to evaporate into pure spirit as his body withered and his eyesight dimmed to blindness. In the last year of his life, he was fed by his mother, morning, noon, and night, from her back doorstep.

A dying man from Nebraska had the ashes of thirteen of his friends, friends whom he had cared for in their living and coached in their dying. At their request, he had their bodies reduced to ashes, all in the same year. He had their ashes lined up boxes on his table because their churches and families refused them funerals. With his own death drawing nigh, he finally took them all to a place called Land's End near the Golden Gate Bridge, and released them into the ocean, called Pacific.

In Michigan, a man named David wanted his union of twelve years with Jon blessed by a representative of God before they died. David lay on the couch while Jim, a gay Presbyterian minister who also has AIDS, moved his hands to the silent sounds of peace. He spoke nourishing words of blessing on these two lives bound by God's grace: "Those whom God has joined together, let no one put asunder . . ." And then, as the minister began to celebrate Communion for those who were present, he spoke the familiar words: "This is my body, broken for you . . ."

and that was the point at which David died. "Do this in remembrance of me."

Lessons for HIV-Positive Persons

As a long-term survivor, when asked what my longevity secret is, I usually offer these brief but important responses:

> Love God or whoever or whatever you name your higher power—Father Sun, Mother Earth, Buddha, or that unidentified chemical impulse in the brain. Love God and don't worry about names.
>
> Take responsibility. Individually we have unique roles to play in changing attitudes not only about sin and guilt but also about safe practices and habits.
>
> Take good care of yourself. Eat correctly and take the prescribed drugs. Get some exercise and stay active.
>
> Don't make friends with just other Persons With AIDS (PWAs); they will die on you. Make friends also with the noninfected. They may benefit from the friendship, and you may learn that other people are also dying and of something other than AIDS.
>
> Don't give up on sex. I have seen that those who abstain and buy into the sin and guilt foisted on them by churches and family, die first and fast. Sexual expression is just as vital to life—and as God-given and God-approved—as air, water, food, rest, and love.

Lessons for Non-Gay Allies

Participating in someone's dying is one of the most beautiful and precious gifts there is. For those who would be brave enough to go against society and walk with us as we complete our journeys, I offer these words of advice:

> Listen carefully to us. Listen without judgment. Believe us. We are the best witnesses.
>
> Don't force us to talk about it. People who are living with death need to be able to talk about their terror, shattered dreams, anger, diminished lives. But they need to talk at their own time and in their own way.
>
> Don't make the mistake of responding by saying: "I know exactly how you feel." You don't, and you can't unless you're HIV positive.

218

Don't consider us dead until we have died.

Do not deny death by not naming it. Don't hide behind euphemisms like "pass away." But, if the one with AIDS chooses to call death something else, respect that as well.

Learn to recognize and deal with your own grief and pain. Those close to the one with AIDS often go through the same stages of response to the dying process as their friend.

Those who sincerely help the dying have to make a lot of changes. You have to make amends—sometimes even for things you didn't do. Say I'm sorry. Say I love you. Say I will miss you. And I hope you will say, "I will remember you."

I would add only one more thing to everyone: Love us as you love your son, brother, father, uncle; that's who we are and have been when you weren't paying attention.

Lessons for and Challenges to the Church

Howard Warren, a Presbyterian minister in Indianapolis, told me of a dying gay man who wanted to see a priest from the Episcopal Church. He was officially still a member but had been rejected by his priest, parish, and bishop. A priest went to the hospital and said to him, "How can I help? What do you want from the church?" Hooked to tubes and within hours of death, the man sat upright and stared at the priest: "An apology would be a good place to start."

An apology *would* be a good place to start. Almost without exception, my gay brothers with HIV tell me to forget about the church; forget about religion; forget about Christianity. They tell me it is *irrelevant* because churches have expelled them and stood over them in judgment and damnation.

And in some ways, they are right. Churches have encouraged families to continue to deny their sons' and daughters' very existence as human beings. And the churches are the most guilty portion of society in covering up AIDS, denying sexuality, and rejecting people who want to be open and visible parts of the body of Christ.

But I will never give up on the church, especially as a congregation of believers who love one another as God loves us. My own spiritual growth has been grounded and enhanced by the support of just such a family of faith. Within it I have strength to go where I know I must go. I will not let the bigots remove me from that love which abides with me even when I am alone. I am more radical than almost anyone you know. I am out to reclaim my portion of the kingdom of God from the bigots.

I personally believe that God is working overtime these days and God has selected us—people living with HIV and AIDS—as "the least of these" to test all the world (Matt. 25:40). AIDS is the ultimate test today of the human spirit:

> The day is coming
> when some of us
> will have the opportunity
> to answer the question:
> "The world considered you
> among the least of my creations
> —how did they treat you?"
> And, you know,
> we will have to answer
> the question.
> For we are the question itself.
>
> We *are* the test.

Conclusion

Knowing your own fate earlier in life than most face it, causes a startling kind of awareness—I call it the gift of certainty. Length of life is not important; living life fully is.

This gift of certainty causes me to mourn the silenced laughter, the work unfinished, the art uncreated, the millions of tomorrows that will never be—too many are dying too young.

This gift of certainty also causes me to spend little time on my own past and others who are gone. I am in this moment only, for the next breath is not assured.

The gift of certainty is what we have been given. From it we can build a magnificent future by filling each moment of each day, seizing each opportunity, and flooding each relationship with total attention and love. For love, nourished in hope, is life's ultimate essential.

And so we, the already gone and the soon-to-be-gone, give the world *our* gift:

> By our love alone,
> by its quality and purity
> and unstinting giving,
> we will show you *a way*
> through the darkness,
> across mountains,
> and to the stars.

Hearing "the thunder of new wings," we face death and transform life while transcending life and death.[3]

NOTES

I deeply appreciate the organizing skills of David Schoeni, a Wake Forest University graduate student, who—in a time when my own skills were failing me—took a dozen of my talks and other writings and wove them together into this essay. He has made whole cloth of my patchwork and I am grateful.

1. See Thomas Flynn, "Foucault as Parrhesiast: His Last Course at the Collège de France (1984)," in *The Final Foucault,* ed. James Bernauer and David Rasmussen, 102–18 (Cambridge, Mass.: MIT Press, 1991).

2. See Thomas Merton, *The New Man* (New York: Mentor Omega Books, 1963), 49.

3. The full epigram, "Sister, I hear the thunder of new wings," comes from the title page of Evelyn Underhill's *The Mystic Way: A Psychological Study in Christian Origins* (London and Toronto: J. M. Dent & Sons, 1913).

17

MAGNIFICENT MANHOOD: THE TRANSCENDENT WITNESS OF HOWARD THURMAN

Alton B. Pollard, III

I have never been in search of identity.
—Howard Thurman

It is the dominant refrain in our nation's halting discourse on race: "The African American community is in a state of crisis." Activists and scholars have painstakingly detailed the deleterious impact of white sociocultural domination on African America. Still, the modern shapers of mainstream mass opinion—television, radio, film, newspapers, and magazines—prefer to depict the carnage as implicitly sociopathic, from the decline of the black family to the rise in black unemployment. Of particular moment is the plight of the African American male, especially younger men and boys. Is it any wonder, given what looks like genocidal impulses on the part of white America, that many advocates allege African American males are in a state of siege, "an endangered species," "vanishing," and "at risk"?[1]

My aim in this chapter is to present a latter-day prophet's response to the death and disillusionment that threaten African America in general and African American males in particular. African American males are in a perilous but far-from-hopeless state. For four hundred years we have endeavored, hope against hope, to bear witness to the often magnificent meaning of African manhood in this land. Now the struggle must be taken up as never before. Brutalized and demoralized by the politics of disparity and disprivilege, our response has often erred on the side of the reflexive and self-destructive. Howard Thurman, mystic exemplar and ancestral griot of the faith, declared that even in the midst of gross societal invalidation, life-affirming resources are yet ours. The real and tragic truth is that many of us, specifically African American men, have forgotten this.

When Howard Thurman died on April 10, 1981, in San Francisco, he left behind an incomparable legacy of hope. During his far-flung career he taught at Morehouse College (1929–33) and Howard University (1933–44) before becoming the first black dean at a major white institution, Boston University (1953). In 1961, he established the Howard Thurman Educational Trust to promote humanitarian endeavors, and he authored twenty-two books over the years. Exceptional among his many involvements, however, was the San Francisco–based church that he cofounded and co-pastored from 1944 to 1953—the Church for the Fellowship of All Peoples—lauded as the first authentically inclusive model of institutional religion in the United States. Universal in both outlook and embrace, the empowering message of Thurman is the essential unity of human life and of all life.

If little else is clear to us about Thurman, it should be that his was a deeply genuine and all-encompassing spiritual life. Key to the movement of his own life was the dynamic encounter between spiritual imperatives and sociopolitical realities. Thurman's prophetic genius was rooted in his understanding of religion's capacity to expose and engage an unjust and oppressive social environment. To believe and to act as he did means that no sociopolitical strategies for change can endure without a spiritual touchstone, without due recognition given to the vital link between personal, historical, and cultural deep-rootedness.

Blackness as Idiom

Thurman was born in Daytona, Florida, at the beginning of this century. The second of three children, he was the only son of Alice Ambrose and Saul Solomon Thurman. His father, a railroad worker who held little regard for churches and preachers, died when Howard was seven. His mother, a sensitive and devoutly religious person, worked long hours as a domestic cook and laundress for white families. Many of the household responsibilities were subsequently shouldered by grandmother Nancy Ambrose, a former slave whose deep and uncompromising sense of personal dignity proved an enormous influence on young Thurman's development.

Thurman grew up experiencing the deep suffering exacted by racial discrimination and injustice. But the hegemony of white racism did not have a determinative influence on Thurman's self-concept. He was well-inoculated against the affronts of bigotry and its bitter fruit—self-doubt, despair, disappointment, social and existential death—by oppositional values deeply embedded in African American culture. Thurman states, "My roots are deep in the throbbing reality of the Negro idiom and from it I draw a measure of inspiration and vitality. I know that a person must be at home somewhere before they can be at home anywhere."[2] His intense awareness of the struggles of African America moved him to utter protestation: "I believe, with my foreparents, that this is God's world. This faith has had to fight against disillusionment, despair, and the vicissitudes of American history."[3]

The racial isolation Thurman experienced as a graduate student in the "liberal" North did little to assuage his feelings. The only African American at then Rochester Theological Seminary in New York, he was urged by a prominent professor to lay aside racial concerns and, instead, apply himself to facing the "timeless issues of the human spirit." Thurman well understood the underlying intent of his mentor's statement. But his own reflections on the matter proved far more discerning and decisive: "A man and his black skin must face the 'timeless issues of the human spirit' together."[4] Says Thurman:

> Always the sense of separateness that is an essential part of individual consciousness must be overcome as it sustains and supports. This is the crucial paradox in the achievement of an integrated personality as well as of an integrated society. To work as if the walls did not exist, to be nourished by the strength of one's ethnic idiom, and at the same time to be victimized by the walls is as exhilarating as it is hazardous.[5]

By drinking deeply from the wellsprings of African American culture and life, Thurman learned to scale the citadel of racism and discrimination in a manner equalled by few.

The Extended Family Network

In contrast to the buffeting winds of race, gendered notions of male prerogative were largely unknown to young Thurman. "I have often wondered," wrote Thurman, "as I contemplate the experiences of loneliness and shyness, how different my orientation to life would have been had I grown up with brothers rather than sisters—or had my father lived longer. But from the beginning I was surrounded by women."[6]

Since his mother was the breadwinner, the daily care of Howard and sisters was given to "Grandma Nancy." Nancy Ambrose was not a woman of letters but she set high academic standards for young Thurman. She also impressed upon him the enabling power of religion, challenging the parochialism of their local church with her own theology of resistance.[7] She insisted that religion, whatever else it does, must begin with the affirmation of an individual's dignity and significance. Her reasoning was derived from slavery's harsh lessons. When she was a child, a white preacher in league with the slave master consistently preached, "Slaves, be obedient to your masters." In contrast, the furtive message of the slave preacher was positive and enabling: "You are not niggers! You are not slaves! You are God's children!"[8]

Thurman's life was also shaped by the extended family network of church and community. As the spiritual face of the African American community, social identity and personal dignity were deeply intertwined with the church's existence. "In the fellowship of the church," Thurman recalled, "particularly in the experience of worship, there was a feeling of sharing in primary community."[9] This religious extended family melded with the life of the larger community in a number of ways. All of the major rites of passage and most community events transpired within its walls. Church members validated Thurman's talents and sensitivities and encouraged their cultivation. The repressive external environment was thus effectively diminished through the agency and affirmation of the black church.

The Male Factor

The extent to which Thurman's thought and character were molded by African American men has been left virtually unexplored by scholars. The great irony is that Thurman's upbringing is a resounding rejoinder to those who doubt African American males can acquire an appropriate masculine identity in a household headed by women.[10] To be sure, this is a complex and controversial point to argue since empirical research in this area remains sparse. But the following anecdote, humorously shared by Thurman, illustrates the historic resilience of the African American family:

> When I was at Earlham College, one of the professors there, a counselor and a psychologist, heard me say that I had been reared without a father. So he said, "Oh, then I have to revise my tests because none of the things that go with a male child reared in a home with women apply to you." Well now, that proves the indomitable quality in my grandmother.[11]

In the absence of his biological father, several men served as elder males for Thurman, from his two stepfathers to "the stranger in the railroad station in Daytona Beach."[12] The most important of these influences, however, was a cousin, Thornton Smith, and the family physician, Dr. Stockings. Thurman held both men in deep esteem as "my masculine idols."

Young men typically choose their role models according to an admired quality or skill and, more often than not, the person's visibility in the larger community. However, it is well known that in the segregationist

South, an African American man who displayed a healthy sense of self-regard and self-confidence risked losing his life. White society would not tolerate an empowered African American presence, male or female. Yet Thornton Smith and Dr. Stockings were two men who consistently refused to conform. Smith, "always his own man," helped African Americans in Dayton to gain the vote, a new school, and black police officers. In similar fashion, Dr. Stockings's disregard for religion upset traditionalists, but his keen intellect attracted the young Thurman. Even after Thurman's decision to enter the Christian ministry (much to the dismay of Dr. Stockings), they remained close friends. Much like the elders in African traditional society, these and other men functioned as important transmitters of African American male identity for Thurman.[13]

Such positive images of responsible male participation accurately reflect the interdependent nature of the African American community during much of this century. Still, the real credit for Thurman's moral, cognitive, and affective well-being belongs to his mother and grandmother. In an important study on the impact of mothers of successful sons, Charles Willie concluded that regardless of whether African American women were single, married, widowed, poor, or nonpoor, they invested in and supported their sons' success by nurturing, providing, and holding them to high occupational and educational expectations.[14] It is the vicious cycle of poverty and not maternal parenting that presents the greatest obstacle to the development of young African American males. Thurman was instilled with high aspirations from an early age, insights that enabled him to establish a different emphasis within the world he knew, ultimately preparing him for a life of profound engagement with the religious and social world.

Spiritual Experience

While the influences of culture, family, and community on Thurman cannot be stated strongly enough, it is clear that his freedom to operate in his racial-ethnic idiom was undergirded by spiritual experience. He writes:

> It gave me my identity, so I didn't have to wait for the revolution. I have never been in search of identity—and I think the explanation is that everything I've ever felt and worked on and believed in was founded in a kind of private, almost unconscious autonomy that did not seek vindication in my environment because it was in me. As long as I keep the environment external to me it cannot control me; but when I internalize it I become captured by it.[15]

This experience, which fundamentally informed and validated his existence, floated away on gossamer wings, Thurman relates, with the first rustlings of reflection.

> I call it spiritual. When I start describing it, explaining it, I become religious. And that is why people always fight about religion. It's a waste of time because when you talk about religion, you are talking about, you are explaining, a spiritual experience . . . *and the explanation is the least relevant thing about it* [emphasis added].[16]

For Thurman spiritual experience is decidedly unique and irreducible. It is neither thought nor feeling nor rational-mystical symmetry; rather, it is a getting through to the creative product of tension and release, the relations of all inanimate and animate life, and the power of endurance in the face of suffering. The spiritual experience centers, in other words, on the transforming process that is at bottom of the dynamics of head and heart: "In all . . . things there is a secret door which leads into the central place, where the Creator of life and the God of the human heart are one and the same. . . . The Head and the Heart are at last inseparable; they are lost in wonder in the One."[17] Thurman's mystic articulations are reminiscent of Plotinus and Spinoza, harmonizing the demands of the heart with the exigencies of the mind, leading one into the primal Logos of existence. His language affirms rationality without disdaining the emotional and mystical; it advances feeling without slighting thought; each seeks all that the other can contribute, without confusing the seeking with the goal of human life—to know God.

According to Thurman, the sacred encounter provides a person with the conviction that however thoroughgoing or even devastating the contradictions of life, they are not ultimate and final. The unity of life, no matter how contradictory on the surface, must yield to the control of God. Life has its own restraints against that which stings and casts down. The individual, grounded in divine reality and empowered with a "proper sense of self," can now begin to act.

Moral-Ethical Concerns

There was a final yield from Thurman's spiritual experience. The dynamics of this experience involved moving beyond theoretical exposition and personal affirmation (without leaving either behind) to the realization of moral-ethical concerns. What has been ascertained in the divine "moment" requires actualization and equilibrium in the ongoing "moments" of persons. In the ever-changing currents one discovers that life denies bifurcation. Socially constructed disjunctions—black and white, sacred and secular, church and world, and the like—are less than accurate, for these are but aspects of a single reality, a single meaning. Thurman emphasizes that life is against all dualisms. Life is One. Therefore, a way of life that is worth living must be a way worthy of life itself. Nothing less than that can abide. Always, against all that fragments and shatters and against all things that separate and divide within and without, life labors to meld together into a single harmony.[18]

This emphasis on unity is of paramount importance to establishing an expansive sense of well-being. In ethical terms, this means that the levels of the personal, communal, and social must be responsibly and actively linked to one another; unity, justice, goodness, and wholeness are experienced as "a growing edge of hope." In sociological terms, one becomes concerned about the development of other persons regardless of race, creed, gender, nationality, sexuality, age, or class. In short, the God-encounter moves beyond merely inspiring revelation to full personal and social accountability. In coming to oneself, a person is called to equally liberating and holistic social engagement. Again and again, Thurman offers such cautionary words as:

[T]he imperative of social action is not merely to improve the condition of society. It is not merely to feed the hungry, not merely to relieve human suffering and human misery. If this were all, in and of itself, it would be important surely. But this is not all. The basic consideration has to do with the removal of all that prevents God from coming to God-self in the life of the individual. Whatever there is that blocks this, calls for action.[19]

To summarize, then, the sources of Thurman's own prophetic witness are several: (1) his cultural roots in African America, (2) the extended kinship network of family, church, and community, (3) the focal and fontal experience of spiritual encounter, and (4) a resultant sensitivity to truth in moral-ethical concerns. Prominent among Thurman's concerns was the advancement of "community," briefly defined as a mode of relatedness in human society characterized by human inclusiveness, justice and mutuality of love, and trust and caring centered in God. This was the deep hunger of Thurman's life, over against the debilitating conditions of external and internalized oppression. The experience of spiritual encounter, the validation of family and friends, including several significant men, released within him resources critical to his "own sense of wholeness," yet the hunger—the givenness of God—persisted. Thurman understood then what many have not accepted even now: to profess to know the love and truth of God is not enough. A person must possess courage enough to risk making truth manifest in human community.

The Challenge

The profound influences on his life came to bear on Thurman's analysis of the plight of African America's youth during the freedom movement of the 1950s and 1960s. The "Movement" was tactically and ideologically two in expression: the civil rights wing was largely Southern, rural, Christian, and demonstrably nonviolent; the black consciousness wing was Northern, urban, and more disposed to violence as a form of mass action and self-defense. Their respective views—the elimination of segregation on the one hand, a sometimes separatist agenda on the other—were in complex respects interwoven and estranged, rending African America and larger society as well. The dilemma, as Thurman interpreted it, was to find a means to change that was grounded in a vision beyond the circumscriptions of race. In the activist's struggle for equality and freedom, authentic change required that one be "inwardly motivated, not ambitiously oriented."[20]

Suffice it to say that the new generation of African American activists did not always possess a rich interior life, a "binding sense of identity." Increasingly, a political and not a spiritual demand empowered the movement (Martin Luther King Jr. and Malcolm X being prominent exceptions), and slowly, painfully, the movement died. As the movement waned, the social advancement of a relative few began to take precedence over the welfare and concerns of the dispossessed black masses. Incremental social gains were accorded some African Americans, but not without serious psychological and spiritual cost. The net result was an uncritical acceptance of white societal (read: "patriarchal") values deeply inimical to millions of African Americans and others living beyond the pale.

Even more immediately devastating were white social attitudes and arrangements working directly to relegate the masses of African America to underclass status. It is at this point that the frustration and rage of African Americans, long present in latent form, became catalytic and, momentarily, cathartic in the movement toward a new black consciousness. Thurman defines the parameters of the new mood:

> In the contemporary push on the part of American Negroes to elevate blackness to a place of supreme significance in self-identity, we see at work an effort to reclaim the body as the home of the self. The battle cry, Black is Beautiful, is an effort to deal with this central issue. In its preliminary stages, the slogan is an attack on the white world which has made of "white" an absolute. It is this absolute that for so long a time has been the key for the identity of the Anglo-Saxon. With such an absolute as a rallying point for the personality, the grounds for establishing a sense of community, exclusive in character, are guaranteed.

Under the aegis of this absolute, the categories for all non-white peoples are defined. The sense of belonging which any non-white peoples are permitted to have can very easily be measured by ground rules established by so-called white supremacy.[21]

If the truth be told, the paramount crisis in the African American community today is what it was thirty years ago (and, with slight revision, the same concerns might well apply to any American group). We have fought segregation and bigotry only to see their more sophisticated return—the ravaging of African American lives of every age and description; structured unemployment and chronic underemployment; environmental, sexual, and psychological forms of genocide. In addition, African American women have had to bring African American men face to face with their own misguided machismo. As cultural commentator Michael Eric Dyson so adroitly notes, African Americans must now "oppose an ironic black patriarchy, on the one hand a faded reflection of white patriarchy in regard to black men wielding institutional power, and on the other hand a faithful imitation of white patriarchy's worst effects, felt most severely in domestic violence by black men aimed at women and children."[22] The struggle for African American men and women thus continues—how best to champion an enabling solidarity forged out of the several crucibles of gender, race, and class, among others.

In this chapter, I have attempted to connect Thurman's legacy to African America's not-so-distant past and present. The children of Africa in America are at a critical juncture today; what is required now are ordinary leaders who make mistakes, assess their errors, and embark on finding solutions. The quietly transformative ministry of Howard Thurman is a pedagogical case in point to Cornel West's unsung contention that "race-transcending prophets" are direly needed.[23]

But Thurman was equally a gender-transcending prophet. By this I mean he was fundamentally a seeker of "the common ground," one who valued the infinite worth of every person regardless of gender, nationality, or creed. Moreover, he envisioned and embraced a common place of meeting in and beyond our maleness, our femaleness, our Hispanicness, our blackness. The worshiping moment was such an opportunity for "the immediate awareness of the pushing out of the barriers of self, the moment when we flow together into one, when I am not male or female, yellow or green or black or white or brown, educated or illiterate, rich or poor, sick or ill, righteous or unrighteous—but a naked human spirit that spills over into other human spirits as they spill over into me."[24] There can be little doubt that, for Thurman, being a black man in America was not without considerable peril. Yet the truth remains that he did not finally rest his identity in pigment or physiology or, for that matter, in general societal expectations but on the irradiating "centering experience."

The Hope

I conclude with a few thoughts on the condition of contemporary African America. A colossal struggle is taking place within the African American community, a struggle that can hardly be said to be simply or even primarily of our own making but a crisis that, if it continues unabated, will render moot the question of who caused it. Undeniably, our problems are rooted in a rejecting social climate that encourages self-rejection; this is how internalized oppression and internalized domination begin.

Distressingly, self-rejection first and best takes root in the lives of the young. The relative powerlessness of youth to resist injustices against themselves or others sets the pattern for a lifetime of feeling helpless in the face of wrongdoing. Thus, what had been a centuries-old struggle to save young ravaged African American lives from white injustice and discrimination has taken an uncertain and insidious turn. The contemporary struggle focuses urgently on internecine strife, crime, abuse, and despair; the cessation of gang bangings, carjackings, and drive-by shootings; the elusive quest for self-respect and accomplishment beyond livin' large and going for the "juice," beyond the destructive downward spiral of drugs and defeat; the misery of chronic unemployment and underemployment; the threat of sexually and psychologically transmitted genocide. It takes few statistics, little imagination, and even less erudition to know that the struggles to which I refer are to varying degrees engulfing every segment of American society. The world of African America—and America at large—is relentlessly shifting and our young are caught in the morass. Noted religion scholar C. Eric Lincoln expresses the dilemma well: "No wonder [young African American males] are alienated. They never really knew what our [older African American men's] values were, and when they discovered it they found out that we didn't know either."[25] It is hardly accidental that the growing trend among African Americans—devoid of a sense of moral continuity—is to distance themselves, as much as possible, from the struggle for intraracial cooperation. What I would call the morality of solidarity has been lost in our acquiescence to a social system that relegates numerous Americans to lives of involuntary servitude, government dependent status, or worse. Still, despite the odds, many of African America's youth, male and female alike, are sowing seeds of hope.

Young African Americans, I believe, hunger for a renewal of activism that is socially progressive and spiritually fulfilling, a movement that is capable of nourishing their famished souls. What insights can young African American men, in particular, gain from the tradition of radical prophetic consciousness that Howard Thurman, David Walker, Frederick Douglass, and Martin Luther King Jr. so magnificently represent (to say nothing of Fannie Lou Hamer, Septima Clark, Sojourner Truth, and Ida B. Wells-Barnett)? Dare they hope to find a forward-looking way out of our current impasse, an impetus to emancipate, elevate, and liberate the race—the human race—collectively?

When we look closely at all our present strivings, from the religio-political to the socioeconomic, prospects for Africa's descendants in America appear to be irrefutably dim. Indeed, if there is any judgment that rests on us today, it may be that we have so marginalized the moral and ethical, so lost our way in pursuit of the American Way, that we believe we can no longer survive. But the great and unrelenting challenge, Thurman is so careful to remind us, is to learn (and learn again) the lessons of the past—good, bad, and otherwise—for the living of these days. The movement of the spirit, the gifts of the ancestors, the wisdom of the elders, the teachings of the griots, the courage of the prophetesses—these are repositories without measure. We end, then, where we began: with the ruminations of Howard Thurman, a magnificent signpost in the luminous darkness, a categorically transcendent witness for our time.

> One may lose fear . . . by a sense of being a part of a company of people who share the same concern and are conscious of participating in the same collective destiny. . . . When a person is able to place at the disposal of a single end, goal, or purpose the resources of his life . . . he relaxes his hold upon his own physical existence because he is caught up in the kind of expanded awareness that is triggered by the commitment that his life becomes important only in terms that fulfill the inscrutable demands of the commitment. Such an experience is spiritual; yea, it is religious. Under such a circumstance, even death is a little thing.[26]

NOTES

1. See, for example, Jewel Taylor Gibbs, ed. *Young, Black and Male in America: An Endangered Species* (New York: Auburn House, 1988); Haki Madhubuti, *Black Men: Obsolete, Single, Dangerous?* (Chicago: Third World Press, 1990); and Andrew Hacker, *Two Nations: Black and White, Separate, Hostile, Unequal* (New York: Doubleday, 1992).

2. Howard Thurman, *The Luminous Darkness: A Personal Interpretation of the Anatomy of Segregation and the Ground of Hope* (New York: Harper & Row, 1965), x.

3. Howard Thurman, *Deep River and the Negro Spiritual Speaks of Life and Death* (Richmond, Ind.: Friends United Press, 1975), 13, 111.

4. Howard Thurman, *With Head and Heart* (New York: Harcourt Brace Jovanovich, 1979), 60.

5. Thurman, *Luminous Darkness,* x.

6. Thurman, *With Head and Heart,* 253.

7. On African American women's theology of resistance, see Delores S. Williams, *Sisters in the Wilderness: The Challenge of Womanist God-Talk* (Maryknoll, N.Y.: Orbis Books, 1993); and Emilie M. Townes, ed., *A Troubling in My Soul: Womanist Perspectives on Suffering and Evil* (Maryknoll, N.Y.: Orbis Books, 1993).

8. Thurman, *With Head and Heart,* 20–21.

9. Ibid., 17.

10. The naysayers are many, from Senator Daniel Patrick Moynihan and researcher M. F. Peters to columnist William Raspberry and writer Shahrazad Ali.

11. Mary Goodwin, "Racial Roots and Religion: An Interview with Howard Thurman," *The Christian Century,* May 9, 1973, 533.

12. See Thurman's dedication in *With Head and Heart.*

13. See, for instance, Yaya D. Diallo and Mitchell Hall, *The Healing Drum: African Wisdom Teachings* (Rochester, Vt.: Destiny Books, 1989).

14. Charles V. Willie, "The Role of Mothers in the Lives of Outstanding Scholars," *Journal of Family Issues* 5 (Fall 1984): 291–306.

15. Goodwin, "Racial Roots and Religion," 534.

16. Lerone Bennett Jr., "Howard Thurman: Twentieth-Century Holy Man," *Ebony,* February, 1978: 85.

17. Thurman, *With Head and Heart,* 85.

18. Ibid., 269.

19. Howard Thurman, "Mysticism and Social Action," Lawrence Lecture on Religion and Society, First Unitarian Church of Berkeley, October 13, 1978.

20. Howard Thurman, "Mysticism and Social Change," Pacific School of Religion, Berkeley, Calif., July 18, 1978.

21. Howard Thurman, "Black Spirituality and Identity," unpublished paper, March 23, 1972.

22. Michael Eric Dyson, *Reflecting Black: African American Cultural Criticism* (Minneapolis: University of Minnesota Press, 1993), xxii.

23. See, for instance, bell hooks and Cornel West, *Breaking Bread: Insurgent Black Intellectual Life* (Boston: South End Press, 1991), 49.

24. Howard Thurman, "The Commitment," The Growing Edge, The Church for the Fellowship of All Peoples, March, 1949.

25. C. Eric Lincoln, "Black Males in Crisis," ITC conference on Research and the Black Church, May 22, 1991, p.11.

26. Thurman, *Luminous Darkness,* 57–58.

PART VI

THEOLOGY
AND ETHICS

Throughout this volume we have raised questions about the adequacy of any one individual or group speaking for all concerning what forms of masculinity might be more conducive to genuine well-being for men and all those whom men encounter. We are convinced that the resources for formulating new understandings must take into account a variety of cultural and situational perspectives. In the four chapters in this part, the authors seek to demonstrate some ways in which the resources of theology and ethics can be used to bring about positive changes in men's lives.

Though they focus on different relationships, Merle Longwood and Michael Clark both view the dominant construction of masculinity in our culture as too limited to help men bring about positive changes in their roles in particular relationships. As an active and nurturant father, Longwood describes and advocates a new understanding of fatherhood in which gender roles are reorganized so that men and women will share equally both breadwinner and childcare responsibilities. He provides a broad overview of the history of fatherhood in Western culture, and particularly in the United States, suggesting the influences the Christian traditions have had in understanding the relationships between parents and children. Within a theological framework that emphasizes the incarnation of God in the embodied lives of people, Longwood argues for egalitarian relationships between men and women and challenges the distinction between private and public spheres of life. He suggests that the ethical principles of justice and the common good, informed by love and articulated in the Christian tradition, should be used to support the development of a new understanding of fathering.

Clark, a profeminist gay man who lives in a long-term committed relationship, develops his chapter in conversation with a number of other gay men engaged in theological and ethical writing about relationships. He stakes out a position between those who propose that gay men assimilate into the society that perpetuates harmful stereotypes concerning sexuality (with the extremes of hypermasculinity and effeminacy) and those who place the gay male sexuality of the 1970s and early 1980s gay male ghetto (before the advent of AIDS) upon a pedestal and refuse to engage in constructive self-critical reflection. Clark argues that it is not enough for gay men to demand justice; gay men must also take responsibility for what they do with their lives. While being careful not to "blame the victim" in discussing gay men's sexual behavior, he nevertheless wants gay men to acknowledge that they have participated in practices that set them up to be exposed to HIV. He calls for a theological ethic that emphasizes love expressed in justice as right relation, the value of long-term couples, fidelity in friendship, and embodied ecological responsibility.

In the last two chapters in this section, Carter Heyward and James Nelson develop proposals for how they would like to shape the agenda for antisexist men who want to construct a more positive masculinity. Heyward, a lesbian, feminist, Christian theologian, does not say much specifically about the role of theology, but her liberationist theological perspective is present in the background of her chapter. She writes about, and to, men who are supportive of feminist or womanist values, to nudge them further in the direction of transforming justice and liberating social change. Acknowledging her disappointment that most feminist men have not moved beyond "liberalism," she identifies three patterns that she views as inadequate: men too embedded in patriarchy, men who lean on women too much, and men who do as they damned well please. She views all of these stances as insufficiently critical of the radical individualism and patriarchal capitalism that she believes informs the status quo. She closes with a series of concrete recommendations concerning what she and other feminists with whom she identifies want and need from men.

Nelson, who has been one of the pioneer antisexist men writing about sexuality and gender issues, develops his views especially in relation to what he would like to see happen in the churches. He is critical of the privatization of sexuality and spirituality, which he views as a legacy of the nineteenth century that still affects the churches in North America. He proposes to develop further an insight of the social gospel of the early twentieth century, which emphasized the social dimension of both sin and salvation, by expanding the notion of "sexually transmitted disease" to include broader phenomena such as social violence, white racism, and environmental abuse. Nelson believes that all three of these social ills are related in significant ways to distortions in male body/sexual dynamics. To respond to these and other important public issues, he proposes that we engage in sexual theology, a dialogical investigation that views the experience of human sexuality and our perceptions of faith as integrally related. He illustrates a way of doing sexual theology, reflecting on the connections between sexuality and broader public issues, by focusing on "the paschal mystery of Christ"—incarnation, crucifixion, and resurrection—in conversation with bodily/sexual experience. He shows how these basic doctrines of Christian theology not only inform our self-understanding but are themselves reformulated in light of our experiences of ourselves as embodied sexual human beings.

A number of questions emerge as we think about how theology and ethics may contribute to constructive changes in masculine roles and practices. How valid are the premises of these authors, who believe that significant social changes are required in masculinity for the sake of humankind and for the whole of creation? What are the possibilities and what are the limitations present in the Western theological traditions for developing new understandings of masculinity? What are the benefits and costs that men might experience if they accept the challenge to participate in masculine roles different from those that are widely accepted in our current culture?

18

CHANGING VIEWS OF
FATHERING AND FATHERHOOD:
A CHRISTIAN ETHICAL PERSPECTIVE

W. Merle Longwood

In an influential book called *Family Politics,* Letty Cottin Pogrebin commented sardonically on the status of fatherhood in our society:

> Have you ever wondered why there are so many men in the "right to life" movement and so few in child care? Or why a man who testifies so passionately about "unborn babies" is usually mute about babies already born and living in sickness and poverty? I attribute these contradictions to the fact that on public issues men act as men and not as fathers. They are protecting their power, not expressing their love of children.[1]

She went on to speculate that these contradictions were a result of masculinist[2] thinking that divides life into neat dualities—power versus love, work versus homework—in which men choose the half that suits them. To illustrate further this masculinist way of thinking, she contrasted the ways men and women take charge of children: "Men are in charge of the concept of the child (they decide when life begins, or which child is 'legitimate') while women are in charge of the reality (three meals a day, fevers, snowsuits, bathtimes, diapers)."[3]

Though this observation about men's relationship to children contains a great deal of truth, it does not provide us with a sufficiently broad context for understanding how we came to view fatherhood in this manner nor does it take into account the important challenges to this way of thinking being raised by those men who are exploring the possibilities of a "new fatherhood."[4] In this discussion of changing views of fathering and fatherhood, I will begin with some observations about how men are becoming more involved and active in child care, and then I will turn to an examination of how the masculinist perspective on the fatherhood Pogrebin described emerged and how the Christian tradition contributed to it. I will conclude with some suggestions about how Christian theology and ethics can provide resources to support a new understanding of fatherhood that benefits children and parents alike.

Before I discuss the changes occurring today, I will identify the perspective from which I write, for I realize that my social location influences how I view these issues. I am a white, heterosexual, Anglo-Saxon, Protestant, middle-class, middle-aged, able-bodied, divorced father. Before it was popular among most of the men I knew, I began to share the breadwinner and child-care roles with my children's mother. I witnessed the birth of my younger daughter before it was accepted policy in the hospital where she was born, and early on I became a deeply involved father, active in the everyday lives of my two daughters, who are now in their mid-twenties. I assumed the larger share of child-care responsibilities for about a decade in my daughters' lives when we were living as an intact family, and I have maintained a close and important relationship with both daughters as a co-parent since their mother and I divorced, ending a sixteen-year marriage.[5] Though I had not thought a lot about parenting before the birth of my daughters, the experience of active fathering taught me how to be a nurturant father when we were an intact nuclear family, how to be a primary caregiver to preadolescent and adolescent daughters when I became a single co-parent following divorce, and how to be a creative long-distance dad when my daughters spent their school-year months with their mother when she moved to a city a thousand miles away from their childhood home. Because my particular circumstances created special burdens as well as unusual opportunities for me to expand my understanding of fathering, I do not claim to speak for fathers in general, but I hope these reflections will be of interest to other men, and women as well, who have their own reasons to explore the changing nature of fatherhood today.

Examples of the "new fatherhood," in which gender roles are reorganized as men and women share breadwinner and child-care roles, are evident almost everywhere one looks—in supermarkets, childbirth and child-care education classes, doctors' waiting rooms, school bus stops, child-care centers, continuing education courses for fathers, and the variety of support groups for fathers springing up around the country.[6] In an interview in the mid-1980s, Samuel Osherson, a psychologist at Harvard who is himself one of these "new fathers," noted this growing trend of greater involvement of men with their children: "I think there's a tremendous yearning in men to have more connection with their children . . . and this is being tapped now. There's very definitely a trend for fathers to become more involved. It's not a tidal wave, but it *is* a trend."[7]

This trend, though still not a tidal wave, has continued in this decade. For many men, involvement in nurturant fathering begins at childbirth or even before, as they monitor the pregnancies of their partners with enthusiasm. In 1960 only 25 percent of American fathers were present at the birth of their children, whereas in 1985 the figure had risen dramatically to 85 percent.[8] This percentage has continued to increase, as the expectation has developed among all social classes that fathers will attend childbirth classes and delivery.[9] This increased physical and emotional contact between fathers and babies effects powerful attitudinal changes in these men.[10]

The extent to which fathers have relinquished their hold on the privilege, power, and responsibility that come with breadwinning and have become companions and co-parents of their children is a matter of debate, but the media—which mirrors as well as influences such changes—is inundating us with materials focusing on the "new father." There are dozens of books and many more articles published each year discussing the role of fathers. More and more films and television programs show men in nurturing relationships with children. These popular presentations help raise consciousness about the possibilities of fathering that involve men not as subordinate "helpers" to their children's mother, but as full participants in the care and nurture of their children, as co-parents or single parents in intact or separated families, beginning their deeper involvement during pregnancy, at birth, or at some later point in their children's lives.[11]

Some scholars suggest that the seeds for the current change of attitudes toward fatherhood in America were planted at the end of the Second World War, with the expansion of suburbs that removed men from their families from early morning to mid-evening and made them feel exiled.[12] In the more immediate past, however, many men began to examine their fathering roles in response to the women's movement, which touched the lives of millions, affecting changes in the family as well as in the workplace. To a lesser extent, a concern for fathering has been fueled by the men's movement, which has encouraged men to reexamine their gender roles, including their roles as fathers, their relationships with other men, and their relationships with the women in their lives.

It is perhaps more accurate to refer to men's movements, rather than a single men's movement, for there are a variety of quite different men's alliances. Kenneth Clatterbaugh has identified six perspectives, each of which has its particular focus and favorite theories about men's issues: profeminist; spiritual (incorporating what is commonly called the mythopoetic); men's rights; group-specific; socialist; and conservative.[13] In relation to fathering issues, the two most important are the profeminist and men's rights groups. The profeminist organizations—such as the National Organization for Men Against Sexism (NOMAS) and the Fatherhood Project in New York City—have taken much from the women's movement agenda and made it their own. NOMAS holds an annual national conference on "Men and Masculinity" and sponsors a variety of task groups, including one on fathers. The Fatherhood Project publishes studies concerning a variety of issues related to men's involvement in parenthood.[14] The men's rights groups, usually focusing on fathers' rights and divorce reform issues, are frequently led by fathers outraged at the legal system that limits their contact with their children after separation or divorce while requiring fathers to pay what they often consider excessive or arbitrarily determined amounts of child support.[15] Both profeminist and men's rights groups support more active fathering, but they part company on some issues. Profeminists take seriously feminist critiques of patriarchy—the public rule of men—and advocate personal and political changes in response, while men's rights advocates often focus on trying to reestablish rights they perceive men as having lost.

Fatherhood in Historical Perspective

A concern for more nurturing parenting emerged slowly in Western culture, first for mothers, and later for fathers. Before the middle of the eighteenth century, European, and to a lesser extent American, family structure was patriarchal and extended.[16] In the agricultural world the family was the basic economic unit, with the father as the unquestioned ruler, and all the members of the family working together to survive. Without tracing all the details of how this patriarchal mode of fatherhood was modified, I will discuss some of the major shifts that have occurred, giving particular attention to those that can be related to certain Christian beliefs and practices,[17] and to the American context.

In the Hebrew and Roman cultures, the seedbeds for the emergence of Christianity, family structures were extended and patriarchal. However, rapid economic changes occurred in Rome after the Carthaginian wars, bringing vast amounts of wealth there and diminishing the power of the patriarchy.[18] Within the Christian community, there were other quite distinctive reasons why the power of patriarchy was challenged. From the beginning the message of Jesus was understood as a call to faith, asking people to reject father, mother, husband, wife, or children, to prepare for the imminent coming of the kingdom of God.[19] Though the New Testament accepted marriage and the procreation of children as honorable and within the purposes of God, in the coming of "the new age" all special relationships, including family relationships, were relativized. Consequently, the early church developed an ambivalent attitude toward the family, regarding it as less valuable than celibacy, which would enable a person to give full attention to God.[20]

It was not until the Renaissance and the Protestant Reformation that a dramatic shift in this thinking took place. While not challenging the assumptions of patriarchy, by then well established in Christianity,[21] the Reformers focused on the Christian life not as renunciation or withdrawal from the world, but as the common life of ordinary people. Martin Luther, for example, believed there was no higher calling than marriage and that raising children was the "noblest and most precious work of them all."[22]

The early church's ambivalence toward the family was thus removed for Protestants, preparing the way for the eventual identification of parental nurturing responsibilities as appropriate only to "female nature,"[23] while the basis for men's more nurturant parenting had to await other sociocultural developments, including the Industrial Revolution, the urbanization of Western Europe, the emergence of new capitalistic economic institutions, and demographic shifts in the age at which marriage occurred, which effected a lower birthrate.[24]

Industrialization brought a significant decline in the authority and responsibility of the father at home. The family became a sphere of life totally dependent on an economic system outside the home.[25] By the nineteenth century there had been a clear cultural shift, resulting in a sharp separation between the private world of the family, dominated by women and children, and the public world of productive work, dominated by men. This sharp division between feminine and masculine, the private self and the public world, was nurtured on the one hand by ideologies of "true womanhood" and an idealized "home," especially for middle-class women,[26] and on the other hand by socioeconomic changes that removed men from day-to-day involvement in their homes.[27]

Fathers, especially among the working classes, now increasingly worked away from home and became less involved in childrearing.[28] The importance of the mother's role in the family expanded, as the mother took over many of the father's previous duties, and the role of the middle-class father became redefined as "the provider"[29] and "head of the household." As American religion, particularly Protestantism, became "feminized,"[30] the mother became the exemplar of religion and piety, in keeping with her role in "the cult of true womanhood."[31] The father assisted the mother in serving as the ultimate disciplinarian and designated moral teacher in the family. He was expected to lead the family in prayers and, in Christian homes, to provide moral instruction based on readings from the Bible. At times he would lead "edifying discourse" around the dinner table or in front of the fireplace;[32] however, his wife was the one who was particularly religious, for it was in this domain that she secured her promised happiness and power.

The nineteenth-century middle-class father had a more active role in relating to his sons than to his daughters. He taught his sons the lessons they needed to know to survive well in the world outside the home.[33] Because of his frequent absence from the home and his own assumptions about his proper role, however, he did not participate effectively in the kind of sharing that characterizes the "new father" I described earlier. This type of fatherhood requires an emotional involvement with the child and role sharing with the alternate parent that is based on principles that I will discuss subsequently, but first I will provide a brief comment about what has happened within the Roman Catholic tradition in the years since the Protestant Reformation.

At the risk of oversimplifying, I will say that in the Roman Catholic tradition the pattern present in the early church which viewed family life with some ambivalence remains intact in official church teachings.[34] Although marriage is viewed as a sacrament, it is still understood as a lesser calling than virginity. The recent special letter to women, written by Pope John Paul II,[35] illustrates this. Anticipating the United Nations Fourth World Conference on Women in Beijing, the letter seemed to be part of a larger strategy by the Vatican to exert its influence on the modern definition of women's role in society and to counteract certain trends in feminist thought. The letter, addressed to women throughout the world, gave credit to the women's movement for its substantially positive achievements, and accepted responsibility for injustices against women committed in the name of the Roman Catholic Church. But the pope made it clear that there would be no change in the church's position barring women from becoming priests. He praised women in various roles, but he singled out "consecrated women" as "following the example of the greatest of women, the mother of Jesus Christ." In addition, in distinguishing between men and women he argued for a "certain diversity of roles," and said that a service Christ had exclusively entrusted to men—"the task of being an 'icon' "—"in no way detracts from the role of women." This argument is consistent with earlier papal teaching that justified exclusion of women from the priesthood because the female body does not resemble the male body of Christ.[36] Thus a woman is understood to be inseparable from her sexual nature, and as a priest she would inappropriately bring sexuality into the realm of the sacred.[37]

Despite their different contexts, the suggestions I want to make about what considerations are necessary for a more adequate understanding of fatherhood in contemporary life can be applied equally well within either Roman Catholicism or Protestantism.

Rethinking Fatherhood: Resources from Christian Ethics

The resources in Christian theology and ethics that can enable us to move toward role sharing and nurturant fatherhood need to be grounded in a prophetic framework that emphasizes equality, justice, mutuality, and human fulfillment, on the one hand, and criticizes institutional and cultural arrangements that oppress, violate, or distort human beings in their relationships, on the other. Underlying this theological perspective is a conviction that the judging, sustaining, liberating, healing, affirming, life-giving presence of God breaks into our lives, as the Word continues to become flesh and dwells among us. As we become aware of God's presence, we realize the destiny for which we have been created, to live as embodied selves who embrace freedom, equality, joyfulness, and peace grounded in justice.[38] The most fundamental ethical principle that flows from this theological perspective is love, in all its multidimensional reality, and this love takes form in human relationships that are respectful, caring, responsible, honest, and faithful.

In bringing this theological perspective and ethical principle to bear on the issue of how parents can enhance the development of children as human persons by being sensitive to their individual needs, the two ethical concepts that emerge as especially important are social justice and the common good.

First, we need to develop an ordering of the patterns of relationships between men and women that is fundamentally egalitarian rather than hierarchical. In much of the history of Christian thought women have been defined as subordinate to men, as humans who lack the fullness of the *imago dei*.[39] A new ordering will view women, as well as men, as autonomous persons, as individuals who can claim rights, as persons who can fill roles outside the home as well as within it based on ability and interest rather than on gender, as equal human beings called to relationships of mutuality within communities of accountability. As Matthew Fox has playfully suggested, we need to explore ways to order our communities to be more like dancing in Sarah's circle than climbing Jacob's ladder.[40]

Secondly, we need to challenge the distinctions between private and public spheres of life, especially as this distinction has rigidly locked women and men into one or the other of these spheres.[41] For too long in our history, we in the Christian community have regarded the family as a place for women and children, and the work done there to be accomplished or at least supervised by women. For men, however, we have interpreted important work as that which takes place outside the family, where the significant work of the world and even of the kingdom of God is accomplished. A transformation of both private consciousness and public policy is needed, with men and women sharing the responsibilities of child care as both fathers and mothers work outside the home. Fathers must understand themselves as not merely helpers but as equal participants in child care, with work and other institutions in the public sphere being restructured to make this possible.[42]

Moreover, we need to rethink our understanding of both work in the family and employment outside the home. We need to give the family the importance it deserves, to see it as a vocation to which both men and women are called to meet the challenges of teaching, modeling, and living out loving relationships, relationships that are valuable in and of themselves but also as the base points for reaching out to the wider world.

We must acknowledge the family as a place where individuals learn and practice the fundamental virtues of love and justice. But we must also acknowledge that the ways in which family life has been ordered in the past distributes burdens and responsibilities unjustly, in ways that destroy rather than enhance its members' capacities and inclinations to develop—intellectually, morally, and socially—as full human beings.

We need to see the world of work outside the home as an arena that is as appropriate to women as it is to men. We must acknowledge that women who work outside the home almost always do so out of economic necessity, and not for the sake of securing luxuries.[43] On the other hand, we need to be aware that men who are unemployed are not necessarily shirking their masculine duties. We must be careful not to denigrate women who are homemakers, but by the same token we must accept men who choose that role as performing equally valuable work.

Thirdly, we need to rethink our understanding of family life in general and parenthood in particular in relation to principles of justice. At the most fundamental level, we need to acknowledge that the patriarchal model of the family, with the father as the ruler in the hierarchy, was not the only model present in the Christian tradition, though it became the dominant one in both the Roman Catholic and mainline Protestant traditions. Feminist scholarship has helped us realize that alternative traditions were available, such as one tradition within the New Testament and the early church, which later got shunted aside, that emphasized equality and collaboration as women functioned as preachers, pastors, prophets, and patrons.[44] And we can go back and resurrect those traditions that have the possibility of fulfilling those requirements of justice which stress equality, equal regard for all persons, and community. Justice so conceived best expresses our fundamental experience of love in which all persons seek the well-being of others in mutuality.[45]

We need to assert that assigning leadership roles in terms of dominance and subordination does not make sense when we understand that all persons are basically equal, regardless of gender. I have become increasingly convinced of the necessity of equality as the basis for true partnership in marriage,[46] and I believe this equality must be expressed in a mutuality of collaboration, including sharing parental responsibilities and other household tasks.

Fathers and children will both benefit from such a redefinition of roles based on principles of equality in the family. Fathers, for example, who participate responsibly in their children's lives, when the children are young and when they are adolescents, will have a profound impact on their children's lives; just as important, these fathers will be significantly influenced themselves to be socially generative in other aspects of their lives as they grow toward maturity.[47] Children will benefit immensely in their moral development when they experience justice implemented in the structures of family life, where they can observe and practice fairness, mutual accountability, appropriate responses to specific needs, and respect for differences within a context of authentic community. In contrast to the patterns that arise in an isolated nuclear family, with the mother as the primary caregiver and the father being physically or emotionally absent during children's early lives, with women wielding power in the lives of their children and men ruling in the public sphere,[48] children's lives can be enriched as they experience both parents doing tasks traditionally associated with "masculine" or "feminine" gender roles.[49]

Involving children in family roles, taking into account their level of maturity, is not a burden but a benefit. Children benefit from learning that neither parent's work is more important, that work that brings in more money is not intrinsically more valuable than work that brings in less or no money, that for a person who earns more, time is no more precious than for a person who earns less, that neither parent needs to choose employment outside the home based on gender considerations, and that all household tasks are gender neutral.[50]

Children can benefit by having mothers take them camping and hiking, and by having fathers take them to doctors' and dentists' appointments. They can also benefit by observing mothers repair cars and mow the lawn, as fathers cook meals and sew buttons on clothes. Their understanding of justice will be deepened by seeing mothers provide new role models as plumbers, mechanics, pastors, professors, and corporate managers, as they also see fathers express their "tender" sides while changing diapers and reading bedtime stories.

In addition, justice within the family needs to be considered in relation to other institutions in society. On the one hand, we need to evaluate the impact of economic, political, and social systems on the family, bringing principles of justice to bear on public policy issues that affect the family. On the other hand, as Wilson Yates has pointed out, we need to understand how families themselves can respond to and shape the changes that affect not only their own destiny but that of the larger society.[51] In this vein, Kathleen and James McGinnis's book, *Parenting for Peace and Justice*,[52] provides helpful suggestions for families in their social mission at the parish, diocesan, and national levels.

Fourthly, we need to examine our family structures and roles in light of the common good, a corollary concept to the notion of justice. The Roman Catholic tradition, far more than any other religious tradition, has given content to this ethical concept, which looks to creating the societal conditions necessary to enhance and justly distribute public or common goods.[53] The quality of the common good arrangements can be measured by how they enhance personal flourishing. Though there was a time in this tradition when it was thought necessary to have a hierarchical ordering with one person at the head of a community, more recent delineations of the common good have affirmed a more egalitarian model as appropriate to modern society. It therefore requires only a further extension of this revised understanding of this concept to apply it to family relationships, showing that the good of families, as well as churches and governments, is best served when leadership is shared and collaborative.

Moreover, family structures that do not encourage and allow for equal sharing of the various functions, without regard to gender, are not conducive to the common good. Family arrangements in which men do not share equally in the care and nurture of children do not serve to enhance the public good, which Douglas Sturm, a Protestant ethicist, has described as "the good of the relationships through which the members of the community sustain one another, contribute to one another, and constitute a creative center for the ongoing life of the community."[54] The common good looks to the quality of the interactive network of institutions to ensure that it secures and enhances justice and human dignity.

Changing our understanding of fatherhood thus requires us to revise the basic principles that illuminate and guide the development of our characters and the direction of our actions. As Samuel Osherson and others have helped us realize, our ideas about fatherhood are rooted in our experience of our own fathers, images of other fathers, and our own gender role socialization.[55] It is, therefore, in the education of children where real changes in understanding fatherhood can take root, as boys and girls experience nurturing men, who want deep involvement in the lives of their children, and whose human qualities transcend sexual identity.[56] Such "new fathers" can help a new generation of children gently appreciate the fragile world about them, understand the value of an appropriate mix of work and play in the home and outside it, and finally help boys who will become men and girls who will become women to become nurturers themselves.

NOTES

1. Letty Cottin Pogrebin, *Family Politics: Love and Power on an Intimate Frontier* (New York: McGraw Hill, 1983), 193.
2. For Pogrebin, as for many feminist and pro-feminist writers, the term

"masculinist" carries a negative, sexist connotation, so it is not really equivalent to "feminist," which does not have that negative connotation.

3. Pogrebin, *Family Politics,* 193.

4. For a helpful discussion of two understandings of "new fatherhood" that emerged respectively in the 1920s and the 1970s in America, see Robert L. Griswold, *Fatherhood in America: A History* (New York: Basic Books, 1993). The second differed from the first, as later twentieth-century feminism transformed male breadwinning as well as female domesticity expectations.

5. See Merle Longwood, "Divorce as an Occasion of Moral Reconstruction," *The Annual of the Society of Christian Ethics 1984,* ed. Larry L. Rasmussen (Waterloo, Ontario: Council on the Study of Religion, 1984), 229–48.

6. Though David Blankenhorn has made a convincing case for the importance of fathers in children's lives, he has encouraged divisiveness and antagonized all but original, heterosexual fathers by arguing that "no other fathering will work" in his recent book, *Fatherless in America: Confronting Our Most Urgent Social Problem* (New York: Basic Books, 1995).

7. Quoted in William E. Smart, "The New Father Figure," *Washington Post,* June 13, 1986.

8. David L. Giveans, "Speaking Out!" *Nurturing News* 8, no. 1 (June 1986): 1.

9. John Snarey, *How Fathers Care for the Next Generation: A Four-Decade Study* (Cambridge and London: Harvard University Press, 1993), 33.

10. See Martin Greenberg, *The Birth of a Father* (New York: Continuum, 1985); Kyle D. Pruett, *Nurturing Father: Journey Toward the Complete Man* (New York: Warner Books, 1987); and Glen F. Palm, "Involved Fatherhood: A Second Chance," *Journal of Men's Studies* 2, no.2 (November 1993): 139–55.

11. See Kathleen Gerson, *No Man's Land: Men's Changing Commitments to Family and Work* (New York: Basic Books, 1993); Geoffrey L. Greif, *The Daddy Track and the Single Father* (Lexington, Mass.: Lexington Books, 1990); Charles S. Scull, ed., *Fathers, Sons, and Daughters: Exploring Fatherhood, Renewing the Bond* (Los Angeles: J.P. Tarcher, 1992); and Judith S. Wallerstein and Sandra Blakeslee, *Second Chances: Men, Women, and Children a Decade after Divorce* (New York: Ticknor & Fields, 1989).

12. Samuel Osherson, *Finding Our Fathers: The Unfinished Business of Manhood* (New York: Free Press, 1986), 179–80.

13. Kenneth Clatterbaugh, *Contemporary Perspectives on Masculinity: Men, Women, and Politics in Modern Society* (Boulder, Colo.: Westview Press, 1990).

14. See Debra G. Klinman and Rhiana Kohl, *Fatherhood U.S.A.: The First National Guide to Programs, Services, and Resources for and about Fathers* (New York: Garland, 1984).

15. See the section "When Daddy Can't Be Daddy Anymore," *Men Freeing Men: Exploding the Myth of the Traditional Male,* ed. Francis Baumli (Jersey City, N.J.: New Atlantis Press, 1985), 163–202.

16. In the development of this section, I am indebted especially to John Demos, "The Changing Faces of Fatherhood: A New Exploration in American

Family History," *Father and Child: Developmental and Clinical Perspectives,* ed. Stanley H. Cath, Alan R. Gurwitt, and John Munder Ross (Boston: Little, Brown, 1982), 425–45; E. Anthony Rotundo, "American Fatherhood: A Historical Perspective," *American Behavioral Scientist* 29, no. 1 (September/October 1985): 7–25; and Jonathan Bloom-Feshbach, "Historical Perspectives on the Father's Role," *The Role of the Father in Child Development,* 2d ed., ed. Michael Lamb (New York: John Wiley & Sons, 1981), 71–112.

17. In discussing the historical developments in Christianity, I have drawn heavily from Margaret A. Farley, "The Church and the Family: An Ethical Task," *Horizons* 10, no.1 (Spring 1983): 50–71.

18. Bloom-Feshbach, "Historical Perspectives," 84–85.

19. Matt. 10:34–39.

20. Farley, "Church and the Family," 53–54.

21. See Karen Jo Torjesen, *When Women Were Priests: Women's Leadership in the Early Church and the Scandal of Their Subordination in the Rise of Christianity* (San Francisco: Harper San Francisco, 1993).

22. William H. Lazareth, *Luther on the Christian Home* (Philadelphia: Muhlenberg Press, 1960), 220, quoted by Farley, "Church and Family," 55.

23. Beverly Wildung Harrison, *Making the Connections: Essays in Feminist Social Ethics* (Boston: Beacon Press, 1985), 42–53. Carl N. Degler discusses the two spheres in American history in *At Odds: Women and the Family in America from the Revolution to the Present* (New York: Oxford University Press, 1980), chap.11.

24. Peter N. Stearns, *Be a Man! Males in Modern Society* (New York: Holmes & Meier, 1979), chaps. 3–5.

25. See Rosemary Radford Ruether, "Home and Work: Women's Roles and the Transformation of Values," *Theological Studies* 36, no. 4 (December, 1975): 647–59.

26. Ibid., 651–53.

27. Demos, "Changing Faces," 432–34; Rotundo, "American Fatherhood," 11–15.

28. Stearns, *Be a Man,* 48. See also Mark Gerzon, *A Choice of Heroes: The Changing Faces of American Manhood* (Boston: Houghton Mifflin Co., 1982), 128.

29. Rotundo, "American Fatherhood," 11; Demos, "Changing Faces," 434.

30. Barbara Welter, "The Feminization of American Religion: 1800–1860," *Clio's Consciousness Raised: New Perspectives on the History of Women,* ed. Mary S. Hartman and Lois Banner (New York: Harper & Row, 1974), 137–57; Ann Douglas, *The Feminization of American Culture* (New York: Alfred A. Knopf, 1977).

31. Barbara Welter, "The Cult of True Womanhood: 1820–1860," *American Quarterly* 18, no. 2, pt. 1 (Summer, 1966): 151–74.

32. Demos, "Changing Faces," 432–33.

33. Ibid., 438; Rotundo, "American Fatherhood," 14.

34. Farley, "Church and the Family," 56.

35. Pope John Paul II, "Letter to Women" (Released July 10, 1995), *Origins* 25, no. 9 (July 27, 1995).

36. See, for example, the Vatican's *Declaration on Certain Questions concerning Sexual Ethics* (Washington, D.C.: United States Catholic Conference, 1975).

37. Torjesen, *When Women Were Priests,* 2–4.

38. See James B. Nelson, *Body Theology* (Louisville, Ky.: Westminster/ John Knox Press, 1992), chap. 1.

39. See Rosemary Radford Ruether, "Misogynism and Virginal Feminism in the Fathers of the Church," in *Religion and Sexism: Images of Woman in the Jewish and Christian Traditions,* ed. Rosemary Radford Ruether, 150–83 (New York: Simon & Schuster, 1974).

40. Matthew Fox, *A Spirituality Named Compassion and the Healing of the Global Village, Humpty Dumpty and Us* (Minneapolis: Winston Press, 1979), chap. 2.

41. An interesting study that demonstrates a way to "do ethics" that does not accept this split between private and public spheres, developed as a biographical "story" of the life of a notable feminist leader, is Eleanor Humes Haney's *A Feminist Legacy: The Ethics of Wilma Scott Heide and Company* (Buffalo: Margaretdaughters, 1985).

42. Though she does not give sufficient attention to restructuring these public institutions, there are many other helpful suggestions about parental role sharing in Rhona Mahony's *Kidding Ourselves: Breadwinning, Babies, and Bargaining Power* (New York: Basic Books, 1995).

43. See Pogrebin, *Family Politics,* chap. 6.

44. See Constance F. Parvey, "The Theology and Leadership of Women in the New Testament," in *Religion and Sexism,* ed. Ruether, 117–49; Torjesen, *When Women Were Priests,* chap. 1.

45. For a powerful example of a sexual theology that stresses the importance of mutuality and selves in relation, see Carter Heyward, *Touching Our Strength: The Erotic Power and Love of God* (San Francisco: Harper San Francisco, 1989).

46. See Carl Rogers, *Becoming Partners: Marriage and Its Alternatives* (New York: Delacorte Press, 1972).

47. Snarey, *How Fathers Care,* chap. 4.

48. See Dorothy Dinnerstein, *The Mermaid and the Minotaur: Sexual Arrangements and Human Malaise* (New York: Harper & Row, 1976), and Nancy Chodorow, *The Reproduction of Mothering: Psychoanalysis and the Sociology of Gender* (Berkeley and Los Angeles: University of California Press, 1978).

49. See James Levine, *Who Will Raise the Children? New Options for Fathers (and Mothers)* (New York: Lippincott, 1976).

50. See Letty Cottin Pogrebin, *Growing Up Free: Raising Your Child in the 80's* (New York: McGraw Hill, 1980), chap. 10.

51. Wilson Yates, "The Family as Power: Towards an Ethic of Family Social Responsibility," in *The Annual of the Society of Christian Ethics 1981,* ed. Thomas W. Ogletree, 121–51 (Waterloo, Ontario: Council on the Study of Religion, 1981).

52. James McGinnis and Kathleen McGinnis, *Parenting for Peace and Justice* (Maryknoll, N.Y.: Orbis Books, 1982).

53. See Merle Longwood, "The Common Good: An Ethical Framework for Evaluating Environmental Issues," *Theological Studies* 34, no. 3 (April, 1973): 468–80; see also John A. Coleman, S.J., "A Common Good Primer," *dialog* 34, no.4 (Fall, 1995): 249–54.

54. Douglas Sturm, "On Meanings of Public Good: An Exploration," *Journal of Religion* 58, no. 1 (January, 1978): 23.

55. Osherson, *Finding Our Fathers.*

56. See the last chapter in Gerzon's *A Choice of Heroes,* in which he discusses "the emerging masculinities"—healer, companion, colleague, and nurturer.

19

GAY MEN, MASCULINITY, AND AN ETHIC OF FRIENDSHIP

J. Michael Clark

Coming out as a gay man usually entails finding oneself excluded from traditional moral discourse. Our exclusion by definition from so-called traditional morality, however, should never be construed as the discovery of a place where "anything goes."[1] Indeed, to claim and to live out one's gay identity as a mode of being-with/in-the-world is not to live in an ethical vacuum: It is not enough only to demand justice for *what* we are—for being gay. We must also take responsibility for what we do—for *how* we have been and for *how* we are—as gay men. In short, doing theology and doing ethics conflate.[2] As theology and ethics do in fact conflate in feminist and profeminist gay male writing, one leitmotif emerges over and over again—accountability. We develop our accountability in and through the dynamics of our lives as bodyselves-in-relation. Accountability is interwoven with our vulnerability, our willingness to be transformed and to grow. It is a sign of our interdependence, our cooperation, our friendship, our solidarity. Our accountability is our love-in-action, befriending ourselves, one another, our community(ies), our earth. It is the embodied ethical posture that enables us to create meaning, to create choices, and to choose life—even in the face of AIDS. It enables us to be more than passive victims and thereby to weave a legacy of resistance for the long-term, multigenerational tasks of liberation. And, because our accountability is part of a relational dynamic—at once vulnerable, transformative, and liberatingly resistant—it necessarily opens us to loving, life-giving self-criticism.

As we discover and nurture our theological and ethical voices in our conversations with one another, we quickly realize that we cannot naively champion the oppressed-who-can-do-no-wrong.[3] Gay men must neither wallow in our victimization nor elevate our embodied marginalization to some inviolable—and thereby utterly ineffectual—pedestal. Neither self-sacrifice nor self-worship will do. What we must deal with instead is a red herring too frequently bandied about our community(ies):

Loving self-criticism, prophetic words both from and to our own embodied lives-in-relation, is absolutely *not* a symptom of unresolved, internalized self-hatred or homophobia. Rather, "the ability to be self-critical, to remain open in a systematic structural manner to revision, is a sign of maturity"; moreover, "the work of revision and self-critique is grounded in strength, not weakness," and not self-hatred.[4] To approach loving maturity rather than self-hatred, our prophetic word to our own community(ies) must be qualified by empathy, by love and compassion, by solidarity and identification with, and by an acknowledgment of our own complicity in ways of being gay that have been inimical to appropriate self- and other-love and therefore have not only hampered our liberational efforts but also placed our very lives in jeopardy.[5] Our prophetic word must also be qualified by an important caveat: As we engage in self-criticism, our ethical reflections must acknowledge the possibility—and insofar as possible guard against the likelihood—that those reflections will be co-opted by those who stand arrayed against us and even perverted to fuel condemnation of our very lives.[6] As but one example, while we gay men need to claim transformative responsibility for our past (and present) sexual behavior, that active wrestling-through must in no way be interpreted or exploited so as to "blame the victims" of AIDS!

Our turn toward loving and nonblaming self-criticism actually begins not with fingerpointing at ourselves or at other individuals, but with a (re)examination of the cultural context in which we find ourselves. For those of us who are gay men, this includes reflecting on the influence of the Western masculine socialization process upon our lives—both how it has shaped us as men and how it excludes us as gay men.[7] One means to break the vicious cycle(s) of masculine socialization in our embodied gay males' lives is to confront the fears veiled by that process. Foremost among these fears are our culturally maintained fear of intimacy and the related fear of any mutuality wherein we might lose control. In the decade prior to AIDS, for example, a significant portion of the gay male subculture institutionalized patterns of behavior that prevented both healthy confrontation with these fears and any possibility of intimacy. Our masculine socialization precluded many of us from any deeper erotic pleasure than fleeting accumulations of genital experience. In our bodyselves we learned to ignore whole-bodied eroticism by distancing our "selves" from our "mere genital functions." At the same time, our socialized male need to control led us to manipulate our minds and bodies with drugs and alcohol, in order to make ourselves perfectly tuned sexual machines. We learned to compensate for the stereotypes around effeminacy and receptivity with extremes of behavior, both as "tops" enacting hypermasculinity and refusing ever to be penetrated as "bottoms" forcing our alienated bodies to receive ever larger items. We overcompensated for our perceived failed masculinity by sexual prowess and sexual achievement. We allowed our entire self-worth to become tied to our sexual attractiveness, while at the same time we became ever more alienated from our bodies as ourselves. The heyday of discos and bathhouses was every bit as exhausting as it was exhilarating.

What we failed to see in all of this is the degree to which heterosexism, particularly in the years following World War II, actually set us up. The bar and bath subculture, for example, kept (and the bars still keep) far too many of us safely one-dimensional (i.e., only sexual), hidden away in the dark late hours where the heterosexual world that does not want to see or even to acknowledge us anyway tacitly agreed to bracket us. If being gay was defined for us by heterosexism as only being sexual, we turned sex into a way of life, completely fulfilling the stereotype of promiscuously sexual, only and always sexual, homosexual males. Prior to AIDS the gay sexual subculture in collusion with masculine socialization taught us to separate sex from love or friendship, consequently leaving many of us with lots of sex but few if any deeply satisfying and mutual relationships; we even competed with our lovers for sexual conquests outside our primary relationships. Our early political discourse simply mirrored these myopic self-understandings as it defended our "right to love"—a thinly veiled phrase for actually defending our freedom of access to sexual license. Only as we grew weary of the endless rounds of the sexual netherworld, and later as we encountered AIDS invading our sexual domain, did we gradually surface from an underworld delimited by heterosexist parameters to realize that what we really need is not more sex but more love— love in committed relationships and in friendships based on justice as right-relation, regardless of whether anything genitally sexual is involved.

One of the most outspoken prophetic voices to emerge from the gay sexual subculture is that of Michael Callen, also one of the best-known long-term survivors who succumbed in late 1993 after twelve years of full-blown AIDS. Callen's writing is tenderly and passionately committed to enhancing both the quality and the longevity of life for his fellow gay men, even as it speaks critically to us. He is, for example, painfully aware of the costs of the closet of heterosexism and masculine socialization, noting that "prior to the gay liberation movement, gay people looked in the mirror of American culture and never—not once—saw our image accurately reflected. . . . The only information . . . said that all gay men are promiscuous." He bemoans our collective failure of imagination, our inability or unwillingness particularly during the 1970s and early 1980s to construct alternative definitions of what being gay could mean. He is saddened by the tyranny of collective belief that not being sexually free enough somehow meant not being adequately or sufficiently gay and that, as a result, "we thought of our bodies as [sexual] machines" and we infused our pol-

itics with just such myopic vision: "One strain of seventies gay liberationist rhetoric proclaimed that sex was inherently liberating; . . . it
seemed to follow that *more* sex was *more* liberating. . . . [In fact] being
gay *meant* having lots of sex."[8]

Accepting mere sexual freedom as the sole meaning of our liberation
not only shortchanged our embodied lives, forfeiting the deeper multidimensional richness of gay being, but also opened our bodyselves to a
plethora of diseases. While some writers in this period actually counseled
us to take pride in our accumulated sexually transmitted diseases (STDs),
Callen argues that these diseases were necessarily taking their toll on our
bodies, making us ripe for something that could not be easily cured by an-
tibiotic remedies.[9] In short, Callen believes that we collaborated with
great abandon in our oppression and in our near retroviral genocide: We
helped set ourselves up by our own complicity, our willingness to accept
heterosexist constructs of what it means to be a gay man—being totally
focused on sex. Ultimately, a sex-negative culture in collusion with gay
sexually reactionary politics made us ripe for AIDS. Even if promiscuity
is not simplistically read as the sole cause of AIDS, at the very least the
gay subculture's obsession with sex orchestrated the conditions by which
we made ourselves vulnerable and it may very well have helped spread
HIV faster among certain portions of our community.

Callen astutely reminds us, of course, that the alternative to equally irresponsible self-pity or victim-blaming, including blaming ourselves, is
accountability. As our theological ethics also attempt to do, he walks the
fine line between accepting responsibility for contributing to the conditions of risk—accepting responsibility for behaving in ways which expose
us to HIV—and being either self-blaming or guilt-ridden because of that
exposure. Ever the balancer, he encourages all of us to move more realistically and more responsibly forward, to see in AIDS "a challenge to *finally* begin living fully" and not just to begin dying.[10] Taking responsibility, acknowledging the ways in which we set ourselves up for exposure to
HIV, while also being critical of the ways in which our heterosexist and
homophobic culture also set us up, is an important "both/and" for our
ethical lives. To accept the hard truth about how many of us lived in the
not-so-distant past and about how we allowed ourselves to be exposed to
HIV, and then to take responsibility for how we live from now on, is to
embody accountability. To take responsibility is most assuredly not to engage in self-hatred; taking responsibility is healing and life giving.

A critical perspective such as Callen's can help us to see our sexual past
and our frequently AIDS-permeated present in fresh ways that enable a
future for us all. We can understand AIDS in our community as one catalyst among others for a shift from a narrow ethics of sexual freedom to
an ethics of caring for one another, including caring for the "casualties,"

at least in part, of the consequences of that sexual freedom. We also realize in this process that our ethics cannot simply sanction every gay lifestyle or every aspect of the gay ghetto; it must instead provide and nurture a genuinely liberating vision. As we begin to articulate such a vision, our efforts will attend to how we experience *both* marginalization and empowerment, rather than focusing on victimization alone. As our understandings of what it means to live ethically as gay men do in fact shift from an emphasis on access to sexual freedom to the complexity of justice-seeking and the tasks of AIDS-related caregiving, our commitments to oppose homophobia and heterosexism will also broaden to advocate solidarity with other people and the earth itself. Beginning to make these connections and to facilitate solidarity entails both celebrating our own diversity and that of others and allowing ourselves to be enriched, even transformed by that diversity, as well as joining in common cause against those forces and structures that oppress any life. Our developing ethics must insist on such solidarity—as both diversity and common cause— particularly with women and the earth, as well as across racial lines and other categories that separate and exclude. We must learn to see and to value diversity as intrinsically valuable, without in any way hierarchical-izing difference such that it becomes an excuse for inequality. For example, if being gay does eventually turn out to be largely biogenetic, we must be at the forefront of insisting that that does not mean being gay is any lesser form of life than any other; we must insist that difference does not mean or require inequality.

Such a critical perspective also helps us see more clearly still what at least some of the real moral issues are: We already know by now that the real moral issue is not that some *are* gay but *how* we are living as gay men. Likewise, the real moral issue is not about AIDS as judgment or punishment upon homosexual behavior; an ethical response to AIDS focuses instead upon the acts of omission and commission that have ignored and/or blamed the victim and in so doing have allowed so many to suffer and die. More specifically still, the real moral issue is not about where, how, or with whom (or even how many or how often) we put our genitals, the real issue is the quality (life-enhancing vs. dehumanizing) of the relationships with ourselves and those with whom we share sexually. While in being true to his own life story Michael Callen conceded that "promiscuity has its place" in the gay male subculture, he immediately went on to add that "the point is, whatever sex one chooses to engage in . . . it should be safer sex and . . . it should proceed from a loving instinct to communication with another human being, rather than being about merely scratching a physical itch, with no regard for the humanity of the individual [one is] scratching the itch with."[11]

Callen's comment brings us back to the need to discern some parameters for gay sexuality. Revaluing our sexuality, not as something restrictive, addictive, or compulsive, but as that active, embodied engagement of our erotic energies which enhances our relationships and nurtures our shared quests for justice as right-relation, is a significant ethical task for all of us, one already elegantly elaborated by feminists and men's studies scholars.[12] Worth reiterating here is that elucidating ethical parameters for our sexuality need not result in a simplistic or moralistic endorsement of monogamy, as if monogamy were somehow sacred in its own right.[13] Indeed, a decision to frame our sexual behavior within the context of a monogamous relationship is purely *pragmatic,* neither divinely given nor carved in stone. A decision to be *non*monogamous simply presents a number of thornier ethical questions: Not only are we confronted with the difficulty of maintaining the special, even sacramental, aspects of our primary sexual and emotional relationships in balance with our outside sexual partners; now we must also ponder how *not* to make those encounters alienating and objectifying, on the one hand, and how *not* to exclude our partners or threaten our primary relationships if our outside encounters do develop humanizing friendships. Whether, or to what extent, such a balancing act can be maintained over time clearly remains an open question.

What is ultimately far more important than the issue of monogamy or nonmonogamy is the value of fidelity. All too often monogamy may not include fidelity in its broadest sense, and only empty relationships remain in such instances. At the same time, fidelity includes far more than simple monogamy. It entails much that is not particularly sexual at all, such as honoring and not abusing the feelings of the partners. It includes not only listening well, but also speaking honestly, from our depths—to be vulnerable rather than to hide what we feel. We must also be faithful to our values within our relationships; we must cherish openness and honesty and we must trust one another deeply; we must be committed not only to our individual growth as persons but also to the growth of our relationship itself. Hence, we must be willing to struggle together, to forgive and to heal one another, and to move together into the future. Monogamy then becomes not simply a restriction upon genital behavior, but rather a pragmatic, mutually chosen means for nurturing the most healthy sexuality-in-relation for two people committed to a common process of growth and liberation together. With this broadened understanding of fidelity, we can discern the liberational insights we need for our journeys as sexual beings-in-relation: "The decision to be monogamous . . . may be our least emotionally confusing way of building and sustaining trust in a particular relationship as the locus of what is, for us, an extraordinary, uncommon experience of erotic power as the love of God."[14]

We also find, not surprisingly, that "fidelity" sounds a lot like "friendship."

Genuine friendship embodies fidelity. Mary Hunt in fact argues both that "all friendships include a sexual dimension, however implicit it may be" and that, conversely, "sexual relations are usually most satisfying when carried out between close friends."[15] Sexual expression can lift a friendship to a qualitatively different place, while friendship in turn enhances that sexual encounter. We are reminded that quality is more important than quantity: The mutuality and depth of caring intimacy inherent in friendship (a special I-Thou relation) enables us to know and to embody a sexuality far more satisfying than any quantity of anonymous or objectified (I-It) relations ever could. In short, friendship emerges as a key umbrella concept for developing our ethically responsible and embodied lives as mature gay men in relation to one another, other persons, and all other life. Unfortunately, however, culturally embedded homophobia often thwarts same-gender friendships—preventing men, for example, from developing deeply intimate and/or physically affectionate friendships—and, for gay men in particular, it thwarts even appropriate self-love. Just as homophobia often thwarts the possibility of friendship among persons of the same gender, so its correlate, heterosexism, imposes upon us a relational standard—marriage—that both disvalues friendships and totally excludes same-gendered commitments. Our heterosexist cultural mindset does not treat any nonheterosexually married friendships as if they matter, and mainstream Christianity, ironically, continues to criticize so-called gay promiscuity while refusing to sacramentalize or support gay coupled commitments. More frustrating still, in our efforts to dismantle homophobia and heterosexism generally and to displace the marriage standard specifically as the only model for acceptable relationships, far too much "politically correct" gay rhetoric has also failed to value our couples as embodied models of friendship.

We must *not* be too quick to dismiss committed couples as if they are by definition not capable of embodying friendship as well as romantic love. To do so is to do ourselves a grave injustice. In fact, the accusation that gay couples are merely "patriarchal dyads" that imitate heterosexual marriage[16] is another disempowering red herring. While, granted, couples need to nurture and be nurtured by their other friendships—those relationships which constitute constructed family and community—all gay coupling does not represent an effort or a desire to imitate heterosexist patterns. If by virtue of being the same gender in our couplings we can avoid the pitfalls of gender roles, our egalitarian relationships might not only embody friendship at its best but also prove the model really worthy of imitation. Indeed, especially for a people whose relationships are almost universally discounted and our very ability to enter into and sustain loving relationships denied in many narrowly moralistic quarters, we need to lift up and celebrate healthy long-term couples—not as imitations but as models of depth, friendship and mutuality, and freedom from gender roles.

(Re)valuing coupling is particularly important for gay men whose same-gender friendships have been disvalued by homophobia: Our homophobic culture mindset has made it easier to engage in objectified, depersonalized, and dehumanized genital sex—frequently and with many different men-as-sex-objects—than to engage in friendship or to sustain a long-term relationship. Whenever two gay men can learn to overcome these impediments to intimacy and depth-in-relation, impediments that are part of the legacy of masculine socialization in our society, we have cause to celebrate their commitments rather than an opportunity merely to dismiss them as hetero-mimesis. Indeed, we need to realize that couples, single men and women, friendships between couples and singles, and various other configurations of friendships are all equally valuable and equally important constituents of community. Finally here, our friendships—both as couples and in community—may be nowhere more important than in the face of AIDS. If "suffering tends to divide the sufferer from those who do not suffer [such that] it is the antithesis of relationship," then we owe it to ourselves and to each other to make our relationships—both our friendships and our couples—work well before loss and death come into our lives. If and when it does, we must also remember that our friendships and our loving do not end with death.[17] Our lives are interconnected in such a way that our impact on the dynamic web of being continues . . . in the embodied lives of our friends.

The ethical concept of friendship is also an ecological concept. Hunt even defines ecology as an "act of befriending the earth and its inhabitants. . . . Ecology is a way of embodying the friendship that the earth deserves"; indeed, "the earth as friend expects the same attention, generativity, community, and justice that any other friend demands" in a relationship modeled not on hierarchical dominion and stewardship, but rather on the utterly equal and intrinsic value of all life. In other words, while we need to be critically astute to those instances and actions whereby humans are unfriendly toward nonhuman life, we also need to develop "new attitudes that may spell the difference between a friendly environment and no environment," both in the present and for the future of life on our planet.[18] Ecofeminist Sallie McFague then synthesizes our understandings of sexual friendship and Hunt's understanding of ecological friendship to describe exactly the kind of movement from a focus on our immediate relational context(s) to a broader focus on global issues by which such new attitudes may develop. Her vision is thus an invitation to the future:

If we were to see *one* other with full attention, that is, loving it, acknowledging that this something [or someone] other than oneself is really real, then it might follow that we would have to acknowledge the reality of many, perhaps all, others. On such a basis we might build an ecological ethic—a way of being in the world that respects the intrinsic value of the many different beings that comprise our planet.[19]

Respecting "the intrinsic value of the many different beings" that together constitute the web of being begins in our embodied lives-in-relation. As we (re)learn to befriend our gay bodyselves and to demand that we be valued alongside all other equally valuable life on our planet, we can also become prophetic embodiments creating a future beyond AIDS . . . for all embodied ecosystemic life-in-relation.

Although I have elaborated a gay ecotheological paradigm in detail elsewhere,[20] certain concerns are pertinent to these present reflections, especially our peculiarly ambivalent relation to "nature." Because a misogynist heterosexism has defined us as primarily and overly sexual, gay men are viewed as chaotic embodiments too close to natural fecundity, just as women are. At the same time, conservative theology has decided our sexual behavior is "unnatural." We are somehow both too close to nature and outside nature! While "unnatural" is really an oxymoron for our lives embedded in the ecosystemic earth, such labeling has nevertheless had very negative effects on us. Insofar as our parents, families, and birthplace cultures have abandoned us to life in cities distant from them, our urban ghettoization all too often further alienates us from the natural world. Longing to return to nature, however, must never degenerate into escapist fantasy; reconnecting with nature must not be merely self-indulgent spiritual reverie engaged in rare moments of solitude or in weekend retreats outside our everyday lives. We can instead create relationships and ecosystems—homes—by making a commitment to the reality of where we find ourselves.

Indeed for many of us, my spouse and I included, learning to raise and tend flower and vegetable gardens—our mini-farms in the midst of the city—has become one embodied, inspirited motivation for ecologically sound praxis on a larger scale. No mere spiritual reverence for nature, gardening unites embodiment and spirituality, as Rebecca Johnson describes: "I garden for sustenance and as a spiritual practice. The annual events of germination, waving green life, fruition, and decay are the only things I really believe in anymore. If I worship at all, it is at the compost pile."[21] Certainly there is both therapy for our urbanized lives and worship in being and working in the yard, cleaning flower beds, planting annuals and perennials, tilling and sowing the vegetable garden, watching daily growth, gratefully savoring newly ripened fruits and vegetables, turning under a summer's worn soil, and raking fall leaves for compost, as well as sitting on the porch watching and listening to the rain. Gay men can indeed be bodyselves-in-relation to other bodyselves-in-nature, even in our urban homes.

There is clearly then an ethically pragmatic aspect to a gay ecotheology. Acknowledging that we cannot "save the world" but that we must nonetheless do what we can do and do it well, an ecological theology and ethics must work to create a "vision that changes the way we see everything and, hence, the way we decide any specific issue and concern"; in short, how we think through these issues necessarily affects how we act.[22] For gay men in particular, real solidarity with the land, with the earth and its embodied pluriform life, must not be mere intellectual assent from within a sterile, ghettoized urban isolation from nature. Rather, it requires accountability and engagement, whether in our home ecosystems or in our care of HIV/AIDS bodies *and their ecosystems* of pets and plants and home. Our all-encompassing engagement and our holistic caring constitute our ecotheological and ethical praxis—our embodied acts of love.

NOTES

1. Mary E. Hunt, *Fierce Tenderness: A Feminist Theology of Friendship* (New York: Crossroad Publishing Co., 1991), 89.
2. Beverly Wildung Harrison, *Making the Connections: Essays in Feminist Social Ethics,* ed. C. S. Robb (Boston: Beacon Press, 1985), 11.
3. Rosemary Radford Ruether, *Liberation Theology* (New York: Paulist Press, 1972), 13, 16, 32, 34.
4. Sharon D. Welch, *A Feminist Ethic of Risk* (Minneapolis: Fortress Press, 1990), 109; cf. 106.
5. Eve Browning Cole and Susan Coultrop-McQuinn, "Toward a Feminist Conception of Moral Life," in *Explorations in Feminist Ethics: Theory and Practice,* ed. E. B. Cole and S. Coultrop-McQuinn (Bloomington: Indiana University Press, 1992), 7.
6. Linda A. Bell, *Rethinking Ethics in the Midst of Violence: A Feminist Approach to Freedom* (Lanham, Md.: Rowman & Littlefield, 1993), 20, 29–30, 33.
7. For a detailed discussion, see J. Michael Clark with Bob McNeir, *Masculine Socialization and Gay Liberation: A Conversation on the Work of James Nelson and Other Wise Friends* (Las Colinas, Tex.: Liberal Press, 1992).
8. Michael Callen, *Surviving AIDS* (New York: HarperCollins, 1990), 2–4, 12 (n. 5).
9. Ibid., 4, 6.
10. Ibid., 2, 10.
11. Ibid., 14–15 (n. 14).

12. See Carter Heyward, *Touching Our Strength: The Erotic as Power and the Love of God* (San Francisco: Harper & Row, 1989); James B. Nelson, *Between Two Gardens: Reflections on Sexuality and Religious Experience* (New York: Pilgrim Press, 1983), *The Intimate Connection: Male Sexuality, Masculine Spirituality* (Philadelphia: Westminster Press, 1988), and *Body Theology* (Louisville, Ky.: Westminster/John Knox Press, 1992).

13. For a detailed discussion, see J. Michael Clark, *A Defiant Celebration: Theological Ethics and Gay Sexuality* (Garland, Tex.: Tangelwuld Press, 1990), 50–54.

14. Heyward, *Touching Our Strength,* 136.

15. Hunt, *Fierce Tenderness,* 49, 82.

16. Ibid., 137–39.

17. Ibid., 2, 18, 32, 122.

18. Ibid., 83–84, 173, 20; cf. 14.

19. Sallie McFague, *The Body of God: An Ecological Theology* (Minneapolis: Augsburg Fortress, 1993), 54.

20. J. Michael Clark, *Beyond Our Ghettos: Gay Theology in Ecological Perspective* (Cleveland: Pilgrim Press, 1993).

21. Rebecca Johnson, "New Moon over Roxbury: Reflections on Urban Life and the Land," in *Ecofeminism and the Sacred,* ed. C. J. Adams (New York: Continuum, 1993), 252.

22. McFague, *Body of God,* 202–3; cf. 201.

20

MEN WHOSE LIVES
I TRUST, ALMOST

Carter Heyward

I want to talk about men whose lives I trust, almost. I want to talk about why I trust them, and why I don't. Men whose lives and work and values are feminist[1] or womanist,[2] the good guys, not the bad ones. I want to look at where, it seems to me, these feminist men "get it" and where they don't, because when they are standing genuinely with us, they are indispensable allies, but when they only think they are, their attitudes and actions can be damaging to women's lives and sometimes their own. These, as I say, are brothers who honestly respect and value women. But they are men in a man's world and, because they are, they have access to a social power (patriarchal, capitalist, racist, and hetero/sexist[3]) that can make or break most women in the world.

I mean by this that men, especially economically privileged, usually white, men in this western society, hold a wildly disproportionate share of wealth and, thereby, social power and privilege. I mean also that these men normally are *empowered* through institutional, cultural, economic, and social positioning to do more harm than women—to inflict more pain on women, children, marginalized and other men, other-than-human creatures, the society as a whole, and the earth. Thus, while much of what I say here about men's attitudes and actions I could say also about many women, including myself, I am writing in this essay specifically about men, not women.[4]

A Few Good Men

But why be critical of men who are our friends? Men who think feminist, vote feminist, learn from feminists, and like feminists? Because our solidarity as women and men in the struggle for justice requires us to cultivate an ability to be critical of ourselves and one another in ways that promote compassion and change. In my experience, few women and fewer men have developed this ability. I hope, in what I am writing, to nudge some brothers in this direction.

Working with men, learning with them, sometimes loving them as friends, I increasingly am frustrated with many (to be honest, most) of them. I believe that feminist men by and large have not moved very far beyond liberalism.[5] Because they don't make critical connections between how the world is structured and how they live their daily lives, these brothers don't embody their feminist commitments with much passion or consistency. More often they depend on women to do the embodying of feminism—that is, to bear the consequences, economically and physically as well as professionally and emotionally. Most feminist men don't suffer for their commitments to women's well-being. For sure, with their sisters, they long for a different world, but how much of their racist privileged men's world are they willing to risk for it? How much of their socially constructed male identities are they willing to have transformed?

Some Disturbing Patterns

The feminism of many men seems often to reflect one or more of three patterns of how these men are related to the world in general and women in particular. The first and most ubiquitous pattern, emerging wherever feminist men live, work, and breathe, is of *men too embedded in patriarchy.* Keep in mind that this essay is not about Rush Limbaugh, Oliver North, Clarence Thomas, or John Bobbitt, but about feminist men, guys who sit among the liberals and, occasionally, radicals (few as they are) in our governmental, religious, professional, and educational institutions, and in our communities and families.

These are the men who really do believe that the institutions of our lives will do right by us if we *women* try harder—that is, if we are simultaneously amazons and ladies. These are the friends who urge us to hang in, be patient, keep the faith, and not be thwarted in our efforts by the misogyny of their male colleagues and by the sexist foundations of the institutions we share with them. These men, many of them, honestly admire us, like us, learn from us and with us, yet still are quick to assure those who hold power over them and us (trustees, CEO's, bishops, department heads, etc.) that the quality and values of the institutions and society need not be compromised by the requirements of feminists, multiculturalists, racial/ethnic minorities, gay/lesbian/bisexual lobbies, environmentalists, and other marginalized interests.

And how do these brothers imagine that they, for the most part white privileged men, and their professional traditions, can represent a very largely nonwhite, nonprivileged, and nonmale humankind? They imagine they can stand for us all because they actually think that they and their traditions, *unlike feminism,* can be objective, fair, and thereby "universal" in their capacity to be for all.

Elsewhere I have written about "patriarchal logic" as the intellectual and political design of our life together, in which white privileged men's *power over* women and everything and everybody else is simply a given.[6] This patriarchal (and in the late twentieth century, advanced monopoly capitalist) power to control, name, organize, reward, and punish is, in truth, *incontestable* among the vast majority of human beings, including most feminist men. And that is what so many of our brothers harbor in the marrow of their bones: that no one, in his right mind, could realistically hope (or seriously want?) to transform patriarchal social relations. Thus resigned, these men assume that all of us would do well to accept "reality" and help make it as just and liberating as possible—for women and, of course, for men. These brothers' real agenda is the *feminization of patriarchy,* not its demise.

The problem with these men's feminism is that, lacking firsthand experience of sexism, they lack also a hermeneutic of suspicion in relation to the shape of our life together as women and men. Without this foundation of a serious liberation politic, liberal feminists think of themselves as pragmatists, realists, measured and balanced in their understandings of what is possible, and caught between "extremes"—between feminist women on the one hand and more conventional forces on the other. Positioning themselves in between others' positions, liberal feminist men often stand nowhere themselves. In failing to take a stand, despite their protests to the contrary, they wind up standing with, and for, the status quo—that is, against feminism.[7]

These men trouble many feminist women because deep in our bodyselves, in our feelings and intelligence, we know that, when the die is cast, most women will lose as long as these brothers are running the show. Women will lose because our male friends are too ready to compromise our well-being. They are willing to compromise our lives not for the good of the whole but for the patriarchal privilege (a set of material entitlements established by gender, race, culture, and class) which these brothers may fail to see clearly—but which they desire—as their own inheritance. We are troubled finally because we realize that, in the ongoing struggle for gender, sexual, racial, and economic justice, these men are more afraid of losing their buddies—other men of their social and professional standing—than of losing us.

It becomes clear to many of us feminist women that the politics of our male friends is often a lot more like the bonding of soldiers or fraternity brothers than a serious, joyful struggle, alongside women, to change the world. In relation to them, we experience ourselves perched perilously close to the edge of imminent betrayal.

The second disturbing pattern evident among feminist men is of *those who lean on women too much*. These guys, it seems, are out of touch with other men, isolated from their brothers, and dependent upon women for some assurance of their own gendered "meanings." I suspect many of these men are scared of their own homoerotic feelings and possibilities, afraid of experiencing tenderness toward men—other men and themselves.

These men seem unable to imagine living without women almost constantly at the center of their lives. They may even espouse feminist theories and do feminist work—such as teaching feminist theology, constructing feminist theory (often in conjunction with women), and lobbying for gender and sexual justice. The trouble with the work of such men is that nowhere in it does there seem to be any serious, sustained attention to what feminism may mean for their own lives as men or for men of any class or culture as a group. These men don't seem to care much about men, other men or themselves. For them, feminism begins and ends with women—women's lives, women's issues, women's initiatives, what women can and must be allowed to bring to the world. They seem to assume that men, regardless of race and class, on the whole are less deeply feeling, less intellectually and politically interesting, and less morally aware than women. And, while many women would concur, few feminist women, I believe, are willing to give up on the brothers quite so easily. We're unwilling to let men off the hook for needing, and being able, to shape up and live nonviolent, decent, woman-affirming lives.

Feminist men who lean too much on women seem to have made a cynical pact with men's oppressiveness as being just the way it is: "reality." Note here the similarity to the first pattern of guys who've accepted patriarchal social relations as, basically, incontestable. The difference between the men who lean so hard on us and our liberal patriarchal brothers is that, whereas the liberals embedded in patriarchy often are high-energy, productive men, the overly dependent feminist men tend to be more depressed and passive. The message these brothers convey is that, if there's any hope for the world, women are it—and they intend to be saved through their attachments to us and what we stand for.

The problem with this pattern of feminist men's politics is that it sucks women's energies, drawing us into mothering yet another generation of grown sons who'd rather live our lives than their own. It's also not a reliable feminism, because its roots aren't fastened in the integrity of the men who hold it but rather in the passion of the women upon whose lives and work they lean. In relation to such men, women often feel exhausted and ripped off—not, be clear, because they like us so much but because they need more from us than we can, or should, give. These are the guys to whom many a woman wants to yell, "Get a life, man!"

If these men are interested in relating to women in ways that genuinely are mutual, they have to become aware of themselves *as men,* who (depending on their race, class, age, and other social/political forces) have access to all the rights and privileges that come with being white, affluent men in this society. Only in the context of such conscientization about how their own gendered, sexual, racial, and class identities have been shaped, and what therefore their "maleness" actually means in this society—to others and to them—can these men actually embody in sexual, economic, and other ways, the feminist commitments they espouse.

The third pattern evident among feminist males is of *men who do as they damned well please.* These are the feminists most likely to terrify, infuriate, and batter women. They are men who don't need us at all when push comes to shove, as too often it does. Though their behavior of entitlement would seem to offer a study in contrast to the actions of depressed men who are overly dependent on women, very often it is not. Lots of men talk and vote feminist, want women constantly in their lives and beds, and don't spend five minutes a day doing anything other than what they want to do. In both instances, we see men who are radically disconnected from their own lives-in-relation and their capacities for intimacy with women *and* other men. Overdependency and entitlement are, I believe, flip sides of the problem of the *radical individualism* that is deadly and epidemic in patriarchal capitalism.

The men who do as they please embrace life, including feminist commitments, on their own terms. These are the dudes who know all about feminism and will be glad to tell you all about it just as they often will tell you whatever you need to know about anything interesting or provocative on the contemporary scene. They're the men who know better than most women what most women need. They're the male professors who think female students and scholars are wonderful but who will choose, as their own successors, good men in their own image over brilliant women whose work may challenge their academic hegemony or transform their scholarly legacy. They're the men in all professions who actually believe in *their* capacity to be "objective" and "discerning" about "reality"—including gender, sex, women, and feminism. They trust and worship themselves and whatever gods, men, or women serve their interests. The Greek image for such men was Narcissus and, following Freud, ruling-class men have imaged "narcissism" as a problem that particularly affects, of course, women.

The narcissist is the husband whose every need comes first, unless he decides that it's okay for it not to—this time. He often is the "gentleman" who exudes a sense of mastery. He is the father who knows best and the son who will be like his father.

He's the brother with the money who decides if and when his women—

267

mother, sisters, wife, sons, and daughters—need it and on what terms. He's the cool, rational spokesman for justice for women who flies into a fury when, once in a while, a *man* is dealt a legal blow by a systemic fluke that puts a woman's interest over a man's. He has nothing but condemnation for men who rape, batter, and harass women and no interest whatsoever in changing his own more nuanced abusive behavior. He's the man who wants absolute equality between the sexes unless he stands to lose something important like money, sex, or reputation. He is the one to whom "belongs" the larger portion because, and only because, he is a brother and not a sister. And he is outraged and *predictably* violent—verbally and emotionally if not physically and sexually—when things don't go his way.

While men who lean on women too much seem, on the whole, to be motivated by a sense of passive resignation to the way things are, the men who, like the gorilla choosing where it wants to sleep, do exactly as they please seem fueled by rage—at the system, at men, at women, at life, at themselves, whatever. And while the first and second patterns that have emerged among male feminists can drain women's energies and frustrate our efforts toward social transformation, this third pattern can cost us our lives—and does more often than we realize, even at the hands of feminist men.

It bears repeating that there is a link between men's violence, men's overdependence on women, and men's embeddedness in patriarchy, albeit of a liberal variety. The connection is the appalling degree of individualism that holds even most of the best men in its grip.

So What's a Good Man to Do?

In a sisterly spirit, I can imagine a brother reading this book and shaking his head in bewilderment: what *is* a guy to do after all? What *do* these women want? Fair enough. Here's what we want, and need, from men:

> We want you to get to know us on our terms—as your sisters, lovers, spouses, mothers, daughters, colleagues, friends, and political comrades. Listen to us. You don't have to "agree" with us. Just be quiet sometimes, and listen.
>
> Set yourselves a project: learn about women's lives—the lives of women very different from the ones you know (or think you know) best as well as the lives of the women closest to you in life. Study women's history, novels, poetry, art, films, and music—and not just any women's work but the labor of women with a passion for justice for women. Let this work touch you, push and change you.

Study feminist and womanist theory. Get to know why sex, gender, class, race, religion, and culture can't be understood—or addressed—separately. Learn what the connections have to do with your life and work, your love and commitments, your values and investments. Let bell hooks, Angela Davis, Beverly Harrison, Manning Marable, Marvin Ellison, Audre Lorde, and others who struggle to understand these dynamics help you see more clearly what's happening to us all.

Get together with a group of men—preferably gay, straight, and bisexual men of different colors—and study your own lives. Explore your internalized homophobia with these men. Learn to love one another as men and brothers. Learn to recognize, and value, the differences you find among yourselves.

If you've been working primarily with, or on behalf of, men, humanity, animals, or the earth, become an activist *also* on behalf of justice for *women* in particular. Do something, for example, on behalf of battered women, incarcerated women, reproductive freedom, homeless women and children, breast cancer research and treatment, or woman-affirming policy making in the institutions in which you spend time.

If you've been working with women and women's groups, become involved *also* with men committed to ending men's violence against women—groups that work with male batterers and perpetrators of sexual violence; incarcerated men who have abused women and children; and organizations of men working against sexism.

If you haven't been active on behalf of either women's lives or men's consciousness, it's time to start, now. And it's not too late, not as long as girl and boy children are being born on the earth.

Dare to imagine your institutions and this society being reconstructed on the basis of visions that you and your feminist colleagues and friends can shape together. Dare to imagine that you can do it, *with other folks*. Do not fool yourselves into imagining that your "realism" or "pragmatism" has deeper roots or more staying power than your sisters' commitments to what can be—with your help.

Get out of the middle. Take sides. Stand with your sisters. Be yourselves, fully human brothers, having neither answers nor control, but hearts and minds stretching beyond patriarchal logic in the ongoing creation of something new and wonderful and radical.

Dare to make mistakes, back down, and make amends.

Have compassion, always, for all people and creatures, including your enemies, but do not be fooled by the constancy of premature "calls" for peace, harmony, stability, and reconciliation. Always ask, at what cost, and to whom?

Be gentle with children, animals, and all living beings. And, if ever you are not, be aware that your behavior is violent and potentially deadly—and stop it. Dare to ask for help if your behavior is violent.

Don't worry too much about getting it right all the time, even feminism. Live a day at a time.

Keep things in perspective. Smile and laugh and cry and wail and sing and grieve and dance and make love, in your heart and with your all your body if you can.

These are the men whose lives we can trust.[8]

NOTES

1. While I appreciate the efforts of some men not to identify prematurely, or misappropriate, feminism as "their" movement, I am glad to recognize as feminists those men whose commitments to women's well-being is central to their work for gender, racial, sexual, economic, and other dimensions of justice. Feminism is a political movement, not a morally uncluttered, simple, or perfect "position" for women or men.

2. Originating in the work of Alice Walker, "womanism" (as distinct from, though not necessarily contrary to, "feminist") denotes a commitment specifically to the survival, quality of life, and well-being of *black women*. Two recent womanist books that speak directly to relationships between men and women in African American communities are Delores S. Williams, *Sisters in the Wilderness: The Challenge of Womanist God-Talk* (Maryknoll, N.Y.: Orbis Books, 1993), and Emilie Townes, *In a Blaze of Glory: Womanist Spirituality as Social Witness* (Nashville: Abingdon Press, 1994). It is important that white feminists *not* appropriate insights of these, and other, womanists, feminists, and women of color but rather try to hear what they are saying not only about their relationships to men in their racial/ethnic communities but also about their relationships to us. It is also important, intellectually and politically, that we women and men of all colors and cultures do what we can together, across historical/cultural lines between us, toward the transformation of unjust systems and relationships of domination and control. No one has been clearer about this than the late African American lesbian feminist poet, essayist, and warrior Audre Lorde (see esp. *Sister Outsider: Essays and Speeches* [Ithaca, N.Y.: Firebrand Books, 1984]).

Reflecting my own social (professional and relational) location, this essay is focused, for the most part, on the attitudes, behavior, and lives of *white men* in institutions (education, religion, publishing, etc.) shaped and secured largely on behalf of white male privilege (economic power, theological naming, institutional policies, etc.) that often is invisible to those who benefit from it.

I'm mindful of ways in which people of different colors, through class privilege as well as the ongoing struggle for gender, sexual, economic, and racial/ethnic justice, *to some degree* can share in the "white privilege" upon which institutions such as the Episcopal Church (my own denomination) and other mainline (white, relatively affluent, male-defined) churches have been constructed. In this context—in which it is possible for some men and women of color, and some white women, to share, *individually,* the benefits that accrue primarily to affluent white men—womanist and feminist struggles often can, and should, be interactive and mutually beneficial. Those whose lives I trust, whatever their gender, sexuality, color, culture, religion, or class, are folks who *know* this and cherish it deep in their politics and spiritualities. It is a deep knowing with roots in our daily lives and in the struggles for justice and compassion.

3. I often use this term—hetero/sexist—to describe social structures and relations that are oppressive and damaging simultaneously to women and to gay/lesbian/bisexual/transgendered people. To use the two different words—sexism and heterosexism—can obscure the inextricability of power dynamics based on gender from those based on sexuality. I certainly recognize and value the political and intellectual integrity of each term, by itself, and often use each. See my book *Touching Our Strength: The Erotic as Power and the Love of God* (New York: Harper & Row, 1989).

4. Any honest and self-aware feminist woman will recognize similar attitudes and actions in her own life and among her woman friends. This fact does not alter or lessen the damage that specifically men, including feminist men, can do in hetero/sexist racist patriarchy.

5. By liberalism, I refer here, in a positive way, to the general acceptance of lessons of the Enlightenment and, more recently, modernism: e.g., respect for science; appreciation of the evolving character of species *and* ideas; and openmindedness to the new and different. But liberalism has its limits, one of which is the failure of most liberals to make serious political, economic connections between one's own embodied being and the larger world. In white-male–dominated middle-strata U.S. culture today, a liberal man is one who wants to change *primarily* either the world or himself, and who doesn't see, or want to see, the radical, systemic forces that are shaping, defining, and grounding him in the world, as part of it. For helpful treatment of the limits and failures of liberal (white) feminism among women, see Kimberle Crenshaw, "Whose Story Is It, Anyway? Feminist and Antiracist Appropriations of Anita Hill," in *Race-ing Justice, En-gendering Power: Essays on Anita Hill, Clarence Thomas, and the Construction of Social Reality,* ed. Toni Morrison (New York: Pantheon Books, 1992), 402–40. Other resources include Carole Pateman, *The Problem of Political Obligation: A Critique of Liberal Theory* (Berkeley: University of California Press, 1979); Zillah Eisenstein, *The Radical Future of Liberal Feminism* (White Plains, N.Y.: Longman Publishing Group, 1981); Nancy C. M. Hartsock, *Money, Sex, and Power*

(Boston: Northeastern University Press, 1983); and Trinh T. Minh-Ha, *When the Moon Waxes Red: Representation, Gender, and Cultural Politics* (New York: Routledge, 1991). One of the most important recent white feminist works that addresses and attempts beautifully to move beyond some of the problems of liberal politics and theology is Ann Kirkus Wetherwilt's *That They May Be Many: Voices of Women, Echoes of God* (New York: Continuum, 1994).

6. *When Boundaries Betray Us: Beyond Illusions of What Is Ethical in Therapy and Life* (New York: HarperCollins, 1993).

7. Other resources on liberalism and feminist liberation politics include Caroline Ramazanoglu, *Feminism and the Contradictions of Oppression* (New York: Routledge and Kegan Paul, 1989); Ruth Smith and Deborah Valenze, "Mutuality and Marginality: Liberal Moral Theory and Working Class Women in Nineteenth-Century England," *Signs: Journal of Women in Culture and Society* 13, no. 2 (Winter, 1988): 277–98; and Ruth L. Smith, "The Evasion of Otherness: A Problem for Feminist Moral Reconstruction," *Union Seminary Quarterly Review* 43, no. 1–4 (1989): 145–62.

8. Special thanks to Beverly Harrison for talking through this essay with me, and to Alison Cheek, Kwok Pui-lan, and other faculty and students in the Feminist Liberation Theology program at the Episcopal Divinity School for continuing to probe these connections between sex, gender, race, class, and power.

21

MALE SEXUALITY AND THE FRAGILE PLANET: A THEOLOGICAL REFLECTION

James B. Nelson

As we approach the twenty-first century, our churches continue to carry the legacy of the Victorians of the nineteenth century regarding certain critical issues related to sexuality and the body. The Victorians reduced sexuality to sex—literally "the privates"—and they insisted that these matters belonged only to one's very private life. They also privatized the spirit, as they placed women on a spiritual pedestal, modifying the ancient formula of patriarchal dualism in which men assumed to themselves superiority in spirit and reason while identifying women with body and emotion. This had important implications for the church in relation to the public world.

It began as a sociopolitical economic process in the Industrial Revolution, as the church gradually lost the established relation to political power it had held since the days of Constantine. The church increasingly became domesticated, limited to the private sphere of home and family. Influenced by nineteenth-century romanticism, the imagery of the feminine underwent a dramatic shift. Now, women—primarily white, economically privileged women—were viewed as more religious, more spiritual, more moral than men (though, strangely, still irrational and emotional). Gone were the witch hunts and the Puritan sermons that had railed against Eve's sinfulness. Eve was now transformed into "the angel of the home," the spiritually feminine one who nurtured the alienated male to compensate for the depersonalized world of industrialism. This Victorian image of Pure Womanhood was a bourgeois class ideal—a delicate, white lady of the leisure class, not the working-class woman of the sweatshop.

Now the church, especially the church of white economic privilege, found itself psychically and socially belonging to the domestic sphere, and the role of the clergy was to pacify the powerless—the women, the children, the aging. Men in the "real world"—the world of politics, business, science, industry—viewed clergy with the somewhat bemused contempt that a masculinist ethic holds for things feminine. Clergy were out of place in the "real" world, and those who "didn't know their place" and interfered in the public world were met with resistance and anger.[1]

This mentality—in which women are placed on a pedestal, with a spirituality limited to the private sphere of life—is still alive today. But these privatizations of body and spirit are profoundly challenged by the apostle Paul, who, despite certain sexual misjudgments, understood that the personal body and the whole body of creation are tied together in resurrection destiny. Thus, his familiar words in Romans 8: "We know that the whole creation has been groaning in labor pains until now; and not only the creation, but we ourselves, who have the first fruits of the Spirit, groan inwardly while we wait for adoption, the redemption of our bodies" (vv. 22–23, NRSV). Paul viewed earth healing and body healing as deeply connected.

In recent decades, our churches have increasingly recognized the public character of many sexuality issues, as they have attempted to speak and act on gender and orientation justice, sexual abuse, commercialization of sex, family planning, population control, abortion, new reproductive technologies, teen pregnancy, pornography, and sexually transmitted diseases. Now we must expand that agenda and grasp more fully connections between our sexual/body issues and the healing of violence on the earth and against the earth.

Years ago when much theology had become precariously privatized, the Social Gospel reminded us that both sin and salvation are socially transmitted. I want to expand this insight to suggest that we are experiencing *sexually transmitted disease* on a scale far greater than we typically think. Going beyond the customary medical sense of the term, I use the term sexually transmitted disease (STD) more broadly. I propose that:

> Social violence is a sexually transmitted disease.
> White racism is a sexually transmitted disease.
> Environmental abuse is a sexually transmitted disease.

I intend neither hyperbole nor metaphor about sexually transmitted diseases here. Quite literally I mean that the alienations and distortions in our sexual existence have direct and deep connections with these social ills. These body/sexual dynamics are not the single cause, but their distortions are much more significant than we have yet recognized, and our hopes for greater earth healing depend significantly on that realization.

Social violence is a sexual/body issue. Men are the agents of perhaps 95 percent of the physically violent actions on the face of the globe. No one-factor explanation will do, but the links of violence with distorted masculinism are undeniable. Consider these examples:

The United States is one of the most violent countries in the world. Our history is replete with presidents who believed war to be the test of both manhood and national vitality. General George S. Patton put it succinctly: "All real American men love to fight." Patton knew well that the successful warrior's psyche includes a powerful blend of hostility toward women, repressed homosexual feeling, and phallic aggression.

Rape is not an act of sexual lust but a violent act of domination. But if genital pleasure is not the primary motive, sexual satisfaction in a broader sense surely is. It is the satisfaction of having power over the woman, and expressing the rapist's anger against the denied parts of his own sexual self.

In the complex web of things that nurture social violence, sexual anxieties, sexual fears, and sexual angers are a common thread.[2] Social violence *is* a sexually transmitted disease.

What about *white racism*? James Weldon Johnson observed that the sex factor is so deeply rooted in the race problem that it is often not recognized, but until white people understood its sexual dynamics they would never understand racism. Consider some of those possibilities:

In the historic sexualization of racism, white men divided women into two kinds—good ones and bad ones, virgins and whores—and this was transferred to the racial scene. White women became the symbol of delicacy and purity, whereas African American women symbolized an animality that white men could exploit both sexually and economically. White male guilt then was projected onto the black male, who was fantasized as a dark sexual beast with insatiable sex drives and large organs, who could never be trusted around white women. Black mothers nurtured their sons to be docile, hoping to protect them from white male wrath. That upbringing in turn complicated black marriages and led to certain destructive attempts to recover black "manliness."

Sexual racism has complicated our response to the AIDS epidemic. Even before AIDS was socially constructed as "the gay disease," it was seen as a plague spreading from Africa and Haiti through dark-skinned, lascivious people—comparable to the way, decades earlier, people of African ancestry were thought to be the primary carriers of syphilis. The black community has been slow to deal with AIDS prevention in gay and bisexual males precisely because openly gay men and lesbians symbolize the weak male and strong female that the slave system and racial segregation produced.[3] So, we reap the harvest of sexual racism in this terrible epidemic.

Racism *is* a sexually transmitted disease.

And what of our *environmental abuse?* Though the issues are scientific, technological, political, and economic, they are also deeply bodily and sexual. Let us remember:

> We are heirs of a powerful and hierarchical sexual dualism that has shaped a pyramid of control and value. God as pure spirit is on top. Then come men, women, children, animals, plants, and finally inorganic being. In this hierarchy, the spirit controls and uses the body, and the male principle controls and uses the female principle.
> The earth is named feminine—earth is "she" and never "he." Father God, but Mother Nature. Sir Francis Bacon made explicit the connection between women's subordination and nature's. He wrote of wresting new knowledge from nature's womb; of seizing her [nature] by the hair of her head; of penetrating her mysteries; of having the power to conquer and subdue her.[4]
> A man's reliance on Mother Nature can remind him of his early dependence on his own human mother. He learned his masculinity by pushing away from her, cutting the ties, and identifying anything feminine as negative. That came to include the earth itself.[5]
> We are now inundated by data about what is happening to the natural environment. Our insatiable appetites for production and consumption poison the air, rain acid upon the lakes, destroy the topsoil, and allow the extinction of species of life to pass unmourned. Yet, it is still so difficult to see nature with wonder, to move beyond self-interest to environmental reverence. Maybe our "knowing" of the natural world is still largely "knowing about," and not the kind suggested by the Hebrew verb that suggested an intimate, erotic, sexual knowledge.

In the complex web of things that have led to our ecological problems, environmental abuse *is* also a sexually transmitted disease.

If we are going to respond effectively to these connections between sexuality and these broader public issues, we need to engage in *sexual theology,* a theology that takes sexual/bodily experience seriously in conversation with and in the reshaping of our perceptions and categories. To illustrate one way to do this, I turn to three central Christian affirmations, often capsuled as "the paschal mystery of Christ"—incarnation, crucifixion, and resurrection—and bring these into conversation with our body experience.

Incarnation

We claim an incarnational tradition. "In the beginning was the Word, and the Word was with God, and the Word was God." And when the Word came to dwell with us, it became flesh—not a book, a creed, a theological system or a code of morality, but flesh. It was and is a jarring claim.[6]

Christ is alive. God's reality is present tense. Incarnation continues. As Nikos Kazantzakis wrote, "Within me even the most metaphysical problem takes on a warm physical body which smells of sea, soil, and human sweat. The Word, in order to touch me, must become warm flesh. Only then do I understand—when I can smell, see, and touch."[7] Yet cognitively affirming God's continuing incarnation in our sexual/bodily lives is one thing. *Experiencing* it may be quite another. Consider some male sexuality issues that illustrate both problems and possibilities.

Western Christian doctrine has not interpreted women's experience well. But neither has it interpreted men's experience well, and for several reasons. First, insofar as men have assumed that their own sex is the norm for all humanity, they have not examined the meanings of their own distinctly gendered experience. Men have been blind to themselves *as men,* as the men's movement is helping us realize.

We must be careful not to trivialize the general movement toward men's transformation by seeing it only through certain manifestations, which are easily parodied. Men's transformation is not just orgies of male bonding, or "wildmen" beating drums in the woods, or beautifully sensitive men gathering for recreational weeping. Rather, it is about helping men to find more wholesome ways to be male in our society. Indeed, the men's movement is of vital importance to the church in ways that have not yet been sufficiently acknowledged.

Second, as Stephen B. Boyd rightly observes, the sexual norm in such theology is not *maleness,* but certain constructions of *masculinity.* Theology has not been so much male-centered or *andro*centric as it has been *masculo*centric. It has reflected the images of masculinity held by privileged males in positions of power. These limited images have historically oppressed many men—marginalized men—especially gay men and men of color.

A third reason, also noted by Boyd, why mainstream theology has provided an inadequate interpretation of men is that the privileged men writing those theologies usually have not been speaking out of their own deepest experience so much as to the public selves that they *think* they should be.[8] And the public selves men think they should be typically have little

277

room for *eros*. We men are not well conditioned to embrace *eros*—the love that yearns, that hungers, that admits incompleteness, that reaches out for fulfillment.

Eros runs counter to the basic social construction of our masculinities. We men learned the fundamental lessons of masculinity through separating, through cutting the erotic bonding with our mothers, through identifying ourselves over against anything feminine—including gayness—that smacked of the erotic. The erotic came to be seen as a contradiction to the manliness that prizes self-sufficiency and rational control of bodily things. We learned to put on masculinity like an old suit of armor—heavy, hot, rusty, stuffy, and inflexible. It made us invulnerable. It also made it hard for us to leap or dance or even make love very well. But we put it on because we thought it was our duty.[9] We learned to control our bodies as objects.

If *eros* makes men anxious about the deepest feelings of bodily life, it also makes Christian men anxious because it raises fundamental questions about the theologies men have written and believed. Our primal male experience of identity through separation and individuation has buttressed the theological perception that God is Absolute Other, utterly transcendent. Divine perfection is completeness: God needs nothing. Thus, we have imaged God as unilateral, nonrelational power, glorified by the weakness and dependency of humanity, deficient in the erotic power of mutuality.

It is threatening to live with a God so imaged, and so masculinized theology compensated by attributing to the divine a one-sided and unilateral love. Divine love, the model for our human love, became sheer *agape,* utter self-giving. Thus our theologies cheapened, devalued, even vilified the erotic and confused it with the pornographic. We confused self-love with selfishness and egocentricity. Hunger, desire, passion, and yearning for fulfillment were banished as inappropriate to Christian spirituality.

Unfortunately, such anti-body theology disconnects men from feeling the immediacy of body issues and prevents men from relying on the body wisdom needed to cope with the "sexually transmitted diseases" of this fragile planet. But "if we are not perceptive in discerning our feelings, or if we do not know what we feel, we cannot be effective moral agents."[10] While social violence, racism, environmental abuse and other social diseases are intimately linked with distorted expressions of masculinity, the antierotic masculinity that white Western males are taught jeopardizes men's capacity to be effective moral agents to undo the damage.

It is also a masculine dualism of the public and the private, well exemplified in Luther's doctrine of the two kingdoms. A man's success in fulfilling his public roles seems to depend on his ability to objectify and control his body and his feelings, as Luther's famous illustration of the

278

Christian hangman attested.[11] The problem—in both Luther and in contemporary society—is that men are conditioned to live their public lives apart from the body, without emotion.

But there is a christic body wisdom. It will be found in those men—and women—who dare to believe that the public self must never lose the embodied person, and that the person must never lose the reality of incarnation.

Crucifixion

If many Christian interpretations of incarnation have missed the good news from and for our bodyselves, it is perhaps even more true regarding crucifixion wherein some understandings have contributed mightily to our sexual sickness. Certain images of the cross have been a primary force—in many women *the* primary force—in shaping women's acceptance of abuse, in believing that pain is redemptive, and that salvation comes in the self-sacrifice of the innocent. Those interpretations have eroticized domination and have kept too many women and children silent in the face of ongoing male violence.

Being formed into the Crucified One means standing for life *with* those who are being killed in body and spirit. Jesus did not run from his death. In faithfulness and integrity he accepted it. He was killed not because he chose death, but because he chose life and in so doing he threatened those who were obsessed with the ways of pain and death. The cross invites resistance to every sadomasochistic power arrangement that teaches pleasure in patterns of domination and submission.[12]

Yet, the cross does speak of redemptive suffering. This is the holy vulnerability of incarnate sacred presence still entering into the depths of human pain. But vulnerability is not an easy issue for men, nor is its companion—power. Reinhold Niebuhr taught us that in humanity there is an equality of sin, but an inequality of guilt. Regarding *sin,* our condition of alienation, the ground is level at the foot of the cross. But *guilt* is not equal—precisely because some of us have more power than others. The distorted acts of the powerful carry more harm.

This distinction is difficult for many men to grasp. Most feminist women, maintaining a social constructionist position, are not saying that men are essentially more sinful than they. But many men *hear* an essentialist message. They hear women brand them as inherently defective, "brutal, competitive, exploitive, insensitive, disconnected from meaningful social relationships, out of touch with their feelings and oblivious to things they do not want to hear."[13] Men hear scorn being heaped on man's robotic brain, his granite heart, and that thing between his legs. And, hearing the indictment, some simply get angry. Others respond with defensive denial or guilty silence when accused of being incorrigible oppressors and embodiments of everything wrong in the world.[14] Still other men accept the indictment and respond with shame.

Guilt over harmful actions is appropriate, but shame over one's very being as a male is not. Neither defensiveness nor shame is helpful. But the power revealed in the cross is not the controlling power that has, in the current gender debates, made men defensive or shameful. It is a different power, one that is vulnerable, relational, and generative. Its aim is not control, but openness to growth and mutuality, a willingness to be influenced as well as to influence.

It is a power that can be known in a man's own bodily revelation. The erect phallus—the "big, hard, up" organ—has been the dominant body symbol for both masculinity and male power. But, when we finally realize how one-sided this is, a new revelation comes. Genitally speaking, we men are *not* big, hard, and up very much of the time. More of the time we are small, soft, and down. And that is revelatory of another side of our masculine spirituality. The classic *via positiva* of Western spirituality is a phallic pattern. It is the way of climbing, the way of transcendence, the way of light, the way of doing. But embracing the other side of our male genital experience, flaccidity, puts us in touch also with the *via negativa*. This is the way of emptying and darkness, the way of vulnerability, the way the being without having to do. One might add that those genital emblems of manly courage, the testicles ("he's got balls"), are the most vulnerable part of a man's body. We need more testicular masculinity—a vulnerable, generative, quiet, and faithful "hanging in there."

Appropriate vulnerability is an important key to sexual ethics, as Karen Lebacqz contends.[15] Nakedness in the Garden of Eden was a Hebrew metaphor for vulnerability, and feeling no shame meant appropriateness. To be "known" is how the Bible frequently describes the sexual encounter: to be vulnerable, open, exposed. That is why the sexual relation is potentially so powerful and needs profound respect and safety.

Sexual vulnerability speaks truth to our current divisive churchly struggles over the issues of sexual orientation. Homophobia is complex in its dynamics, but I am convinced that one ever-present element of it is the fear of our own body vulnerability.

And it is no accident that usually the fear of homosexuality is stronger in men than in women. According to the social construction of normative masculinity, the ideal man is invulnerable, in control of all things bodily. Gayness, however, suggests womanization; that other men might be treated as sex objects, just like men treat women; that men may be penetrated. Until our vulnerable bodies are fully integrated into ourselves and embraced as *us,* these homophobic dynamics will continue.

The cross exposes our invulnerabilities. But it does more. It invites resistance to every form of violence against the incarnate bodies of God in the world. It invites that healing justice that comes from standing with and suffering with. It invites our transformation, the suffering journey into our own homophobic fears. Some of us men have been learning how deeply connected are homophobia and male sexism, how much homophobia in men is the projection of an anxious quest for masculinity, that we did not need to fear our desires for emotional intimacy and physical touch with other men, and that our lives could be immeasurably enriched when those fears were diminished. Indeed, we are learning to fear ourselves less and love ourselves more, and that is a gift.

That these issues of power, fear, and vulnerability—so pronounced in heterosexism and male homophobia—are deeply connected with such sexually transmitted social diseases as violence, racism, and environmental deterioration, I have little doubt. It may yet be that the conversation of our sexual bodies with the christic meanings of the cross will illuminate them further.

Resurrection

As I turn now to the third element of the paschal mystery, *resurrection,* I want to explore death anxiety as a pervasive issue for men. A few examples will illustrate its importance:

> Men avoid death. I personally know what it is to be a death avoider. My father died suddenly when I was twenty-one. It was not until twenty-five years later that I finally began to grieve. Big boys don't cry.
>
> Men's attraction to pornography is often a defense against death anxiety. Because we have so genitalized our understanding of sexual feelings, our bodies feel dead when we do not feel genital excitement. Pornography makes us feel like having sex when we don't feel like having sex—and we don't like the feeling of not feeling like having sex. We want to feel alive.[16]
>
> Men are more likely to be workaholics, obsessed with occupational achievement for justification and finding jobs the central clue to their identities. I suspect that work becomes "an immunity pact against death." An obsession with work is a distraction from mortality, and work's achievements become one's hope of immortality. Work as a defense against death has its strange reality, as witnessed by the depression, even loss of the will to live, upon many a man's unemployment or retirement.

Such may be some death anxieties particularly pronounced in many men. But why does death anxiety seem to have a gender preference? Undoubtedly, the reasons are complex, but they probably include these:

> We know our fate and fear it. We men will die, on the average, seven years earlier than women will, and the cause is not primarily our male biology but our gendered masculinity and its behaviors.
>
> We do not experience the frequent and radical bodily changes that women do—menstruation and, for many women, pregnancy and birthing. Death is the most radical bodily change of all, and we fear what we have not experienced.
>
> Death seems to be the final defeat of every traditional male value—competition, winning, and performance.
>
> The fearfulness of death seems linked for many men to the unending and unsatisfied search for their father's blessing. Men want their father's love. But, unsure of it, they also want to prove they can get along without it. Hence, Dylan Thomas cries out, "And you my father, there on the sad height / Curse, bless, me now with your fierce tears, I pray." By no accident these words come together with his protest against death, "Do not go gentle into that good night / Rage, rage, against the dying of the light."[17]

Where does all of this lead us? Men's anxieties run deep into the social construction of our masculinities, but what is constructed is not fated. It can be transformed. That is the hope of resurrection. What the resurrection of the body means after death is a mystery. But whatever the symbol means, it does affirm bodies. In whatever mysterious form God's eternal love holds us, we are not now and will not be disembodied spirits. Matter matters to God.

The trouble with those theologies that urge us to kill off the body by denying its goodness and spiritual significance is that we do not kill the body so much as consign it to hell. And hell is the place of the dead who cannot accept their death—the place of the "undead," as H. A. Williams has observed.[18] How, then, can we bodyselves live in newness now?

Consider the naming of our bodily connectedness to the universe. Each of us is more than a trillion individual cells, all trying to live in harmony with one another. Our bodies are communities with the whole earth. Our bodily fluids carry the chemicals of the primeval seas, our bones have the same carbon as the ancient mountains, our blood contains the sugar that once flowed in the sap of now fossilized trees, the nitrogen binding our bones is the same that binds nitrates to the soil. Even in—often precisely in the midst of—our diseases and bodily dysfunctions, our flesh reveals our destiny for wholeness and connection. It is the vision of *shalom.*

In one of his last books Teilhard de Chardin reminded us that while we have been taught that the body is a fragment of the universe, in future we shall have to see it differently. My body is not simply part of the universe that I possess totally. My body is the totality of the universe that I possess partially.[19]

Death names the world godless. Resurrection names the world as God's body. It is a metaphor that speaks of our profound interdependence with everything. Grace Jantzen[20] and Sallie McFague[21] suggest that the metaphor of the universe as God's body might remind us of powerful truths of both faith and experience:

> That God is not just a distant being, but is being itself—the One in whom we live, move, have our being.
>
> That God is somehow physical as we are. That the very world itself is the sacramental presence of the invisible God.
>
> That bodies matter to God, so salvation is just as concerned about basic bodily needs as with matters of spirit.
>
> That God is vulnerable and in some sense at risk. God's body may be poorly cared for, even ravaged.
>
> That the earth is sacramental. It is sacred ground. We might have the breathtaking awareness that we *do* live in God, move in God, have our being in God. We would no longer see God as worldless or world as Godless, no longer see bodies as Godless or God as bodiless. We would live differently.

How, then, shall we describe our sexual bodies? In the christic conversation of sexual theology, some of us may wish to name incarnation, crucifixion, and resurrection. And to the extent that we know the gospel in our bodies, we shall know it well. The ancient prayer says, "It was God's good pleasure to take on our human flesh." It was. And it still is.[22]

NOTES

Certain portions of this essay are adapted from my third Earl Lecture at Pacific School of Religion, Berkeley, California, January, 1994, and my lecture at *Theology and Sexuality* Launch Conference, Newcastle upon Tyne, September, 1994.

1. See Rosemary Radford Ruether's *New Woman, New Earth* (New York: Seabury Press, 1975), 75ff, to which I am indebted for insights in this and the preceding paragraph.

2. For more thorough discussion of the dynamics of these forms of sexual and bodily oppression, see my *Embodiment* (Minneapolis: Augsburg, 1978, and London: SPCK, 1979), chap. 9, and Christine M. Smith, *Preaching as Weeping, Confession, and Resistance* (Louisville, Ky.: Westminster/John Knox Press, 1992).

3. See Harlan Dalton, "AIDS in Blackface," *Daedalus,* Summer, 1989: 217.

4. Quoted in Elizabeth A. Johnson, *Women, Earth, and Creator Spirit* (New York: Paulist Press, 1993), 15.

5. For a helpful discussion of the psychosexual dynamics summarized in these paragraphs, see Elizabeth Dodson Gray, *Green Paradise Lost* (Wellesley, Mass.: Roundtable Press, 1979, 1981), chaps. 3–4.

6. See Robert McAfee Brown, *Spirituality and Liberation* (Philadelphia: Westminster Press, 1988), 77f.

7. Nikos Kazantzakis, *Report to Greco,* trans. P. A. Bien (Oxford: Bruno Cassirer, 1965), 43.

8. See Stephen B. Boyd, "On Listening and Speaking: Men, Masculinity, and Christianity," *The Journal of Men's Studies* 1, no. 4 (May, 1993).

9. The armor metaphor is Sam Keen's. See *The Passionate Life: Stages of Loving* (New York: Harper & Row, 1983).

10. Beverly Wildung Harrison, *Making the Connections* (Boston: Beacon Press, 1985), 13.

11. See Boyd, "On Listening and Speaking."

12. See Joanne Carlson Brown and Carolyn R. Bohn, eds., *Christianity, Patriarchy, and Abuse* (New York: Pilgrim Press, 1989). Also, Beverly Wildung Harrison, *Making the Connections,* 218, and Carter Heyward, *Touching Our Strength.* (San Francisco: Harper & Row, 1989), 56.

13. Richard A. Shweder, "What Do Men Want: A Reading List for the Male Identity Crisis," *New York Times Book Review,* Jan. 9, 1994.

14. See Boyd, "On Listening and Speaking."

15. See Karen Lebacqz, "Appropriate Vulnerability: A Sexual Ethic for Singles," in *Sexual Ethics and the Church: After the Revolution,* A Christian Century Symposium (Chicago: Christian Century, 1989), 21. I am indebted to Lebacqz's suggestive treatment in these two paragraphs on vulnerability.

16. See John Stoltenberg, *Refusing to Be a Man* (New York: Penguin Books, 1989), 110.

17. Dylan Thomas, "Do not go gentle into that good night," in *Collected Poems* (New York: New Directions, 1957).

18. H. A. Williams, *True Resurrection* (New York: Harper & Row, 1974), 32f.

19. See Pierre Teilhard de Chardin, *Science and Christ* (New York: Harper & Row, 1968), 12f.

20. See Grace Jantzen, *God's World, God's Body* (Philadelphia: Westminster Press, 1984).

21. See Sallie McFague, *The Body of God* (Minneapolis: Fortress Press, 1993).

WHERE DO WE GO FROM HERE?
SOME CONCLUDING REMARKS

As we come to the end of our work on this collection, we want to make a few closing observations about themes that have emerged and trajectories for future work in this area. We are in no way attempting to explore exhaustively the richness of the content and implications of the material the authors have put before us. Rather, we lift up a few of the dynamics, themes, and issues that have struck us with particular poignancy.

The Instability of Masculinity

First, masculinity has been involved in recurring crises. We have seen that, throughout various historical periods, the strains, even contradictions, inherent in cultural definitions of men's roles have led to conflicts between women and men, between and among groups of men, and within individual men. The sexist imperatives endemic to masculine expectations in dominant, as well as in many oppressed groups, lead to the oppression of women and significant alienation between men and women. As we have seen, men's "othering" or objectification of women can take the form of idealizing distorted images of women (Wiethaus, Kirkley) or seeking the affirmation and nurture of feminist women (Heyward), with the result of maintaining men's dominance. Men often maintain stereotypical images of women that rationalize the unjust treatment of women and press women to "accommodate" to their own mistreatment (Mowrey). Even in men who recognize the injustice of sexism, a residual masculine individualism keeps them from being effective allies in dismantling patriarchal structures so destructive to the lives of women and men (Heyward).

Between and within groups of men, hegemonic masculine norms cause deep divisions. To the extent that these norms include racist, heterosexist, classist, and anti-Semitic imperatives for men in dominant groups, they encourage these men to see as their duty the maintaining of dividing walls of mistreatment and discrimination between them and nondominant groups of men (e.g., Euro-American men from African American and Native American men; heterosexual men from gay, bisexual, and transgender men; owning-class men from working-class men; and Christian men from Jewish and Muslim men). Within the same groups, these norms of hegemonic masculinity polarize men. Among gay men hypermasculine men conflict with effeminate men (Clark); among poor men predators prey on victims (Nonn); among Jewish men mice cower before supermen (Brod); among dominant groups, there are conservatives (e.g., Moral Purity men, American fundamentalists) locked in combat with liberals (e.g., Freethinkers, Heyward's liberal men).

Within the personal lives of individual men, definitions of masculinity often cause certain contradictions. Heterosexual men seek intimacy and sexual fulfillment, which requires mutuality and equality, in unequal, patriarchal relationships with women and therefore experience lack of fulfillment (Boyd). Many men develop idealized images of women, but devalue real women and exercise an alienating threat power over them (Smith, Wiethaus, Kirkley, Fout). Many institutionally religious men believe they must embody masculine dominance, but their worship and submission to a male God paradoxically feminizes them (Eilberg-Schwartz, Muesse). They also must rely solely on linear (left-brain), technical reason but affirm mystery at the center of many of their faith traditions (Muesse, Kirkley). Men in nondominant groups believe they must succeed at masculine tasks as defined by dominant groups, yet face obstacles preventing that success due to discrimination based on their race or ethnicity, sexual orientation, class, or physical abilities (Munir, Pollard, Jocks, Brantley, Nonn).

Fundamental Theological Questions

A second constellation of issues emerges concerning the role of religion in supporting or resisting unstable masculine identities. We mention here five areas suggested by these essays that need further exploration: images of the divine, theological anthropology, ethics, historical studies, and myth and ritual.

Images of the Divine

In the Jewish and Christian monotheistic traditions, imaging God in exclusively masculine terms has legitimated, even sacralized, the dominance of men and the "othering" of women. This imaging is problematic for women (Wiethaus), as well as for men (Eilberg-Schwartz, Mirsky). Is this imagery an essential element of these traditions? If so, must those seeking gender justice between women and men search outside these traditions for more inclusive images and understandings of the divine? If not, what resources exist within these traditions for developing more inclusive images of the divine? Many feminist scholars have written on these questions, and we refer the reader to those works.[1]

In this volume, several authors have touched on these issues. Mirsky argues that female images of the divine, such as the Goddess, hold great promise for a more just and, therefore, a more wholesome male spirituality. Moore and Gillette contend that in order for male images of God, such as the father, to have more constructive meanings, distorted views of masculinity must be rejected in favor of deeper, fuller notions. Mirsky insists that male images of God must always be seen in relation to female images rather than in "masculine" isolation. Eilberg-Schwartz agrees with Moore and Gillette that male images of God must be informed by more appropriate understandings of masculinity and with Mirsky that male images must be related to strong images of the female. Much more work needs to be done concerning these issues as they relate to male identities and men's relation to these traditions.

Theological Anthropology

In the area of theological anthropology—the understanding of the nature of humankind—all of our authors agree that the dominant definitions of masculinity contain at least some destructive elements. Yet, our essays do reveal differences in the diagnosis of those elements and prescriptions for their change. Underlying at least some of these differences is a disagreement about the relationship between cultural definitions of masculinity and maleness. Are masculine expectations the expression of inherent and distinctive male attributes, or are they simply complex social constructions that serve to perpetuate the economic, political, or other interests that produce them? One's position in this essentialist/social constructionist debate can yield quite different visions of and strategies for positive transformation. For example, reflecting the essentialist perspective, Moore and Gillette believe that access to the "deep masculine" structures of male consciousness is the way toward more just and generative identities for men. In contrast, from a social constructionist perspective, Mirsky encourages men to reject the culturally contrived polarization of femininity and masculinity and to embrace female images of the divine for their own spiritual growth. In effect he asks, Would it not be more conducive to gender justice simply to speak about men's humanity or their male humanness and leave off all talk about masculinity?[2]

Some of our authors focus on another aspect of theological anthropology—notions of sin and the human capacities and incapacities implied in them. From a Christian perspective, Heyward points out that the tendency to view sin theologically in such individualistic terms means that the larger, structural dynamics of oppression that shape individual lives go relatively unattended and, therefore, unchanged. In other words, inadequate notions of sin are another major obstacle to gender justice. Nelson develops a theological perspective on sin that addresses both the personal and political dimensions of male experience. In his expanded notion of sin as a sexually transmitted disease, he incorporates social dynamics that help explain men's participation in sexist, racist, and environmental violence. Recent authors of Christian liberation theologies have explored the corporate dimensions of sin by reappropriating the New Testament language of the "principalities and powers."[3] For instance, Marjorie Suchocki interprets the doctrine of original sin as "structures of consciousness which bode to our ill-being."[4] Among these structures of consciousness, she includes sexism, heterosexism, racism, anti-Semitism, and classism. Because these structures of consciousness permeate many cultural definitions of hegemonic masculinity, this kind of analysis holds great promise for future studies of the relationship between theology and masculinity.

Ethics

Our essays have raised questions about the role of gender in a range of ethical issues related to notions of right order, the common good, or, in Christian theological terms, the "reign of God." We consider some of those issues under the traditional theological rubrics of justice and love, and their relation to notions of the common good.

With respect to meanings of justice, or "right order," that have informed interpretations of masculine and feminine, many of our authors have challenged two-sphere thinking and the models of dominance and subordination that are often implicit in this thinking (Mowrey, Longwood, Heyward, Nelson). Historically, influential religious figures have consciously or unconsciously used real or perceived differences between men and women to rationalize unjust power relations between women and men. For example, prevailing Western religious traditions have prescribed a dominant role for men in public life and institutions and limited women's influence to a private, domestic sphere. This split has been particularly exacerbated by the industrialization of the West in modern times.

Consequently, some social constructionist scholars believe that any talk of differences between men and women leads inevitably to unequal power relations. They tend to see definitions of gender roles serving the economic, political, and/or cultural interests of those in power. Therefore, these scholars prefer not to speak about nature or what might be "natural" for men as opposed to women, but rather prefer to speak of just political and social arrangements regardless of perceived differences. Other scholars, from an essentialist perspective, believe that the only way to get any leverage against that which distorts human life is to discern what is inherent in the natures of those who are clearly biologically different. These differing approaches raise the following questions: How do we talk together about these issues in ways that acknowledge what seem to be differences between women and men, while not perpetuating unjust power relations between us? Are there ways to understand and even celebrate differences while avoiding distorting masculine and feminine stereotypical images?

In addition to reflections on justice, we also see attempts to develop notions of love that do not involve accommodating submission to unjust power arrangements. Here, we draw on Cooper-White's distinctions (introduction to part 1) among power-over/power-for, power-within, power-with, and power-in-community to characterize some of the descriptions and prescriptions our authors offer of love directed toward right order.

We see emerging ethical visions of friendship (power-in-community)— across social barriers involving gender, race/ethnicity, sexual orientation, class, age, and species—wherein there develop structures of accountability to and within more inclusive communities (Mowrey, Munir, Clark, Nonn, Longwood, Nelson). Resources for this vision are gleaned from various religious perspectives. For example, Munir explores the power of Malcolm's view of obedience to the One, Allah, as an impetus for racial reconciliation. Mirsky turns to Goddess traditions as the basis for gender reconciliation. Jocks articulates the ways the Kahnawà:ke myths and rituals hold differences—between male and female, human and nonhuman—in creative tension, leading to life-affirming syntheses, rather than alienating dualisms. Nelson offers a Christian view of the cross that does not eroticize domination, but invites compassionate resistance to every form of sadomasochistic exploitation.

In this revisioning of both justice and love, our authors draw on a variety of religious and spiritual traditions in service of the common good. They lead us to several pressing questions that confront our species today: Can we find ways of recognizing and valuing differences of sex, race/ethnicity, sexual/affectional orientation, class, and culture while overcoming the destructive effects of unjust uses of power-over by dominant groups? In addition to the imperative of developing an egalitarian ethical vision (power-with), can we forge visions of the common good that move us toward moral commonality and more peaceful habits of cohabitation and cooperation (power-in-community)? Our survival and the survival of our planetary home depend on our answers.

These essays make clear that constructive conversation and action require a material basis of equality between and among the conversation partners: men with women; Euro-Americans with African Americans, Native Americans, and Hispanics; heterosexual with gay, lesbian, bisexual and transgender persons; first-world with third-world persons; owning class with persons from the middle and laboring sectors of the working class, and the poor; Christians with Jews, Muslims, and others. Consequently, men, particularly men who are from dominant groups, must make political commitments to share the privileges and responsibilities of the institutional power (power-for) of which we have had an inordinate share. We and other members of dominant groups must also commit ourselves to alliances with members of oppressed groups to develop structures of accountability for those who exercise power-for to promote the good of all. In addition, we need to mine our religious traditions for those prophetic visions of the common good and those supporting personal and communal spiritual disciplines that empower us in those commitments and draw us toward ways of being and acting that are more just and mutually enhancing for all beings—human and nonhuman.

Two areas of scholarship that can help in that search are historical studies and studies in myth and ritual.

Historical Studies

Historical studies done at the intersection of men's lived experience, cultural constructions of masculinity, and religious texts, institutions, and practices yield important data for both the deconstructive and constructive work that needs to be done. As we have seen, exploration of the ways dominative definitions of masculinity shape and are shaped by religious ideas (Boyd, Wiethaus, Kirkley, Fout, Muesse, Parsons) illuminate the destructive potential religion has when used as an ideological support for oppression. That work must be extended into many more historical periods and religious traditions. It is important that these studies also discover and explain the ways religious narratives and their interpretations, along with institutional forms and practices, have empowered adherents to resist oppressive and alienating dynamics (Boyd, Parsons).[5]

Myth and Ritual

In these essays, myth and ritual emerge as resources for positive change. Many of our authors share an appreciation for the transforming power of religious myth and ritual. Unfortunately, what has become clear in several of our essays (Parsons, Jocks, and Muesse) is that dominant definitions of masculinity often privilege binary, critical reason, thus devaluing, as feminine, unitive, intuitive reason, through which the power of myth and ritual are experienced. Members of oppressor groups have often used binary, critical reason to rationalize and to defend their dominance over subjugated groups of human beings and over nonhuman beings. Several of our authors have explored spiritual disciplines or traditions that serve as correctives to this masculine overdependence on and, therefore, distortion of, critical reason and its use in the maintenance of ideologies of oppression.

We organize the following comments according to those practices utilizing alternative modes of understanding that emphasize unitive, intuitive human capacities; recognize the finite, conditioned nature of human life; and analyze differential power relationships in the service of justice.[6]

The essays of Pollard and Brantley illustrate the value of intuitive, mystical modes of understanding in the development of more holistic male identities. Pollard points out that through individual (power-within) and communal (power-with) spiritual disciplines, Howard Thurman was able to resist internalizing racist definitions of manhood and find a "common ground" with women and men of his own and other racial and ethnic groups (power-in-community). Mystical perspectives and experiences (power-within) also empowered Brantley to overcome internalized homophobia and embrace himself and his mortality, freeing him for a fuller life, including social justice work.

As Nelson points out, spiritual perspectives enabling men to acknowledge and accept their limitations, especially their mortality, play a central role in resistance to alienating structures of oppression and help men work toward reconciliation within themselves and with others. This embrace of finitude can lead men away from the masculine imperatives of autonomy and separateness toward a recognition of the deep need for connection to contemporary and historical communities. Our essayists have demonstrated this need in several ways. Among culturally nondominant groups, our authors have variously described the power of historical and contemporary communal ties. Munir reveals the way experience in the Nation of Islam empowered Malcolm X to take pride in his identity as an African American man, while Sunni Islam led him to a more inclusive vision of racial reconciliation. Jocks illuminates the value of the nondualistic perspectives of his own Kahnawà:ke (Mohawk) tradition for contemporary reflections on gender relations. Clark uncovers spiritual and theological resources inherent in just, committed relationships that counteract the alienating effects of sexist and heterosexist masculine patterns of relating. Among culturally dominant groups, Parsons and Moore and Gillette explore the transformative possibilities of men in community, mining the wisdom of biblical and nonbiblical traditions through ritual practices fostering both intuitive and critical modes of understanding.

While men's communal ties are important, we recognize that homosocial groups of men have historically functioned to maintain the unjust control of threat power in the hands of a few. A number of our authors, therefore, point to the necessity of men's participation in the creation of communities that cross barriers of sex (Heyward), sexual orientation (Brantley), race (Pollard, Munir), generations (Longwood), class (Nonn), and even species (Nelson). On building communities that cross barriers of oppression and culture, Jocks raises an important caution: when members of dominant groups appropriate cultural forms of subjugated groups, without making commitments to work in solidarity with those groups to stop their oppression, this furthers their exploitation and breeds resentment.

Much work needs to be done at the intersection of men, religion, and masculine identities; we hope that this book demonstrates the constructive value of that work, contributes some clarity about the directions that work might take, and identifies some resources for doing it.

NOTES

1. For feminist scholars searching outside the Jewish and Christian traditions for images of the divine, see, for example, Carol P. Christ, "Symbols of Goddess and God in Feminist Theology," in *The Book of Goddess Past and Present: An Introduction to Her Religion,* ed. Carl Olson (New York: Crossroad, 1989); Mary Daly, *Gyn/ecology: The Metaphysics of Radical Feminism* (Boston: Beacon Press, 1978); Naomi R. Goldenberg, *Changing of the Gods: Feminism and the End of Traditional Religions* (Boston: Beacon Press, 1979); Daphne Hampson, *Theology and Feminism* (Oxford and Cambridge: Basil Blackwell Publisher, 1990). As examples of feminist scholars elaborating more inclusive images of God from within the Christian tradition, see Rita Nakashima Brock, *Journeys by Heart: A Christology of Erotic Power* (New York: Crossroad, 1988); Rebecca S. Chopp, *The Power to Speak: Feminism, Language, God* (New York: Crossroad, 1991); Jacquelyn Grant, *White Women's Christ and Black Women's Jesus: Feminist Christology and Womanist Response* (Atlanta: Scholars Press, 1989); Elizabeth A. Johnson, *She Who Is: The Mystery of God in Feminist Theological Discourse* (New York: Crossroad, 1992); Virginia Ramey Mollenkott, *Godding: Human Responsibility and the Bible* (New York: Crossroad, 1987); Gail Ramshaw, *God beyond Gender: Feminist Christian God-Language* (Minneapolis: Fortress Press, 1995); Rosemary Radford Ruether, *Sexism and God-talk: Toward a Feminist Theology* (Boston: Beacon Press, 1983); Susan Brooks Thistlethwaite, *Sex, Race, and God: Christian Feminism in Black and White* (New York: Crossroad, 1989). For similar work from feminist scholars working within Judaism, see Lynn Gottlieb, *She Who Dwells Within: A Feminist Vision of a Renewed Judaism* (New York: HarperCollins 1995); Judith A. Kates and Gail Twersky Reimer, eds., *Reading Ruth: Contemporary Women Reclaim a Sa-*

cred Story (New York: Ballentine Books, 1994); and Judith Plaskow, *Standing Again at Sinai* (San Francisco: Harper & Row, 1990).

2. See introduction to part 5.

3. See, among other sources, the MudFlower Collective, *God's Fierce Whimsy: Christian Feminism and Theological Education* (New York: Pilgrim Press, 1985), 40; Rosemary Radford Ruether, *Sexism and God-Talk: Toward a Feminist Theology* (Boston: Beacon Press, 1983), 234; John Howard Yoder, *The Politics of Jesus* (Grand Rapids: Wm. B. Eerdmans Publishing Co., 1972); James H. Cone, *God of the Oppressed* (New York: Seabury Press, 1975) 232; and Walter Wink's trilogy, *Naming the Powers* (Philadelphia: Fortress Press, 1984); *Unmasking the Powers: The Invisible Forces That Determine Human Existence* (Philadelphia: Fortress Press, 1986); and *Engaging the Powers: Discernment and Resistance in a World of Domination* (Minneapolis: Fortress Press, 1992).

4. Margaret Suchocki, "A Feminist Re-Interpretation of the Doctrine of Original Sin," Robinson Lectures at Wake Forest University, 1990, and *The Fall into Violence: Original Sin in a Relational Theology* (New York: Continuum, 1994).

5. For examples of this kind of work, see Michael S. Kimmel and Thomas E. Mosmiller, eds., *Against the Tide: Pro-Feminist Men in the United States, 1776–1990: A Documentary History* (Boston: Beacon Press, 1992), in which the editors bring together documentation of, for example, the role played by Protestant clergy in nineteenth-century America who worked for the abolition of slavery and for women's rights. See also Michael S. Kimmel, *Manhood in America: A Cultural History* (New York: Free Press, 1995)

6. See Parson's "Re-membering John the Baptist," n. 2, reference to Edward Farley's, *Fragility of Knowledge*. The next several paragraphs are indebted to Farley's description of four ways of understanding reality (hermeneutical modes): (1) the critical, Enlightenment mode that stresses empiricism, abstraction, and linear thought; (2) the Romantic mode that restores the multidimensionality to our thinking by emphasizing our unitive, creative, synoptic capacities; (3) the traditional mode that recognizes the way our lives and the categories of our thinking have been shaped by others, including historical communities; and (4) the praxis mode that analyzes the ways in which our interpretations of reality are informed by specific interests within relationships involving power. Farley observes that mode 1 has been privileged in the academy since the Enlightenment and the other three modes serve as correctives to the distorting effects of that hegemony.

FOR FURTHER READING

General

Abbott, Franklin, ed. *Men and Intimacy: Personal Accounts Exploring the Dilemmas of Modern Male Sexuality.* Freedom, Calif.: Crossing Press, 1990.

———, ed. *New Men, New Minds.* Freedom, Calif.: Crossing Press, 1987.

Allen, Marvin, and Jo Robinson. *In the Company of Men: A New Approach to Healing for Husbands, Fathers, and Friends.* New York: Random House, 1993.

Askew, Sue, and Carol Ross. *Boys Don't Cry: Boys and Sexism in Education.* London: Open University Press, 1988.

Astrachan, Anthony. *How Men Feel: Their Response to Women's Demands for Equality and Power.* New York: Doubleday, 1986.

Baumli, Francis, ed. *Men Freeing Men: Exploding the Myth of the Traditional Male.* Jersey City, N.J.: New Atlantis, 1985.

Bell, Donald H. *Being a Man.* Lexington, Mass.: Lewis Publishing Co., 1982.

Blumenfeld, Warren J., ed. *Homophobia: How We All Pay the Price.* Boston: Beacon Press, 1992.

Brod, Harry, ed. *The Making of Masculinities: The New Men's Studies.* Boston: George Allen & Unwin, 1987.

Brod, Harry, and Michael Kaufman, ed. *Theorizing Masculinities.* Thousand Oaks, Calif.: Sage Publications, 1994.

Carnes, Mark C., and Clyde Griffen, eds. *Meaning for Manhood: Constructions of Masculinity in Victorian America.* Chicago: University of Chicago Press, 1990.

Cherfas, Jeremy, and John Gribbin. *The Redundant Male: Is Sex Irrelevant in the Modern World?* New York: Pantheon Books, 1984.

Chesler, Phyllis. *About Men.* New York: Simon & Schuster, 1978.

Clatterbaugh, Kenneth. *Contemporary Perspectives on Masculinity: Men, Women, and Politics in Modern Society.* Boulder, Colo.: Westview Press, 1990.

Clawson, Mary A. *Constructing Brotherhood: Class, Gender, and Fraternalism.* Princeton, N.J.: Princeton University Press, 1989.

Connell, R. W. *Gender and Power: Society, the Person and Sexual Politics.* Stanford, Calif.: Stanford University Press, 1987.

———. *Masculinities.* Berkeley and Los Angeles: University of California Press, 1995.

Corneau, Guy. *Absent Fathers, Lost Sons: The Search for Masculine Identity.* Trans. Larry Souldice. Boston: Shambhala Publications, 1991.

David, Deborah S., and Robert Brannon, eds. *The Forty-Nine Percent Majority.* New York: Random House, 1976.

D'Emilio, John. *Sexual Politics, Sexual Communities: The Making of a Homosexual Minority in the United States, 1940–1970.* Chicago: University of Chicago Press, 1983.

Diamond, Jed. *Inside Out: Becoming My Own Man.* San Raphael, Calif.: Fifth Wave, 1983.

Di Stefano, Christine. *Configurations of Masculinity: A Feminist Perspective on Modern Political Theory.* Ithaca, N.Y.: Cornell University Press, 1991.

Doyle, James A. *The Male Experience.* 3d ed. Madison, Wis.: Wm. C. Brown & Benchmark, 1995.

Doyle, Richard. *The Rape of the Male.* St. Paul: Poor Richard's Press, 1976.

Ehrenreich, Barbara. *The Hearts of Men: American Dreams and the Flight from Commitment.* Garden City, N.Y.: Anchor Doubleday, 1983.

Farrell, Warren. *The Liberated Man.* New York: Bantam Books, 1975.

———. *The Myth of Male Power: Why Men Are the Disposable Sex.* New York: Simon & Schuster, 1993.

———. *Why Men Are the Way They Are.* New York: McGraw-Hill, 1986.

Fasteau, Marc Feigen. *The Male Machine.* New York: McGraw-Hill, 1974.

Fausto-Sterling, Anne. *Myths of Gender.* New York: Basic Books, 1985.

Fogel, Gerald I., et al., eds. *The Psychology of Men: New Psychoanalytic Perspectives.* New York: Basic Books, 1986.

Franklin, Clyde W., II. *The Changing Definition of Masculinity.* New York and London: Plenum Press, 1984.

———. *Men and Society.* Chicago: Nelson-Hall, 1988.

Friedman, Richard C. *Male Homosexuality: A Contemporary Psychoanalytic Perspective.* New Haven, Conn.: Yale University Press, 1988.

Friedman, Robert A., and Leila Lerner, eds. *Toward a New Psychology of Men: Psychoanalytic and Social Perspectives: A Special Issue of The Psychoanalytic Review.* New York: Guilford Press, 1986.

Gerzon, Mark. *A Choice of Heroes: The Changing Face of American Manhood.* Boston: Houghton Mifflin Co., 1982.

Gilder, George F. *Men and Marriage.* London: Pelican, 1986.

Gilmore, David D. *Manhood in the Making: Cultural Concepts of Masculinity.* New Haven, Conn.: Yale University Press, 1990.

Goldberg, Herb. *The Hazards of Being Male: Surviving the Myth of Male Privilege.* New York: Signet, 1976.

————. *The Inner Male: Overcoming Roadblocks to Intimacy.* New York: New American Library, 1987.

Griswold, Robert L. *Fatherhood in America: A History.* New York: Basic Books, 1993.

Grubman-Black, Stephen D. *Broken Boys/Mending Men: Recovery from Childhood Sexual Abuse.* New York: Ivy, 1990.

Hagan, Kay Leigh, ed. *Women Respond to the Men's Movement: A Feminist Collection.* San Francisco: Harper San Francisco, 1992.

Halperin, David M. *One Hundred Years of Homosexuality: And Other Essays on Greek Love.* New York: Routledge, 1990.

Hearn, Jeff, and David Morgan, eds. *Men, Masculinities, and Social Theory.* London and Boston: Unwin Hyman, 1990.

Hopcke, Robert H. *Men's Dreams, Men's Healing.* Boston and London: Shambhala Publications, 1990.

Hudson, Liam, and Bernadine Jacot. *The Way Men Think: Intellect, Intimacy, and the Erotic Imagination.* New Haven, Conn., and London: Yale University Press, 1991.

Hunter, Mic. *Abused Boys: The Neglected Victims of Sexual Abuse.* Lexington, Mass.: D. C. Heath, 1990.

Johnson, Robert. *He! Understanding Masculine Psychology Based on the Legend of Parsifal and His Search for the Grail, and Using Jungian Psychological Concepts.* New York: Harper & Row, 1986.

Kaufman. Michael, ed. *Beyond Patriarchy.* Toronto: Oxford University Press, 1987.

Kauth, Bill. *A Circle of Men.* New York: St. Martin's Press, 1992.

Kimbrell, Andrew. *The Masculine Mystique: The Politics of Masculinity.* Los Angeles: J. P. Tarcher, 1995.

Kimmell, Michael S. *Manhood in America: A Cultural History.* New York: Free Press, 1995.

————, ed. *Changing Men: New Directions in Research on Men and Masculinity.* Newbury Park, Calif.: Sage Publications, 1987.

————, ed. *Men Confront Pornography.* New York: Meridian, 1990.

————, ed. *The Politics of Manhood: Profeminist Men Respond to the Mythopoetic Movement (and Mythopoetic Leaders Answer).* Philadelphia: Temple University Press, 1995.

Kimmel, Michael S., and Michael A. Messner, eds. *Men's Lives.* 3d ed. Boston: Allyn & Bacon, 1995.

Kimmel, Michael S., and Thomas E. Mosmiller, eds. *Against the Tide: Pro-Feminist Men in the United States, 1776–1990: A Documentary History.* Boston: Beacon Press, 1992.

Kipnis, Aaron R. *Knights without Armor: A Practical Guide for Men in Quest of Masculine Soul.* Los Angeles: Jeremy P. Tarcher, 1991.

Kipnis, Aaron R., and Elizabeth Herron. *Gender War, Gender Peace: The Quest for Love and Justice between Women and Men.* New York: William Morrow & Co., 1994.

Klein, Carole. *Mothers and Sons.* Boston: G. K. Hall, 1985.

Kohn, Alfie. *No Contest: The Case against Competition.* Boston: Houghton Mifflin Co., 1986.

Korda, Michael. *Male Chauvinism: How It Works.* New York: Random House, 1973.

Langley, Roger, and Richard C. Levy. *Wife Beating: The Silent Crisis.* New York: E. P. Dutton, 1980.

Lee, John. *At My Father's Wedding.* New York: Bantam Books, 1991.

———. *The Flying Boy: Healing the Wounded Man.* Deerfield Beach, Fla.: Health Communications, 1989.

Levant, Ronald F., and William S. Pollack, eds. *A New Psychology of Men.* New York: Basic Books, 1995.

Levinson, Daniel J., et al. *The Seasons of a Man's Life.* New York: Ballantine, 1978.

Lew, Mike. *Victims No Longer: Men Recovering from Incest and Other Sexual Child Abuse.* New York: Harper & Row, 1988.

Maccoby, Eleanor E., and Carol Nagy Jacklin. *The Psychology of Sex Differences.* Stanford, Calif.: Stanford University Press, 1974.

Majors, Richard, and Janet Mancini Billson. *Cool Pose: The Dilemmas of Black Manhood in America.* Lexington, Mass.: Lexington Books, 1992.

Majors, Richard G., and Jacob U. Gordon, eds. *The American Black Male: His Present Status and His Future.* Chicago: Nelson Hall, 1994.

May, Larry, and Robert Strikwerda, eds. *Rethinking Masculinity: Philosophical Explorations in Light of Feminism.* Lanham, Md.: Littlefield Adams, 1992.

McGill, Michael E. *The McGill Report on Male Intimacy.* New York: Harper & Row, 1985.

Metcalf, Andy, and Martin Humphries, eds. *The Sexuality of Men.* London and Sydney: Pluto Press, 1985.

Meth, Richard L., and Robert S. Pasick. *Men in Therapy: The Challenge to Change.* The Guilford Family Therapy Series. New York: Guilford, 1990.

Miedzian, Myriam. *Boys Will Be Boys: Breaking the Link between Masculinity and Violence.* Garden City, N.Y.: Anchor Doubleday, 1991.

Miller, Stuart. *Men and Friendship.* Los Angeles: J. P. Tarcher, 1983.

Mirandé, Alfredo. "Qué Gacho Es Ser Macho: It's a Drag to Be a Macho Man." *Astlan* 17.2 (1988): 63–89.

Modeski, Tania. *Feminism without Women: Culture and Criticism in a "Postfeminist" Age.* New York and London: Routledge, 1991.

Nardi, Peter M., ed. *Men's Friendships. Research on Men and Masculinities.* Vol. 2. Ed. Michael S. Kimmel. Newbury Park, Calif.: Sage Publications, 1992.

Nemiroff, Greta Hofmann, ed. *Women and Men: Interdisciplinary Readings on Gender.* Markham, Ontario: Fitzhenry and Whiteside, 1987.

Nichols, Jack. *Men's Liberation: A New Definition of Masculinity.* London: Penguin Books, 1975.

Osherson, Samuel. *Finding Our Fathers: The Unfinished Business of Fatherhood.* New York: Free Press, 1986.

———. *Wrestling with Love: How Men Struggle with Women, Children, Parents, and Each Other.* New York: Fawcett Columbine, 1992.

Pleck, Joseph H. *The Myth of Masculinity.* Cambridge, Mass.: MIT Press, 1981.

———, and Jack Sawyer, eds. *Men and Masculinity.* Englewood Cliffs, N.J.: Prentice-Hall, 1974.

Pruett, Kyle D. *The Nurturing Father: Journey toward the Complete Man.* New York: Warner Books, 1987.

Raphael, Ray. *The Men from the Boys: Rites of Passage in Male America.* Lincoln and London: University of Nebraska Press, 1988.

Richardson, Laurel. *The Dynamics of Sex and Gender.* New York: Harper & Row, 1988.

Rochlin, Gregory. *The Masculine Dilemma.* Boston: Little, Brown & Co., 1980.

Roszak, Betty, and Theodore Roszak, eds. *Masculine/Feminine.* New York: Harper & Row, 1969.

Rotundo, E. Anthony. *American Manhood: Transformations in Masculinity from the Revolution to the Modern Era.* New York: Basic Books, 1993.

Rutherford, Jonathan. *Men's Silences: Predicaments in Masculinity.* London and New York: Routledge, 1992.

Sanford, John A., and George Lough. *What Men Are Like.* New York: Paulist Press, 1988.

Schenk, Roy, and John Everingham, eds. *Men Healing Shame: An Anthology.* New York: Springer Publishing, 1995.

Secunda, Victoria. *Women and Their Fathers: The Sexual and Romantic Impact of the First Man in Your Life.* New York: Dell Publishing Co., 1992.

Segal, Lynne. *Slow Motion: Changing Masculinities, Changing Men.* New Brunswick, N.J.: Rutgers University Press, 1990.

Seidler, Victor J. *Recreating Sexual Politics: Men, Feminism and Politics.* London and New York: Routledge, 1991.

————. *Rediscovering Masculinity: Reason, Language and Sexuality.* London: Routledge and Kegan Paul, 1989.

————. *Unreasonable Men: Masculinity and Social Theory.* London and New York: Routledge, 1994.

————, ed. *The Achilles Heel Reader: Men, Sexual Politics and Socialism.* New York: Routledge, 1991.

Snarey, John. *How Fathers Care for the Next Generation: A Four-Decade Study.* Cambridge, Mass., and London: Harvard University Press, 1993.

Snodgrass, Jon, ed. *A Book of Readings for Men against Sexism.* Albion, Calif.: Times Change Press, 1977.

Staples, Robert. *Black Masculinity: The Black Male's Role in American Society.* San Francisco: Black Scholar's Press, 1982.

Steinmann, Anne, and David J. Fox. *The Male Dilemma: How to Survive the Sexual Revolution.* New York: Jason Aronson, 1974.

Stoltenberg, John. *The End of Manhood: A Book for Men of Conscience.* New York: Penguin Books, 1994.

————. *Refusing to Be a Man: Essays on Sex and Justice.* Portland, Oreg.: Breitenbush Books, 1989.

Thompson, Keith, ed. *To Be a Man: Developing Conscious Masculinity.* Los Angeles: J. P. Tarcher, 1991.

Thompson, Mark. *Gay Spirit: Myth and Meaning.* Stonewall Inn Editions. New York: St. Martin's Press, 1987.

Tolson, Andrew. *The Limits of Masculinity.* New York: Harper & Row, 1977.

Religion, Spirituality, and Theology

Arnold, Patrick. *Wildmen, Warriors, and Kings.* New York: Crossroad, 1991.

Baker-Fletcher, Garth Kasimu. *XODUS: An African-American Male Journey.* Minneapolis: Fortress Press, 1995.

Bly, Robert. *Iron John: A Book about Men.* Reading, Mass.: Addison-Wesley, 1990.

Bolen, Jean Shinoda. *Gods in Everyman: A New Psychology of Men's Lives and Loves.* San Francisco: Harper & Row, 1989.

Borresen, Kari Elisabeth, ed. *The Image of God: Gender Models in Judaeo-Christian Tradition.* Minneapolis: Fortress Press, 1995.

Boswell, John. *Christianity, Social Tolerance, and Homosexuality: Gay*

People in Western Europe from the Beginning of the Christian Era to the Fourteenth Century. Chicago: University of Chicago Press, 1980.

Boyd, Stephen B. *The Men We Long to Be: From Domination to a New Christian Understanding of Manhood.* San Francisco: Harper San Francisco, 1995.

Brod, Harry. ed. *A Mensch among Men: Explorations in Jewish Masculinity.* Freedom, Calif.: Crossing Press, 1988.

Brown, Joanne Carlson, and Carole R. Bohn, eds. *Christianity, Patriarchy, and Abuse: A Feminist Critique.* New York: Pilgrim Press, 1989.

Bucher, Glenn R., ed. *Straight/White/Male.* Philadelphia: Fortress Press, 1976.

Carmody, John. *Toward a Male Spirituality.* Mystic, Conn.: Twenty-Third Publications, 1990.

Clark, J. Michael. *Beyond Our Ghettos: Gay Theology in Ecological Perspective.* Cleveland: Pilgrim Press, 1993.

————. *A Place to Start: Toward an Unapologetic Gay Liberation Theology.* Dallas: Monument Press, 1989.

Clark J. Michael, with Bob McNeir. *Masculine Socialization and Gay Liberation: A Conversation on the Work of James Nelson and Other Wise Friends.* Las Colinas, Tex.: Liberal Press, 1992.

Comstock, Gary David. *Gay Theology without Apology.* Cleveland: Pilgrim Press, 1993.

Culbertson, Philip. *Counseling Men.* Minneapolis: Fortress Press, 1994.

————. *The New Adam: The Future of Male Spirituality.* Minneapolis: Fortress Press, 1992.

Dalbey, Gordon. *Father and Son: The Wound, the Healing, the Call to Manhood.* Nashville: Thomas Nelson Publishers, 1992.

Dittes, James E. *The Male Predicament: On Being a Male Today.* San Francisco: Harper & Row, 1985.

————. *When Work Goes Sour: A Male Perspective.* Philadelphia: Westminster Press, 1987.

Doty, William G. *Myths of Masculinity.* New York: Crossroad, 1993.

Eilberg-Schwartz, Howard. *God's Phallus and Other Problems for Men and Monotheism.* Boston: Beacon Press, 1994.

Fortunato, John E. *Embracing the Exile: Healing Journeys of Gay Christians.* San Francisco: Harper & Row, 1982.

Glaser, Chris. *Coming Out to God: Prayers for Lesbians and Gay Men, Their Families and Friends.* Louisville, Ky.: Westminster/John Knox Press, 1991.

————. *Uncommon Calling: A Gay Man's Struggles to Serve the Church.* San Francisco: Harper & Row, 1988.

Harding, Christopher, ed. *Wingspan: Inside the Men's Movement.* New York: St. Martin's Press, 1992.

Hilton, Bruce. *Can Homophobia Be Cured? Wrestling with Questions That Challenge the Church.* Nashville: Abingdon Press, 1992.

Horner, Tom. *Jonathan Loved David: Homosexuality in Biblical Times.* Philadelphia: Westminster Press, 1978.

Keen, Sam. *Fire in the Belly: On Being a Man.* New York: Bantam Books, 1991.

Krondorfer, Bjorn, ed. *Body and Bible: Interpreting and Experiencing Biblical Narratives.* Philadelphia: Trinity Press International, 1992.

————, ed. *Men's Bodies, Men's Gods: Male Identities in a (Post-) Christian Culture.* New York: New York University Press, 1996.

Liebman, Wayne. *Tending the Fire: The Ritual Men's Group.* St. Paul: Ally Press, 1991.

McNeill, John J. *The Church and the Homosexual.* 4th ed. Boston: Beacon Press, 1993.

————. *Freedom, Glorious Freedom: The Spiritual Journal to the Fullness of Life for Gays, Lesbians, and Everybody Else.* Boston: Beacon Press, 1994.

————. *Taking a Chance on God: Liberating Theology for Gays, Lesbians, and Their Lovers, Families, and Friends.* Boston: Beacon Press, 1988.

Meade, Michael. *Men and the Water of Life: Initiation and the Tempering of Men.* San Francisco: Harper San Francisco, 1993.

Monick, Eugene. *Phallos: Sacred Image of the Masculine.* Toronto: Inner City Books, 1987.

Moore, Robert, and Douglas Gillette. *King Warrior Magician Lover: Rediscovering the Archetypes of the Mature Masculine.* San Francisco: Harper San Francisco, 1990.

Murphey, Cecil. *Mantalk: Resources for Exploring Male Issues.* Louisville, Ky.: Presbyterian Publishing House, 1991.

Nelson, James B. *Body Theology.* Louisville, Ky.: Westminster/John Knox Press, 1992.

————. *The Intimate Connection: Male Sexuality, Masculine Spirituality.* Philadelphia: Westminster Press, 1988.

Owen-Towle, Tom. *Brother-Spirit: Men Joining Together in the Quest for Intimacy and Ultimacy.* San Diego: Bald Eagle Mountain Press, 1991.

Raschke, Carl A., and Susan Doughty Raschke. *The Engendering God: Male and Female Faces of God.* Louisville, Ky.: Westminster John Knox Press, 1995.

Rohr, Richard, and Joseph Martos. *The Wildman's Journey.* Cincinnati: St. Anthony Messenger Press, 1992.

Roscoe, Will, ed. *Living the Spirit: A Gay American Indian Anthology.* Stonewall Inn Editions. New York: St. Martin's Press, 1988.

Rowan, John. *The Horned God.* New York: Routledge & Kegan Paul, 1987.

Scroggs, Robin. *The New Testament and Homosexuality.* Philadelphia: Fortress Press, 1983.

Welch, Don. *Macho Isn't Enough: Family Man in a Liberated World.* Atlanta: John Knox Press, 1985.

Wren, Brian A. *What Language Shall I Borrow? God-talk in Worship: A Male Response to Feminist Theology.* New York: Crossroad, 1989.

Men's Studies: Bibliographies

August, Eugene R. *The New Men's Studies: A Selected and Annotated Interdisciplinary Bibliography.* 2d ed. Englewood, Colo.: Libraries Unlimited, 1994.

Ford, David, and Jess Hearn. *Studying Men and Masculinity: A Sourcebook of Literature and Materials.* Bradford, England: University of Bradford, 1991.

Feminist Studies: Bibliographies

Fisher, Clare B. *Of Spirituality: A Feminist Perspective.* Metuchen, N.J.: Scarecrow Press, 1995.

Henking, Susan. "Bibliographic Resources on Gender and Religion." In *Teaching the Introductory Course in Religious Studies: A Sourcebook.* Ed. Mark Juergensmeyer, 275–79. Atlanta: Scholars Press, 1991.

Nordquist, Joan. *Feminist Theory: A Bibliography.* Santa Cruz, Calif.: Reference & Research Services, 1992.

———, ed. *Feminist Theory: Women of Color: A Bibliography.* Santa Cruz, Calif.: Reference & Research Services, 1995.

INDEX